To Jesse — Gary Esparza
Thanks for caring about
us old River Rats.

MW01145944

DUTY HONOR SACRIFICE

Ralph Christopher

authorHOUSE®

AuthorHouse™
1663 Liberty Drive, Suite 200
Bloomington, IN 47403
www.authorhouse.com
Phone: 1-800-839-8640

© *2007 Ralph Christopher. All rights reserved.*

No part of this book may be reproduced, stored in a retrieval system, or transmitted by any means without the written permission of the author.

First published by AuthorHouse 10/11/2007

ISBN: 978-1-4343-2801-4 (sc)
ISBN: 978-1-4343-2802-1 (hc)

Printed in the United States of America
Bloomington, Indiana

This book is printed on acid-free paper.

Edited by Rodney Richey
  Cover, back, maps and photo pages all designed
and reconditioned by Dave Chase.
  Cover photo: Two Alpha Patrol boats leading a column of assault craft down a stream during an early morning troop insertion.
  Back photo: Monitor Flame thrower.
  Left center: Sergeant Julio Diaz leading 3rd Platoon Charlie Company 3/47th Infantry, 9th Infantry Division on patrol.
  Right center: River Division 532 Boat Captain Jerry Gandy patrolling the Vinh Te Canal in PBR.

LAOS

South Vietnam

I

CAMBODIA

II

III

IV

QUANG TRI
HUE
THUA THIEN
DA NANG
QUANG NAM
QUANG TIN
CHU LAI
QUANG NGAI

KONTUM

BINH DINH
QUI NHON

PLEIKU

PHU BON

PHU YEN

DARLAC

KHANH HOA

NHA TRANG

QUANG DUC
TUYEN DUC
VINH THUAN

LAM DONG

BINH THUAN

PHUOC LONG
BINH LONG
TAY NINH
BINH DUONG
LONG KHANH
BINH TUY
HAU NGHIA
BIEN HOA
GIA DINH/SAIGON
LONG AN
PHUOC TUY
CHAU DUC
KIEN PHONG
KIEN TUONG
DINH TUONG
GO CONG
KIEN GIANG
AN GIANG
SA DEC
VINH LONG
KIEN HOA
An Thoi
PHONG DINH
VINH BINH
CHUONG THIEN
BA XUYEN
GULF OF THAILAND
BAC LIEU
AN XUYEN

SOUTH CHINA SEA

Map 1

Map 2

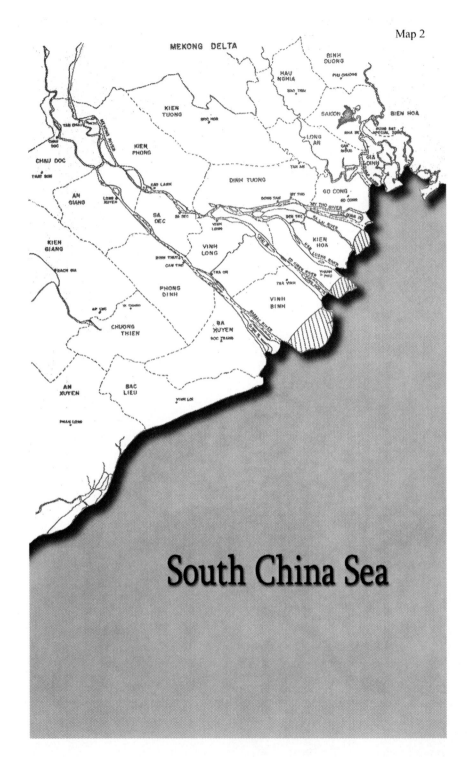

South China Sea

PROLOGUE

I dedicate this book to all who fought in the river and coastal wars in the jungles and rice paddies of South Vietnam, and to my many shipmates and friends who volunteered their stories to me. Without them, this book could not have been possible.

I do not claim these stories are precisely true. They are my findings from researching the Vietnam War and interviewing the men that served there. All the views expressed in this book are mine; they are simply what I believe to be true. Whenever the validity of a story was in question, I told the veteran's point of view. These stories are not offered for personal glory or to brag, but to honor those silent heroes of our past, who should not be forgotten. There is still much pain and anger left over from the Vietnam War, and the welcome home we did receive was disgraceful. Many still cannot talk about the war, and the controversy drove way too many of our ranks to an early grave.

Please forgive me for what may be left out, forgotten, or unknown. It was a long time ago, and although some memories of that time are crystal clear, some are foggy, like a bad dream. At times it is hard to believe that these men performed these tasks, but most agree that they would go back and do it again. My apologies to all for dragging them back through the swamps of South Vietnam. Spending time with these warriors was an honor for me and reinforced the pride that I have always felt.

Please do not confuse us with the forces that we were sent to face. We were good men in an ugly war. Our military men and women are the best there have ever been and have always been held accountable. Vietnam was no different. We apologize for nothing and are only sorry that we were not able to bring the world to peace, as every generation of U.S. Veterans has tried to do.

This is the second in a series of books recording stories from the Vietnam river and coastal war. The names of the men you will read are real. Many of the words are theirs as well. I am merely a storyteller, putting those words to paper, trying very hard to recapture the feelings and mood of the time. I researched and recorded veterans about events that happened forty years ago. They did not go off to kill, but rather to help the struggling and oppressed people of South Vietnam, a nation that had been at war for 2,000 years. We were asked to go stop communist aggression, so we did. My years in service to my country were some of the most unselfish, honorable years of my life, and I have continued to live in the shadow of that time.

I wrote my first book "River Rats" while being treated by the good people that work for the Veterans Administration, which were very kind to me and my family. Although it took many years and several treatments that I could have never afforded, the doctors, nurses, and hospitals helped to overturn my illness. Because of their diligence, these fine people made possible my successful recovery, and I thank them for another chance at life. I will forever be in their debt.

Many times we hear of the price paid by those who served in these forgotten and unknown places in that unpopular war. These heroes fulfilled a part of our country's destiny and truly deserve to be respected and celebrated by all Americans, for they were of the highest caliber that this world has ever known. I hope through this book you will be able to see them more clearly and not paint them with the politics or feelings of the time. They were young men who went off and accomplished their mission. And for the ones who were allowed to return home to raise families and work for America, they are all unsung heroes as well, walking among us every day, going about their lives, asking for nothing. Please take the time to thank them for their service and talk to them. For what stories they have, and there are only a few left who can tell them.

To the families of the men we lost, it is hard to find the words to express what your loved ones mean to us. For me, they were the heroes of my youth, and I thank you for the short time I was allowed to share their company. I will never forget them, and I hope my fellow countrymen will not as well. They will remain in my heart as my brothers throughout time.

They were simply men who went and did their job. Praise is hardly enough.

RUBIN BINDER

It was a sunny summer's day in July 2006, and brown water veterans of the river patrol forces of Vietnam gathered in Seattle to honor one of their own. Boatswain's Mate Third Class Rubin Binder was the last survivor of the most famous river patrol boat of them all, PBR 105. With his passing, we had lost another of the greats. We held our heads high, wearing our black berets with pride for a legend who would live on long after we remaining river sailors are gone.

The commanding officer of River Section 531, the Delta Dragons, retired Navy Commander Fred McDavitt, related many fond memories of his friend and shipmate at Binder's eulogy. Less than a year earlier Binder called McDavitt and they talked about what they both wanted at their funeral services. They both agreed that McDavitt would most likely pass first as he was ten years older. Retired Navy Commander Tom Anderson, also a commanding officer of River Division 531, the same ten river patrol boats commanded three years earlier by McDavitt, presented a flag to Kris Binder, Rubin's widow, while Binder's children, Michelle, Melissa, Carl, and Kelsey, sat in silent reverence for their dad.

A small diverse crowd of friends and admirers stood, listening attentively, for Binder had many friends in all walks of life. Retired Rear Admiral Morton E. Toole who had traveled from far-off Washington D.C., also commanded Binder while serving as commander of River Division 53. He, too, had come to pay his respects, as a twenty-one gun salute, taps, and bag pipes played "Amazing Grace" beautifully. U.S. Navy sailors, in full dress whites, stood at attention in the background, ready to salute the man who had come to represent brown water naval forces of the past, as the Navy once again prepared for river combat in a far-off land. It was a day to celebrate Rubin's life and pay tribute to his legend.

Rubin Binder had volunteered to serve in Vietnam and reported aboard River Section 531 and was assigned to PBR 105 in the city of My Tho in 1966. There he became life-long friends with the boat captain of PBR 105, Boatswain's Mate First Class James Elliott Williams, a father figure who took Seaman Binder under his wing. This was a most unlikely relationship, since Williams was a thirty-eight year old Methodist from South Carolina and Binder was a twenty year old Jewish kid from Coney Island. Boat Captain Williams had led his crew, consisting of Electronics' Technician Second Class Roy Castleberry, who served as radio/radar operator and aft gunner, and the engineer, Machinist Mate Fireman Clem Alderson, into dangerous waters against communist forces many times. Williams' ability to find the enemy was uncanny, and the crew of PBR 105 was a bunch of scrappers. Rubin stepped up quickly and manned the forward twin .50 caliber machineguns, the most important and targeted gun aboard. Of the 161 patrols Rubin went on, he was involved in fifty-nine firefights, and although it was Boat Captain Elliott Williams leading the way, it was a young Binder on the forward .50s delivering devastating blows to the Viet Cong guerrillas and North Vietnamese infiltrators, who operated against the Republic of Vietnam and their struggling government in Saigon.

The thirty-one foot Mark I river patrol boats and crews, were the first of their kind and cut a path for those who followed. Their mission was to keep the rivers and canals free so the farmers and fishermen could move safely and bring their products of fish, rice, and fruit to market. The Viet Cong communists would rob and tax the people, abducting the young men to serve as VC fighters against their will. Anybody who objected was murdered on the spot, all in the name of communism.

Rubin Binder grew up on Coney Island, the son of Jewish parents who had survived Hitler's concentration camps, a fact of which he was immensely proud. His mother, Florence, wore long sleeves to cover the camp tattoos she had received while in those inhumane hellholes. Although she had never talked about Auschwitz, I am sure her survival helped shape the character of her young son, who became a leader among men and lent a helping hand to many he came in contact with throughout his life. In some ways, his fate was similar to that of his parents, in that he witnessed many horrors that plagued him much of his life. He had seen violence and death in a war that few understood, other than the men who served there with him, and this, too, probably contributed to his early death. For years, Binder was reluctant to talk about a war for which we were criticized and called names. It was too hard to explain, so we just stopped talking about it. Then in the eighties, movies about the war started to surface, dragging many of us back through it again, only not quite the war we fought. It had only been in the nineties, when people started to look at us differently and embrace the men we are. Thanks to our children and grandchildren's generations, we were finally starting to get a little recognition, people thanking us for our service and welcoming us home. No more is the military looked down on, thought of as dishonorable, and ridiculed. Our kids started asking questions and began to understand us a little better, maybe because they were now in a difficult fight with terrorists who used tactics similar to the ones we had faced. Contrary to popular belief at the time, we were not bad men, just men serving in a bad situation, fighting a brutal, heartless enemy who used terrorist tactics against us and the people of South Vietnam.

I guess we should go back to the beginning and tell the story of the gallant river battle fought on Halloween night, 1966, by PBRs 105 and 99, led by Medal of Honor recipient, boat captain and patrol officer James Elliott Williams, whose motto was "Lead from the Front."

While patrolling the Mekong River just before dusk, PBR 105 took fire from two sampans. Williams quickly gave chase and ordered the fire returned, killing the crew of one sampan with the other fleeing. While pursuing the second sampan around a bend into a tributary of the Mekong, the patrol surprised the 261st and 262nd North Vietnamese Army Regiments, just beginning to move by boats down river. The feisty Williams, in his last year of service, cut through the enemy forces, running over sampans at full throttle, twisting and turning PBR 105 to present a poor target, with PBR 99 right on his heels. All the while, Rubin and the rest of the crewmen on both patrol boats manned all guns and were blasting away at the target-rich environment.

Facing overwhelming odds, Williams led his patrol against concentrations of enemy junks and sampans, carrying fifteen to twenty enemy soldiers each, cutting through the middle, chopping boats in two. All the while, guerrillas armed with mortars and small arms fired on the Americans from fortified riverbank positions. When the enemy troops returned fire, many times they didn't lead the fast boats far enough ahead, resulting in missing and hitting their own forces on the opposite side of the two speeding boats. This rocked the sampans and small junks with the waves of the boats' wakes, throwing the enemies aim off. One communist rocket did find its mark, but it had been fired at such a close range that it did not detonate, passing through the bow of PBR 105 and out the other side, exploding on enemy forces. Meanwhile, Williams radioed for support from the heavily armed Navy Seawolf attack helicopters, who scrambled immediately.

After passing through the first inlet, the two PBRs turned into a second and larger staging area, with larger junks and more communist soldiers. Again the two speed boats waded into the enemy forces, who were caught off-guard taking heavy casualties. By the end of the run, the two Huey Seawolf gunships had arrived, and Williams kicked off another attack in the fading light. The Seawolves flew low to the deck with their Zuni rockets, as their door gunners blasted away through the enemy, who were retreating into the trees returning fire, taking devastating hits. Many more firing runs were made into the night as Williams ordered the searchlights turned on to press the attack, even though it made the patrol boats better targets. In spite of this, and a dwindling supply of ammunition, his patrol confronted the enemy onshore and routed its entire force, destroying sixty-five boats and inflicting 1000 NVA and Viet Cong casualties. The two fiberglass patrol boats and their crews had done what most would have considered impossible. They were later proclaimed the heroes of one of the greatest Navy victories of all time: the Halloween Massacre.

There were many more times when Williams, Binder and the Delta Dragons of River Section 531 chased down Viet Cong party members and VC tax collectors, who terrorized the Vietnamese villagers, taking their money and supplies to support the Viet Cong. Willie, as Williams shipmates called him, was famous for his expert boat handling and shrewd use of speed, as well as courage in facing the enemy. Time and time again, James Elliott Williams and PBR 105, along with the Delta Dragons, caught and decimated communist forces. On one sunny day, they caught more than 400 Viet Cong crossing in the open.

Through the years Williams, Binder, McDavitt, and many who served in those first river sections stayed in touch and remained friends, proud of their service together. They did not call or think of themselves as "River Rats," as that title was already being used by the legendary U.S. Air Force, Red River Delta "River Rat" pilots, who flew bombing missions into North Vietnam in 1966-67. Most river sailors referred to themselves by their unit name, such as the "Delta Dragons" in the case of River Section 531. When they referred to themselves, collectively they used the terms "Brown Water Sailors" or "Brown Water Navy."

James Elliott Williams retired in 1967 and was honorably promoted to chief petty officer in 1975. Later, he worked as a U.S. Marshal and with his wife and childhood sweetheart Elaine, raised five children. He was asked to speak in public on many occasions, tearing up the King's English, as the burly South Carolinian put it. But Williams minced no words. Of his men he would say:

"These men, they wasn't no dumb-bunnies. They had a lot of common sense, and they worked hard at what they were doin'. And that was at a time when they were sayin' that ever'body was crazy and dopeheads, and in Vietnam in partic'lar, which just wasn't true.

"I think the men that deserve the credit in Vietnam was the youngsters," said Williams, who was an "old man" of thirty-five when he reported for duty on the river. "They've never got the credit they rightfully deserve. They did such a good job if you were willing to show them, to lead, to get out front. They didn't ask you why. They done what you told 'em. And they did a good job of it. The young people that I got, they were throwaways, they were rejects. Their commanding officers wanted to get rid of them, and they turned out to be the greatest young men in this country. In a year and four days, we lost only one man. I'm not trying to brag, but we accounted for some 1,400 kills and 180 captured. You could not have done that without teamwork."

Willie and Rubin survived to return home, although they were both wounded while in combat. Cruising Vietnam's notorious Mekong Delta meant trouble. But Williams was used to trouble and left Vietnam as one of the war's most decorated heroes. The crew of PBR 105 would cast a giant shadow that was hard to surpass, setting an example for future river sailors, instilling pride in the units. It was considered an honor just to serve in the same force they helped establish. In many ways, serving in these units shaped many who went on to do great things. For this, I will always be grateful to Williams, Binder, McDavitt, Toole, and the rest of the Brown Water Sailors who served in Vietnam. For the fame they earned trickled down, to be shared by me and the rest of the Naval forces that served in the Republic of Vietnam.

In 1999, when Chief James Elliott Williams passed away, Melissa Binder said her father broke down and cried. On December 11th, 2004, USS James E. Williams, DDG 95, was commissioned in Charleston, South Carolina. Over 100 Brown Water Sailors wearing their Black Berets were present at the ceremony.

MEMORIES OF VIETNAM

It was September 13th, 1969, and Radioman First Class Jerry Gandy was celebrating his birthday along with his friends at the "War Zone," the enlisted men's club at the Naval Inshore Operations Training Center at Mare Island in Vallejo, California. The class had graduated with flying colors and was throwing a going-to-war party when it was discovered that Gandy was born on Friday the 13th. The group decided to have both parties together, so Jerry's inebriated friends placed a candle on a cold biscuit and presented it to him.

The next morning, Jerry, with a terrible hangover and a crushed biscuit in his pocket, got up to board a flight for the Republic of Vietnam. Petty officer Gandy had been trained to assume the responsibilities of boat captain of a thirty-one-foot fiberglass Navy Patrol Boat River, a PBR. This was a highly respected position in the Brown Water Navy and one that would require making life-and-death decisions. The legend and acomplishments of the river patrol boats were not widely known, but the sailors of the United States Navy who had volunteered to serve with the river divisions were very aware of that legacy and the job they would be assigned. The PBRs were the great nemeses of communist forces in South Vietnam, as they had severed their supply lines and deprived them of the rivers and canals that they had once controlled. There was no mistaking the danger of the job, since the enemy saw the boats as a great prize and waged a determined effort to keep track and destroy them. Petty officer Gandy was aware of all of this, yet he and his shipmates volunteered to serve with the brown water fleet.

Upon arrival in the Republic of Vietnam, Jerry was picked up at Tan Son Nhut Air Force Base and transported to the U.S. Navy receiving detachment, Annapolis Hotel, for outfitting and assignment to a river division. He was issued a .38 caliber pistol with shoulder holster and was advised that he would be assigned to River Division 532, the "Dragonflies." Jerry and his friend, Gunner's Mate First Class Hugh Edge, together tried to act inconspicuous and enjoy their stay at Annapolis Hotel, for secretly, Jerry was scared as hell and knew he was heading into combat. After two days, they came for him and placed him on a C130 airplane heading into the boonies.

As with all newly arriving sailors, his mind started to play tricks on him. The plane started to zigzag, and he saw flashes as they were about to land. Damn, he thought, we're under attack, and I am going to be killed on my first day in the bush. But one of the crewmembers explained the flashes were just strobe lights on the runway.

River Division 532 was based at Ha Tien at the western end of the Vinh Te Canal near the Gulf of Thailand, or, as it had been called in ancient times, the Gulf of Siam. There were ten river patrol boats attached to the famed River Division 532, and their job was to patrol the treacherous Rach Giang Thanh, which flowed into Cambodia, as well as the Vinh Te Canal, which skirted along the Vietnam/ Cambodia border. This was a heavy communist infiltration zone and very "hot," as enemy-controlled areas were called. Rows of nipa palm trees grew along the edge of the narrow river that had already taken many lives. It was part of Operation SEA LORDS, Admiral Elmo Zumwalt's plan to interdict the communists transporting men and arms into the Mekong Delta to disrupt and control the rice crops and indigenous people of the region.

The first couple of months, for the most part, were uneventful, as the PBR crews patrolled their zones, checking cargo manifests of the local fishermen and farmers and sitting in their night guard posts, to catch the communist crossing from Cambodia into Vietnam. Although the crews experienced only a few skirmishes and mortar attacks on their makeshift base, they knew their presence deterred the enemy, which helped the locals get their crops, fish, and goods to market.

During one mortar attack, the River Division 532 boats took off into the bay of the Gulf of Thailand for protection. There was an LCU, (landing craft utility) boat that brought up materials and

Seabees from the Naval Construction Battalion, to build Advance Tactical Support Base Ha Tien, so patrolmen would have a place to rest from many hot, sun-fried hours patrolling the rivers and canals and long, tedious nights of setting in wait on ambush, fighting off mosquitoes and every kind of insect imaginable. Before the base's construction, they had been living on boats or in tents on the beach. They bathed in the river, the canal, or wherever they could find water, which was not really all that clean.

They ran their boats up alongside the landing craft in the bay and were pulled aboard one by one by the crew of the landing craft. When it became Jerry's turn, a fellow on deck took his hand and started to pull him aboard. Suddenly, Jerry fell back to the deck of the PBR, where he busted his butt and injured his muscles and pride. He jumped up to ask the sailor why he had turned loose of his grip, but, as he got a better look, he immediately knew why. Jerry had enlisted the man into the Navy at his last duty station in Murfreesboro, Tennessee promising him Electronic Technician School. Although the man's scores and basic battery tests qualified him for the rating, for some reason, he had been denied the school and had instead been assigned to the LCU Jerry was attempting to board. Damn, it's a small world.

On February 23, 1970, Jerry and his crew were slated to be off, but because 532's patrols for the night were one light, 532's executive officer asked Jerry to throw a crew together and fill the slot, which Jerry did with two Americans and one Vietnamese sailor. Jerry manned the helm of PBR 634, the second boat of a two-boat night patrol under the command of Patrol Officer Ensign Bomarito, who was on PBR 121 with Boat Captain Data Processor Third O'Brien. The boats proceeded north on the Rach Giang Thank River toward the assigned sector on the Vinh Te Canal. When they emerged around a bend, both boats came under intense rocket and automatic weapons fire. The first rocket hit Boat Captain Gandy's craft in the bow, knocking it sideways. The second rocket hit them aft of the coxswain's flat, blowing away the splinter shield and rendering the port engine inoperative. The third communist rocket hit aft, blowing the fantail gunner over the stern into the water, knocking the boat back into its intended line of travel. Meanwhile, the lead boat had been struck by a high explosive anti-tank round from a recoilless rifle and was ablaze.

Initially the forward twin .50s gunner on Gandy's boat froze. Jerry yelled at the forward gunner and hit him in the back of his helmet with the headset from the radio. The gunner came alive and commenced to burn up the barrels of the twin .50 caliber machineguns as Gandy maneuvered the patrol boat in a position to bring devastating return fire on the enemy. Steve Green, the engineer of the lead boat, was hanging onto the rail over the coxswain's flat while attempting to steer the burning PBR toward the shore using his feet. Petty Officer Gandy managed to maneuver his boat between the enemy fire and the burning lead boat, while Steve Green steered the disabled craft, which was down to one operating engine, toward the river bank.

Boat Captain O'Brien of the lead boat was seriously wounded, as were Patrol Officer Ensign Bomerito and Gunner's Mate Seaman Bowling. Gandy got on the radio and reported their situation to their Tactical Operations Center at Ha Tien as he did, he turned to notice that Bomerito was in the water. As the adrenaline bubbled over, Gandy jumped into the water and retrieved Ensign Bomerito, pushing him up and into the PBR. This was no small feat, considering that Bomerito was well over six feet tall and weighed over 200 pounds, while Petty Officer Gandy stood five foot six and only weighed 145 pounds.

Gandy brought the remainder of the wounded sailors aboard and headed through the gauntle - with one operating engine - toward a clear zone to facilitate medical evacuation of the wounded men. By the time they had arrived at their destination, they had expended all ammo and their guns were hot. Once in position, the wounded were evacuated in two Seawolf helicopter gunships. Although Boat Captain Gandy had sustained injuries and had blood running down the side of his face from ruptured ear drums, he stayed with his boat. After being blown over the side, Gandy's fantail gunner had traveled miles down stream before being picked up by two PBRs rushing to aid the ambushed patrol. The gunner survived. Unlike the Viet Cong, who usually attacked and fled, the enemy had stayed and continued to fight, leading everyone to believe that they were a well-trained North Vietnamese unit. There were no enemy weapons or bodies left behind.

When all the wounded had been taken aboard the choppers for medevac, Gandy and his crew started his damaged river patrol boat on the long trek back to their base camp on the one operating engine. Since the boat had taken a B40 rocket in the bow, leaving a large entry hole at the water line, Gandy was instructed to beach the boat upon arrival, to prevent sinking. He got the best running start he could on one engine and rammed the patrol boat's nose up onto the beach.

But upon inspecting the damage, he had found that there was a hot B40 rocket still lodged in the bow. At this point, Gandy started to turn a little pale thinking what could have happened while running aground. The area was evacuated while a trained EOD - Explosive Ordinance Disposal team member - carefully removed the rocket.

Shortly after the events of February 23rd, Jerry Gandy was promoted to Chief Petty Officer and moved up to Patrol Officer in charge of two boat patrols.

In June 1970, the Dragonflies of River Division 532 received orders to join President Richard M. Nixon's incursion into Cambodia. U.S. Naval forces had entered every major river flowing from Cambodia into Vietnam, and River Division 532 was assigned the Bassac River. Executive Officer of 532, Lieutenant Richard D. Greenburg, was in command of the ten-boat patrol riding the lead boat. Greenburg assigned Chief Gandy as Patrol Officer, riding in the last boat in the column. This was to allow the entire column of boats to turn 180 degrees, if they ran into serious trouble, so that Chief Gandy could lead the division out. But the trip into Cambodia was uneventful.

On the way out, Engineman Steve Green asked Chief Gandy if they could stop at one of the numerous pagodas along the banks, so he could get a Buddha for a souvenir. Not thinking about the Buddha being a religious artifact, Gandy agreed, and the boat pulled in. Steve jumped off and whisked the Buddha aboard. Suddenly Vietnamese sailors began to leap over the side, into the water. Chief Gandy immediately realized his mistake and had Steve return the Buddha.

Soon after its Cambodian adventure, River Division 532 was moved to Chau Doc City on the eastern in of the Vinh Te Canal, where it meets up with the Bassac River. The sailors were housed on YRBM 16, a yard, repair, berthing, and mess barge, where they enjoyed their first hot food, hot showers, and air-conditioned racks in some time. It was there that Jerry Gandy got into the first serious trouble of his tour. One day, the chief went ashore with his old boat crew to visit the MACV, military assistance command Vietnam compound located in the village of Chau Doc. While there, they had a few too many Ba Mui Ba beers and were drunk as they made their way back to the pier to be picked up by one of their boats. As they waited, they noticed a Boston whaler boat tied to the pier. It's funny how close a boat crew can become, because they all jumped on the boat with Gandy at the helm. It was only right that their old boat captain, the chief, would be the driver as they sped away full bore to make firing runs back and forth between YRBM 16 and the MACV compound.

They were drunk enough to ignore the Army first sergeant on the pier and River Division 532's executive officer on the barge alongside YRBM 16, waving for them to come in. A funny thing happened, though: The outboard motor cable snapped, and the chief lost steering. Thinking quickly, the chief wrapped his arms around the outboard motor and, manually turned the boat. However, they all forgot that, without the controls, they couldn't slow the boat or stop. Out of control, the whaler hit the barge and was sheared off at the water line. The top of the boat, with the chief and his ex-crew, was propelled onto the barge, right in front of the crew's executive officer.

They were all put on report and sweated it out for a long time, while the craftsmen aboard YRBM 16 reassembled the Boston whaler. Chief Gandy meanwhile apologized to the Colonel at the MACV compound. Because of their good combat records, the crew's report slips were thrown out, and they were able to breathe easier and concentrate on the work at hand.

In July 1970, the Dragonflies were moved to Advance Tactical Support Base Phouc Xuyen, on the Grand Canal in the Plain of Reeds. The Brown Water Navy had dubbed this zone Operation Barrier Reef. Jerry Gandy, along with his buddy Mel Underwood, who was also assigned duty on the Grand Canal with the Strike Assault Boats of STABRON 20, took their R and R in Hong Kong, where it took them days to realize that the enemy wasn't going to jump out from behind every tree and bush they passed. It's funny how that happens.

On July 17th, 1970, Gandy was again patrol officer of a two-boat patrol, riding the lead boat with Boat Captain Quarter Master First Milliken, en route to their assigned waterborne guard post to set up their night ambush position. Four-and-a half-miles east of Phouc Xuyen, their patrol came under heavy automatic weapon and rocket fire. Chief Gandy was struck with shrapnel that penetrated his flak jacket. As a result of the hit, he lost a good portion of his right lung, about half of his liver, and three sections of his ribs, while the shrapnel tattooed him all over his body. He lay there, begging someone to knock him out, since he was struggling to breathe, but no one would.

He was flown to the Third Medical Evacuation Hospital in Ben Thuy, wondering if he was going to make it. After being bounced from hospital to hospital, he underwent an operation at the Naval Hospital in Jacksonville, Florida, two operations at the United States Air Force Hospital in Wiesbaden, Germany, and a final operation at the U.S. Air Force Hospital, at Maxwell Air Force Base in Montgomery, Alabama. Chief Jerry Gandy spent the next three years in recovery.

During his tour in the Republic of Vietnam, Gandy had participated in 178 combat patrols and engaged in armed conflict against the North Vietnamese and Viet Cong communist aggressors on seven separate occasions. During those patrols, he had boarded and searched numerous junks and sampans, interdicted cross-river traffic, inserted and extracted friendly forces in hostile territory, provided fire support for besieged units and outposts, and enforced curfew. In addition, he conducted psychological warfare operations and civic action programs.

Jerry went many years with limited contact from his brothers and shipmates from Vietnam. After finally hooking up with an old buddy, he found out why. Radioman First Tom Collins and Gandy had gone through PBR training at Mare Island together and were deployed to Vietnam around the same time. Gandy found Collins' address and mailed Tom a letter.

"Man, we thought that you had been killed in Nam," Tom responded. "I have made several trips to the 'Wall' in D.C. looking for your name." Gandy began to understand then why he had heard from so few people, as he reassured Tom that he was very much alive.

After recovering from the wounds he received in the Republic of Vietnam, Jerry Gandy returned to the United States Navy, receiving a promotion to Master Chief. He later accepted a commission as a Warrant Officer. After retiring from the Navy, he served twenty years with the U.S. Postal Service. During this time, he had tenure as Postmaster of Williamsburg, Virginia, and manager of the Main Post Officer in Virginia Beach. He is now retired and dedicates much of his time to veterans' organizations.

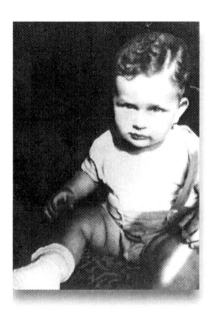

Rubin Binder as a baby as Seaman Recruit and on the
left bottom with James E. Willams, Roy Castleberry and Maurice Koch

Vinh Te Canal patrol. Engineman "Frog" Gergewich on buffalo. Jerry Gandy at ATSB Ha Tien. PBR with live B40 in bow and two hits aft.

INDOCHINA

The Indochinese peninsula extends down from the Asian continent into the South China Sea. It forms the southeastern extremity of Asia with Laos, Cambodia, Thailand, Myanmar, and Malaysia, sharing the peninsula with Vietnam. Over 2,000 years ago, Indian and Chinese immigrants began moving into the region, which was rich in soil deposits and ideal for growing rice. Although the ancient Indian state of Funan dates back to the first century in the Mekong Delta and the Chams Islamic Indian culture settled in central Vietnam, both famous for the tradition of piracy, the country was more influenced by the Chinese. Thus, the Chinese civilization, and its military forces, kept a close eye on Southeast Asia and tried to extend its ruling power there.

Two of the most famous heroines of Vietnam's history are the legendary Trung sisters, who, on the backs of elephants, led the first national uprising against the Chinese, who conquered them in the year 40 A.D. The Vietnamese had been suffering under the harsh rule of Chinese governor To Dinh when they rose up and were later crushed, placed under direct Chinese administration for the first time. Some feel that, if the sisters had not resisted the Chinese when they did, there would be no Vietnamese nation today.

Vietnam lies on the eastside of the Indochinese peninsula and extends 1,200 miles south from the Chinese border to the Gulf of Thailand, roughly the area of California. There are two deltas in Vietnam that are enriched with fertile silt; the Red River Delta in the north and the even more important Mekong Delta in the south. That delta is supported by the mighty Mekong River that winds 2,500 miles from the Himalayas to the South China Sea. Like the American colonists, the Vietnamese were migrants, moving from China's southern provinces into what would become Vietnam. First they settled in the north around the Tonkin Gulf, then in the central mountainous regions. Then, in the 19th century, after centuries of war, they won the virgin territory of Vietnam's larger and richer rice bowl, the Mekong Delta, away from the Cambodians. Today, the delta produces a million tons of rice a year and is home to many of the indigenous people who had migrated to Vietnam.

Vietnam is a beautiful country with mountains, plains, and deep valleys lush with green fields and rice paddies. About half of Vietnam is covered in jungle, with tropical vegetation and inhospitable humidity that drains one's strength and rots one's clothes. The beaches along the coast are beautiful and considered by many to be the French Rivera of the Far East. Much of the southern third of the country is connected by streams and canals, many built during the French colonial period, and they provide an excellent network for navigation and irrigation. Junks and sampans maintain communications among villages and carry surplus rice to Saigon, which was Vietnam's largest port and only forty miles from the South China Sea.

From the early days of the Vietnamese culture, the people struggled to retain their independence. Under the Tran dynasty, 1225-1400 A.D., the country prospered and flourished as the Tran rulers carried out extensive land reform, improved public administration, and promoted the study of Chinese literature. But the Tran are best remembered for their defense of the country against the Mongols. By 1225, the Mongols controlled most of northern China and Manchuria and were eyeing southern China and Chumpa, which is now south and central Vietnam. The Mongol armies of Kublai Khan later invaded Vietnam, sacking the capital at Thang Long, known today as Hanoi, on three occasions, only to find that the Vietnamese had anticipated their attacks and evacuated the city beforehand. Disease, shortage of supplies, the climate, and the Vietnamese strategy of harassment frustrated the aggressors on the first two invasions. The third Mongol invasion of 300,000 men and a vast fleet was also defeated by the Vietnamese under the leadership of General Tran Hung Dao. The Vietnamese drove iron-tipped stakes into the bed of the Bach Dang River, located in northern Vietnam, and then with a small Vietnamese flotilla, lured the Mongol fleet into the river just as the tide was starting to ebb.

Trapped by the iron-tipped stakes, the entire Mongol fleet of 400 craft was sunk, captured, or burned by fire arrows. The Mongol army retreated to China, harassed en route by Tran Hung Dao's troops.

The 14th century was also marked by wars. The quality of the Tran rulers had deteriorated by the end of the century, with them allowing the landlords to take advantage of the peasants by holding the titles of the land with duty owed to the landlowner. This caused a number of rebellions. General Ho Quy Ly seized the throne and proclaimed himself founder of the short-lived Ho dynasty, lasting less than ten years. He instituted a number of reforms that were unpopular with the landlords, including a limit on how much land a family could own and the overseeing of rental of land to peasants. He printed proclamations in Vietnamese rather than Chinese, and provided free schools in provincial capitals. Unhappy with the reforms, landowners appealed to China's Ming Dynasty for help. Restoring the Tran dynasty, the Ming reasserted Chinese control soon after.

Le Loi, one of Vietnam's most celebrated heroes, is credited with rescuing the country from Ming rule. Born of wealthy landowners, he served as a senior scholar-official until the arrival of the Ming, whom he refused to serve. After years of building a resistance movement around him, Le Loi and his forces finally defeated the Chinese army. But rather than order the captured Chinese soldiers and administrators be put to death, he generously provided ships and supplies to send them back to China. Le Loi then assumed the Vietnamese throne, establishing the Le dynasty.

The greatest of the Le dynasty rulers, was Le Thanh Tong, who reorganized governmental powers and upgraded the civil service system. He ordered a census of people and landholdings to be taken every six years, revised the tax system, and commissioned the writing of a national history. He also ordered the creation of the Hong Duc legal code, which was based on Chinese law but included distinctly Vietnamese features, such as recognition of the higher position of women in Vietnamese society than in Chinese society. Under the new code, parental consent was not required for marriage, and daughters were granted equal inheritance rights with sons. Le Thanh Tong also initiated the construction and repair of granaries, dispatched his troops to rebuild irrigation systems following floods, and provided for medical aid during epidemics.

European missionaries had occasionally visited Vietnam for short periods of time, with little impact, beginning in the early 16th century. The best known of the early missionaries was Alexandre de Rhodes, a French Jesuit of the Roman Catholic order who was sent to Hanoi, where he quickly learned the language and began preaching in Vietnamese. He is also responsible for the current Vietnamese written language. Initially, Rhodes was well received, and he reportedly baptized thousands of converts. But his success most likely led to his expulsion a few years after arriving. After being expelled from Vietnam, Rhodes spent the next thirty years seeking support for his missionary work from the Vatican and the French Roman Catholics, as well as making several more trips back to Vietnam appealing his case.

The 17th century was also a period in which European missionaries and merchants became a serious factor in Vietnamese life and politics. Although both had arrived in the previous century, neither foreign merchants nor missionaries had much impact on Vietnam at first. The Portuguese, Dutch, English, and French had all established trading posts. But fighting among the Europeans and Vietnamese resistance made the enterprises unprofitable, with all of the foreign trading posts closed by the end of the century.

Decades of continual warfare between the ruling families of Vietnam had taken a toll on the peasants. Unable to pay their taxes, many had been forced off their land, which made it easy for a few wealthy landowners, nobles, and officials to purchase large quanties. Because officials were exempt from paying land taxes, the more land they acquired, the greater the burden that fell on those peasants who had been able to retain their land. In addition, the peasants faced new taxes on items such as charcoal, salt, silk, and cinnamon, and on commercial activities such as fishing and mining. The deteriorating condition of the economy led to neglect of the network of irrigation systems. The lack of repairs caused catastrophic flooding, which resulted in famine with large numbers of starving people wondering aimlessly about the countryside. This led to many revolts throughout the century, with widespread suffering in both the south and north.

The Tay Son rebellion was led by three brothers from the village of Tay Son in Binh Dinh Province. The eldest brother, Nguyen Nhac, began an attack on the ruling Nguyen family by capturing Quang Nam and Binh Dinh provinces in 1772. The principle goal and slogan of the Tay Son was to seize the property of the rich and distribute it to the poor. In each village, the Tay Son controlled oppressive landlords and officials, who were punished and had their property taken away. The Tay Son also abolished taxes, burned the tax and land registers, freed prisoners from local jails, and distributed the food from storehouses to the hungry. As the rebellion grew in strength, it gained the support of many army deserters, merchants, scholars, and local officials.

Within ten years, the Tay Son had control over the southern part of the country, including Gia Dinh, later called Saigon. The ruling Nguyen family were all killed by the Tay Son rebels, except Nguyen Anh, the sixteen-year-old nephew of the last Nguyen lord. Escapeing to the Mekong Delta, Nguyen Anh was able to gather an army of followers and retake Saigon. The city changed hands several times in the next five years, when the Tay Son brothers finally destroyed Nguyen Anh's fleet and drove him to take refuge on Phu Quoc Island. Nguyen Anh then met with French missionary bishop Pigneau de Behaine and asked him to be his emissary in obtaining French support to defeat the Tay Son. Pigneau de Behaine took Nguyen Anh's five-year-old son, Prince Canh, and departed for French India to plead for support for restoring the Nguyen family to power. Finding none, he went to Paris to lobby on Nguyen Anh's behalf. King Louis XVI agreed to provide ships, several thousand men, and supplies in exchange for Nguyen Anh's promise to give France the port of Tourane, now Da Nang, and the island of Poulo Condore. But the local French authorities in India, recieving secret orders from the king, refused to supply the promised ships and men. Determined to see French military intervention in Vietnam, Pigneau de Behaine himself raised funds for ships and supplies from among the French merchant community in India, hired deserters from the French navy to man them, and sailed back to Vietnam within a few years.

In the meantime, the Tay Son had overcome the crumbling Trinh dynasty and seized all of the north, thus uniting the country for the first time in 200 years. The Tay Son made good their promise to restore the Le dynasty. Then the three brothers installed themselves as kings of the north, central, and southern areas of the country, while continuing to acknowledge the Le emperor. Two years later, the reigning Le emperor fled north to seek Chinese assitants in defeating the Tay Son. Eager to help, a Chinese army invaded Vietnam, seized Hanoi and installed the Le ruler as King of northern Vietnam. That same year, the second eldest Tay Son brother, Nguyen Hue, proclaimed himself Emperor Quang Trung. Marching north with 100,000 men and 100 elephants, Quang Trung attacked Hanoi at night and routed the Chinese army of 200,000, which retreated back to China. Immediately following his victory, Emperor Trung sought to reestablish friendly relations with China, requesting recognition of his rule.

Quang Trung died before the end of the century, without leaving a successor strong enough to lead the country. By this time, Nguyen Anh and his supporters had won back much of the south from Nguyen Lu, the youngest of the Tay Son brothers. When Bishop Pigneau de Behaine returned to Vietnam, Nguyen Anh was in control of Saigon. In the following years, the bishop brought Nguyen Anh a steady flow of ships, arms, and European advisers, who supervised the building of forts, shipyards, cannon foundries and bomb factories, and instructed the Vietnamese in how to manufacture and use modern weapons. After a steady assault on the north, Nguyen Anh's forces took Phu Xuan and Hanoi a year later.

Peasant rebellion flared from time to time throughout the first half of the 19th century, brought on by government repression and such disasters as floods, droughts, epidemics, and famines. One of the most serious problems for the Nguyen rulers was dealing with the French traders, missionaries, diplomats, and naval personnel who came in growing numbers. The influence of missionaries was seen as a critical issue by the court and officials. In the southern part of the country, Christians enjoyed the protection of Viceroy Le Van Duyet, until his death. Soon after, the Nguyen government began a serious attempt to rid itself of French missionaries and their influence. A series of orders forbid the practice of Christianity, forcing the Christian communities underground. Almost 100 priests and members of the church were executed by the Vietnamese during the following twenty-five years. The missionaries stepped up their pressure on the French government to send military troops for protection. French traders once more became interested in Vietnam with French diplomats in China expressing the view that France was falling behind the rest of Europe in gaining a foothold in Asia. French Navy commanders, deployed with the squadron in the South China Sea, also began to campaign for a stronger role in protecting the lives and interests of the missionaries and merchants. After receiving approval from Paris, naval intervention grew steadily. In 1847, two French warships bombarded Da Nang, destroying five Vietnamese ships and killing an estimated 10,000 Vietnamese. The purpose of the attack was to win the release of a missionary, who had actually already been released. For the next ten years, hostilities toward missionaries continued.

Within ten years, Louis-Napoleon had been convinced that invasion of Vietnam was the best course of action. French warships were ordered to take Da Nang without any further efforts to negotiate with the Vietnamese. Da Nang was captured and Saigon a few months later. In both cases, Vietnamese Christian support for the French, predicted by the missionaries, failed to happen. Vietnamese resistance and outbreaks of cholera and typhoid forced the French to abandon Da Nang. Meanwhile, fear was growing in Paris that, if France withdrew, the British would move in. Also believed in Paris was the theory that France had a duty to bring the benefits of its advanced culture to the less fortunate lands of Asia and Africa. This was a common justification for the colonial policies of most of the Western countries. French business increased their pressure on the government for action. Thus in early 1861, a French fleet of seventy ships and several thousand men reinforced Saigon and, in a series of bloody battles, gained control of the surrounding provinces.

A year later, Emperor Tu Duc signed the Treaty of Saigon, agreeing to French demands, giving up three provinces around Saigon, as well as for the opening of three ports to trade, free passage of French warships up the Mekong to Cambodia, freedom of movement for the missionaries, and a large compensation payment to France for its losses in attacking Vietnam. Even the French were surprised by how easily the Vietnamese agreed to the treaty. After resisting Chinese invasions for hundreds of years, the Vietnamese gave in to the French.

Not all Vietnamese resisted French colonization; some welcomed it. The Vietnamese rulers, after years of unfavorible leadership, had lost the support of the people. The French reported hundreds of thousands of Christian converts in Vietnam. Repression of Catholics during Tu Duc's reign of power also created a large opposition group ready to cooperate with the French, and those who did were often rewarded with lands vacated during the French invasion. Much of this land was given to French colonial settlers in large amounts. Gradually a French-Vietnamese landholding class developed. But the Vietnamese were only appointed to the lower levels of the government. Seeking to finance the new government and officials, the early French governors of Vietnam viewed the colony as a source of necessary income. Rice exports, forbidden under Vietnamese rule, reached large numbers. State controlled monopolies and higher taxes on opium, salt, and alcohol, eventually came to provide seventy percent of the government's operating income.

In 1883, the French and the Chinese fought in the Sino-Chinese war. The French had settled through most of Vietnam and Cambodia, but their trade was being disrupted by the Chinese in northern Vietnam. In response, the French attacked and destroyed the Chinese navy as it lay anchor at Foochow, China. Under the treaty of Hue, the French consolidated their protection and control over all of Vietnam and Cambodia, with Laos added six years later after the French blockaded Bangkok and defeated the Siamese. This was the beginning of the formation of French Indochina, with the French taking over the leadership roll in Southeast Asia.

The French continued to impose colonial rule over Vietnam well into the 20th century, but the Vietnamese national sense of identity had not been crushed. Anti-colonial sentiment soon began to emerge, with poor economic conditions contributing to Vietnamese hostility toward the French. Although French colonization brought improvements in transportation and communications, and contributed to the growth of commerce and manufacturing, colonialism seemed to bring little improvement in livelihood to the mass of the population. In the countryside, peasants struggled under heavy taxes and high rents. Workers in factories, in coal mines, and on rubber plantations labored in extremely bad conditions for low wages. By the early 1920s, Vietnamese nationalist parties began to organize and demand reform and independence. In 1930, the revolutionary Ho Chi Minh formed an Indochinese communist party.

In 1937, the second Sino-Japanese war began between the Republic of China and the Empire of Japan. On September 22nd, 1940, after an ultimatum from Japan, the French Vichy government, which had been operating independently as the colonial government, granted the Japanese permission to use air bases in Indochina and to maintain troops. Within a year, the French Vichy government yielded military control of Indochina to the Japanese.

December 7th, 1941, the United States was suddenly attacked by forces of Japan at Pearl Harbor. Eight hours later, the Japanese attacked facilities in the Philippines, Hong Kong, Malaysia and the Netherlands' East Indies. Americans were mad as hell and wanted to avenge the attacks. World War II raged on until 1945, with fierce fighting on all sides.

In the United States, at 1535 hours, on April 12th, 1945, President Franklin D. Roosevelt passed away at the little White House in Warm Springs, Georgia. Later that afternoon, Harry S. Truman, the Missouri senator who had reluctantly volunteered and been elected vice president, was sworn in as the 33rd president after serving less than three months as vice president. It was the end of an era...and the beginning of another.

By the end of April, Major Archimedes Patti, U.S. Office of Strategic Services, OSS, met with Ho Chi Minh to open talks and request the Vietminh's assistance in locating and recovering downed American pilots. During the meeting, Ho showed his support for America and later asked Patti to take a message back to the American people that the Vietnamese loved the Americans and would never fight them. Archimedes Patti, who headed up the OSS operations from its Kunming headquarters in Yunan province in southern China, and in Hanoi Vietnam, developed a close relationship with Ho, becoming somewhat friends. This OSS meeting marked the beginning of a modest and brief American encounter with Ho Chi Minh and his Vietminh, who wanted recognition of the Vietminh as legitimate representatives of the Vietnamese and wanted America's help in achieving independence. Both Patti and Ho were encouraged by the meeting and expected good things out of the U.S.-Vietminh collaboration.

May through July 1945, severe famine struck Hanoi and surrounding areas, eventually resulting in two million deaths from starvation, out of a population of ten million. The famine generated political unrest and peasant revolts against the Japanese and remnants of French colonial society. Ho Chi Minh capitalized on the turmoil by successfully spreading his Vietminh movement.

In July, Major Allison Kent Thomas directed a seven-man OSS team, which parachuted into Ho Chi Minh's jungle headquarters north of Hanoi at Tan Trao. The "Deer Mission" team was to train the Vietminh and provide them with explosives and small arms. While there, the team's medic provided medical assistance to Ho Chi Minh, who on first contact was found to be very ill. It has been said that the medic may have saved Ho Chi Minh's life. By this time, the three men in an intelligence group known as GBT - code named from the first letter of the last names of the three men on the team, Laurence Gordon, Harry V. Bernard, and Frank Tan - had made contact with Ho and learned of his eagerness for further contact with Americans in the war against Japan. In addition to their advisory role and a few weapons, the OSS gave Ho Chi Minh an official appointment as OSS agent nineteen and the code name "Lucius."

The Office of Strategic Services was established in June 1942 with William "Wild Bill" Donovan as director. During their OSS missions into Indochina they were able to observe the Vietminh while they trained them. In return, Ho Chi Minh, General Vo Nguyen Giap, and the Vietminh assisted in rescuing U.S. pilots who had been shot down in the war against Japan. During the meetings, the OSS agents studied the Vietminh and learned how dedicated they and their leaders were to gain Vietnam's independence. It is believed that the brief encounter was a lost opportunity.

In retrospect, Vietnam and the Pacific war were not the most important priority of the United States after Pearl Harbor. From the get-go, the defeat of Hitler was the top priority holding together the U.S., British, and Soviet alliance. It is unlikely the U.S. ever seriously considered going into French Indochina, which was in the area of responsibility of the Allied Southeast Asia Command headed by Admiral Louis Mountbatten. Therefore it was difficult for Ho Chi Minh to get America's attention. Although President Roosevelt was a strong advocate of independence in Indochina, the U.S. government had been reassuring France that its colonial possessions would be returned after the war. After Roosevelt passed away and Truman entered office, the United States quickly re-affirmed its commitment to restoring French sovereignty over Indochina, which Truman maintained had never really been in question. With the Russians establishing themselves throughout Eastern Europe and the Western wartime alliances hanging by threads, there was little else Truman could do without jeopardizing the cooperation of post-war France and Britain in containing Soviet expansion.

The OSS-Vietminh collaboration lasted only until the Japanese surrender on August 15, 1945. However, some OSS officers did remain in Kunming and were even in Hanoi at the time of Ho Chi Minh's August Revolution.

From July 17th to August 2nd, 1945, the Potsdam Conference was held in Germany, with Joseph Stalin of the Soviet Union, Winston Churchill of the United Kingdom, and President Harry S. Truman of the United States in attendance, representing the three largest and most powerful of the victorious allies. The leaders gathered to decide how to administer defeated Nazi Germany, which had agreed to unconditional surrender nine weeks earlier on May 8th,

VE Day. The goals of the conference also included the establishment of post-war order, peace treaties issues, and countering the effects of war. They also offered Japan an opportunity to end the war by an unconditional surrender. French Indochina was considered a minor item on the agenda. By the end of the conference, Britain was assigned with the responsibility for French Indochina south of the 16th parallel, while China had the rest. Representatives from France requested the return of all French pre-war colonies in Indochina. Their request was granted. Vietnam, Laos and Cambodia once again became French colonies following the removal of the Japanese.

At 0815 hours, August 6th, the U.S. exploded the 15-kiloton "Little Boy" atomic bomb over the Urakimi district of Hiroshima. It was dropped from the Enola Gay, a B-29 superfortress bomber commanded by Colonel Paul W. Tibbets.

At 1102 hours, August 9th, the U.S. exploded the 21-kiloton "Fat Man" atomic bomb over the Urakimi district of Nagasaki. On that same day, the Soviet Union declared war on Japan. The next day, Japan surrendered unconditionally, stating, "The Japanese Government is ready to accept the terms enumerated in the joint declaration which was issued at Potsdam on July 26th, 1945." But the Japanese response contained a condition affirming the prerogatives of the Emperor as a sovereign ruler.

August 11th, James F. Bryne, U.S. Secretary of State, responded to the Japanese that the surrender was to be unconditional, per the Potsdam declaration. Three days later, the Japanese Government agreed to unconditional surrender.

In August 1945, at a spontaneous non-communist meeting in Hanoi, Ho Chi Minh and the Vietminh began their August revolution, assuming a leading role in the movement to wrench away power from the French. With the Japanese still in control of Indochina, Emperor Bao Dai, 13th Nguyen emperor of Vietnam, went along with the plan, thinking if the Vietminh were working with the OSS, they could guarantee independence for Vietnam. There was no real uprising per se; Ho Chi Minh's guerrillas simply occupied Hanoi and other cities proclaiming a provisional government in North Vietnam.

September 2nd, 1945, on the deck of the USS Missouri in Tokyo Bay, Japanese representatives signed unconditional surrender. Chinese Nationalists accepted surrender of Japanese Occupation Forces north of the 16th parallel in Vietnam. The British accepted surrender south of the line.

Also that day, Ho Chi Minh declared independence from France and established the Government of the Democratic Republic of Vietnam in Hanoi, issuing his Declaration of Independence, which drew heavily upon the American Declaration of Independence as well as Sun Yat-sen's "Three-people Doctrine." Ho Chi Minh made many appeals to Truman requesting recognition and U.S. aid against the French, citing the Atlantic Charter and the United Nations Charter. Through OSS channels, he proposed that Vietnam be accorded the same status as the Philippine Islands for an undetermined period prior to full independence. While his requests were officially ignored, the United States also refused to assist French military efforts in Vietnam.

From a realistic perspective, with all that was going on in the world in 1945, just what reaction could one expect a letter carried by low-level OSS agents, if it did in fact make it to Washington? It was certainly not in the realm of what we would call our vital interest. Soon, the state of affairs changed as the United States began to preoccupy itself with the growing communist threat in Europe and Asia. Destracted with Uncle Ho's apparent communist nature and the fear that once established he would set up a Kremlin-controlled communist state, the U.S. allowed Ho to drift further from its control and into the waiting arms of the Chinese Red Army.

After the Japanese surrendered to the allies, their forces in Indochina allowed nationalist groups to take over public buildings in most of the major cities. But while the Japanese allowed the nationalist groups free run of the country, they kept former French officials imprisoned.

In September 1945, Major A. Peter Dewey led an OSS team; which arrived at Tan Son Nhut and was greeted by Japanese military and Vietnamese civilians, to recover U.S. prisoners of war. The primary mission was to locate and facilitate the return of POWs in the Saigon area. There were two sites of primary interest: Camp

Poet in Saigon, and Camp 5-E, just outside of Saigon. Together, they held 209 prisoners.

Two days later, the last of the U.S. POWs flew out of Tan Son Nhut. It is assumed that the Japanese were the ones who facilitated the recovery and transfer of the POWs, since they still controlled the country. The American OSS team remained on, possibly waiting for the British to arrive, probably collecting intelligence. Some members of Dewey's team met with the Committee of the South, a Ho Chi Minh organization, which solicited their help in keeping the French out of Indochina. On September 12th, the Indian Ghurkha Division, some 26,000 men in all, under British Major General Douglas D. Gracey, arrived. Until that time, Dewey's team was the only allied presence in Indochina. Shortly after the Indian troops' arrival, a company of French paratroops arrived. General Gracey released and armed the French troops the Japanese had held captive during the war. Some 1,400 French paratroop POWs from Japanese camps around Saigon, under Colonel Jean Cedile, with some of the 20,000 French citizens living there, took control of a government building in Saigon and went on a vengeful rampage, killing Vietminh suspects and ordinary Vietnamese civilians in Saigon. The defeated Japanese forces were re-armed to assist and restore order. The Vietminh respond by calling a national strike and organizing a guerrilla campaign against the French. Although Dewey protested the action, British General Gracey did nothing to stop it. After the clash with communist and nationalist forces, the French seized power in the south, with British help. General Jacque Philippe Leclerc declared, "We have come to claim our inheritance." The Indochina War had begun.

FIRST BLOOD

In September 1945, the Vietminh seriously wounded Captain Joseph R. Coolidge, a member of Major Dewey's OSS team because he spoke French. Dewey and Captain Herbert J. Bluechel visited Coolidge in the 75th Field Hospital the next morning. At noon, Dewey learned that his flight from Tan Son Nhut was again delayed, and he decided to go to the OSS quarters for lunch. En route, they drove through a road block they had previously passed earlier that day. This time they observed Vietnamese in a ditch. Dewey called out something in French, and they opened fire, killing him instantly. Bluechel, who was unhurt, made it back to the OSS base. Major A. Peter Dewey became the first U.S. casualty of the Indochina War. The Vietminh later apologized, calling his death a mistake saying they mistook Dewey for a Frenchman after he spoke to them in French.

By October, a bilateral British/French agreement recognized the French administration of the southern zone. In the north, 180,000 Chinese troops went on a rampage. Ho Chi Minh's Vietminh were hopelessly ill-equipped to deal with it. Ho accepted an allied compromise for temporary return of 15,000 French troops to rid the north of Chinese. The Chinese troops of Chiang fled, looting as they departed. Almost immediately Ho was attacked by pro-Chinese elements within his Democratic Republic of Vietnam for his dealings with the hated colonialists. He replied, "You fools! Don't you realize what it means if the Chinese stay? Don't you remember your history? The last time the Chinese came, they stayed a thousand years."

In March 1946, France recognized Vietnam as a free state within the Indochina Federation and the French Union. The French and Ho Chi Minh's forces continued to battle over Ho's demand for total independence.

After the war, there were two major powers in the world: the Soviet Union and the United States of America. Although they were allies in the fight against Hitler and the Nazi war machine, it was a shaky relationship at best between the three WWII powers of Truman, Churchill and Stalin. With Churchill's wartime coalition government being voted out of office and new Prime Minister Clement Attlee of the Labor Party replacing him, this put Stalin in a powerful position. Churchill, the mainstay of the allied effort, was gone, and Truman had been in office for only a few months.

Stalin sought to expand Soviet dominance by spreading communism around the world. The United States tried to keep the Soviet sphere in check with military alliances. With the communist seizure of China in 1949 and the invasion of South Korea by North Korean and Chinese forces the following year, U.S. leaders concluded that the Indochina Peninsula and possibly all Southeast Asia soon might also sink under the rising communist tide. It was during this time that President Truman provided U.S. aid and sent thirty-five U.S. advisors to Vietnam to support French forces fighting the Vietminh. Back in the USA, Senator Joseph "Tail-gunner Joe" McCarthy alleged communist penetration of the government, and scientists continued testing the atomic bomb, while the Soviet Union played catchup in the development of its own nuclear weapons.

In President Truman's inaugural address on January, 20th, 1949, he stated:

It may be our lot to experience, and in large measure to bring about, a major turning point in the long history of the human race. The first half of this century has been marked by unprecedented and brutal attacks on the rights of man, and by the two most frightful wars in history. The supreme need of our time is for men to learn to live together in peace and harmony. The peoples of the earth face the future with grave uncertainty, composed almost equally of great hopes and great fears. In this time of doubt, they look to the United States as never before for good will, strength, and wise leadership. It is fitting, therefore, that we take this occasion to proclaim to the world the essential principles of the faith by which we live, and to declare our aims to all peoples.

The American people stand firm in the faith which has inspired this Nation from the beginning. We believe that all men have a right to equal justice under law and equal opportunity to share in the common good. We believe that all men have the right to freedom of thought and expression. We believe that all men are created equal because they are created in the image of God. From this faith we will not be moved.

The American people desire, and are determined to work for, a world in which all nations and all peoples are free to govern themselves as they see fit, and to achieve a decent and satisfying life. Above all else, our people desire, and are determined to work for, peace on earth, a just and lasting peace, based on genuine agreement freely arrived at by equals. In the pursuit of these aims, the United States and other like-minded nations find themselves directly opposed by a regime with contrary aims and a totally different concept of life. That regime adheres to a false philosophy which purports to offer freedom, security, and greater opportunity to mankind. Misled by this philosophy, many peoples have sacrificed their liberties only to learn to their sorrow that deceit and mockery, poverty and tyranny, are their reward. That false philosophy is communism.

Truman believed that France, and perhaps the rest of Western Europe, was in danger of falling to the communist. Truman made many decisions based upon this theory and most likely felt that the best way to prevent this from happening was to support the French in Indochina. In many ways, the French and Western Europe gave him no choice.

In June 1949, the new state of Vietnam was officially established in Saigon with Bao Dai as chief of state.

In January and February 1950, the Soviet Union and China recognized the Vietminh regime. Ho Chi Minh, his back against the wall, unwilling to consider further deals with the French and wary of the Red Chinese giant within arm's reach of his northern border, was forced to embrace communism as the government of the Vietnamese people. At the same time, the United States and United Kingdom recognized Vietnam, Cambodia and Laos as states within the French Union.

On Monday, May 15, 1950, President Truman grasped the hand of his Secretary of State, Dean Acheson, and said "Bon voyage. I know you're going to have a successful trip and make a contribution to the peace of the world. Best wishes."

Acheson answered respectfully, "This is another indication of your support, which has never failed me. I will carry out your instructions and your wishes." Then he flew off, in the President's DC-6 aircraft Independence, to confer with fellow diplomats of the North Atlantic community. Western chancelleries hoped that the overseas talks would be more than just another regional conference. The North Atlantic Treaty had stopped the progress of the first wave of communist expansion on the European front. Meanwhile, the Red tide had rolled unchecked over much of Asia. Western diplomats were learning that the front against communism was meaningless unless worked out on a global basis.

"Free men and free nations everywhere," said Dean Acheson at his departure, "will face increasingly crucial tests in the years immediately ahead. What we seek in London is to accelerate the mobilization of vast untapped moral and material resources in the free world. We must develop those reserves to the best of our ability. We should be doing so even if international communism did not exist. As things are, we must do so with utmost vigor."

In Paris that week, the U.S. Secretary of State stopped for a two-day parley with French leaders. His next stop would be London. There, Acheson would first confer with Foreign Secretary Ernest Bevin, and then France's Foreign Minister Robert Schuman would join them for three-way discussions. Later, Acheson would meet with representatives of the nine other North Atlantic signatories. The meetings, which would continue for two weeks, would include a survey of the whole perimeter of the Russian-controlled world. One of the matters that would be of uppermost importance was that the French wanted immediate U.S. help in the defense of Indochina, which was more and more tied in with the defense of France and Western Europe. To support the Vietnam regime of Emperor Bao Dai against the forces of communist Ho Chi Minh, the French were using the bulk of their 130,000 man army, spending about 500 million francs a year. Paris argued that Indochina's defense was a joint western concern and that only U.S. aid could make it effective. After his exchange of views with Schuman, Acheson announced that the U.S. had agreed and would give economic and military help to Indochina.

In August 1950, U.S. Navy Section, Military Assistance and Advisory Group, Vietnam, was established and headed by Commander John R. Holland. In October, Brigadier General Francis G. Trink assumed command of Military Assistants and Advisory Group Indochina.

Recognizing they could not successfully prevail in set battles against the French, in April 1951 the Vietminh decided to change tactics, beginning guerrilla warfare. The Vietminh forces were in control of about half of South Vietnam, and while the French enjoyed an advantage in equipment, thanks to Chinese assistance and a bottomless pit of men, the Vietminh were catching up, becoming a highly mobile force while the French were road-bound and dug in. America was paying around seventy percent of the French war cost.

In the 1950s, Catholic clergyman, Francis Cardinal Spellman used his political contacts outside of the country to influence Americans like Representative John F. Kennedy and other Congressional leaders to support a little-known Catholic Vietnamese politician named Ngo Dinh Diem. Diem was raised in a strict Catholic upbringing and graduated top of his class in law school in Hanoi. By his thirties, he was minister of the interior in the government of Emperor Boa Dai. Diem had turned Ho Chi Minh down when Ho tried to recruit him for the communist party. Instead, he traveled to the United States and lectured at universities, lobbying for support from America's political and religious leaders, gaining access to important political circles in Washington, D.C., making a favorable impression.

From the early days of western contact with Vietnam, the Catholic missionaries had turned to politics to secure the throne of Vietnam for a Catholic successor. These policies, begun by the missionaries, had led to a subtle division within Vietnam. It was against this backdrop that the United States continued the slow process of involvement, with President Dwight D. Eisenhower taking office in 1953.

March 9th, 1954, the French national Assembly authorized the government to negotiate an Indochina peace settlement in Geneva.

Less than a week later, French forces and the Vietminh locked horns in the battle of Dien Bien Phu. The French undertook to create an air-supplied base deep in the hills of Vietnam for the purpose of cutting off Vietminh supply lines into the neighboring French colony of Laos. The Vietminh, under General Vo Nguyen Giap, surrounded and besieged the French, who were unaware of the Vietminh's possession of heavy artillery and their ability to move such weapons to the mountain crests overlooking the encampment. Thousands of Vietnamese soldiers and peasants cleared - and dragged big guns through - what was believed to be impassible jungle and up hills around Dien Bien Phu Valley, completing an impossible feat. Because of this, the Vietminh were able to fire down accurately onto French positions, shells raining down like hail. Tenacious fighting on the ground followed, reminiscent of the trench warfare of World War I. The French repeatedly repulsed Vietminh assaults on their positions, which were taking high casualties on both sides as French troops were slowly being whittled down. Although thousands of French volunteers parachuted into the turkey shoot, which for many became their last, trench after trench collapsed, burying men and weapons under them. Within forty-eight hours, four French battalions had been lost and the Montagnard units supporting them retreated for the hills deserting the French to fend for themselves. One by one, French strongholds were lost, and then the Vietminh overran the airstrip, cutting the French off. Colonel Charles Piroth, commander of the French artillery, personally accepted the blame for losing the positions and made the rounds of his fellow officers, confessing his responsibillity. At dawn, Piroth laid down on his cot and, with his teeth - he had lost a arm in WWII - pulled the pin from a grenade that he held against his chest with his right arm.

Later in the month, General Paul Ely, French Chief of Staff, flew from Paris to Washington, requesting the U.S. to respond if the Chinese intervened with air power. He was assured that the United States would respond immediately with American air power if the Chinese did involve themselves. Admiral Arthur W. Radford, chairman of the Joint Chiefs of Staff, unveiled a new plan - conceived by joint American-French military staffs in Vietnam - named Operation Vulture, in which 200 aircraft, launched from the carriers Essex and Boxer in the South China Sea, would conduct bombing raids around the perimeter of Dien Bien Phu, cutting Vietminh communications and artillery installations, to relieve the siege. In private, President Eisenhower said he would approve of the operation only with congresional approval. Congressional leaders voiced their oppositon that America should not support France alone. When contacted, the French preferred to negotiate and the British refused to support the plan fearing that it would sabotage the Geneva talks. Operation Vulture was shelved.

In the first week of April, after a long night of battle, French fighter-bombers and artillery inflicted gruesome losses on one Vietminh regiment caught on open ground. At that point, General Giap decided to change tactics. Although Giap still had the same objective to overrun French defenses east of the river, he decided to emphasize entrenchment and sapper attacks. At this point, the morale of the Vietminh soldiers broke. The French intercepted radio messages which told of units refusing orders, and communist prisoners said that they were told to advance or be shot by the officers behind them. The extreme casualties they had suffered had taken a toll. Worse yet, the Vietminh had no medical aid stations. Vietminh morale was shaken by the knowledge that, if wounded, the soldier would go uncared for. To avert the crisis, General Giap called in fresh reinforcements from Laos.

French supplies and reinforcements continued to be supplied by air, although as the French positions were overrun, fewer and fewer of those supplies reached them. Flights became increasingly dangerous for the paid volunteer American civilians in Fairchild C-119s and French air force pilots, mostly in C-47s. In order to improve accuracy and to avoid the monsoon cloud cover, the pilots were forced to fly lower and lower, slower and slower. The World War II veteran American pilots, whom French soldiers at Dien

Bien Phu said took more chances than their French counterparts, reported that the Vietminh threw worse flak over the valley than had the Nazis over their industrial cities a decade earlier.

Meanwhile, the situation at Dien Bien Phu worsened as General Giap continued the tactic of building a series of trenches so that his troops could choke off the French strongholds, bunker by bunker. Every night, the Vietminh would move a little farther forward and dug in. By mid April, the Vietminh were reinforced by the monsoon rains, which grounded French air support. Men on both sides fought in trenches full of water, bogged down by mud as French provisions and ammunition started to run low, but there was no thought of surrender. In late April, when the Geneva Conference convened, General Giap reinforced his troops and in May, launched a dual attack, with the Vietminh outnumbering the French ten to one. Still the French resisted, and the battle raged on.

A week later, Giap opened fire with Russian rockets while the French were forced to dig in and conserve their ammo for the final attacks. Bugles blared through the night as four Vietminh regiments attacked, raining down on the last few fortresses like a dark cloud. One last French barrage wiped out the assault wave. A few hours later, the Vietminh detonated a mine shaft, literally blowing up one of the fortresses designated Eliana II. Allegedly all fortress strongpoints at Dien Bien Phu were named after a former mistress of the French garrison commander, Colonel Christian de Castries. The Vietminh attacked again and again, and within a few hours had overrun the defenders. Beatric, Gabrielle and Anne-Marir had all fallen. By dawn, the French had only two field guns left, with no tanks and very little ammunition. During the last hours of the battle, the camp physician reported cases of men dying at their posts from exhaustion, starvation, or injury.

By 1700 hours, May 7th, 1954, Colonel Christian de Castries reported by radio that the Vietminh were within yards of his transmitter, and that he and his men would fight to the end. By nightfall, all central French positions had been overrun, ending all communications. That night, the garrison at Isabelle made a breakout attempt. Out of the 1,700 men in the garrison, less than 100 escaped to Laos. De Castries and his staff were taken prisoner as the battlefield fell silent as a graveyard with the smell of death in the air.

The next day, the Vietminh divided more than 11,000 prisoners from the French garrison, most of whom were wounded, into groups. It was the most French POWs the Vietminh had ever captured. Able-bodied soldiers were force-marched over 250 miles to prison camps to the north and east, intermingled with taunting Vietminh soldiers, to discourage French bombing runs. Hundreds died on the way. The wounded were not given basic triage until the Red Cross arrived, removing almost 1000 wounded and giving aid to the rest. The remaining French soldiers were sent into detention, with prison camps being even worse. The Legionnaires, many of German origin, were constantly starved, beaten, and heaped with abuse, with many dying. Of the remaining prisoners, less than half survived.

During the historic defense of Dien Bien Phu, the French suffered 2,293 dead, 5,195 wounded, and 11,800 captured. Vietminh reported their losses at almost 8,000 killed and over 15,000 wounded.

The day before Dien Bien Phu fell, James B. "Earthquake McGoon" McGovern, named after the character in Li'l Abner comic strip, squeezed his six-foot, 250-pound frame into the modified pilot's seat of a Fairchild C-119 "Flying Boxcar" at Hanoi's airfield, as he had twice daily for weeks. The big, burly giant of a man with a hearty laugh, and his copilot, Wallace A. Buford, flew out in support of the besieged Dien Bien Phu, knowing all too well of the dangers they would be facing. Once the six-plane formation reached the valley, Earthquake McGoon eased the control stick forward, descending for his run. Suddenly, McGovern radioed, "I've got a direct hit." A shell had slammed into one of the engines, sending oil spurting everywhere. Just as he was gaining control, a second shell hit, damaging the tail. As the plane began losing altitude, Earthquake McGoon radioed the pilot of the plane following and asked which ridge was lower.

The pilot responded, "Turn right," but it was too late. The controls were crippled, and the plane wouldn't hold the turn.

As his buddies watched and listened helplessly, Earthquake McGoon coolly said, "Looks like this is it, son." The left wing struck first, and the plane tumbled down the hill, bursting into flames. James B. McGovern and Wallace A. Buford were the only Americans to die in combat in the French Indochina War.

A fourth American was killed in Indochina by a land mine in May 1954. Robert Capa was a combat photographer for Life magazine who first achieved fame in September 1936 as a correspondent in the Spanish Civil War. One of his photos showed a loyalist soldier falling after being shot. In World War II, Capa covered the fighting in Africa, Sicily, and Italy, with his images of the Normandy invasion, after he landed at Omaha Beach at 0630 hours, June 6th, 1944, among his most memorable works. He proclaimed he would never go into harm's way again, but when Life magazine asked him to go one more time, he agreed. It was his last assignment.

After the defeat at Dien Bien Phu of France, the first western nation to be defeated by a south-eastern communist country, the French continued to negotiate at the international conference in Geneva, Switzerland, but had lost much ground.

The Geneva Accord was an agreement among Cambodia, the Democratic Republic of Vietnam in the north, France, Laos, the People's Republic of China, the State of Vietnam in the south, the Soviet Union, the United Kingdom, and the United States, but was signed only by the French and Ho Chi Minh's Democratic Republic of Vietnam. After the Geneva Accord, Vietnam became two countries, divided at the 17th parallel, with Saigon becoming the capital city of the new southern government of a divided nation. Because of this, American representatives insisted on a 300-day period of free movement between North and South Vietnam so the Catholics in the north could move south to safety and the communists of the south could move north to join Ho Chi Minh.

From the outbreak of the Korean War, the drums of the Cold War beat fiercely, with decisions being made in Moscow and Washington, D.C., that affected the entire world. From the beginning of the conflict in Southeast Asia, the U.S. Navy played a key role in supporting American strategic objectives. When it came time, the Navy answered the French government's call to assist in evacuating the hundreds of thousands of Vietnamese and ethnic Chinese who chose to live in the predominately non-communist south. It is also highly likely that Uncle Ho had many of his spies and followers also enjoying the free ride south. From August 1954 to May 1955, U.S. Navy ships mounted a massive sea lift between the ports of Haiphong and Saigon to carry out Operation Passage to Freedom, allowing 800,000 Vietnamese to travel south of the demarcation line, while the much smaller group of communist supporters of the south moved north. American planes dropped leaflets that read, "The Virgin Mary is moving south."

After Diem had solidified power, South Vietnam's million and a half Catholics continued to receive preferential treatment. This caused discontent, and the mood of the Buddhist majority became rebellious. The other third of South Vietnam's population was made up of indigenous religious sects who also did not trust the Viet Catholics, but were resisting the communists as well. Both the Cao Dia and Hoa Hao religious sects had their own armies and were the masters of several southern and western provinces in central and southern Vietnam. What they didn't control was in the hands of the Vietminh.

The Cao Dia religious sect was organized in 1926 and had built its temples northwest of Saigon in Tay Ninh Province, where Tay Ninh City stood as the third largest city in South Vietnam. Caodaism is a religion which combines elements from many of the world's main religions, including Buddhism, Confucianism, Christianity, Hinduism, Islam, Judaism, Taoism, as well as Geniism, an indigenous religion of Vietnam.

The Hoa Hao Buddhist religious sect was established in the late 1930s by Huynh Phu So, whose influence extended over a considerable part of the delta, particularly along the rivers. Prophet Huynh Phu So traveled the delta preaching eloquently and attracting large audiences who gradually acknowledged his supernatural talents. In his salvation mission, he cured thousands of diseases. He published six books, and his writings were considered extremely soul stirring and impressive. Thanks to his teachings, which met the spiritual needs of the time, he succeeded in a very short time converting about two million people.

After World War II, Vietnam was plunged into an unstable period, and the Vietnamese were afraid of becoming slaves transferred from one master to another. Huynh joined hands with other nationalist to create the Front for National Union. During this time, the Hoa Hao had aligned with the Vietminh against the French until they became disenchanted with Vietminh politics and broke away. Because his beliefs and teachings could ruin the communist, the Vietminh sought every possible means to suppress the charismatic Huynh Phu So.

Early in 1947, Hoa Haos in the western provinces of South Vietnam rose up against the dictatorial policy and methods of the communists. In order to avoid bloodshed while the people fought a common enemy, French colonialism, Huynh went to preach peace and calm down his followers' anger. But in April, the Vietminh succeeded in trapping Huynh Phu So in an ambush and killing him. Fighting became brutal after that, with many revenge killings, in spite of the fact that most victims were innocent of any wrongdoing.

The Binh Xuyen was an organized-crime group which also stood as a barrier to the communist. With the approval of Emperor Boa Dai, head of Vietnam's French-supported government, the Binh Xuyen leader Bay Vien made arrangements with Bao Dai, giving the Binh Xuyen control of their own affairs. In return, the Binh Xuyen helped run Saigon's police force and controlled most of the roads out of town where they collected safety taxes. Back in September, 1945, the Binh Xuyen had massacred 150 French and Eurasian civilians, including children, in a suburb of Saigon.

Emperor Boa Dai, who had been living the good life in France, was urged by America and France to offer Ngo Dinh Diem the premiership in 1954, which he reluctantly did. Diem thought his dream had come true that he would lead South Vietnam to independence. In 1945, some of Ho Chi Minh's officers had executed a number of nationalists that were not part of the Vietminh, including the Constitutional Party leader, the head of the Party for Independence, and Diem's brother, Ngo Dinh Khoi, so

Diem considered Ho Chi Minh a murderer and had vowed to work for independence of his country against the communists. One of the first orders of business was to replace the Binh Xuyen pirates and end the safety taxes. The Hoa Hao and Cao Dai leaders united in support of a Binh Xuyen coup against Premier Diem, while the French indirectly supplied arms to the sects.

Boa Dai secretly hoped that Diem would fail and that he could regain power. He had planned to undercut Diem by supporting General Nguyen Van Hinh, who had graduated the French Air Academy and had served with French colonial forces in Algeria and Tunisia. Married to a French woman, and a hard-line anti-communist, General Hinh was determined to form a coalition government with anti-communist sects, and the Binh Xuyen as a third force, resisting communist aggression. With Bao Dai, his army, and his chief of staff ready to betray him, Diem turned to what seemed to be his only friend at the time, Colonel Edward Lansdale of the Central Intelligence Agency. With General Hinh poised to pounce on Diem, the shrewd Colonel Lansdale stepped in with the help of General "Iron Mike" O'Daniel, commander of the U.S. Military Assistance and Advisory Group, and saved Premier Diem by threatening to cut off U.S. aid. The coup was averted when Bao Dai summoned the rebellious General Hinh to France. With General Hinh restrained, the Hoa Hao and Cao Dai religious sects decided to continue their bid for power alone. With the sects' thousands of soldiers, armed by the French, the Hao Hao and Cao Dai leaders bargained for a share of the political power. Diem bribed Cao Dai strongman General Trinh Minh, and the general switched sides, parading 5000 black-uniformed Cao Dai troops into Saigon in support of Diem. This upset the rest of the leaders of the sects, who decided to back the Binh Xuyen and humble Diem in his own backyard, Saigon.

By the end of April 1955, Saigon erupted in a shootout between Diem's forces and the Binh Xuyen when the rebels launched a mortar attack on Diem's presidential palace beginning a short civil war. For three and a half hours, into the mid afternoon, the South Vietnamese soldiers battled hundreds of Binh Xuyen mobsters carrying Tommy guns, just outside of the National

Army headquarters. Bodies littered the streets as crossfire killed innocent bystanders, while people went about their normal lives in crowed cafes. Fighting became house-to-house as four battalions of government paratroopers attacked and the battle for Saigon raged on. By mid May, the paratroopers had overrun one Binh Xuyen position after another and had the gangsters on the run. By June, the Binh Xuyen had been defeated and were retreating, taking refuge in their old pirate liar in the Rung Sat swamp. Their leader, Bay Vien, flew to Paris after his unsuccessful attempt to take power. Many of the defeated fighters of the Binh Xuyen joined the Vietminh.

After the rout of the Binh Xuyen, Diem's forces took the offensive against the Hoa Hao and Cao Dai strongholds, slaughtering many, sending the sects into panic and gaining the upper hand. Many ran to Cambodia, and the notorious General of the Hoa Hao, Ba Cut, the terror of the west, was captured and later guillotined, putting an end to the revolt and making Diem an instant hero. This gained Diem much support in the United States as the last 10,000 French troops marched out of Saigon, being accused of providing explosives to the Binh Xuyen. This ended France's rule of Vietnam and the beginning of the new government of South Vietnam. The Eisenhower administration was convinced that Premier Diem was the man for the job and Emperor Boa Dai was a villain and had to go.

Leading U.S. Democrats like Senators Mike Mansfield and Hubert Humphrey voiced support for Premier Diem on the senate floor back in Washington, and many proclaimed Diem was the only man that could save Vietnam from the communists. American military officers in Saigon expressed disdain against the departing French and displayed a "this-time-we'll-get-it-right" demeanor, as United States dollars started pouring into South Vietnam.

In Diem's campaign to transform Emperor Bao Dai's monarchy into a republic, Diem held elections in October 1955 to allow the South Vietnamese people to choose between Bao Dai and himself. Colonel Edward Lansdale suggested that Diem should provide two ballot papers, red for Diem, which signified good luck, and green for Bao Dai, which was considered bad fortune. Lansdale hoped this would influence the results of the election in Diem's favor. When the voters arrived to the polling stations to place their votes they were told by Diem supporters to place the red ballots in the box and to throw the green away. Those brave enough to go against these orders and place the green papers in the ballot box were roughed up and treated harshly. After the election, Diem proclaimed that he had received more than ninety percent of the vote. His American advisors warned him that his figures would be questioned and suggested that he should claim a much lower number, which Diem refused to do.

After sweeping the election, President Diem formed a popular elected legislature and began drawing up a new constitution. President Eisenhower had once told him: "President Diem, you have exemplified patriotism of the highest order." The Republic of Vietnam was proclaimed in Saigon by Diem in October 1955.

As dictated by the Geneva Accords of 1954, the division of Vietnam was only meant to be temporary, pending free elections for a national leadership. The agreement stipulated that the two military zones that were separated by a temporary demarcation line, which eventually became the Demilitarized Zone, or DMZ, should not in any way be interpreted as constituting a political or territorial boundary, and specifically stated that elections would be held in July 1956, which North Vietnam repeatedly reminded Diem. Nevertheless, Diem refused to enter into negotiations to hold the elections and had no intention of consulting with the Democratic Republic of Vietnam concerning them. Instead, Diem started arresting his opponents, putting thousands into jail. The U.S., which expected elections to be held and had originally supported them, shifted its position in the face of Diem's opposition. The north was solidly unified behind Ho Chi Minh, but the south was divided, with many upset at Diem, who most felt could not win in an election against the popular Ho Chi Minh. It was felt that Ho would receive about eighty percent of the vote. Questions were raised about the legitimacy of any election being held in the communist-run North Vietnam and of evidence being gathered about the oppressive nature of the northern regime. Diem was encouraged by the United States unwillingness to elect a communist leader to lead Vietnam. The government of South Vietnam justified its refusal to comply with the Geneva Accords by the fact it had not signed them.

Given the politics of the time, it is beyond the realm of comprehension that any U.S. administration would consider aiding a confessed communist such as Ho Chi Minh. I am sure this is particularly true after the Eisenhower administration started receiving reports of Vietnamese being killed by the Vietminh during their land reform program after taking power in North Vietnam. At that time, to have supported Uncle Ho would have undermined the international effort to bring some sort of resolution to the first Indochina War. We had supported France during that war, and for us to turn to the communists would have been detrimental to our efforts in NATO. Both North and South Vietnam governments were corrupt and continued to rule with an iron fist, while the Vietnamese people suffered as a result, with many in the south coming to the conclusion that violence was the only way to persuade Diem to agree to the terms of the Geneva Conference.

In late 1956, the Americans reorganized their military assistance advisory group program under the command of General Samuel T. "Hanging Sam" Williams and began rebuilding a force to repel any invasion from the North Vietnamese. Assassinations of village officials' escalated and American agricultural machines in villages near the Cambodian border were deliberately destroyed. Terrorism and sabotage from communist infiltrators became inescapable as security at the homes and offices of American officials in Saigon were doubled. Several U.S. Army advisors in the town of Bien Hoa were ambushed and killed.

The Ho Chi Minh Trail, still a secret to most of us at the time, was up and running as infiltrators poured into the central highlands, clashing with the Army of the Republic of South Vietnam, ARVN, which had been trained and equipped by the United States. South Vietnam's army of 150,000 men, and regional and providence paramilitary forces totaling 90,000, were ill-equipped to fight a guerrilla army. The Viet communists had the advantage of thick forest and a vast river delta of endless fields and rice paddies, crisscrossed by rivers and canals, with safe havens just across the border in the jungles of Cambodia and Laos. The American-trained South Vietnamese Marines, with American advisors, mounted an attack in the guerrilla-ridden Ca Mau Peninsula and killed 300 insurgents, capturing 400 and accepting the surrender of 700 more. But when ARVN forces launched a series of full-scale operations into the Plain of Reeds, they met stiff resistance, including opposition from the Hoa Hao inhabitants themselves.

The strategy of the communist infiltrators was not to defeat the South Vietnamese Army in battle, but to gain support of the civilian population. By using terror selectively, the guerrillas hoped to win over the peasants of the countryside and turn them into a source of food and recruit fighters for overthrowing the South Vietnamese government. In pacification efforts, the South Vietnamese government had large numbers of peasant families resettled into fortified village compounds in the most active insurgent areas. The villages were to offer schools, hospitals, and electricity, and they would protect the peasants from the communist insurgents and their cruelty. The government began to retrain the Civil Guard and self-defense groups to help defend hamlets and villages, and American advisors were made available down to battalion levels. By 1957, U.S. Navy advisors had replaced the departed French advisors providing advisers to all six Vietnamese Navy river assault groups and eleven coastal groups.

In late January 1960, during the celebration of Tet, the Chinese lunar New Year, communist guerrillas rose up, raiding rubber plantations and attaching government outpost. They then overran a battalion headquarters near the Cambodian border and made off with arms and ammunition. In Long An Province, southwest of Saigon, there was a week of assassinations in which twenty-six village and hamlet chiefs, teachers, and public officials were killed. Many more were slated for execution but escaped. By March, insurgents had killed an average of twenty-five local officials each week. Tay Ninh suffered the greatest defeat during this Tet offensive when the fortress at Trang Sup was overrun by insurgents, who destroyed the radio installation and made off with a thousand rifles. This had a devastating effect as communist agents moved freely through the countryside, recruiting fighters into insurgent groups that grew quickly, numbering 5000 in the Mekong Delta alone.

In November 1960, five crack Vietnamese paratroop battalions, backed by tanks and Viet Marines, encircled the presidential palace and demanded administrative reforms. Diem craftily bargained with the rebels all night as his radio called out to all loyal troops to come to his aid. By the next morning, two infantry divisions loyal to the regime had reached the capital. South Vietnamese Marines who had fought with rebels the day before turned their guns on the insurgents and the paratroopers were driven back, ending the coup. In December 1960, due to continued dissatisfaction with the South Vietnamese government, the National Liberation Front was established by Ho Chi Minh and his followers, marking the birth of the Viet Cong communists.

A SHINNING STAR

In 1961, Americans had many things occupying their minds. They watched a war in Algeria, rebellion in the Belgian Congo, and Southeast Asia falling apart. In addition, Washington had cut off diplomatic relations with Cuba, eventually leading to a missile crisis. Russia shot down a U-2 spy plane capturing pilot, Francis Gary Powers, with President Eisenhower refusing to apologize for the incident. An outraged Nikita Khrushchev boasted that the Soviet Union would crush the United States and pledged support for all wars of "national liberation" throughout the world, lending support to North Vietnam. Back home in America, there was much discontent as segregation burned through the South.

It was during this time that a bright shinning star of democracy rose to power in America as we all crowded around the TV on January 20th 1961, and watched the inauguration of a new president, John Fitzgerald Kennedy. President Kennedy was no stranger to war or the evils surrounding it. He had skippered a Navy torpedo patrol boat in the South Pacific during World War II. The son of a weathy Massachusetts politician, he was loved by America and rose to power quickly. Handsome with a beautiful wife, he was the darling of the Democratic party and inspired the new generation of baby boomers. In his inaugural speech, Kennedy had said:

"The torch of leadership has been passed to a new generation, born in this century, tempered by war, disciplined by a hard and bitter peace, proud of our ancient heritage and unwilling to witness or permit the slow undoing of those human rights to which this nation has always been committed, the same revolutionary beliefs for which our forebears fought are still at issue around the globe."

I was only eleven years old at the time, sitting on my mom's floor, and had no idea what he was talking about, but I was stunned by his words and in the manner in which he used them.

President Eisenhower had advised the young president-elect, describing the anti-Castro guerrilla forces training in Guatemala and the mess that he would be passing on in Laos, but mentioned very little about Vietnam, Diem, or the Viet Cong. When Kennedy inquired about Southeast Asia, Eisenhower suggested, "You might have to go in there and fight it out," which made Kennedy furious. Only two weeks before, Russian Premier Khrushchev had challenged the new administration, boasting of communism's inevitable triumph. John Kennedy took office in a time when people were building bomb shelters in their backyards, and the Cold War was boiling over, creating crisis after crisis.

First, there was the Bay of Pigs, which nobody wanted to talk about, and then the search for a cease-fire in Laos. Then Kennedy and Khrushchev's standoff summit meeting, where little was accomplished, and, in August, the building of the Berlin Wall to divide East and West Berlin, with additional barriers dividing the frontier between the Federal Republic of Germany and the Democratic Republic of Germany. It was in this atmosphere that reappraisal of Vietnam was made. The Vietnamese, the Pentagon, and his own advisors all pressured Kennedy to take military steps to save Vietnam from the communist insurgents. In his own speech, he had committed to stopping communist aggression when he promised to "pay any price, bear any burden, meet any hardship, support any friend, oppose any foe, to assure the survival and the success of liberty."

After being sworn in, the new president was advised of the grave situation in Vietnam. Kennedy approved proposals to increase aid to build a stronger South Vietnam and to counter insurgency. He then beefed up Fort Bragg's Special Forces ranks and set in motion the creation of a new unit in the United States Navy that was to be trained in counterinsurgency and guerrilla tactics. If South Vietnam was to survive, it would have to change its thinking and switch to fighting unconventional warfare.

In February 1961, Lieutenant Junior Grade Roy Boehm, the first SEAL, received orders from Lieutenant Commander William Hamilton, commanding officer of Underwater Demolition Team Twenty-one, UDT-21, and Commander Underwater Demolition

Units Atlantic fleet, to put a group of men together from UDT-21, men who were prepared to go anywhere, do anything, at any time. For guidance, Boehm was told that if he and his men were called to a task that they could not perform, then he had failed. Boehm would go on to train many more SEALs and river combat sailors.

President Diem had little competition in South Vietnam's elections in 1961 and was easily elected to a six-year term. President Kennedy met with General Douglas MacArthur, who advised Kennedy it would be a mistake to fight in Southeast Asia. This message was echoed by George Ball, deputy undersecretary of State for economic affairs, who felt any involvement in Southeast Asia would be costly and not succeed. As far as George Ball was concerned, Vietnam was a tribal war, and the United States should not be involved.

Kennedy went on to hold a televised press conference against a backdrop of large maps showing the communist gains supported by the Soviet Union. Within two weeks, Kennedy had alerted 10,000 U.S. Marines in Okinawa while moving the Seventh Fleet into the South China Sea. Kennedy, facing a crisis at the Bay of Pigs, vetoed military response to Cuba and maintained his aggressive posture in Laos. In April, 1961, the Soviet Union agreed to a cease-fire in Laos. Although Kennedy had won that stand-off, he had decided that Laos was too fragile a place from which to oppose the communists. If that line was to be held, it would have to be from South Vietnam.

At that point, President Diem had a change of heart and requested a bilateral treaty with the United States. Two weeks later, he asked for an additional fighter-bomber squadron, civilian pilots for helicopters and transport aircraft, and U.S. combat units. The chiefs in Washington estimated 40,000 U.S. soldiers would be required and possibly 125,000 more if North Vietnam or the Chinese jumped into the fight. Kennedy decided to send General Maxwell Taylor to assess the situation, with a plane full of experts to accompany him. The day they arrived, Diem went before the National Assembly to proclaim a state of emergency. The monsoon had flooded along the Mekong River, killing the livestock and destroying the rice surplus for the next year. Some 200,000 homes were underwater and 1.5 million Vietnamese were hungry. One week later, Taylor returned to Washington and told Kennedy that the introduction of a U.S. military task force, without delay, offered far more advantages than difficulties, far more opportunities than risks. He concluded that their plan to save Vietnam would not succeed without it.

In May 1961, President Kennedy sent 400 Green Beret Special Forces soldiers to South Vietnam to train local forces in counter-insurgency methods.

President Kennedy was worried that Vietnam would become another Berlin, having to send in American forces with no end in sight. It had been a tough first year in office for the young president, with Cuba, Laos, Berlin, and now Vietnam. Kennedy was forced into taking a stand against the communists, but feared that there could not be an American solution to every world problem. The president's misgivings were shared by others in Washington who felt the war would have to be won on the village level by the people of Vietnam. Secretary of Defense Robert McNamara recommended support of South Vietnam by deploying 200,000 troops, suggesting that if Vietnam fell to the communists, it would have serious repercussions around the world. This was not what the president or Secretary of State Dean Rusk wanted to hear, and Rush persuaded McNamara to reconsider his position.

They jointly drew up a memorandum retaining a commitment to prevent the fall of South Vietnam to communism, but deferred committing U.S. ground forces to South Vietnam unless North Vietnamese aggression grew. They did decide to dispatch support troops and equipment, including helicopters, transport aircraft, air reconnaissance equipment, along with increasing the number of American military advisors. It was also decided that there would be a study for committing major ground forces in the future. In return, President Diem was expected to initiate reforms and join in a partnership with American military in the conduct of the war. George Ball warned the new American president that within five years they would have to commit troops. Kennedy's reply was, "That just isn't going to happen George." Following a meeting between John Kennedy and South Vietnam envoy Nguyen Dinh Thuan, an agreement was reached for direct training and combat supervision of Vietnamese troops by U.S. instructors. On October 24, 1961, the sixth birthday of the Republic of Vietnam, President Kennedy sent a letter to President Diem pledging that the United States was determined to help South Vietnam preserve its independence.

In his January 11th, 1962, State of the Union address, President Kennedy had stated that few generations in all of history had been granted the role of being the great defender of freedom in its maximum hour of danger. And he then included that this was good fortune. U.S. military personnel in South Vietnam totaled over 10,000, but in accordance with President Kennedy's pledge to provide American military assistance to South Vietnam, the number would rise quickly, with America being pulled deeper and deeper into the conflict.

THE BUILD UP

In December 1961, the escort helicopter aircraft carrier USS Core, CVHE-13, cautiously steamed up the Saigon River, trying not to wash out any of the small sampans and junks with her wake. She towered above the small boats, even though she was loaded to the gills. On her deck was a squadron of Shawnee "flying Banana" helicopters with U.S. Army pilots and maintenance personnel waving from the rail at the Vietnamese people who stopped to stare. It was the beginning of a new era, with America raising the stakes. The U.S. Military Advisory Assistance group had tripled in size to more than 4,000 men, and within a year would grow to more than 10,000. U. S. advisors stepped up the training for South Vietnamese forces and supplied them with small arms, machineguns and radios. Many Naval advisors and Army Green Berets, trained in paramilitary tactics, moved into South Vietnamese hamlets and villages and began living alongside their Vietnamese Regional Force counterparts, while they trained them in conducting counter-guerrilla warfare and led them into battle against the National Liberation Front-backed Viet Cong who infested the Mekong Delta and who were always watching.

U.S. military personnel began assisting the South Vietnamese on all levels as American Marines participated in training exercises, coordinating artillery fire and air support, and acted as liaisons with the U.S. Navy for amphibious maneuvers. American Navy Advisors worked on ship maintenance and accompanied the South Vietnamese Navy on sea patrols and river force operations, helping to organize the Vietnamese junk fleet. A U.S. Marine advisor from Texas, Lieutenant Colonel Marion C. "Dirty" Dalby, set up a boat manufacturing operation to provide desperately needed swamp and canal transports in the Mekong Delta.

Thousands of American soldiers worked alongside the Vietnamese at every level, from command operation planning to village and hamlet execution of operations and defense. The advisors not only trained, but participated in pacification and civic action programs living alongside the Vietnamese, sharing their food and accompanying their patrols, suffering the same hardships and dangers. It was not unusual for the advisors to take point and lead the way, teaching the Vietnamese how to be aggressive and take the fight to the enemy. This was no easy job, and there was much friction between the Americans and South Vietnamese, but out in the rice paddies and bush, the danger shared by the two helped earn respect, bringing the anti-communist forces together. Back in Saigon, it was a different matter.

Washington had instructed the advisors to take a more passive role, training and advising the South Vietnamese forces but returning fire only when fired upon by the enemy. This didn't last long, as American advisors started taking hits. Seeing this, their fellow countrymen started firing much sooner, throwing all logic out the window. Although Washington did not consider Vietnam a war, for the men serving there, it sure felt like one. And as the American casualty rate started to rise, it started looking like one. Even Attorney General Robert Kennedy on a visit to Saigon had stated that the United States would stay in Vietnam until we had won. Many of the people back home in the States did not know this small nation halfway around the world. But for the Americans serving in Vietnam, it was obvious that they were in a fight, and probably a long one, at that.

The Army's Green Beret Special Forces knew all too well of Vietnam and had been serving there since the late 1950s. They had been training the South Vietnamese forces in commando tactics and had helped form a counterinsurgency program. They participated as advisors on patrols, operating with Saigon forces. But their main objective in Vietnam was to develop and operate with civilian and regional forces of the countryside. The indigenous people of Vietnam were all too vulnerable to communist aggression and often were physically forced to serve as Viet Cong fighters. Working with primitive Montagnard tribes, the Coa Dia and Hao

Hao religious sects, and many others was normal procedure for the Green Berets. Going into small villages and hamlets, strengthening their defenses and organizing economic and social programs to raise the standards of living, made loyal fighters of the tribe people who were often persecuted by the South Vietnamese government and left out of the decision-making processes. They lined up to join forces with the Green Beret, as twelve-man Green Beret A-teams were set up throughout South Vietnam, supplying training and weapons, creating strong allies and catching the communists off-guard as they lost footholds in what used to be secure territory. Within a year, a network of villages with thousands of trained and armed defenders had been set up, spanning from the DMZ on the northern border of South Vietnam to the tip of the Ca Mau Peninsula, at the far southern end of the country.

The year of 1962 was the year of the Tiger, and communist forces began a series of attacks to turn the people against President Diem and drive the Americans out of Vietnam. By the end of February, two renegade South Vietnamese pilots flying American-made WWII planes, bombed the presidential palace. The Viet Cong intensified efforts to strangle Saigon and control the rice crops of the Mekong Delta, to insure adequate supplies for their own forces and create shortages - and fear - in Saigon.

The South Vietnamese government and Washington countered by carving out a series of strategic hamlets, in jungles once controlled by the Viet communists. In Operation Sunrise, relocated peasants built compounds and moved into fortified hamlets protected by barbed wire, sharpened bamboo stakes, and newly trained self-defense militia units. The fortified hamlets offered schools, clinics, markets, and protection, with land given to each family who moved into the compound. The strategic hamlets were considered revolutionary at the time and put many peasants to work creating a new spirit in the south. In Ca Mau Peninsula alone, an area long controlled by the Viet Cong, over 10,000 people settled into strategic hamlets. By year's end, thousands of these hamlets had been built, funded by America. Many Washington politicians, including both Secretary of Defense McNamara and Deputy Secretary of State Ball, had made tours and reported back to President Kennedy that the strategic hamlets were an excellent way to bring South Vietnam together and under Diem's control, countering Viet Cong aggression. The government in Saigon was very happy and started calling it the year of the strategic hamlet.

Through the year, the armed forces of South Vietnam continued growing and getting stronger, and soon the combined forces of the Army of the Republic of Vietnam, Civil Guard and Self Defense groups and militias numbered over 300,000. But for the most part, it was the Vietnamese Army that carried the fight to the Viet Cong. Utilizing the helicopters and M-113 armored personnel carriers provided by the United States, soldiers began an aggressive campaign against the insurgents. For the first time in years, they began operations in enemy strongholds north of Saigon in Tay Ninh Province and in the far south, in the Viet Cong-infested U Minh Forest, along the Gulf of Thailand. Being unfamiliar to the new aggressive tactics of the ARVN, the Viet Cong were harassed repeatedly and retreated time and again, defeated and demoralized.

During April, while they were launching Operation Sunrise north of Saigon, 8,000 men of 7th ARVN Division, supported by Vietnamese Navy river boats with American naval advisors aboard and fighter planes overhead, penetrated the Viet Cong-held Plain of Reeds, eighty miles west of Saigon. After three days of fighting through rice paddies, muddy fields of the vast plain, and bamboo and reed forests, government forces killed eighty-five Viet Cong and captured thirty more. In July, battalions of South Vietnamese soldiers and marines were airlifted into Kien Hoa Province to hunt down the groups of guerrilla forces taking refuge. In August, they started a two-week campaign that was supported by U.S. helicopters and military advisors sweeping the Cau Mau Peninsula in search of enemy "caches" and hiding places. Over 200 Viet Cong were killed, and tons of medical supplies and ammunition were captured. Successful operations were conducted in Tay Ninh Province, along the Cambodian border, where government troops had not operated in years. Thanks to the new helicopters, track vehicles, and American advisors, the Republic of Vietnam was gaining the upper hand.

During the summer of 1962, the Declaration on the Neutrality of Laos was signed in Geneva by the United States and thirteen other nations, which protected the Ho Chi Minh Trail in eastern Laos from American intervention. President Kennedy also signed the Foreign Assistance Act, which provided assistance to countries on the rim of the communist world, under direct attack. A U.S. Special Forces camp was set up at remote Khe Sanh, to monitor North Vietnamese infiltration down the Ho Chi Minh Trail.

In October 1962, President Kennedy was again put to the test when he ordered the United States Navy to intercept and turn around Soviet Union supply ships transporting missiles, after viewing an intelligence spy plane photo showing hidden missile sites in Cuba. He then set in motion a Naval blockade of Cuba and demanded that Premier Khrushchev remove all the missile bases from Cuba, just ninety miles from America. One of the key U.S. ships involved in the quarantine was the USS Joseph P. Kennedy Jr., DD850, named in honor of the President's eldest brother, who was killed in WWII.

It was a defining moment as we all held our breath and prayed that the stand-off would not lead to nuclear holocaust. By the end of October, the Russian premier conceded to President Kennedy's demands by ordering all Soviet ships away from Cuban waters and agreeing to remove the missiles from Cuba's mainland.

For over a year, the Viet Cong watched and studied the Americans and their helicopters, knowing that the day would come when they would have to make a stand. Shortly after Christmas, in December 1962, South Vietnamese Army Intelligence located a Viet Cong radio transmitter with evidence of a Viet Cong company in the hamlet of Tan Thoi, a little under a mile northwest of Ap Bac hamlet. The 7th ARVN Division, commanded by Colonel Huynh Van Coa, with division advisor Lieutenant Colonel John Paul Vann leading the way, devised a plan to trap the Viet Cong by landing the ARVN infantry regiment to the north in air assault from CH-21 Shawnee helicopters, while a regiment of two task forces of regional forces, commanded by the providence chief, Major Lam Quang Tho, moved on foot, in columns, from the south. The armored cavalry, with thirteen armored tracked personnel carriers, were to transport a company of infantry and lead the attack, leaving a field to the north open for a Viet Cong retreat that would be engaged by South Vietnamese artillery. This would leave three Vietnamese companies held in reserve, with artillery and air support on call.

Ap Bac hamlet was located roughly thirty-five miles southwest of Saigon, in the rich rice fields of the Mekong Delta. It was mostly a flat wetland of rice paddies supported by canals running off the river.

Contrary to intelligence reports, the Viet Cong regular force was dug in and ready, consisting of not one, but three, main force Viet Cong companies, over 300 fighters well equipped with captured U.S. weapons, reinforced with machineguns, 60mm mortars, and several local VC guerrilla units by their side. The Viet Cong got word of John Paul Vann's plans to attack and carefully prepared defensive positions along the Cong Luong Canal to the north, which was ringed by dense tree lines. The vegetation along the canal offered good concealment for spider holes and fortified fighting positions, difficult to see from both the air and ground, and gave the Viet Cong a clear field of fire across open rice paddies.

At the time, the Shawnee CH-21 "flying banana" assault helicopter was the workhorse of Vietnam. It carried twenty-two fully equipped soldiers into battle or twelve men on stretchers with two medics for medical evacuations. The flying bananas, first developed for Vietnam in 1961 in support of South Vietnamese forces, were relatively slow, at just over 100 miles per hour. The Shawnee was just over fifty-two feet long and almost sixteen feet high, with a range of about 265 miles. She was powered by one Curtis-Wright R1820 Cyclone supercharged, 1150 horsepower, piston engine, with two tandem fully-articulated, three-bladed, counter-rotating rotors. Its cables and fuel lines were so vulnerable to small arms fire that it was joked that one had been brought down by a Viet Cong spear. Later models were armed with .50 caliber machineguns in the door and made a little more durable.

At 0700 hours, January 2nd, 1963, the regional forces started advancing, while the Shawnee helicopters made one trip safely, lifting one company of infantry into position. Within an hour, Task

Force Alpha, of the regional forces, walked up on an ambush as the Viet Cong opened up from both the tree line and Cong Loung Canal, pinning the regional forces down. In the first few minutes of the battle, the company commander was killed. After that, the regional forces tried to flank the guerrillas but were unsuccessful in many attempts. Artillery was called in but misdirected, landing on the far side of the enemy. The task force commander was then wounded, stopping the maneuver in its tracks. Major Lam Quang Tho, leading the provincial forces, refused to allow the advance to continue any further and set up blocking positions, changing the mission. The major may have feared South Vietnam's President Ngo Dinh Diem, who was known for removing and demoting ranking officers if they took high losses in battle. By then, the helicopters had landed the 7th ARVN Battalion, so division commander Colonel Huynh Van Coa decided to drop back in a reserve force posture to the north side of the canal, in the rice paddy west of Ap Bac.

Shortly after 1000 hours, the Shawnee helicopters approached, escorted by five UH-1 Huey helicopters. The pilots, knowing only of the enemy position in the southern tree line, flew over the canal and Ap Bac, drawing fire along the way and landing the big helicopters 200 yards west of the village, as the troops quickly disembarked under fire. The Hueys began making strafing runs along the enemy positions, but because of the cover of the trees and deep holes shielding the enemy, they had only limited success. One of the flying bananas was shot up too badly to get off the ground, so a second Shawnee landed to pick up the crew. All of a sudden, communist antiaircraft guns and mortars hidden along the canal and in the tree line opened up with murderous fire, damaging the second helicopter as it landed. Now they were being pounded by automatic weapons and mortar fire as a Huey came in to rescue the two downed crews. While it hovered, the enemy found its mark again, striking the main rotor, causing the Huey to flip over and crash on its side. Another Shawnee made it out but, because of damage from enemy guns, was forced to land just a short distance away. The disembarked infantry company found itself in deep trouble and had to take cover in a shallow irrigation ditch, also pinned down.

The division advisor, Lieutenant Colonial John Paul Vann, radioed to senior advisor of the armored cavalry, Captain James B. Scanlon, that the helicopters were down about 1500 yards to the southeast of the regiment. Because of steep banks and an argument between Scanlon and Captain Ba about moving the tracks across the Cong Ba Ky Canal, the column made poor time. As the first tracks approached the copters, mortars and enemy fire raked the two leading vehicles and their dismounted infantrymen. The tracks then backed up, abandoning the wounded South Vietnamese forces, which were still drawing heavy fire. Minutes later, they advanced, firing their .50 caliber machineguns and again meeting with heavy fire. The Viet Cong began focusing on the machine gunners atop the track vehicles, killing fourteen of them before day's end. Meanwhile, another Shawnee copter landed, trying to rescue the downed crews. But it took so much fire that it had to immediately take back off, barely clearing the contact zone, eventually landing safely away from enemy fire. By noon, five helicopters had been shot down, with wounded sprawled over the wet swamplands.

At one point, Captain Scanlon disembarked his track and ran to the aid of the wounded helicopter crews, with the help of American Army advisor Sergeant Bowers, pulling them out and carrying them to the armored vehicles. By then, more tracks had crossed the canal and tried to move forward, but they, too, were repelled. The Viet Cong concentrated fire on each vehicle as they advanced one at a time.

By mid-morning, it was apparent the tracks would not be able to overrun the Viet Cong positions, so the South Vietnamese commanders, with approval of the advisors, decided to request reinforcements from an Airborne battalion. Despite the objections of both Colonel John Paul Vann and Colonel Daniel B. Porter, who was IV Corps Tactical Zone advisor, the corps commander decided to drop the South Vietnamese Airborne battalion to the west, behind the mechanized squadron rather than to the east of the canal, where it would have completed the encirclement. At dusk, the 8th Airborne Battalion parachuted into the rice paddies. By morning, the Viet Cong had taken advantage of the open escape route and slipped out of the area and the Civil Guardsmen sent to block the escape route had disappeared. Colonel Vann, trying to salvage something positive, commandeered every American advisor in the vicinity. Maintenance personnel, cooks, communications men, and even a water purification specialist, all joined together and formed Vann's motley force of irregulars, who bravely went out and rounded up thirty-two Viet Cong prisoners.

Because of the number of South Vietnamese troops involved and helicopters downed, the battle drew attention. Lieutenant Colonel Vann considered the operation a malicious hoax and later stated that because of the failure of the armored track vehicles and South Vietnamese's forces to move forward, and the parachute drop on the wrong side of the river, the South Vietnamese had reinforced defeat rather than ensured victory. The Viet Cong had suffered eighteen killed and thirty-nine wounded. The South Vietnamese losses were eighty dead with 100 wounded. Three U.S. advisors were killed in the battle, and eight were wounded, with five helicopters shot down.

In many ways, the fighting at Ap Bac had shown the problems that the advisors were facing and the poor leadership of the South Vietnamese commanders in coordinating their forces. Politically, the battle was reported as a victory, but in truth, relations between U.S. advisors and South Vietnamese command was strained, and many felt that improvements would need to be made if South Vietnam was to win the war.

American newspaper front pages reported the battle as the first major combat victory by regular force Viet Cong guerrillas over South Vietnamese forces. Vann fumed, proclaiming the battle to be a miserable damn performance by South Vietnamese forces, just like always. The Viet Cong had maintained battlefield discipline and fired with deadly accuracy, while government troops panicked and stalled, resulting in heavy casualties. In after-action reports, U.S. advisors, who had observed the performance of the Vietnamese on the battlefield, placed the blame on the shoulders of the South Vietnamese commanders, whom they accused of poor coordination, even worse leadership, and a lack of aggressiveness.

In May 1963, Buddhists rioted in South Vietnam after they were denied the right to display religious flags during their celebration of

Buddha's birthday. As demonstrations spread, South Vietnamese police and army troops shot at Buddhist demonstrators in Hue, resulting in the deaths of one woman and eight children. Back in Washington, there was mounting pressure for the Kennedy administration to disassociate itself from Diem's family-run government. Diem's younger brother Nhu, who controlled the American-trained South Vietnamese Special Forces, ordered brutal crackdowns on Buddhist sanctuaries, imposing martial law. Nhu's crackdowns sparked widespread anti-Diem demonstrations, with several Buddhist monks publicly burning themselves to death as an act of protest. The sacrifices were captured on film by news photographers and the images shocked the American public, as well as President Kennedy.

By July, South Vietnamese General Tran Van Don, a Buddhist, contacted the CIA in Saigon about the possibility of staging a coup against Diem, whose regime was described as almost a police state with strict censorship of the press and absence of political opposition. Those opposing Diem faced arrest and imprisonment. Fearing the worst, Kennedy sent for help.

In August, new U.S. Ambassador Henry Cabot Lodge, a tough Massachusetts Republican who had lost his Senate seat to a young John Kennedy in 1952, arrived in South Vietnam and met President Diem for the first time. Lodge advised Diem to fire his brother Nhu and to reform his government, but Diem arrogantly refused to even discuss the matter. Lodge then reported to Washington that Diem had not done anything he had asked and that he did not believe the war could be won under his administration. President Kennedy responded by giving Lodge a free hand to manage the unfolding events in Saigon and described Diem as out of touch with the South Vietnamese people in a TV interview with Walter Cronkite. Then Kennedy went on to comment that if we withdrew from Vietnam, the communists would gain control of Southeast Asia.

Rebel South Vietnamese generals, led by Duong Van "Big" Minh, the former ARVN field commander who had crushed the Binh Xuyen crime lords and run them out of Saigon, continued planning the coup after receiving assurances that U.S. aid would continue and that Washington would not interfere with the overthrow of

President Diem. Generals Minh, Tran Van Don, former commander of I Corps, and Le Van Kim, former commandant of the National Military Academy, had all been deprived of their duties by Diem and placed in figurehead positions. Minh, the leader, was a man of action, whereas Don was adept at administration and the liaison with the Americans, while Kim was in charge of political planning for the successor government and considered the most intelligent of the three. Between the three generals, they had enlisted an impressive group of additional generals and fellow officers who supported the takeover. Seeing this, Ambassador Lodge reported to Washington that a coup was imminent.

On the afternoon of November 1st, 1963, after a morning meeting between Lodge, Admiral Harry D. Felt, the commander of U.S. Pacific forces, and Diem, the coup began as Vietnamese marine, airborne, and army troops roared into Saigon backed by tanks, surrounding the presidential palace and seizing control of the police headquarters. By late afternoon, fighting had erupted between rebel forces and the palace guard as rebel tanks raked the central avenues with bursts of machinegun fire. Two rocket-firing T-28 fighter-bombers dived toward the palace, only to be driven off in a hail of 20mm antiaircraft shells. Small arms fire began to crackle around the city, and the thump of mortars reverberated in the humid air. During this time, Diem telephoned the rebel generals yet failed at attempts to talk them out of the coup, then rejected all appeals for him and his brother to surrender. Diem then called Ambassador Lodge and asked what the attitude of the United States was. Lodge responded that he was not well enough informed to be able to tell him much, as it was 4:30 a.m. in Washington, and the U.S. government could not possibly have a view. Lodge then expressed concern for Diem's safety. Diem responded "I am trying to restore order."

Meanwhile, Diem and Nhu made frantic attempts to rally loyal army commanders throughout the country. But no one came to their rescue. Sometime early in the evening, Diem and Nhu slipped out of the presidential palace unnoticed, through secret tunnels, and went to a safe house in the Cholon district, owned by a wealthy Chinese friend.

In the early morning hours of November 2nd, one of Diem's aides betrayed his location to the generals, and the hunt began as the brothers moved to a nearby Catholic church. At 0600 hours, realizing their situation was hopeless, Diem and Nhu called General Don and offered to surrender from inside the church. Colonel Duong Ngoc Lam, the head of the Civil Guard and a trusted friend, was the first out of the armored personnel carrier sent to arrest them. Following him was General Mai Huu Xuan, one of the original plotters and a bitter enemy of the brothers, who were placed in the back of the armored personnel carrier with their hands tied behind their backs. While traveling to Saigon, the vehicle stopped and Diem and Nhu were assassinated, both shot in the back of the head. Their deaths were officially described as accidental suicide.

According to reports, it was General Xuan who gave the order, but it is believed that the command came from General Minh. At the White House, a high-level meeting was interrupted with news of Diem's death, President Kennedy turned white and was noticeably shaken by the news, immediately leaving the room. Later he recorded in his private diary, "I feel that we must bear a good deal of responsibility."

Saigon celebrated the downfall of Diem's regime, but the coup resulted in leaving South Vietnam in a power vacuum during which a series of military and civilian government leaders tried to seize control. Meanwhile, the Viet Cong used the time to increase their hold over the rural population as the Republic of Vietnam became increasingly dependent on the United States, which was forced to providing millions of dollars in aid.

CHANGE OF COMMAND

On November 22nd, 1963, while riding through Dallas in a convertible limousine with his wife Jackie and Texas Governor John Connally, President John F. Kennedy was assassinated, ending the dreams of a generation. America stopped in a moment of silence as all eyes were glued to the TV. It was a day when America wept openly, as eyes recently full of happiness turned sad and warm tears ran down my thirteen-year-old cheeks. I was shocked and stunned, but more than that, I was mad that we had been robbed of one of the best presidents of my time.

Later that day, America watched Lyndon B. Johnson being sworn in as 36th U.S. President. He would become the fourth president to cope with Vietnam, using many of the same advisors who had served Kennedy. Johnson vowed publicly not to lose Vietnam.

In the first week of January 1964, Major Generals Tran Van Don and Le Van Kim joined Big Minh to form a short lived troika of power between the three generals. By the end of January, Major General Khahn Nugyen overthrew the three and became the new leader of South Vietnam.

In March, secret-U.S. backed bombing raids began against the Ho Chi Minh Trail inside Laos, conducted by mercenaries flying old American fighter planes. Defense Secretary McNamara visited General Khanh in South Vietnam and said "We'll stay for as long as it takes." President Johnson increased aid, believing a communist victory in South Vietnam would damage the credibility of the U.S. globally, with America's prestige and his reputation on the line. The National Security Council recommended the bombing of North Vietnam, but Johnson only approved the planning phase by the Pentagon. In April, Ambassador Lodge proclaimed he would not be surprised to see the Mekong Delta totally cleared of communist forces by the end of 1965.

As summer began, 56,000 Viet Cong were spreading their guerrilla war throughout South Vietnam, reinforced by North Vietnamese Army regulars who were pouring in via the Ho Chi Minh Trail. Responding to the escalation, President Johnson approved CIA clandestine operations, using South Vietnamese commandos in speed boats to harass sites along the coastline of North Vietnam.

General Maxwell D. Taylor, chairman of the Joint Chiefs of Staff, was appointed by President Johnson as the new U.S. ambassador to South Vietnam. During his one-year tenure, Taylor had to deal with five successive governments in politically unstable South Vietnam. President Johnson also appointed Lieutenant General William C. Westmoreland to be the new U.S. military commander in Vietnam. Westmoreland, a West Point graduate, was a highly decorated veteran of World War II and Korea.

On July 30th, 1964, South Vietnamese commandos in Nasty Class fast patrol boats, which had been purchased quietly from Norway to lend the illusion that the United States was not involved, raided two North Vietnamese military bases located on Hon Me and Hon Ngu Islands, just off the North Vietnamese coast in the Gulf of Tonkin. Under cover of darkness, the four boats slipped out of Da Nang and headed north, racing up the coastline, crossing the demilitarized zone, then angling farther out to sea as they left the safety of South Vietnamese waters. Five hours later, they neared their objectives just before midnight, with the four boats cutting their engines. To the northwest was Hon Me Island, with Hon Ngu to the southwest. The crews quietly made last-minute preparations and then split up, sailing off into the darkness in different directions. It was twenty minutes into the new day when PTF-3 and PTF-6 reached Hon Me and began their run at the shore.

Since the mid-1950s, the South Vietnamese Navy, under CIA guidance, had been conducting clandestine operations against North Vietnam. Initially operating with junks, the Republic of Vietnam operations used increasingly more sophisticated craft, including modified Swift boats. But the limited operating range of these craft limited their effectiveness and increased their likelihood for detection.

In 1964, the U.S. moved the responsibility for the clandestine operations against North Vietnam from the CIA to the U.S. military as represented by Military Assistance Command - Special Operation Group, MACSOG, and later, Study and Observation Group established in January 1964. With this change, the U.S. provided a number of fast patrol boats that extended range of the clandestine operations.

To counter the new boats, the North Vietnamese established radar and communications facilities to detect the new threat and relocated naval assets, including Soviet-made P4 motor torpedo boats and Chinese-built Swatow motor gunboats, to counter the expanded South Vietnamese operations.

Although aerial reconnaissance provided some information regarding the changes in the North Vietnamese order of battle, it was decided to utilize DeSoto Patrol destroyers in the Tonkin Gulf to obtain definitive electronic intelligence information. The DeSoto Patrol had previously operated in the waters along the shore of China and North Korea. The first DeSoto Patrol in the Tonkin Gulf was conducted at the end of February 1964.

During the morning of July 31st, 1964, the destroyer USS Maddox, DD-731, the latest specially fitted destroyer, had rendezvoused with the tanker USS Ashtabula, just south of the DMZ, where they were topping off fuel when they saw four Nasty Class patrol boats heading back to Da Nang from the Gulf of Tonkin. The USS Maddox had planned to sail to sixteen points along the North Vietnam coast, ranging from the DMZ north to the Chinese border. At each point, the ship would stop and circle, picking up electronic signals before moving on.

Everything had gone smoothly at first until 0354 hours on August 2nd, when the destroyer was just south of Hon Me Island. Captain John J. Herrick, Commander Destroyer Division 192, who had gone aboard USS Maddox, concluded that there could be a possible hostile attack. So Maddox turned seaward, hoping to avoid a confrontation until daybreak, while radioing nearby USS Ticonderoga, CVA-14, alerting its crew of the situation incase air support was needed. At 1045 hours, Maddox returned to the coast, this time north of Hon Me. By 1600 hours, Maddox's radar detected five patrol boats that turned out to be P-4 torpedo boats and Swatows, which were closing and appeared to be preparing for an attack. When the enemy boats were within 10,000 yards, the destroyer fired three warning shots across the bow of the lead vessel. In response, the North Vietnamese boat launched a torpedo. The Maddox fired her guns again in self defense, hitting the second North Vietnamese boat just as it launched two torpedoes. Badly damaged, the boat turned and began limping back to home port. Changing course in time to evade the torpedoes, Maddox again was attacked, this time by a boat that fired another torpedo and machineguns. But fortunately, only one bullet hit Maddox during the unprovoked attack, and there were no causalities. As the enemy boat passed astern, it was raked by gunfire from USS Maddox that killed the boat's commander. The North Vietnamese turned for shore with Maddox in pursuit.

U.S. Navy fighters from the carrier USS Ticonderoga, led by Commander James Stockdale, arrived on the scene and attacked, strafing three torpedo boats and sinking the one that had been damaged in the battle with Maddox earlier. The aircraft then returned to USS Ticonderoga positioned off the coast of South Vietnam. The battle was over in twenty-two minutes. It is difficult to imagine that the North Vietnamese could come to any other conclusion than that the 34A and Desoto missions were all part of the same operation.

Back at the White House, twelve hours behind Vietnam time, President Johnson received reports of the attack and decided against retaliation, sending a diplomatic message to Hanoi warning of grave consequences from any further unprovoked attacks. Johnson then ordered USS Maddox to resume operations joined by a second destroyer, USS Turner Joy, DD-951, as the two ships begin a series of vigorous zigzags, sailing off North Vietnam's coast.

At 2108 hours on August 4th, Maddox and Turner Joy were on a southeasterly course approximately sixty miles from the North Vietnamese coast when three high-speed radar contacts were detected around fourteen miles eastward of the two ships.

At 2119 hours, the contacts, which were displayed on the radar screens on both ships, indicated probable hostile intent by changing course and closing range to take up positions that would permit launching torpedoes. Maddox and Turner Joy opened fire when it was evident from maneuvers of the approaching contacts that they were pressing in to attack. About one minute later, USS Maddox, a torpedo running on her sonar, detected by Captain Herrick, Commander, Destroyer Division 192, and others in CIC, Combat Information Center, informed USS Turner Joy that a torpedo had been launched and was headed in its direction. Lieutenant Junior Grade John Jerome Warry III, serving as the forward gun officer on Turner Joy, sighted a torpedo coming from the direction of the radar contacts while Turner Joy turned to avoid being hit. Seaman Larry O'Litton, who was with Lieutenant Warry and a seaman apprentice who was ships' lookout portside, sighted the torpedo passing parallel to USS Turner Joy at a distance of 300 feet. The torpedo passed along the destroyer, from aft to forward, on the bearing USS Maddox had reported.

During the attack, a searchlight was observed by all the sailors on the signal bridge and maneuvering bridge, including the commanding officer of USS Turner Joy. The beam of the searchlight did not touch the ship, but was seen to swing in an arc toward Turner Joy and was immediately extinguished when aircraft from a combat air patrol, orbiting above the ships, made their approach. When the combat air control aircraft overhead dropped flares, the attacking torpedo boats were actually seen and described by a number of Turner Joy crewmembers. None of the personnel had previously seen a torpedo boat before this time, since Turner Joy was not involved in the August 2nd action with USS Maddox, but on the basis of their observations, each one independently drew an accurate sketch of a motor torpedo boat similar to those known to be operating with the North Vietnamese Navy, which were similar to the torpedo boats that had attacked USS Maddox on August 2nd.

Commander G.H. Edmondson, commanding officer of Attack Squadron 52, and his wingman, had been flying combat air patrol in the vicinity of Maddox and Turner Joy at the time of the torpedo attack. Both officers were flying at altitudes ranging between 700 and 1,500 feet when they sighted gun flashes on the surface of the water as well as light anti-aircraft bursts at their approximate altitude. On one pass over the U.S. destroyers, both pilots positively sighted a snaky wake, one and one-half miles ahead of the lead destroyer, USS Maddox. The weather was overcast with limited visibility, but surface visibility was sufficient for U.S. Marines, Sergeant Matthew B. Allasne and Lance Corporal David A. Prouty, who were manning machineguns on Maddox, to see lights pass up and down, circling the ship. Both believed the lights to be from one or more small boats going at high speed.

Although immediate doubts arose concerning the validity of the attack on Maddox and Turner Joy, the Joint Chiefs of Staff recommended a retaliatory bombing raid against North Vietnam. Press reports in America greatly embellish the second attack with eyewitness accounts, although no journalist had been onboard the destroyers at the time. President Johnson decided to retaliate, ordering the first bombings of North Vietnam by the United States on oil facilities and naval targets along the North Vietnamese coast. An hour before the Pierce Arrow attack was to commence, LBJ went on national TV and announced that it was going to happen. Many in the Navy stood open-mouthed, watching what was considered to be a breach of security, while fifty U.S. Navy fighter bombers prepared and launched the attack.

Two Navy jets were shot down during the bombing raids, resulting in the death of Lieutenant Richard Sather of Pomona, California, and, one of the first American prisoners of war, Lieutenant Everett Alvarez of San Jose, California. Alvarez was taken to the internment prison in Hanoi that was later dubbed the "Hanoi Hilton" by hundreds of American airmen who became POWs during the Vietnam War. Opinion polls indicated eighty-five percent of America supported President Johnson's bombing decision; newspapers were also in support, but very few knew of the raids.

August 7th, 1964, in response to the two incidents involving the USS Maddox and USS Turner Joy, the U.S. Congress overwhelmingly passed the Gulf of Tonkin Resolution, allowing the President to take all necessary steps to prevent further attacks against U.S.

forces. The only two U.S. Senators to vote against the Resolution were Ernest Gruening of Alaska, who said "all Vietnam is not worth the life of a single American boy," and Wayne Morse of Oregon, who confronted McNamara at a meeting after being tipped off that the USS Maddox had been involved in a South Vietnamese commando raid against North Vietnam, and not an innocent victim as believed. McNamara adamantly denied the U.S. Navy had any part in, or was aware of, if there were in fact any, raids.

Although there were conflicting reports about the attacks on USS Maddox and USS Turner Joy, there is no disputing what Maddox was doing in the Gulf of Tonkin. It was participating in DeSota patrols monitoring North Vietnamese defenses. Like most DeSota patrols of the time, the purpose of secrecy was not only to conceal the operation from the enemy, who was well aware of it, but also from the American people, while the Johnson administration denounced North Vietnamese reports of U.S. terrorist attacks as communist propaganda.

In truth, most Americans believed that our involvement in the Vietnam War began with the Tonkin Gulf incident. The fact is, U.S. involvement had begun much earlier. Following the 1954 international conference in Geneva, CIA Director Allen Dulles sent Air Force Colonel Edward Lansdale to Vietnam as Deputy Director of the Office of Special Operation with orders to implement clandestine operations against North Vietnam. Highly experienced in such operations, Lansdale had performed similar duties, eliminating the communist in the Philippines.

One of President Kennedy's first directives to the CIA after taking office had been for the agency to initiate more clandestine operations in North Vietnam, to give Ho Chi Minh a taste of his own medicine. Many felt this was the way to fight the communists, and they may have been right. After all, North Vietnam was crossing over into Laos and Cambodia, sneaking men and arms down the Ho Chi Minh Trail. Why should the south play fair?

In late 1964, Saigon erupted in chaos amid the government's gross instability, with two disgruntled South Vietnamese generals staging an unsuccessful coup. In the U.S.S.R., Soviet leader Nikita Khrushchev was ousted from power and replaced by Leonid

Brezhnev, while China tested its first atomic bomb and massed troops along its border with Vietnam, responding to U.S. escalation. Back home in the United States, President Lyndon B. Johnson was nominated at the Democratic National Convention and during his campaign declared: "We are not about to send American boys 10,000 miles away from home to do what Asian boys ought to be doing for themselves." In November, Johnson was re-elected as president of the United States in a landslide victory over Barry Goldwater, and Viet Cong attacked Bien Hoa air base, twelve miles north of Saigon, in a pre-dawn mortar assault which killed five Americans and two South Vietnamese, and wounded nearly 100 others.

By December, 10,000 North Vietnamese Army soldiers had arrived in the Central Highlands of South Vietnam via the Ho Chi Minh Trail, carrying sophisticated weapons provided by China and the Soviet Union. Before the month was out, there was another military coup in Saigon by General Khanh, supported by a group of young South Vietnamese officers. An angry Ambassador Taylor summoned the young officers to the U.S. embassy then scolded them like school boys, warning them that America was tired of coups. Viet Cong terrorists set off a car bomb explosion at the Brinks Hotel, an American officers' residence in downtown Saigon, during the happy hour in the bar. Two Americans were killed with fifty-eight wounded. By year's end, there were 23,000 American military advisors supporting South Vietnamese forces, who were facing an estimated 170, 000 Viet Cong and NVA soldiers, which had begun battalion-sized attacks against South Vietnamese villages around Saigon, scoring victories against an increasingly unstable South Vietnamese government.

MOBILE RIVERINE FORCE

As far back as the Revolutionary War, America forces have conducted riverine operations. They were used in the War of 1812 on the Chesapeake Bay, Lake Erie, and the waterways of New Orleans against the British. From 1835 to 1842, Army and Navy forces fought together in the Florida Everglades against the Creeks and the Seminoles. A short time later, 2,500 sailors and Marines landed while being supported by fire from a rivercraft force at Juan Bautista in the War with Mexico, from 1846 to 1848. But not since the Civil War, when Union ironclads and Confederate steamers fought for control of Vicksburg on the Mississippi River, had America assembled a river fleet comprised of both Army and Navy troops. Then after a century of being away from river operations, the United States Navy began building up a brown water riverine force to combat the communist insurgents in the Rung Sat Special Zone, and in the Mekong Delta of the Republic of Vietnam.

When the United States government made the decision to help the South Vietnamese government counter communist aggression in the Mekong Delta, it was necessary for the U.S. Navy to face up to an environment very different from any in which it had operated. The Army of the Republic of Vietnam had been fighting for years, along with the regional and popular forces of South Vietnam, which all hated and actively pursued the Viet Cong guerrillas of the National Liberation Front, as well as the North Vietnamese infiltrators sent down from Hanoi.

It was rumored that North Vietnam was starving. The Mekong Delta was a low flatland of rice paddies and known as the rice bowl of Southeast Asia. The Republic of Vietnam had been successful in its efforts to govern the cities and larger villages, but had difficulty enforcing the law in the muddy swamps and paddy lands. American Naval advisors and Army Special Forces had been fighting alongside government troops and territorial forces for years. But it was not until U.S. Navy and Army entered the war that the South Vietnamese started to gain control of the vast Mekong Delta and began defeating the communists.

South Vietnam's government was located in Saigon at the northeastern edge of the Mekong Delta. The Long Tau channel to the south was the major deepwater shipping channel connecting Saigon to Vung Tau anchorage and the sea. It was the main route navigated by the large ocean going ships that were full of ammunitions and supplies being shipped from all over the globe to support the struggling Republic of Vietnam.

The Long Tau Channel wound forty miles through the Rung Sat, where the Viet Cong launched devastating attacks on shipping, thus earning it the title of the "Forest of Assassins." The Rung Sat was a dense, humid mangrove covered wasteland with tidal swamps where roads were virtually non-existent and sampans were the major mode of transportation. U.S. Navy and Coast Guard units from Task Forces 115 and 116 waged a tough determined war against the Rung Sat assassins and kept the channels open, but special equipment would be needed to dislodge the Viet Cong guerrillas from the outlying countryside. This is where the Mobile Riverine Force of Navy Task Force 117 and the 2nd Brigade of the 9th Infantry Division came into the picture. They had been designed and tasked to conduct assault operations throughout the low-lying areas of Vietnam. The Army-Navy team performed beach landings that resembled scenes from World War II, with boat ramps dropping and men running off in a hail of bullets to root out the enemy in their hidden holes and fighting bunkers in the jungles and marshy wetlands of South Vietnam.

To the south and west of Saigon was a beautiful flatland of rice paddies with miles of connecting rivers, streams, and canals, surrounded by mangrove forests full of nipa palm, pineapples, and coconut and banana trees. Most of the land during the rainy season, from May to October, was either just above or just below the water level. The waterways were rich in mineral and silt deposits that had washed down from as far away as Tibet, making the land extremely fertile. The entire region was ideal for growing rice.

The Mekong Delta was home to roughly fifty percent of the population of South Vietnam, with about seventy percent of the rice-producing fields located there. It extended from Saigon southwest to the Gulf of Thailand and the border with Cambodia. The permanent residents, who were mostly farmers and fishermen, lived almost entirely off the land. They grew their own rice, the mainstream of their diet, and supplemented it with fruit and fish, which was plentiful. They also ate pork, chicken, and duck, which were raised by nearly every household. The locals built their hooches from the fronds of the palm trees. Mud from the river banks was used to seal the fronds together.

Over the years the delta, with exception of the cities, had become a Viet Cong stronghold. The Parrot's Beak of Cambodia was less than fifty miles away from Saigon and a known communist infiltration zone and sanctuary for insurgents trying to make their way into the capital city Saigon to disrupt the Republic of Vietnam's government, to gain control of South Vietnam's people and their rice.

The first river forces were assigned to protect shipping on the waterways into Saigon through the Rung Sat and around My Tho. As they pushed into the delta, they needed river assault divisions to land troops on the beach to pursue the many pockets of Viet Cong Main Force Battalions taking refuge there. The delta's marshland was interlaced with one of the world's most intricate systems of rivers, streams, and canals, making a perfect refuge for the Viet Cong. Since there were few roads in the wetlands, the assaults on the Viet Cong bases would have to come from those waterways. Thus was born the concept for the Mobile Riverine Assault Force.

In the summer of 1965, the members of United States Military Assistance Command, Vietnam, MACV, drafted a plan for 1966 and reported that, in their opinion, there could be no substantial progress in the IV Corps Tactical Zone unless U.S. ground forces were introduced. Brigadier General William E. DePuy, assistant chief of staff for military operations, directed his planners to survey the delta for land suitable for basing ground troops. After careful study, it was decided that, after dredging river sand as fill material, they could build an area large enough to base a division. Only problem was, it would take some time to procure additional dredges from the United States to complete the job. So in addition to a land base, it was believed that other means of operating in the delta were needed. The planning staff turned to the French experience and the fact they had used riverine craft fairly well on the shallow inland waterways. The staff decided to take it one step further and planned to use not only small craft, but also a group of larger mobile landing craft that would house and support a mobile riverine force, very much like the Navy had done in World War II with amphibious forces.

LSTs, Landing Ships Tanks, would be drafted back into service and become very important to the river and costal war. More rugged and useful than their designers dreamed, they had continued to serve through the years, seeing duty in Korea after World War II. The Mekong Delta would become an amphibious war where landing ships took priority over destroyers, carriers, and just about everything else. In some ways, they were large slow targets. But they always got there delivering a heck of a punch. Along the coast and down the rivers the LSTs would steam, taking their fighting boats and copters with them.

But the LSTs would not be enough; barracks ships would also be needed. Self-propelled barracks ships would be used to house troops, and support operational staff. With up to seventeen FM radio antennas on each ship the staff had links to all ground, naval, and air elements of the force. Additional barges would be tied alongside the barracks ships to facilitate troop movements to and from the assault craft, and to provide storage space to support the boats. As the concept of an American river flotilla took form, the planners concluded that these barracks ships could be altered to furnish a helicopter flight deck and weapons for defense.

Captain David F. Welch of the United States Navy, who worked for MACV, believed that the force afloat concept merited a full study and discussed the matter with Rear Admiral Norvell G. Ward, chief of the Naval Advisory Group, Vietnam, who agreed that the idea had possibilities and that they needed help on the waterways.

In early December 1965, General DePuy briefed General Westmoreland and his commanders, on the concept of a Mekong Delta Mobile Afloat Force that would employ an Army brigade, coupled with a Navy squadron, deploying from mobile riverine bases. Westmoreland found the idea most imaginative and directed a team be sent to brief Headquarters, Pacific Command, and solicit its support. The team was headed by General DePuy, who after a period of discussion, received acceptance by the Commander in Chief, Pacific. It was felt that barracks ships, supported by small landing craft, patrol boats and helicopters, could be utilized to house part of the force and would enable the riverine force to conduct operations within a defined radius of the floating bases. The Joint Chiefs of Staff tentatively approved the employment of an Army division in the Mekong Delta, to put the plan in operation.

Back in Washington, the vice Chief of Naval Operations, Admiral Horacio Rivero Jr., supported the concept of a joint Army-Navy force and approved a proposal to send a planning group to Saigon to work with the MACV staff. The Navy team arrived in Vietnam, January 1966. Together the two groups studied the experiences of the French and Vietnamese with river assault forces, and drew up a proposal of what they thought would be needed to support such a force. The MACV-Navy team continued to plan, following the guidance of the Commander in Chief, Pacific, Admiral Ulysses S. Grant Sharp Jr., and in time their plan would prove to be a comprehensive blueprint for the preparation of both Army and Navy components, and the conduct of future riverine operations.

In the summer of 1966, MACV reported that about one-third of all Viet Cong actions against the government in South Vietnam occurred in the IV Corps Tactical Zone, and estimated that the Viet Cong controlled twenty-five percent of the population there. In many areas, government forces claimed control by day, but acknowledged that the night belonged to the Viet Cong, with exceptions of the larger cities. However, these cities were occasionally subject to terrorist incidents, mortar and rocket attacks, or assaults upon outlying guard posts. The Viet Cong continued choking off the flow of rice to market, making importation of rice necessary. Conditions in the delta were not improving, and something was going to have to be done to change the situation there. It was against this background that the basic decision for creation of an American Mobile Riverine Force was made.

By mid 1966, U.S. Naval forces would include Task Force One-Fifteen, TF-115, with its fast fifty-foot gray "Swift boats", and eighty-foot Coast Guard cutters, with the mission of patrolling coastal areas on the South China Sea and Gulf of Thailand in Operation Market Time, severing communist supply lines from the sea. The fast thirty-one-foot river patrol boats of Task Force One-Sixteen, TF-116, code named Game Wardens, were to interdict the enemy on the thousands of miles of rivers, streams, and canals of South Vietnam's navigable water highways controlling Viet Cong cross-river movements, and assisting government forces in repelling enemy attacks on river outpost of the Regional and Popular Forces. In addition, Game Warden patrols would provide intelligence and check sampans, junks, and water-taxis day time river traffic. Minesweeping of shipping channels and other support forces fell under TF-116 as well.

In late '66, Task Force One-Seventeen, TF-117, would come into being. The ships and heavy waterborne tank boats, of the Mobile Riverine Force, would support a variety of tactical riverine operations, remaining in enemy base areas for weeks deploying ground troops to route out Viet Cong battalion-size forces, which were embedded throughout the Mekong Delta. In addition, planners had envisioned that river assault craft would be used in reconnaissance and patrolling missions, in resupply operations, would reinforce Game Warden and Market Time operations when necessary, and would support operations to open and secure important water routes. To meet the needs to interdict logistical supply routes and to take the battle to the enemy, the U.S. Navy planners had to develop an entirely new type of warfare to combat the enemy in the Mekong Delta. Since most of the Navy's equipment at that time was not well suited for use in the delta's mud and water, they had to create new equipment to support this new type of warfare. To meet this challenge, the U.S. Navy contracted for the building and modification of existing boats for river patrols and to carry assault troops into battle. They also had to quickly retrain sailors in jungle warfare tactics and riverine warfare.

During this time of rebuilding, many new river squadrons and divisions for the three new task forces were born. But certainly one of the most unique military forces of the river costal war was the Army-Navy Mobile Riverine Force, which was tasked to strike Viet Cong strongholds the length and breadth of the delta region. The great "green fleet" deployed to far-ranging places taking the fight to the enemy, slowly chipping away at their numbers. As a result, the Viet Cong would be pushed farther and farther from the principal waterways that they used, and would have so much liked to have continued to control.

Due to the size of the Mobile Riverine Assault Force, which had doubled in size by late 1968, they would divide their ships and boats into two separate task groups, normally operating independently of each other. Mobile Riverine Group Alpha would come to consist of River Assault Squadrons Nine and Eleven, with six ships – USS Benewah, USS Colleton, USS Nueces, USS Askari, USS Sphinx, and a LST supplied by Command Seventh Fleet on a three-month rotation basis. Three battalions of infantrymen from the 2nd Brigade, 9th Infantry Division would embark in these ships and comprised the ground force element of the task group. It was probably no coincidence that the division had been designated the 9th U.S. Infantry Division, since General Westmoreland had seen extensive service with the 9th Infantry in World War II in both France and Germany.

Mobile Riverine Group Bravo would include River Assault Squadrons Thirteen and Fifteen with five ships – USS Mercer, USS Satyr, APL-26 and APL-30, both non-propelled barracks barges, and a LST provided on a rotational basis. Task Group Bravo would also support Army elements of the 9th Infantry Division. And in addition, both task groups would support Vietnamese Marine Battalions, the Army of the Republic of Vietnam, and Popular and Regional Forces of the countryside.

River Assault Flotilla One was designated the naval component of the Mobile Riverine Force and would grow to consist of River Assault Squadrons Nine, Eleven, Thirteen and Fifteen, with ten shallow draft ships and 200 river assault boats, all of which were painted dark green to blend in with the dense jungle foliage that lined the banks of the rivers, canals, and delta streams. As the force grew in strength, there were roughly 2000 officers and enlisted sailors that exhibited zeal, initiative, and good judgment as they performed the many difficult tasks which were necessary to make the force efficient and effective. Each River Assault Squadron was divided into two River Assault Divisions of 250 men and twenty-five assault boats. Squadron Nine was the first to deploy, consisting of River Assault Divisions 91 and 92. Squadron Eleven was second with Divisions 111 and 112. Squadron Thirteen was next, consisting of River Assault Divisions 131 and 132, and last was Squadron Fifteen with Divisions 151 and 152.

The repair ship USS Askari (ARL 30) was the first "on station" repair ship for the assault craft assigned to River Assault Flotilla One. Converted from a LST and painted green, she operated in Vung Tau harbor and provided temporary housing. On a well-equipped repair shop the size of a football field, crewmen stayed busy around the clock repairing and maintaining boats returning from assault operations. Most of the work was done at night and in the early mornings after the day's operations. Still, morale was high, with the repair crews felting a sense of accomplishment that repairs were kept at a high standard to protect the crews who went into harm's way and fought in the assault craft. Everyone knew what was at stake and believed in what they were doing. The Internal Combustion Engine Repair Shop could manufacture most small parts not readily available, and handle any problem. The guys there were a proud seasoned bunch of veterans, but if you asked them, they would tell you they were just trying to do their jobs the best they knew how, and they did. Later, USS Satyr, ARL 23, USS Sphinx, ARL 24, USS Krishna, ARL 38, and USS Indra, ARL 37, all converted LSTs, joined the Mobile Riverine Force.

Equally as important were the self-propelled barracks ships USS Benewah, APB 35, and the USS Colleton, APB 36. When they arrived in Vung Tau, it was the beginning of the mobile base for the new riverine force. The ships would provide living quarters and command and control facilities for the Army-Navy team conducting the operations. The two barracks ships, which could berth over a thousand men each, were converted LSTs and had shallow enough drafts so they could establish a base of operations wherever needed, on the waterways in Vietnam. When the units returned to the mobile riverine base, the men relaxed aboard the barracks ships where clean bunks, hot food and showers, movies, a snack bar and air conditioning was available to them. In time, USS Mercer, APB 39, and USS Nueces, APB 40, would join River Assault Flotilla One.

The river assault divisions were made up of three basic types of modified World War II Landing Craft Medium (LCM-6) and the "Alpha" assault patrol boat, which was the fastest of the heavies at eighteen knots. It was designed and constructed specifically for the Mobile Riverine Force in Vietnam. About half of the boats in each division were armored troop carriers (ATC) called "Tangos," which had front landing ramps for river assaults and canopies to protect their passengers. Within a few months after arriving in-country, some had been specially reconfigured with helicopter decks to accommodate medical evacuations, resupply and personnel transfers. Each Tango was capable of lifting a platoon of forty fully-equipped infantrymen into virtually any waterway in the delta.

To protect the Tangos and troops against enemy rockets and recoilless rifles, rebar cage-like bar armor was used at strategic points as a trigger shield to cause premature detonation, plus a fourteen-inch layer of Styrofoam and a special hard-grade steel plate had been installed. The Tangos were armed with 20mm cannons and .30 and .50 caliber machineguns, manned by Navy gunners who also served as the crews of the boats. Communist weapons fire usually originated from mud and concrete bunkers that frequently lined the narrow and heavily vegetated stream banks. At least one troop carrier would be designated as a floating aid station, and one of the Tango boats was converted into and designated as a refueling tanker with a capacity of 10,000 gallons, allowing the assault craft longer stays away from the supporting ships stationed on the larger rivers as floating supply centers.

Protecting the troop-laden Tangos were Monitor assault boats, named for the Civil War Ironclad, that were designated the battleships of the green fleet and would lead the column into battle. With more conventional tapered bows, the Monitors were more heavily armed and armored, including automatic 40mm cannons, and either a 105mm Howitzer or Navy 81mm mortars, with .50 and .30 caliber machineguns as well. The boat-mounted Howitzers were not normally used for long-distance fire support missions, but more for close in fighting with heavily fortified bunkers, projecting beehive and high explosive rounds into fortified Viet Cong bunkers, busting them open. Some Monitors were equipped with flame throwers and dubbed the Zippo, with their napalm spitting out along the banks, burning away the foliage that concealed hidden enemy fighting positions where the enemy lay in wait, prepared to ambush the Tangos and their troops.

Command Communication boats (CCB) were used for floating command post for the ground force and boat group commanders, incharge of the many units dispersed around the battlefield. Armed with bow 40mm turrets, they had an amidships section devoted to communications equipment and maps. Both Army and Navy operations and fire direction officers worked side by side on these boats. Command helicopters also exercised through the use of Command Communication boats, which could also be used to provide fire support when needed.

Serving as the destroyer/minesweeper boat of the fleet was the high-speed assault support patrol boats (ASPB) nicknamed the Alpha boat. Normally four to six Alpha boats provided mine countermeasures for the river assault divisions and escorted the slower Tango convoys during troop transport phases of operations. Later, after the troops had disembarked, all of these heavy assault craft would set blocking, surveillance positions, intercepting water traffic near an assault operation and preventing the enemy from withdrawing and escaping across major rivers and streams, during the heat of the battle. Assault craft not involved in operations would remain in the rear to protect the mobile afloat base. Each squadron consisted of approximately fifty boats with 500 sailors, including the squadron staff, which normally consisted of twelve men.

Duty on the heavily armored boats was brutal. There was very little air circulation inside the hulls of the slow moving metal boats, and the heat could be like that of an oven in the hot, harsh environment, of the delta, especially after three or four days of operations, searching out and destroying the enemy, which was the normal time a battalion conducted operations. But nevertheless, the sailors who manned the assault crafts were a tough, determined bunch of fighters that took pride in their job and would prove that the boats maneuvered and stood up well to enemy opposition. Considering the danger involved, moral was high with many becoming lifelong friends.

The Army contingent of the Mobile Riverine Force would consist of three embarked battalions of combat ready infantrymen from the 3/47th, 4/47th and 3/60th Infantry Battalions, 2nd Brigade, 9th Infantry Division, as well as a battery of artillery on mobile river barges from the 3/34th Artillery Division. The barges were towed by LCM-8s operated by the Army's 1097th Transportation Company.

When the Mobile Riverine Force was planning to execute an attack, command would select the area for each of the many operations on the basis of the latest intelligence information regarding current locations of enemy forces, in coordination with Army commands and Vietnamese authorities. Planners would then go to work drawing up the details of the operation. Some of the things considered were the number of friendly troops and assault craft required to do the job, how many boats of each type would be needed, and what waterways were navigable due to depth, width, or other factors such as vegetation growing in the water. The Mekong Delta's tidal range was very severe and would have great bearing on operations. Frequently, transits would be planned to cross shallow areas at high tide, or pass beneath a low bridge at low tide. Once in an area south of Can Tho, a bridge was jacked up a few feet so that the boats could pass underneath.

The Army and Navy staffs would then go over the operation in complete detail to see if they could find any weakness or fault in their plans. At the conclusion of the meeting, the plans were typed, duplicated, and distributed to the commanders who would participate in the operation. The operational area also had to be cleared with local Vietnamese military leaders to avoid conflicting with any operations that might have been planned for the same vicinity.

Twelve hours prior to the beginning of the mission, they would have a final briefing for all their commanders, who in turn, would brief their respective units. Since many of their operations were predawn landings, troops often boarded boats between midnight and four o'clock in the morning. Regardless, boat crews and infantrymen were served a hot breakfast by Navy cooks before they departed.

Then three assault boats at a time would come alongside the pontoons, floating beside each barracks ship, and embark the troops. Although they operated in darkened ship conditions, they used red lights of low candle power to provide a small amount of visibility so the infantrymen could assemble their packs and climb safely aboard. Once the Tango transports were loaded, the boats formed into a column and began the trip to the operation area.

Leading the formation would be two to four Alpha, or Tango boats, assigned minesweeper duties, and followed by a Monitor, leading the group of transports. Other Monitors with flamethrowers were interspersed among the troop transports to protect the troop-laden convoy. The division commander controlled the actions of the division from aboard a Monitor. Often the squadron commander was embarked on the Command Communications boat, which was usually near the middle of the column. The artillery barges towed by the Army LCM-8's were usually escorted by assault craft which did mine sweeping. This element would have left its base earlier so that they would be in place and ready to fire prior to the time the troop convoy began moving into the narrow waterways, near the operational area.

En route to the landing site, many of the soldiers would be resting or catching a few final hours of sleep. The first part of the journey would normally be on one of the larger rivers, where the boat crewmen would relax somewhat, although all gun mounts were manned and ready for action, should the column be attacked. As the boats neared their objective area, they would turn into one of the smaller streams or canals with everyone alert, with all guns jacked and ready to fire. In many areas of the delta, where it was heavily populated, they could not open fire unless fired upon first. In some unpopulated Viet Cong-dominated regions, where they had good reason to expect enemy ambushes, they would recon by machinegun fire. By firing at suspicious spots and into tall grass or wooded areas along the banks of the streams, they could sometimes surprise the enemy into firing early and exposing their positions.

When they finally reached the area where the landing was to be made, the force would soften up the beach for the ground assault with jet air strikes, helicopter gunships, artillery, or by machinegun and Napalm fire from the boats. The boats always stood ready to provide supporting fire before, during, and after the landing. The safety of the troops was foremost in everybody's mind. The Monitors, along with the command and minesweepers boats, continued to cruise in mid-stream with every weapon on the ready, while the transports beached and the troops disembarked. After the troops were all gone ashore, the heavies took up blocking positions to prevent the enemy from escaping by sampan. On most operations, the troops would stay ashore for two or three days, although the boats might move them to many different locations during that period of time.

By the end of three or four days of operations, every sailor and soldier was ready to return to the ships for rest. On the same Navy pontoons the Army had embarked the Tangos earlier in the week; the Navy had installed and connected a hose for washing the mud off the troops when they returned to the barracks ship from their arduous missions. Then it was jump in line for hot chow, read a few letters, and finally catch some well-deserved shuteye, falling to sleep in air-conditioned berthing quarters.

A STORM ON THE HORIZON

In paintings dating back to the thirteenth century, there are depictions of the Vietnamese fighting on the rivers and canals of Vietnam. General Tran Hung Doa was an early Vietnamese warrior sailor who became a hero fighting on these waterways, and was considered the father of guerrilla warfare. But riverine warfare in Vietnam really began with the French conquest of Saigon in 1859, and continued through the nineteenth century. After World War II, the French and Vietminh fought for control of these very same rivers in the Red River Delta of the north in Tonkin, and more importantly, the Mekong Delta of the south. To fight these river battles, the French organized naval assault divisions called Dinassauts. These Dinassauts were once again revived by the fledgling South Vietnamese Navy as River Assault Groups, or as they were called by the American Naval advisors, RAGs. By the end of the Eisenhower administration, there were five RAGs plus a riverine transport group consisting of over a hundred assorted types of landing craft and patrol boats armed to fight in shallow waters under jungle conditions.

The RAGs normally worked with a battalion of South Vietnamese Marines functioning as a landing assault group. Together these components made up the Vietnamese Navy river assault force. By 1961, there were forty-five U.S. advisers, all from the U.S. Navy or Marines, working with the Vietnamese Navy, some with the river force. The Navy remained the poor sister among the Vietnamese armed services, and the river force was the poorest of the poor. Until late 1963, the riverine units were consistently undermanned. Much of their equipment was left behind by the Japanese and British from World War II or French in the fifties. When a sixth RAG was formed in 1962, more than half its craft were French leftovers. In 1963, when Captain Joseph B. Drachnik headed the naval advisory group, 145 Americans worked at every level from Vietnamese command down to the RAGs. On a typical day in 1963, when the riverine forces had about 150 vessels, only a small portion of them were on riverine operations, while nearly fifty worked as utility craft in various ports or were loaned out to village level units.

It seems that Vietnamese Army division commanders preferred airmobile operations to riverine; hence the river assault groups were usually employed in support of small-unit operations by Regional or Popular Forces under the control of province chiefs. Often they were used simply as escort for commercial craft. Citing poor use of existing units, Washington rejected assistance for the formation of a seventh RAG, although President Johnson later approved funds for a seventh in the spring of 1964.

Since the creation of the Vietnamese Navy in 1953, U.S. Naval advisors assigned to the Naval Advisory Group had sought to improve the material readiness of the fleet, promote sound doctrine and motivate Vietnamese officers to become more aggressive in their operations against the enemy. The brave action of Navy Lieutenant Harold D. Meyerkord, a senior adviser with River Assault Group 23, was exhibited when he was killed in a nasty canal action during March 1965, while leading his South Vietnamese Naval counterparts in battle. Many called the RAGs daring gunboat forces and Meyerkord a leader and teacher of men. But Meyerkord continually took chances while leading the Vietnamese from the front, which resulted in him dying on a muddy canal with a bullet in his brain. Before the year was out, four more Naval advisors would be loss while serving with the RAGs.

During February 1965, a U.S. Army pilot flying over Vung Ro Bay near Qui Nhon noticed an island moving slowly from one side of the bay to the other. Upon closer observation, he saw the island was a cleverly camouflaged ship. Air strikes were called in and the vessel sunk. Tons of ammunitions and supplies were found, with documents reporting that the trawler was North Vietnamese and had engaged in supplying enemy forces twenty-two times. Any doubt of communist supply activity by sea was gone, while U.S. commanders continued to believe the seas and rivers could be interdicted better by U.S. Naval forces than by the South Vietnamese.

In early 1965, U.S. Navy activity in Vietnam was limited to support functions in the Saigon area, construction and medical activities, and advising the Vietnamese Navy and Marine Corps. To stop the flow of enemy arms and supplies by sea, a tight security and surveillance system was needed. This would be no easy chore, with 1,200 miles of Vietnamese coastline to patrol and over 60,000 junks and boats to check and control. To provide this coverage, the Coastal Surveillance Force was established on March 24th, 1965. Called "Market Time," after the native boats using the waterways for fishing and marketing, this task force provided a single command to integrate sea-air-and land-based units and coordinate U.S. Navy with South Vietnamese Navy craft. This was the first U.S. Navy operations to commence and engage counter-infiltration in Vietnamese waters and was under the operational control of the commander of Task Force 71, a Seventh Fleet Force.

Because the U.S. Navy ships could not get close enough to shore, they contacted the U.S. Coast Guard, which had a fleet of eighty-two-foot high-endurance cutters known as WPBs. It was said to be a rapid solution to a critical problem. Accordingly, Coast Guard Squadron One was commissioned on May 27th, 1965, with seventeen WPB cutters and 245 crewmembers to support Operation Market Time. They began with five weeks of training in Vietnamese culture and language at Alameda, California, followed by weapons training at Camp Pendleton Marine Base. Then they spent a week in SERE, Survival, Evasion, Resistance and Escape training, starving and learning what it would be like if they were captured. While the Coast Guard sailors were in training, the WPB cutters were getting retrofitted with .50 caliber machineguns over, and 81mm mortar launchers under. A Coast Guard Chief Warrant Officer came up with the idea for the over/under, with the machinegun and mortar launcher becoming a very lethal combination.

With new guns and other refinements, the cutters were loaded as deck cargo on merchant vessels and ferried across the Pacific to Subic Bay in the Philippines. There the sailors married up with their boats, configured them, and set sail cruising 11,000 miles through storms and rough seas to Da Nang, South Vietnam. Arriving on July 20th, 1965, they became Division Twelve, patrolling as far north as the Demilitarized Zone. Division Eleven arrived eleven days later in the Gulf of Thailand and began patrolling up to the Cambodian border. Stationed at An Thoi on Phu Quoc Island, the cutters had arrived painted in their traditional bright white, as if they were back in the States. On Coast Guard Cutter Point Orient's first night patrol, she came under heavy mortar attack in the moon light. The cutters were quickly painted dark gray and continued patrols. After it was found how effective their 81mm mortar tubes were, they were called on repeatedly for fire support. The WPBs searched out enemy craft boarding junks, encountering hundreds of boats daily. But night was scary, with the chances of encountering the enemy greatest.

On July 30th, 1965, Task Force-71 was disestablished and shifted to Task Force-115 under the operational control of Rear Admiral Norvell G. Ward, Chief of Naval Advisory Group and the first Commander of Naval Forces, Vietnam, who was located in Saigon. Planning commenced for an expansion of Market Time to the Rung Sat Special Zone, the maritime approach from the South China Sea to Saigon by way of the Long Tau and Soi Rap Rivers.

By late summer of 1965, activity had increased at the Navy amphibious base in Coronado as a new breed of Swift boats, and sailors that would crew them, began arriving for training in an effort to fulfill the urgent request from the Commander of the Military Assistance Command, General William Westmoreland, for shallow draft water craft. The first two Swifts, of an eventual fleet of over one-hundred destined for service in Southeast Asia, had been rushed for staging in the Philippines directly from the Sewart Seacraft factory in Berwick, Louisiana. Coronado was to be used as the work-up base for the initial deployment of the fifty-foot aluminum-hulled Patrol Craft Fast (PCF) and their crews.

Called "Swifts" by the crews who served on them, they were originally designed for use by U.S. oil companies as transport to service offshore oil rigs in the Gulf of Mexico. Lacking a suitable craft for inshore patrol work, and faced with an immediate need to deploy such a boat to Vietnam, the Navy contracted Sewart for twenty modified crafts with a .50 caliber machinegun mount atop the aft section of the pilot house, and an over-under .50 caliber/81mm mortar mount aft on the fantail. The crew consisted of one officer in charge of five enlisted men, normally a boatswain's mate, quartermaster, gunner's mate, engineer and a radioman, of which most had volunteered and carried a gun also.

Of the initial eighteen Swifts, which were capable of speeds of twenty-five knots plus, PCFs 1, 2, 7 and 8 were to be retained in Coronado to form the first increment of training boats to be used by the Naval Amphibious Warfare Training Center. After being checked out, the remainder of the Swifts would be sent on to Subic Bay, joining PCFs 3 and 4 that were already there, before being transported to their final destinations in South Vietnam. A small group of sailors, called "Swifties," were matched up with PCFs 3 and 4 in the Philippines ahead of the arrival of the larger group of men. After a short familiarization period, PCFs 3 and 4 were transported as deck cargo to Phu Quoc Island, where the partially built base at An Thoi had been set up to receive them. They arrived on October 20th, 1965, and immediately began combat patrols in the waters between the island and the mainland of South Vietnam.

The Coastal Surveillance Force of Task Force 115 was composed of a wide variety of ships and craft, ranging from Vietnamese "basket boats" to U.S. destroyer escorts, fitted with half the power plant of a war-built destroyer, and with fewer guns and torpedo tubes. These ships and craft exclusively patrolled the coastal waters of the Republic of Vietnam. This expanded mission resulted in the employment of two Mark IV large personnel landing craft, which made the initial patrols. The Mike boats were metal-hulled successors to the thirty-six-foot "Higgins" boats, which were plywood and commonly used for beach landings in World War II, but also served as utility boats in South Vietnam. The Mike boats operated from the Vietnamese Naval Repair Facility in Saigon and concentrated their efforts to the port of Saigon and its approaches.

By September '65, with the war heating up, a command conference of top Navy officers, including representatives from the Pacific Theater, the Pacific fleet, and the Military Assistance Command, Vietnam, recommended that an American river patrol force be created and based on the rivers, using large landing ships as accommodation vessels. The initiative led to the formation of Task Force 116, Operation Game Warden, which was initially designed to supplement Vietnamese units in patrols of the Mekong Delta and the Rung Sat waterways, using high-speed river patrol boats as the principal patrol units.

On October 29th, at the request of the Secretary of the Navy, the Coast Guard ordered nine additional Coast Guard WPB cutters to join Coastal Squadron One, to carry out surveillance operations in support of Market Time forces. The cutters sailed from Subic Bay, Philippines, en route to Cat Lo, South Vietnam.

During November, the Navy continued planning for the second major influx of operational units by awarding a contract to the United Boat Builders in Bellingham, Washington, for the construction of 130 Mark I high-speed Patrol Boats River called PBRs. These boats would become the principle patrol units of river interdiction, allowing the farmers and fishermen to move their goods to the market, but interdicting enemy movement, depriving the communists of the waterways.

In November 1965, the U.S. 173rd Airborne Brigade was ambushed by 1,200 VC just outside of Saigon. Beginning on the 5th, the 173rd Airborne had initiated "Operation Hump," a search and destroy mission fifteen miles north of Bien Hoa. The 1st Battalion, Royal Australian Regiment was deployed south of the Dong Nai River while the 1st Battalion, 503rd Infantry, conducted a helicopter assault on a landing zone northwest of Dong Nai and the Song Be Rivers, but little happened at first. On the 8th, contact was made when the 173rd Airborne moved up Hill 65 encountering numerous fortified Viet Cong fighting positions. When artillery and air strikes were called in for support, the VC commander countered by ordering an attack, as the Viet Cong attempted to out-flank the 173rd Airborne from two directions. This brought the two opposing forces face-to-face, resulting in shoulder-to-shoulder attacks up the hillside, as American and Viet Cong clashed in hand-to-hand combat. The Americans held against two assaults and kept fighting till the intensity reduced and the VC finally withdrew. Forty-eight Paratroopers were lost with many more wounded. The Viet Cong lost 410 fighters. Army medic Lawrence Joel became the first living black man since the Spanish American war to receive the Medal of Honor for saving so many lives in the midst of battle that day.

From November 14th through the 18th, 1965, the battle of Ia Drang took place at two landing zones northwest of Plei Me in the Central Highlands between the 1st Battalion 7th Calvalry, the 2nd Battalion 7th Calvalry, and the 1st Battalion 5th Cavalry of the United States Army and communist forces consisting of the 33rd, 66th, and 320th Regiments of the North Vietnamese Army, and the Viet Cong H15 Battalion. It was a horrendous battle that caught the attention of many in Saigon and around the world and made the powers to be wonder what they would be facing in the Mekong Delta.

Harbor Clearance Unit One, HCU-1, was established on December 1st, '65 to provide a harbor and river clearance capability. Assigned the permanent duty station of Subic Bay, the unit was composed of four harbor clearance teams with two light crafts. Each team consisted of two officers in command of fourteen enlisted, all of whom were qualified divers.

On December 18th, the river patrol force of Task Force 116 was established to carry out Operation Game Warden with Admiral Ward as the task force commander.With these operations came the requirement for construction of new naval bases for both Market Time and Game Warden units. Also by the end of '65, the U.S. Army 13th Combat Aviation Battalion had begun to operate in support of Republic of Vietnam forces in the delta, with four assault helicopter companies and one reconnaissance airplane company.

In late December, six Swifts assigned to Patrol Craft Fast Division 101, PCFs 5, 6, 9, 10, 11 and 12, were loaded into the USS Catamount, LSD 17, and transported from Subic Bay to just offshore of Phu Quoc Island. The well deck ramp of the Catamount was then lowered, and the Swifts proceeded at full bore into the harbor and tied up to the pier just in time to celebrate Christmas Eve '65 in their new home at An Thoi. The first Swift boat division to arrive in Vietnam was now on station and open for business.

Because of the speed of the deployment of the Swifts, conditions at the base as the boats arrived were primitive at best. The only accommodations available ashore for the crews and support personnel were tents scrounged from wherever the Navy could find them and assembled by the crews themselves. Facilities for maintenance and repair of the boats simply did not exist. Fuel, ammunition, and other supplies were provided by periodic visits to the offshore support vessel USS Krishna, ARL 38, where command staffs were set up for both Patrol Craft Fast Division 101 and Coast Guard Squadron One. Meals initially were C-rations plus whatever else could be scrounged from the Krishna or the local people.

Perimeter security was provided by the South Vietnamese Navy, which already had a small base established at An Thoi. Basic services such as cleaning and laundry were contracted out to locals from the small adjacent Vietnamese Navy dependents' village. Secretary of the Navy Paul Nitze made a visit to An Thoi, and after he spent a few days living in the tents swatting mosquitoes, and had participated in one or two patrols on the boats, stuff started arriving to make life a little more bearable. First it was materials to construct World War II-type Quonset huts. A combination of sailors from the Krishna, Seabees from the U.S. Navy construction battalion, local workers and Swift boat sailors soon had buildings up and ready for occupancy. It was never firmly established how a boat load of San Miguel beer arrived from the Philippines, but it was very much appreciated by those working on the new base. Thank you Mr. Secretary. Cheers!

SOI RAP RIVER

With the new year of 1966 came additional boats of all types and less space at the single pier at An Thoi. One of the significant tasks for the newly arrived Coast Guard cutters and U.S. Navy Swift boats was to set up facilities to dock, replenish, maintain, and repair the boats as they continued patrols in a harsh new environment. The boats and crews would require constant care in order to sustain the tempo and level of operations envisioned by the planners of the interdiction strategy. In the meantime, the boats and crews did the best they could with what they had available, which was not very much.

One of the most difficult jobs that they had to address and bring up to speed quickly was to define, develop, and refine the roles of the patrol boats in this new kind of waterborne warfare. There was no rule book on how to stop the flow of communist supplies and men into South Vietnam. But it did not take long for the Coastal Surveillance Force to work out these details. As lessons were perfected, they were passed on to sailors preparing to arrive in Vietnam to join the force. It was a difficult time to be a sailor participating in this new type of naval warfare, in a strange land with unknown dangers waiting to strike at any moment. It is a tribute to the sailors who manned these fast boats in the early stages of the coastal river war that they brought their mission up to speed in such a short time. But although lessons were learned, they didn't come cheap.

While patrolling in the Gulf of Thailand on Valentine's Day 1966, PCF 4 was destroyed when it hit a shore-detonated water mine, with four sailors killed and two wounded. The lost were Boatswain's Mate First Tommy E. Hill, Engineman Second Jack C. Rodriguez, Gunner's Mate Second Dayton L. Rudisill and Seaman David J. Boyle.

SEALs commenced operations in support of Task Force 116 during February.

On February 22nd, Coast Guard Division Thirteen, with nine WPB cutters, arrived at Cat Lo South Vietnam, becoming the first patrol boats in the area. After receiving a warm welcome by the local Vietnamese, they immediately began night patrols to interdict supply operations of communist forces in the Rung Sat. A joint Swift boat - Coast Guard cutter patrol was established on March 7th, on the Soi Rap River, which was being considered for an alternate route to Saigon from the sea.

Coast Guard cutter Point White was in Vietnam only a short time when she started conducting patrols on the VC-controlled Soi Rap. The cutter used a plan of steaming out of the patrol area and covertly returning. Soon she spotted a fully armed and heavily manned motorized junk crossing the river as she sped forward to intercept when the junk opened fire with small arms and automatic weapons. Gunner's Mate Lester Gates returned fire from his bow-mounted .50 cal machinegun and set off an explosion. An intense firefight followed with bullets flying as Boat Captain Lieutenant Hickey, fearing one of his men would be shot, turned the cutter and at full speed headed toward the junk to ram. But at the last minute he turned the cutter slamming the two boats together sideways, causing water to swamp the junk, throwing many of its occupants over the side. With the burning junk sinking, the Coast Guard crewmen began rescuing the Vietnamese on the craft when a VC who had lost both his legs in the explosion started firing at point blank range. Left with little choice, they shot and killed him. One of the men they rescued from the water turned out to be a key Viet Cong leader of the Rung Sat force who was badly burned from the explosion. The crew of the Point White treated his wounds, and the man was so appreciative of how the crew and the American hospital had treated him that he gave up all his info of the Rung Sat Special Zone.

Since this was the cutter's third night patrol in the Rung Sat, Electronics' Technician Second Jerry Sampont wondered to himself, "Holy crap, is this what it is going to be like the rest of the year?"

On March 15th, cutter Point Partridge engaged and damaged another junk, but shallow water allowed the contact to escape. Three days later, Point Partridge detected a sampan with two people embarked attempting to cross into the Rung Sat. When the cutter approached to investigate, the sampan opened fire with small arms. The fire was returned, with one Viet Cong killed and the other captured. The effectiveness of the Soi Rap patrols could also be measured in the stepped-up harassment of patrol units. On numerous occasions, the boats came under small arms and automatic weapons fire from the banks. Because of the patrols, intelligence reports indicated a shift in Viet Cong infiltration patterns into the Rung Sat Special Zone with traffic entering from the east, originating in Viet Cong strongholds in Phouc Tuy Province.

On March 18th, in a ceremony held at Nha Be, Captain Burton "Burt" Witham, Jr., relieved Admiral Ward as Commander of Task Force 116. The first eleven PBRs of Game Warden's river patrol force arrived on March 21st, followed by an additional nine units on March 30th. During March, training and area indoctrination for PBR crews was conducted in the Vung Tau area, where numerous boat alterations were under consideration and experimentation. The first of eight permanent Game Warden Naval support bases was established at Cat Lo, which was partially completed, with the land for the other bases already acquired and in the planning stages.

On March 22nd, Point Hudson drew fire from a junk on the Soi Rap River. In the heated exchange that followed, an estimated ten Viet Cong were killed.

During Operation Jack Stay, commencing on March 26th, river patrol forces on the Soi Rap and other Rung Sat rivers were expanded. Because of this maneuver, several sharp surface engagements resulted. On the Soi Rap, PCF 31 traded fire with a junk that was seriously damaged but managed to escape into shallow waters. On the following day, PCF 31 returned the fire of another junk and cut the craft in two, killing five VC. On the Dong Tranh River, also in the Rung Sat, PCF 26 ran into an intense ambush from .50 and .30 caliber machinegun fire. She suppressed the attack with machinegun and mortar fire but suffered two personnel wounded with light material damage.

Also during the month, three Coast Guard cutters of Division Thirteen killed twenty-seven Viet Cong, captured seven, and confiscated a considerable amount of contraband. By the end of March, a dozen fifty-seven-foot wooden hull minesweeping boats (MSB) had begun operating from the facilities at Nha Be, making two sweeps daily of the Long Tau Channel and, in the process, providing more complete coverage of the shipping route.

From January 1964 through April '66, there were seventy-seven river mining incidents reported in South Vietnam, resulting in twenty Vietnamese boats destroyed, fifty-seven damaged, 115 men killed, 138 wounded, and forty-three missing in action. In almost all cases, the communist mines were controlled from shore. Because of the dimension of the mine threat and the limited countermeasures available to the South Vietnamese Navy, the U.S. Navy had directed their minesweepers to the Long Tau and Soi Rap Rivers. Although no mines were discovered at the outset, electric cables were pulled up on two occasions.

The Navy's Military Sea Transportation Service continued to provide the basic flow of supplies to South Vietnam upon which all friendly fighting forces in-country depended. During March '66, cargo manifested for South Vietnam totaled 691,000 tons. This was a much greater amount than in previous months, with unloading time cut in half to fifteen days.

On April 1st, in ceremonies aboard USS Lowe, DER 325, in Saigon harbor, Rear Admiral Norvell G. Ward established and assumed command of Naval Forces, Vietnam. This was done at the request of General Westmoreland, who earlier in the year proposed that a major Navy command with a flag officer be established in Saigon under the command of Commander in Chief, U.S. Pacific Fleet, and under operational control of Westmoreland and MACV.

With the continuing growth of the Navy establishment in Vietnam, and the problem of a Naval component commander remote from the center of Naval Operations, the need existed for a change in structure to provide an organization more responsive to the needs of commander MACV and the Navy. Admiral Ward would exercise operational control under MACV of the Coastal Surveillance Force, the River Patrol Force, and other Navy units as they were assigned. It was proposed that it be titled U.S. Naval Forces, Vietnam. In addition it was proposed that a junior flag officer command Naval Support Activity, Da Nang, and that Navy captains be assigned to command Task Forces 115 and 116 at the earliest date. The proposal was then forwarded to the Joint Chiefs of Staff in Washington and received their approval, while details were being worked out.

During the first week of April, the first ten graduates of the Army's special basic intelligence course for Vietnam, conducted at Fort Holabird, arrived in country. They were assigned to the ARVN Sector Operation Intelligence Centers in Coastal and Mekong Delta sectors. But daily intelligence reports were being sent to out-of-country commands to be analyzed.

The departure of the Seventh Fleet Marine Amphibious Force from the Rung Sat on April 7th signaled the termination of Operation Jack Stay. Highly successful in terms of equipment and facilities destroyed, Jack Stay also resulted in sixty-three VC killed. The likelihood was great that the Viet Cong forces would attempt to re-infiltrate into the Rung Sat Special Zone and establish once again their secure bases. To counter this possibility, the river patrols established during Jack Stay were maintained and continued patrols after the completion of the operation to deny the Viet Cong the use of the Rung Sat waterways. The ten patrol stations were to be manned by five WPB cutters, four Swifts, two Mike boat landing craft, and the UH-1B Army helicopter fire teams with the MSB minesweepers assisting.

Operation Game Warden had entered its fledgling stages during April as the first PBRs became operational. As the new crews received area indoctrination and training, construction of new bases in the Mekong Delta continued at a rapid pace in preparation for the arrival of the first Game Warden patrol units.

On April 10th, the PBRs of River Patrol Section 541 commenced orientation patrols with the Swift boats and Coast Guard cutters on the Long Tau River stations. The PBR crews adapted well to the river patrol situation, assuming two Rung Sat patrol stations at the outset, relieving two Swifts and two WPB cutters for Market Time operations. This resulted in seven stations manned continually by United States units, two by PBRs, three by WPB cutters and two by Swifts. PBRs occupied one additional station vacated by Vietnamese Navy units shortly after. Vietnamese Navy units assumed patrols on the upper Soi Rap River, freeing up one Swift and one WPB cutter, while also continuing to patrol the eastern reach of the Vam Co and Dong Tranh Rivers.

PBRs initially operated from the Inshore Support Ship USS Belle Grove (LSD-2), until April 19th when USS Tortuga (LSD-26) relieved Belle Grove. By the end of the month, the units moved to Nha Be operating from the Game Warden facilities at that location.

On April 16th, Captain Clifford L. Steward relieved Admiral Ward as commander of Task Force 115, Operation Market Time. By this time, twenty new Swifts had arrived in country. Patrol Craft Fast Division 101 was stationed at An Thoi with seven Swifts. Division 102 was in Da Nang with ten boats, and Division 103 was out of Cat Lo with thirteen craft. Division 104 was established at Cam Ranh Bay with thirteen Swifts. While base facilities were underway being constructed at Camh Ranh Bay, berthing and support facilities were located aboard an APL, a non-propelled barracks ship anchored in the bay. Half of the space aboard the ship had been modified to provide repair shops and support facilities. Viet Cong sapper swimmers were a constant threat.

The Soi Rap River patrol stations continued to meet with success as the Viet Cong persisted in their attempts to utilize the Rung Sat waterways. On April 17th, PCF 23 illuminated a contact attempting to cross the Soi Rap that maintained speed and opened fire with small arms. Four people in the sampan jumped overboard as PCF 23 returned fire. The sampan was taken in tow but sank with shore fire preventing a search of the area.

Also in April, Point Comfort was fired upon by a Cambodian patrol in the Gulf of Thailand, and Point Partridge captured a VC colonel of engineers. Coast Guard and Navy personnel also fought a fire that destroyed several houses in the village of An Thoi.

The Vietnamese Navy hospital ship Hat Giang, LSMH 400, deployed on April 20th for the Mekong Delta. She first operated in Ba Xuyen Province and later in Vinh Binh Province, with approximately 1,600 people receiving medical treatment and 175 given dental care. Civic action material was distributed to 450 needy families. A platoon was embarked to give performances of folk dances and music while two Chieu Hoi, Open Arms broadcasts were conducted. Over twenty-two tons of civil action materials had been received during the month for distribution to the needy. Approximately seven tons of materials were distributed in the village of Tam Thon Hiep in the Rung Sat. One child from the Rung Sat and two from Saigon received successful cleft lip operations.

On April 21st, the First Battalion of the Vietnamese Marines, along with the Vietnamese 5th Airborne Battalion, accounted for 150 Viet Cong killed with advisors estimating another 300 killed by artillery on a two-day search-and-destroy operation near Quang Ngai. Five Marines were killed and thirty wounded with the battalion remaining in the area on static security for the remainder of the month. The 2nd and 3rd Vietnamese Marine Battalions were deployed to Da Nang Airfield because of political unrest, until returning to their base camp in Saigon for Capital security where they conducted one search-and-destroy operation south of Saigon. The 4th and 5th Battalions participated in Operation Jack Stay, being deployed by copters to the Long Thank Peninsula, twice making contact with the enemy. The 5th Battalion conducted a series of four amphibious landings, utilizing Vietnamese RAG boats, in the vicinity of An Thit Village.

During one operation south of Saigon, the Vietnamese Marines used the new Dong Ngai boats to transport one battalion across a river and down streams. The fourteen-feet-long boats of fiberglass construction were powered by forty-horsepower outboard engines and cable of carrying eight combat loaded Marines at a speed of twenty knots. There was one platoon of fifty boats. Unit morale within the Vietnamese Marine battalion remained high with good leadership. The majority of the operations were executed with enthusiasm and a good grasp of tactics, although coordination and control in dense jungle and swamp areas left something to be desired.

April 26th saw the arrival of an additional twelve PBRs at Cat Lo. These units commenced shakedown cruises from the base at Cat Lo and from USS Floyd County, LST 762, which had arrived in-country on April 12th to become the second inshore support ship. River Patrol Division 51 was activated on April 27th, aboard USS Tortuga in preparation for the first transit into the Mekong Delta in May. The new units were designated River Section 512. While crew performance during the initial month of PBR operations was regarded as excellent, numerous problems arose in the boats themselves. Initial boarding and search operations indicated that the narrow vinyl beading which served as a fender was not adequate protection when boarding and searching larger junks, or when alongside a support ship. This resulted in damage to the side of the boats. To correct this, discarded helicopter tires were obtained for use as fenders. Armor plating around the forward gun mount was removed on all PBRs to improve gunner and coxswain visibility and communications. M-72 anti-tank rockets were being carried on all boats until approval and installation of the Mark 18, 40mm rapid fire grenade launcher, and .50 caliber machineguns were being installed in place of the aft .30 caliber guns.

SEAL Team One, Detachment Delta operating from Nha Be, staged ambushes in the Rung Sat at two-and three-day intervals throughout April. Ambush sites were often based on intelligence data obtained by aircraft equipment with infrared detection devices. Except for one successful ambush during Jack Stay, the SEAL team efforts had been fruitless. It was certain that an atmosphere for clandestine operations did not exist. To counter this, a plan was put into effect where the team got underway from Saigon for operations. Early one morning, the team made contact with a sampan with three occupants. It was taken under fire and sunk with all three occupants killed. On another night, the SEALs ambushed a sampan firing at a man, killing him. The body was recovered and taken to Nha Be, where it was identified as that of a friendly Vietnamese intelligence agent working in the Rung Sat. Although meetings were held between the two friendly forces discussing the problem, it was decided to exclude the Vietnamese from information regarding clandestine SEAL operations for the safety of the SEAL team.

To support the operations of Navy and Coast Guard units, two U.S. Army helicopter fire teams were established to patrol the Soi Rap and Long Tau channels. The first team, which had operated fromUSS Belle Grove during Jack Stay, switched over to USS Tortuga when she relieved Belle Grove and was joined by a second detachment aboard USS Floyd County on April 12th. Throughout the month, they supported the Long Tau and Soi Rap patrol stations and SEAL ambushes. On April 22nd, the birds scrambled to support two Swifts which had grounded while conducting survey operations at the mouth of the Cua Tieu River. The timely arrival of the fire teams suppressed shore fire, which the boats had been receiving, until they were freed and able to move.

Late in the afternoon of April 29th, the Army helicopter fire teams made their most successful strike of the month. Numerous camouflaged sampans were spotted on a narrow waterway on the Long Thanh Peninsula just west of Can Gio Village. Despite moderate ground fire, continual strikes were flown until darkness made further accurate fire difficult. During the action, ten sampans were destroyed with two Viet Cong confirmed, and many more believed, killed.

By the end of April, the first Long Tau River static defense post had been established at a point eleven miles southeast of Nha Be. Manned by one Regional Force company with two U.S. Army advisors, the outpost offered conditions that were less than desirable, with no permanent structures. In addition, all food and water had to be supplied by river patrol units near the outpost until better arrangements could be made.

On May 8th, 1966, Task Force 116 commenced operations in the Mekong Delta. Initially the PBR and gunship fire teams commenced operating from LSDs, Landing Ship Dock, near the river mouths. Each landing ship was equipped to change screws, shafts, engines, and other mechanical parts of patrol boats by virtue of fully equipped machine shops. Operating the small PBRs in the open seas was less than desirable, and in time, LST landing ships replaced the LSDs as bases and began operating on the rivers.

Necessary steps were also taken to establish personnel allowances for Operation Game Warden. Of eighty-four officers and 1159 enlisted billets, sixty-nine officers and 688 enlisted men were assigned to the river patrol sections serving on river boats, with the balance being assigned to man the naval support bases. Headquarters Naval Support Activity, Saigon was destined to transfer its functions to the Army by May of '66, but most of its personnel and facilities were to be incorporated into Naval Support Activity Saigon, to provide logistic support for U.S. Navy activities in II, III, and IV Corps Tactical Zones. Naval Support Activity Da Nang operations were expanded to support all free-world military forces in the I Corp Tactical Zone. Although Headquarters Naval Support Activity, Saigon, had lost eight sailors from 1963 to 1966, Naval Support Activity Saigon lost its first man, Gunner's Mate Third Lester A. Wright, on July 31st 1966. Naval Support Activity Da Nang had lost quite a few more by that time.

On May 10th, Coast Guard units again fought a significant Naval engagement. Point Grey was on patrol near the Ca Mau Peninsula when she sighted a 110-foot trawler heading on various courses and speeds. Suspicions aroused, Point Grey commenced shadowing the trawler. After observing what appeared to be signal fires on the beach, she hailed the vessel but received no response. The trawler then evaded and ran aground when Point Grey sailors attempted to board her. Heavy automatic weapons fire from the beach had prevented the boarding with three sailor's wounded onboard Point Grey during the firefight that followed. Point Cypress and U.S. Navy units rushed to assist, laying heavy suppressing fire during the encounter, resulting in the trawler exploding. U.S. Navy salvage teams later recovered a substantial amount of war material from the sunken vessel. The incident was the largest single known infiltration attempt since the Vung Ro Bay incident.

A month later, Coast Guard crews on Point League, Point Hudson and Point Slocum engaged in an intense gun battle with a Viet Cong trawler. The firefight lasted several hours before the trawler was forced aground and burst into flames. Coast Guard and

Vietnamese units extinguished the fire and then unloaded 250 tons of contraband. During another attempt, Point Partridge captured a junk containing communist Chinese weapons, and at still another attempt, Point Grace captured a sampan and took three prisoners, rifles and ammunition.

Market Time units continually stopped enemy vessels trying to transport supplies and men into South Vietnam. The success of the operation forced the North Vietnamese to rely heavily on the Ho Chi Minh Trail as an alternative route to transport supplies. As many of the trawler kills were in southern Vietnam near the Ca Mau Peninsula, this forced the enemy to carry supplies over an extraordinarily long distance. Although suffering many hardships and losses along the way, communist troops and supplies continued to pour into South Vietnam.

On May 20th, 1966, U.S. minesweepers became Minesweeper Squadron Eleven, Detachment Alpha. Every morning as dawn broke over the Long Tau, the minesweeping boats had already been on the river for four hours sweeping for enemy mines. They would put in another eight to ten hours before calling it a day. For the merchant ships anchored at the mouth of the river, dawn signaled the start of the trip up the channel to Saigon. Merchant vessels were not allowed to make the hazardous transit at night. Minesweeping was not glamorous but vital, with crews putting in long tedious hours in a very dangerous environment. To get to the merchant ships, the enemy had to first strike at the Navy MSBs.

The Game Warden MSBs worked two abreast, using chain drag or float method of minesweeping. The chain drag cut wires from mines which were command detonated from the river bank. The O-float cut loose mines anchored at the bottom of the river. Seven sailors made up the crew of the forty-four-ton boats, with a petty officer first class usually boat captain. The armament consisted of two .50 cal and four .30 cal machineguns and a 40mm grenade launcher, plus whatever hand weapons the sailors carried.

In 1966, the Vietnamese Navy consisted of more than 23,000 officers and men, of whom 7,000 were Marines. Their fleet included twenty-one seagoing ships, fifteen mine warfare boats, 138 amphibious ships and craft, 488 junks, and about seventy-five other ships and craft. Vietnamese Naval forces attached to the Mekong Delta included six river assault groups and eleven coastal groups known collectively as the Junk Fleet. The assault groups' primary mission was to support Vietnam Army and Marine riverine operations. Almost 1,000 U.S. Navy men were attached to the Naval Advisory Group, many of whom were assigned to operate with units of the Vietnamese Navy.

Two critical areas of concern to the U.S. Naval advisors were maintenance and personnel. The maintenance for larger ships of the Vietnamese Navy was considered to be unsatisfactory. The hulls of many junks in the coastal groups were in a bad state of deterioration, with engine malfunctions common. The major difficulty with personnel was their lack of motivation. Many Vietnamese officers and petty officers were considered to be good, but the overwhelming majority showed little or no desire to become leaders.

Another problem was the security of the coastal group junk division bases scattered along the entire coastline of South Vietnam. Many of these bases were in areas of communist control. During March '66, one base underwent a heavy mortar attack while another was the subject of internal sabotage. In the latter instance, the commanding officer of the coastal group was killed. U.S. advisors who were assigned to each coastal group continued to seek improvements in security.

The ships of the Seventh Fleet continue to be supplied while steaming off the coast of South Vietnam in Operation Market Time, and off the coast of North Vietnam in Yankee Station in the Tonkin Gulf. During June, Service Group Three made a total of 598 underway replenishments in the western Pacific, 119 of which were conducted at night.

On July 1st, 1966, U.S. Navy Detachment 29 of Helicopter Combat Support Squadron One, HC-1, home ported at the Naval Air Station Imperial Beach, California, departed to Tan Son Nhut Air Base near Saigon as the Navy's first gunship fire team. Arriving on the afternoon of Wednesday, July 4th, 1966, after a flight that began on Sunday, July 1st, HC-1 Detachment 29, consisting of eight pilots and eight air crewmen, were quartered at a three-story hotel in Saigon. The eight pilots were in one room on the second floor with one bathroom, and the air crewmen were in similar accommodations on the third floor. After somewhat getting settled in, they were transported daily to Tan Son Nhut for ground school with the H-1 helicopters.

At first they found it odd riding in the back of a pick-up truck with chain-link fence around the bed to prevent someone from tossing in a grenade and ruining everybody's day. But they were on an important assignment and valuable to the future of the river patrol mission and stranger things had happened in the past. They had attended ground school training the Marine version of the H-1 copter at Camp Pendleton, Marine Base in California before their departure; however the Army version had significant differences with the main one being the electrical system, so they had to learn about it after arriving in-country.

Lieutenant Kent Vandervelde managed to solicit some time at Fort Rucker, Aviation War Center in Alabama prior to the teams' departure, but he was the only one of the pilots that had any H-1 copter flight time. But still they adopted and after completing the ground school, they started flying with the "Deans" of the 120th Army Helicopter Aviation Company based at Tan Son Nhut. The Deans supported Headquarters, Military Assistance Command and provided transportation for VIPs and USO personnel, as well as provided the ground school. At first they flew "slicks" with no flex guns or rockets, with mixed crews, Army pilot, Navy co-pilot, Army aircrew gunner, Navy aircrew gunner. Together they flew out to an area where there was a runway to practice take-offs, landings and auto-rotations. On one day, they had to abandon practice because of sniper fire, but most of the time is was business as usual. After they had gone over the basics, they flew a few missions with the Deans to build up flight time.

After initial in-country training, Detachment 29 moved out to Ben Hoa and flew missions with the Army's "Playboys" of the 197th Aviation Company. It was the Army's only aviation company in which all three platoons were gunship platoons. There, still with mixed crews, the first order of business was to practice shooting the forward-firing flex guns and rockets in a free-fire zone. Of course, the door gunners also got to fire their M60 machineguns out the side doors. After passing with colors, they started flying missions fully armed. Their primary mission was to cover the Saigon shipping channel and the Rung Sat Special Zone, a free-fire area that had been defoliated.

On one of Navy Lieutenant Frank Koch's first flights found him patrolling the forty-mile channel through the Rung Sat with a mixed crew, an Army First Lieutenant as the helicopter aircraft commander in the right seat, and Navy co-pilot Koch in the left seat. The Army lieutenant had had a late night at the club the previous evening, and the boring mission was putting him to sleep, so he passed control to his co-pilot Koch, to grab a little shut-eye. Of course this was fine with Lieutenant Koch as he took over the controls and continued patrolling the area. After flying for a couple of minutes with the Army pilot peacefully asleep, Koch noticed that the rockets were armed. In order to turn off the armed switch, which was located on the center console between Frank and the sleeping Army pilot, it would be necessary for Frank to trim up the aircraft so he could change hands on the stick and use his right hand to turn off the switch. Normally, this would not be a difficult maneuver; however the trim button on the H-1 copter was located in a different place on the stick from the trim button on the H-2 copters that Koch was used to flying. On the H-1 copter, the trim button was located on the left side of the stick. In order to trim the aircraft for "hands-off" flight, the button on the left side of the stick was depressed and the stick was adjusted to provide the attitude required and then the button was released. In the H-2 copter, the trim button was the "Chinese hat" on top of the stick. To trim the H-2 copter, the trim button was pushed and released in the direction the pilot wanted the stick to move until the stick was where he wanted it. On the H-1 copter, the "Chinese hat" fired the rockets. Unfortunately, when attempting to trim the aircraft, Lieutenant Koch forgot that slight difference for a few minutes and accidentally fired a rocket from the pod on the right side of the aircraft. Needless to say, the Army pilot awoke startled! Fortunately, they had been over the Rung Sat, which was a defoliated swamp and pretty much uninhabited except for an occasional woodcutter gathering wood to sell. The Army lieutenant reported the incident to "Control," and the area was checked to see if any woodcutters had been present. Luckily none were, so everything worked out okay, except for the embarrassment Koch suffered that night at the club when the word got around.

After getting checked out by the Playboys, Lieutenant Koch went on to fly with the gun platoon of the Army's "Firebirds," including participation in a GRF troop insertion. Then Detachment 29 of Helicopter Combat Support Squadron One started flying independent from the Army as a Navy gunship fire team in late August. Initially based off shore on landing platform dock, ships, USS Tortuga, LSD-26, USS Comstock, LSD-19, Detachment 29 was later transferred to shallow draft LSTs that were able to navigate the rivers in support of a river patrol boat sections, which were also stationed onboard the LSTs. USS Harnett County, LST-821, USS Hunterdon County, LST-838, and USS Jennings County, LST-846, just to mention a few, were all assigned to fulfill important jobs.

Helicopter Combat Support Squadron One, Detachment 27, was the second Seawolf fire team to deploy about a month later, and after completing training with the Army, was based at Nha Be. This was followed by Detachment 25, which deployed a little later still and after training was based at Vinh Long in the Mekong Delta. Due to the delay in obtaining additional helicopters from the Army, Detachment 21 didn't deploy until November.

Lieutenant Commander Bill "Rocky" Rockwell was the Officer in Charge of Detachment 29, call sign Seawolf One-six, and his wingman was Lieutenant Kent Vandervelde, Seawolf One-seven. The second team was Lieutenant Jim Potters, call sign Seawolf Two-six, with his wingman Lieutenant Frank Koch, Seawolf Two-seven. The crews were twenty-four on, twenty-four off, with each detachment consisting of two gunships equipped with forward firing flex guns and rockets manned by two pilots up front, and two gunners in the cabin, who also manned machineguns and hung out the doors attached to safety harnesses. Originally assembled to support the river patrol and coastal forces, they were on a twenty-four-hour-alert basis and could scramble in minutes, becoming one of the most feared units of the U.S. Navy in South Vietnam.

INTERDICTION

The Office in Charge of Construction, Vietnam, as the Department of Defense's construction agent in Southeast Asia, had negotiated more than 150 million dollars in military construction completed in South Vietnam since 1956. As of August '66, construction was proceeding at a rate of 17.5 million dollars per month, but would increase to forty million a month by year's end. U.S. civilian contractors totaled more than 33,000 workers in Vietnam, in addition to seven Navy mobile construction battalions, and 15,000 Army Engineer Corps personnel. Construction of deep draft piers at Hue, Da Nang, Vung Tau, Cam Ranh Bay and several other locations was underway and to be completed to complement the port of Saigon. In addition, LST ramps at Vung Tau and Da Nang were also under construction, as well as airfield complexes at Cam Ranh Bay, Qui Nhon, Chu Lai and Da Nang. Earlier shipping problems were improving, with the average turnaround time for ships cut to twelve days. Market Time units, augmented by the arrival of sixteen Swift boats at the end of July, continued to operate at a high level of activity during August. Numerous hostile fire and evading junk incidents were reported, with patrol units frequently delivering gunfire missions in support of friendly forces. A series of incidents had also indicated that Game Warden patrols were becoming increasingly more successful in one phase of their mission, that of interdicting Viet Cong river crossings.

At 2315 hours on August 3rd, Coast Guard Cutter Point Jefferson received hostile fire from the beach on the Ke Ga Peninsula, sixty miles northeast of Vung Tau, and returned fire. At 1815 hours on the 8th, PCF 39 received mortar fire from the same general area. At 1000 hours the next day, PCF 58 received machinegun fire ten miles north of Qui Nhon and returned fire. The following day, PCF 62 was taken under fire in the same area and at 1655 hours, again received fire while closing in on the beach to investigate suspicious contacts.

On August 11th, Coast Guard Cutter Point Welcome was patrolling at the North Vietnamese boarder, adjacent to the Demilitarized Zone, when an Air Force O2B fixed-wing forward air controller failed to identify the cutter and illuminated it. He then called in one U.S. Air Force B-57 bomber and two F-4 jets at 0340 hours and mistakenly ordered an attack. Point Welcome was underway at eight knots, and when illuminated, turned on her docking and running lights. The ensign and Coast Guard flag were properly displayed with the executive officer on the bridge and the commanding officer outside signaling the aircraft with the Aldis Lamp. During the initial strike, the commanding officer was mortally wounded, with the executive officer and all others on the bridge severely wounded. The senior chief, Chief Boatswain's Mate Pat Paterson, came to the bridge at 0350 hours and assumed command, immediately accelerating to full speed, as he commenced evasive maneuvers to avoid the illuminated area and the attacking aircraft.

The attack continued for one hour under continuous illumination, with the aircraft making from seven to nine passes. The signal searchlights and all electronics and communication equipment were disabled during the initial pass. A gasoline-can fire on the fantail was extinguished by the survivors, who were also busy caring for the wounded, strapping them into life jackets. At 0415 hours, Chief Paterson paired the least wounded with the more serious and beached the cutter near a friendly Vietnamese regional outpost, giving the order to abandon ship as the men began slipping into the water. But the attempt to reach shore was thwarted by automatic weapons and mortar fire from an unknown source.

Prior to losing communications, Point Welcome had got off a message reporting that she had been illuminated, fired upon and hit. Commander Task Force 115 directed Point Caution and Point Orient to the scene, and patrol units from Vietnamese Navy Coastal Group 11 were dispatched as well. Twenty minutes later, Point Orient and Point Caution had located Point Welcome and started rescuing survivors with the help of Coastal Group 11 junks, who also fired mortar illumination rounds and moved the wounded to an area for copter medical evacuation. Commanding Officer Lieutenant Junior Grade David Brostrum and Engineman Second Jerry Phillips were lost in the friendly fire incident, with an additional nine crewmembers, the Vietnamese liaison officer, and one newsman wounded as well. Although the cutter was heavily damaged, she was able to get underway and escorted to Da Nang under her own power.

The stepped-up intensity of Market Time patrols led to an increased number of junks attempting to evade contact with patrol units. During this time, An Thoi-based Market Time units began operating in support of Operation Sea Mount on Phu Quoc Island. The operation was conducted by eight U.S. Special Forces personnel and a 220-man Mike Force of specially recruited indigenous people, augmented by Vietnamese National policemen from Duong Dong Village on Phu Quoc Island. In addition to gunfire and patrol support from Market Time Swifts and WPB cutters, Seventh Fleet Destroyers and Vietnamese Fleet Command ships provided gunfire support while U.S. Air Force and Army aircraft provided air strikes.

A sweep of the island was conducted from An Thoi north, followed later by a series of amphibious raids on the east coast of the island. In the final phase, a base camp was established near Duong Dong and probes were made into the heaviest Viet Cong-concentrated areas. The operation marked the first major military operation to attempt clearing Phu Quoc Island. Sixteen Viet Cong were known killed, but after the prisoners were interrogated, it was revealed that seventy-five VC had actually been terminated, with an undetermined number wounded. Two U.S Special Forces members were lost, with another wounded. Seven other friendly forces were wounded, with the costly operation considered a major success.

Twenty-four PBRs arrived in-country during August '66, bringing the total to ninety-five Game Warden river patrol boats patrolling in the Republic of Vietnam. Eight PBRs arrived aboard the victory ship SS Brazil Victory on August 16th, eight on the 17th aboard SS Duke Victory, and eight aboard SS American Victory on the 19th. The number of operational Game Warden bases increased to seven as river patrol boats made the transit to new bases at Vinh Long and Sa Dec on the Mekong River, and Long Xuyen on the Bassac River. River Patrol Section 513 became operational at the beginning of the month, with ten patrol boats making the trip from Cat Lo to Vinh Long, stopping at My Tho for fuel. Then River Patrol Section 521 reported operationally ready a few days later with nine PBRs and made the transit from Cat Lo to Sa Dec. River Patrol Section 522 was activated at Cat Lo with ten PBRs, followed a few days later by River Patrol Section 523 with five patrol boats. Both sections made the long trip to Long Xuyen, arriving by the end of the month. All river patrol sections underwent outfitting and operational testing at Cat Lo before activation and had come up to speed quickly.

USS Tortuga had supported Game Warden operations at the mouth of the Bassac River until the end of August, when she was transferred to an anchorage off the mouth of the Long Tau to provide additional security for the shipping channel. River Patrol Section 512, operating from Tortuga, continued to experience difficulty patrolling in heavy weather, losing thirty-nine hours during the month due to rough seas. Several PBRs from Tortuga experienced hull cracks, resulting in absorption of water by the Styrofoam. The cracks apparently were caused by boat handling. Repeated hoisting and lowering of the boats and misplacement of PBRs in the skids failed to distribute weight evenly throughout the boats. Up to 100 gallons of water had been drained from patrol boats after operations. A team of military and civilian specialists arrived to implement and install a planned maintenance system for PBRs, and to instruct personnel in the mechanics of the system.

The PBRs had become increasingly more important in pushing further up river, cutting off the Ho Chi Minh Trail. An increase in operational activity had occurred as the PBRs successfully continued their mission of interdicting Viet Cong river movement, while there was a noticeable increase in Viet Cong harassment of patrol units. Thanks to Navy pilots assuming operation of the first Naval helicopter fire teams, and the SEAL detachment working the Rung Sat Special Zone, Operation Game Warden began experiencing a high level of success seeking out and destroying enemy facilities.

In early August, PBR 39 and PBR 41, operating twenty-three miles southeast of Can Tho on the Bassac River on night patrol, detected three beached sampans. As beaching in the area was unusual, PBR 39 closed and illuminated the sampans, receiving heavy small arms and machinegun fire from the bank. The PBRs returned the fire, retired and then rendezvoused with a patrol consisting of two armored personnel landing crafts from Vietnamese River Assault Group 25. The combined units returned to the area to attack and again received heavy fire, including several anti-tank grenades from two locations. The firefight continued until the patrol units had expended the majority of their ammunition and were forced to withdraw. Three additional RAG units, including a Monitor and four additional PBRs supported by an AC-47 Spooky fixed-wing gunship with Mini-guns were dispatched to the scene, but the Viet Cong had withdrawn. Due to the location of the action, the tidal conditions and the volume of enemy fire, it was evaluated that the PBRs had broken up a Viet Cong crossing attempt.

At 1050 hours on August 15th, a spotter aircraft observed a sampan dropping off eleven armed men on Dung Island at the Bassac River mouth. The aircraft relayed the message to Vietnamese Coastal Group 36, which in turn relayed it to a PBR patrol from USS Tortuga. The aircraft marked the area with smoke and the PBRs opened fire on the Viet Cong, who were wading through the water with rifles over their heads, killing at least three. A patrol from Vietnamese Coastal Group 36 recovered the sampan motor and a Viet Cong flag.

PBR patrol Alpha, fifteen miles upstream from the Bassac mouth, observed a sampan evading into underbrush along the south bank at 1500 hours on August 17th. Later, two additional sampans were discovered hidden along the bank. Permission was then obtained from the Long Phu District Chief to engage the contacts. The initial .50 cal machinegun fire from PBRs resulted in a secondary explosion which destroyed all three sampans and reportedly killed three VC.

The increased Viet Cong activity in the Rung Sat carried over to the PBRs as patrols units on the Soi Rap River made significant contact on several occasions. At 1900 hours on August 18th, a PBR patrol detected two contacts crossing the Soi Rap into the Rung Sat eight miles south of Nha Be. The patrol approached to within seventy-five yards of the contacts and illuminated the area exposing two sampans, one with four occupants and the other with two. Simultaneously, light automatic weapons and small arms fire was received from both sampans. The fire was returned, and the patrol proceeded south out of range, calling in another two PBRs to assist.

Upon arrival of the second patrol, the PBRs reentered the area, discovering the two sampans abandoned, with no further opposition encountered. Among the contents of the sampans were rifles, ammunition, medicine, assorted documents and 200 pounds of food. The action was evaluated as a Viet Cong attempt to run supplies into the Rung Sat. The same area, one of the narrowest stretches of the Soi Rap, was the scene of intensive harassment on the next night as well. Just before midnight, four PBRs on patrol received heavy automatic weapons fire from both banks. The fire was suppressed, but then the patrol began receiving fire from another location on the east bank. Two additional PBRs joined the patrol, and an air strike was called in on the ambush positions. There was no damage to the PBRs, nor were there any friendly casualties. A few nights later they again detected a sampan crossing the Soi Rap, and upon closing, received small-arms fire from both banks. The fire was returned while another PBR patrol, accompanied by a helicopter fire team, was dispatched to the area with a U.S. Air Force C-47 flare ship providing illumination. The PBRs suppressed all fire from the banks and sampan. A search for the sampan, believed damaged during the firefight, was unsuccessful.

For Gunner's Mate Seaman Guy Arrans on the forward twin .50 cal machineguns of PBR 24, assigned to River Section 541, August 19th was his first firefight and one he would not soon forget. It was then he had learned for the first time that the enemy tracers were green as he watched the muzzle flashes from the bank being fired at his boat with tracers zipping by. It was also the first time he experienced the reality of the thunder of the .50 cal machineguns lighting up the night as he watched the red-orange flaming muzzle flashes of the aft .50 cal, and amidships M60, machineguns firing away, which was a sight to see for an eighteen-year-old kid from Paw Paw, Michigan. Then after a few minutes of suppressing fire, which seemed much longer, they had moved down river and the fire had ceased. Arrans looked down and realized he had not fired his guns. In all the excitement of green tracers and watching the aft gunner firing like crazy, he had forgotten to open fire. Embarrassed when asked by the boat captain what happened, he replied, "I had no target."

But Arrans learned fast when, three nights later, his boat went to intercept a sampan and received enemy fire from the banks. For on that night, the patrol boats answered, with Arrans lighting up the .50 cal machineguns. Though the sound of the big guns was deafening, what Arrans remembered most was the flare ship overhead putting out all those flares, while they searched for the illusive VC sampan, which they never found. To him it seemed if the night sky had turned to day, although the smoke from all the gunfire and flares made it appear like a thick fog in an old horror movie.

When Seaman Guy Arrans had first arrived at Nha Be in August '66, River Section 541 was on twelve-hour patrols, six days a week with one day off. There was a little Vietnamese joint (which Guy couldn't bring himself to call a café) on the base. He would go there from time to time and order fried eggs and french fries, since he had already been told to pass on the steak part of steak and eggs, not knowing what meat he might be served. A Coke was a quarter, unless you wanted to take the bottle with you, at which time you would need to pay a fifty-cent deposit on the bottle.

The river patrolmen were paid per diem and had to purchase whatever food they wanted. As Arrans recalled, the food wasn't much to talk about, so he acquired C-Rations by the case, with his favorites being the meat and potatoes with gravy, and the ham and lima beans. He thought the pound cake sucked, as did the cookies, so he traded them for fruit cocktail most of the time. While on patrol, they warmed their main course on the manifold of the boat engines, or on a hot plate when they were back at the base in their tent where they slept. One of their boat captains, by the name of Travis, loved his coffee so much that he had a percolator on his boat. He would unplug the radar during day patrols and plug his coffee maker in. Their cover boat would hear Charlie Tango over the radio and knew that it was coffee time and to come alongside with their cups.

When not on patrol, the patrolmen would clean and perform maintenance on their weapons. They could either sleep before or after patrol, depending on whether they were on day or night duty. Some days, it was so hot in their tent that it made it difficult to sleep. They played cards on old wire spools turned up to make tables and every day was the same as the last. Guy Arrans celebrated his nineteenth birthday patrolling the Soi Rap River.

The trip into Nha Be consisted of walking out the gate to arrive immediately in beautiful downtown, which was a single street full of bars and not much else. On base was an old Quonset hut called the "EM Club" for enlisted men. The club would bring in a Vietnamese band to play American songs, and they actually did a pretty decent job. Or was it the beer? They would also bum around the base in cutoff dungarees and clean and paint the boat for something to do during slow periods.

One time, this mamma-san in Nha Be, who did the laundry for them and let them pay her on paydays, asked Arrans to help her. She wanted to know if he knew some guys who had charged their laundry and had not been back to pay her. Unfortunately, the people who had charged were listed as Donald Duck, Mickey Mouse, Roy Rogers, Rin Tin Tin and other similar names. It took him quite some time for her to understand who Mickey Mouse was, but thanks to Arrans, she finally realized what was going on.

Arrans remembers moving into new barracks at Nha Be right before his tour of duty was over. It was only for one month, but it was great to have showers and toilets, instead of that big old outhouse over the ditch, which the tide cleaned out, or that old shower, which consisted of a tank up in the air that got filled when the drinking water was trucked in from Saigon. The temperature of the shower depended on the amount of sunshine on the tank. Even through all of this, Arrans still had many fond memories of the people he trained with, and of those he served with in Vietnam.

At 0200 hours on August 21st, three ARVN outposts ten miles southeast of Can Tho on May Island came under simultaneous attack by an estimated two Viet Cong companies. Upon request of the Tra On District Chief, PBRs 30 and 31 initiated a blocking action on the southeastern side of the island, while an AC-47 Spooky gunship assumed surveillance on the northwestern side. Game Warden river patrol boats were requested for medical evacuation of twenty-three seriously injured Regional Force and Popular Force troops, with PBRs 39 and 41 assuming the medical evacuation mission. While en route, they received fire from the bank, which they were able to suppress. Meanwhile, PBRs 30 and 31 maintained their barrier, checking 635 persons leaving the island the next morning, detaining thirty-three for identification card discrepancies.

At 1900 hours on the same day, PBRs 34, 38, and 40 received heavy automatic weapons and small-arms fire from both banks of the Bassac River, fourteen miles southeast of Can Tho. The boats suppressed the fire, withdrew upstream and requested an artillery strike. Thirty 105mm artillery rounds were placed on target by the Tra On battery. The incident was evaluated as an attempt by Viet Cong fleeing from an ARVN operation, trying to cross the river to escape.

The night of August 22nd provided My Tho PBRs with the most significant Game Warden action of the month, when they captured a large number of intelligence documents. The initial action occurred at 2008 hours when PBR 101 and PBR 105 of River Section 531, the Delta Dragons, received light machinegun fire from positions on Thoi Son Island five miles west of My Tho. As PBRs 103 and 107 drifted in the area to watch for a possible Viet Cong crossing, PBRs 101 and 105 again approached the area of the original attack and again drew fire. Artillery support was then called in on the enemy positions. Continued PBR patrols, augmented by RAG units from My Tho, drew more sniper fire but detected no crossing in the area.

At 2213 hours, PBRs 103 and 105 again began patrolling, this time twelve miles west of My Tho, and received fire from approximately seventy-five rifles on the north bank of the river. During the ensuing firefight, the patrol leader detected a contact moving rapidly from north to south, with PBR 105 moving in to intercept it. Upon illumination, a single shot was received from the sampan and additional fire was received from ten or more positions on the south bank. PBR 103 returned fire to the south while PBR 105 strafed the north bank and the sampan, killing two green-uniformed occupants. PBR 105 then grabbed the sampan and proceeded eastward out of range of enemy fire. The PBR patrol leader, Boatswain's Mate First Williams, was wounded in the action.

Among the contents of the sampan were thirty-one top secret documents with overlays, fifty-eight confidential documents and nine unclassified documents. All documents were from the Viet Cong 261st Main Force Battalion of the Dong Thap regiment, which indicated that the two VC killed were high-ranking members of the battalion.

Another type of activity was proving more difficult for the Viet Cong as PBRs continued to impede the movement of Viet Cong tax collectors. PBRs 34 and 40 observed a sampan twelve miles southeast of Can Tho with one male occupant aboard calling other boats alongside. The PBR patrol immediately suspected that he was a VC tax collector. Upon approaching, the sampan darted to the bank. The pursuing PBRs then came under fire from positions in the area, evaluated as special covering fire for the VC tax collector. The patrol suppressed the fire and kept the area under surveillance. On two other occasions during the month, fire was received from suspected VC tax collectors as well.

The Viet Cong made one known attempt during the month to mine a PBR. At 0005 hours on August 29th, PBRs 29 and 111, operating on the Co Chien River, twenty miles southeast of Vinh Long, sighted a lighted sampan twenty yards from the river bank. The patrol approached to within a hundred yards and illuminated the sampan, which was empty and not moving with the current. The patrol then closed to within fifty yards for a closer inspection, but still no mooring or anchor lines were visible. When the sampan was illuminated for a second time, a large explosion occurred twenty yards from the lead patrol boat, followed by light weapons fire from the shore. The fire was suppressed as the PBRs cleared the area.

Prior to the patrol, the crew had been briefed by U.S. Army intelligence officers at Vinh Long that the Viet Cong had four mines weighing 160 pounds each, which would probably be planted in the Mekong River. The Vietnamese RAG commander at Vinh Long had provided the information that the mines might be used to sink a PBR. Thanks to his intelligence information, he probably prevented the lost of a PBR and saved its crew. Throughout the month, PBR patrols were increasingly harassed by Viet Cong positions along the river bank, proving once again that they were hurting the enemy and depriving him the use of the rivers.

On the Long Tau at 0620 hours on the very same day, a PBR patrol detected an unoccupied, drifting sampan with cargo covered by a tarpaulin and bushes. Unable to determine if the sampan contained cargo or a possible booby-trap, the patrol took it under fire from a distance and destroyed the sampan, not wanting to take any chances. The patrol officer was slightly wounded by grenade shrapnel from his own M-79.

During the month, helicopter fire teams had repeatedly fought in the Long Toan Secret Zone at the mouth of the Bassac River in response to a request from the district chief. The choppers delivered devastating strikes against a reported Viet Cong company in their base area while receiving enemy fire from the village and the adjacent river bank. Still, they were successful in destroying four structures and damaging over a dozen others. Multiple sampans were also destroyed, with a high percentage of the Viet Cong killed or wounded. Fixed-wing aircraft were called in and contributed greatly to the action by delivering additional strikes.

The Game Warden helicopter fire teams operating in the Rung Sat detected another camouflaged sampan twelve miles southeast of Nha Be late in the month, with Vietnamese authorities requesting that it be destroyed. While taking the sampan under fire, the helicopter spotted three structures, apparently used for storage. Vietnamese authorities requested that they also be taken under fire, and the subsequent strike resulted in a large secondary explosion from the largest structure. Assessment indicated that the area was also used for rice storage. A U.S. Air Force strike was called in to complete the destruction.

SEAL Team Detachment Golf, operating from Game Warden's base at Nha Be, made contact with Viet Cong units twice while on ambushes in the Rung Sat, and discovered and destroyed one large rice storage area. In the first week of the month in the early morning hours of a new day, the SEAL Team came upon three camouflaged sampans sixteen miles southeast of Nha Be. A Viet Cong in the lead sampan spotted the SEAL ambush and fired a warning shot. All the occupants then jumped overboard and escaped into the mangrove. The SEAL Team followed the escaping Viet Cong but was unable to establish contact. The three captured sampans, two of them motorized, contained 2,800 pounds of rice, a small quantity of medicine and several notebooks.

At 1100 hours on August 18th, a SEAL reconnaissance team discovered two large silos and one bunker in an area fourteen miles southeast of Nha Be. The structures were of reinforced wood and contained an estimated 200 tons of rice. At 1300 hours the SEAL Team was extracted by a landing craft to allow naval gunfire and fixed-wing aircraft to destroy the rice. At 1735 hours, the SEAL Team was inserted to evaluate the destruction efforts and to destroy the remaining rice and structures.

The next morning, the SEAL Team discovered a series of bunkers and an automatic weapons emplacement along the Dinh Ba River, thirteen miles southeast of Nha Be, while on a reconnaissance mission. After not finding the enemy, the team was extracted and reinserted into a region farther upstream where a loaded sampan near a hut had been spotted by copter. Fresh tracks were discovered, with the sampan spotted 500 yards from the SEAL Team. But before the team could move in to investigate, a short burst of fire was heard, followed by automatic weapons fire from both banks of the river directed at the team. In the firefight that followed, Radioman First Class Billy W. Machen of SEAL Team One, Detachment Golf, was lost, the first SEAL casualty in the Rung Sat. The SEALs were then extracted by Mike boat, bringing Machen out with them.

The first incident of mutual interference between Market Time and Game Warden units occurred the night of August 24th. Intelligence indicated a possible infiltration attempt in the vicinity of the Bassac River, so intensified patrols were stationed near the river's mouth. PCF 38 was assigned to area just off the coast, while two PBR patrols were assigned surveillance in the estuaries. At 2100 hours, PCF 38 detected two contacts near the river's mouth and closed to investigate. A challenge was initiated with no response. Immediately, two additional contacts were detected and challenged. All four contacts were PBRs, but the Swift boat was unable to determine this fact in the darkness of night. At a range of one mile, an illumination round was fired, followed by a second round at 1,500 yards.

PBRs 22 and 25, on patrol near the Can My Thanh Canal, spotted a blinking red light 400 yards from shore, followed by a second blinking light on the beach. They mistook the PCF's challenge for an attempt by a possible enemy craft to signal Viet Cong on the shore. The illumination rounds were then spotted, and the PBRs suspected that they had been caught in an ambush. A firefight ensued between the PBRs and Swift boat. One crewman was wounded on PBR 22, and several additional hits were sustained. The PBRs reported to USS Tortuga that they were in a firefight with an unidentified junk. After receiving the message, Tortuga contacted the command of Market Time aboard USS Floyd County to determine if there were any additional friendly forces in the area. The inquiry was intercepted by the Officer in Charge of PCF 38, who replied that he had been in a firefight with two unidentified contacts. The PCF then established FM radio communication with the PBRs. An investigation was conducted and measures were taken to prevent future mutual interference.

On August 30th, Navy pilots and crewmembers from Detachment 29 of Helicopter Combat Support Squadron One began operating, without Army pilots aboard, as Game Warden helicopter fire teams aboard USS Tortuga, relieving the U.S. Army crews who had previously flown in support of the Navy. By the end of the September, Navy Seawolf gunships were flying in support of friendly forces in the Rung Sat from Nha Be and USS Comstock (LSD 19) as well. During this time, Seawolf gunships came to the aid of several friendly outposts under attack and a downed Army helicopter in III Corps, just north of the Rung Sat. As enemy fire was surpressed in all assaults, the enemy broke off and withdrew after the arrival of the Navy gunships, but sadly, a Detachment 25 crewmember, Aviation Ordinance Third Class Roger D. Childers, was lost.

On August 31st at 1855 hours, PBRs 31, 35 and 40 were proceeding downstream on the Bassac twelve miles southeast of Can Tho when a sampan with two men aboard was observed crossing from Phong Nam Island to the south bank. When the patrol closed, the sampan attempted to evade and warning shots were fired. Enemy fire was immediately received from the bank and in the ensuing firefight the sampan was destroyed. Artillery fire from the Tra On battery was then called in on the enemy positions.

During September, river patrol boats provided increasing support for Vietnamese outpost under attack in their patrol areas, as well as medical evacuation of indigenous personnel. These efforts continued to impress the Vietnamese and U.S. advisors in these areas. But PBRs were targeted and received small-arms fire eight miles from Can Tho on the Bassac above Tra On, where the Viet Cong had told the locals that they were going to "get a PBR."

At 2315 hours on the 5th, PBRs 79 and 80 proceeded to help a Popular Force outpost under attack from two directions twelve miles south of Sa Dec on the Mekong. Upon arrival, the PBRs took the VC under fire and drew enemy fire in return. After a flare ship arrived, the Viet Cong broke off the attack, leaving one Popular Force soldier killed with two wounded and two dependents wounded also. The PBRs provided medical evacuation of the wounded to Sa Dec. Two days later, PBRs took the Viet Cong under fire at an outpost on the Bassac that ended their plans to overrun the friendly post. And a few days later in the same vicinity, the VC began a mortar attack on still another outpost when PBRs rushed to the scene and broke up the attack by directing fire at the Viet Cong, silencing their mortars and causing a secondary exposition. RAG units from Can Tho were then dispatched for outpost security.

On September 8th at 1445 hours, PBRs 30, 34 and 36, operating in support of an ARVN 9th Infantry operation eleven miles southeast of Can Tho, observed a sampan departing a canal in the vicinity of the operation. The two occupants of the sampan jumped overboard as the PBRs closed and fired warning shots. The sampan was captured and was found to contain 300 pounds of rice. The two men escaped. Also that morning at 0517 hours, MSB 49 reported an underwater explosion while on a routine chain drag on the Long Tau. Later that day SS Exhibitor, a civilian cargo ship, received enemy harassment fire from the west side of the Long Tau. A PBR patrol arrived and laid M-79 grenade fire into the enemy positions.

Continued attacks by Viet Cong forces using fortified shore positions resulted in the first PBR crewman killed in action since the beginning of Game Warden operations. On September 11th at 1915 hours, PBRs 29 and 82 of River Section 512 came under automatic weapons fire on the Co Chien River, twenty-six miles south of Vinh Long. In the ensuing firefight, Boatswain's Mate Third Charles Baker was lost while manning the forward .50 caliber machineguns. Game Warden patrols continued making contact with the enemy on a steady pace with River Section 532 activated at Cat Lo by the end of the month. Also, modified Jacuzzi pumps were installed in three PBRs with a noticeable increase in speed.

On September 22nd MSBs 14 and 15 were making their third pass of the Long Tau channel when MSB 15 experienced an explosion on the starboard turbine stack while sweeping the west bank. At the same time, MSB 14 observed three explosions within fifteen feet of her position on the east bank. Light trails of smoke were observed behind the rockets, which were fired from defoliated underbrush at low tide, with additional automatic weapons fire received from both banks. Engineman Second Ronald A. Heintz of MSB 15 was lost in the action, with nine other crewmen wounded. The sweeper was carrying a second crew for indoctrination.

A average of sixty-seven U.S. units were on Market Time patrols during September, with many units receiving hostile fire and contributing gunfire support on ten different occasions through the month. On the 24th, cutter Point Grey dispatched a whaler to investigate several sampans near the beach just off the coast of the U Minh Forrest and fired warning shots as several men jumped overboard and were fired upon. The sampan was destroyed from a secondary explosion when it was taken under fire from the whaler. Two days later, cutter Point Kennedy assisted in recovering four survivors of a downed Army helicopter seventy miles south of Vung Tau. One soldier was lost.

On September 26th, Swift boats of PCF Division 105 based at Qui Nhon set up a blocking force from the sea supporting the First Calvary Division's successful three sided trap of enemy units in Binh Dien Province, 300 miles north of Saigon. Dubbed Operation Irving, Swifties had to board and search more than 150 junks and sampans a day, while patrolling over thirty-six hour periods with only a few hours ashore for a hot meal while their PCFs were refueled between patrols. At the end of the operation, the Market Time coastal craft had netted more than 300 Viet Cong suspects, which they turned over to the U.S. Army's interrogation center at Phu Cat.

The Swift sailors at Qui Nhon normally worked twenty-four to thirty hours, spent a day on stand-by and were off the next day. The maintenance crews for the Swifts averaged twelve hour workdays, seven days a week. The base itself was located at the center of Qui Nhon harbor, at the foot of three mountains. Sanitary facilities and oil drum showers remained outside the Quonset hut type barracks, with showers salt water. The men might spend their time off going to the little village, which sprang up just outside the gate, to eat french fries and squid. Or go to the base's open-air theater, which had wooden benches under the stars with a plywood, whitewashed screen. Or they volunteered to spend their spare time building a school, and then took up a collection to hire a teacher.

In addition to interdicting enemy trawlers, junks and sampans, detaining and transferring prisoners, the Swift crews were also called on to fire mortar rounds or bullets over the beach in support of friendly troops or into suspected VC positions. Or they might rescue distressed fishermen or pick up refugees. A Division 105

Swift once rescued 156 Vietnamese refugees fleeing the Viet Cong just as their overloaded junk filled with water and sank on a dark, stormy night.

By the end of monsoons in 1966, the Mekong Delta had been hit hard with flooding. This gave Game Warden forces a distinct advantage, especially in Kien Tuong Province, where the Viet Cong strongholds in the Plain of Reeds discovered a new enemy riding the crest of flood waters. U.S. Navy patrol boats traveled across flood-swollen canals and submerged rice paddies to cover the vast, sparsely-populated province, searching for the Viet Cong where few Vietnamese and no U.S. combat units had gone before.

Led by Lieutenant Commander Morton E. Toole, commander of the Kien Tuong special operation, eight PBRs used the flood waters to locate and destroy enemy forces. Their mission was to search out the Viet Cong abandoned campsites and bunkers. They would work with the Civilian Irregular Defense Groups, who were advised by the U.S. Army Special Forces. On six search-and-destroy operations, the PBRs acted as a blocking force for friendly forces, preventing the Viet Cong from escaping. They also served as mobile gunboats using their .50 caliber machineguns for extra firepower.

"I like to think the PBRs with their .50 caliber machineguns kept the VC from ambushing the Civilian Irregular Defense Group troops," said Commander Toole.

While patrolling through the Grand Canal to the eastern edge of the plains, three PBRs on the Vam Co Tay River encountered the heaviest action of the operation. They were investigating two sampans crossing the river when ten VC in a rice paddy opened fire on them. The PBRs returned fire and killed two VC and wounded several others. A U.S. Air Force spotter plane arrived soon after, with an Army helicopter fire team following closely behind. The spotter estimated that a VC company was in the area and called in air strikes, which were delivered by U.S. Air Force fighters.

The PBRs sighted sampans moving north along narrow streams and, along with the Civilian Irregular Defense Group troops, who were in small support boats, pursued to intercept. The PBRs then provided fire support while the troops searched the sampans and a group of small huts. As the search continued into the night, one VC was killed and two captured. Four PBRs set up a blocking force through the night to prevent the VC from escaping across the Vam Co Tay. But a search the next morning found very little. Since light contact had been made in the flooded Plain of Reeds, the Navy concluded that the VC had left their long-time refuge and fled to neighboring provinces.

Lieutenant Commander Toole had the highest praise for the Army helicopter gunships which acted as forward eyes from the sky for the PBRs as they swept across the rice paddies and barren plains as far as the eye could see. Several times, the PBRs came under fire with the gunships flying in to provide fire support.

"Without Army air, there would have been some serious moments; cooperation couldn't have been more successful," Commander Toole said.

During these operations, pontoon platforms were brought in for the helicopters so they could be close to the PBRs. Six different Viet Cong campsites were searched by the patrols, resulting in fifty-five structures and six bunkers destroyed. More than a ton and a half of rice was captured and turned over to the Vietnamese flood victims. In addition, the patrol boats distributed over 1,500 pounds of food, milk and soap to the Vietnamese. While at Moc Hoa, all supplies, including fuel, spare parts, food and water, to sustain the boats and their crews was flown in by Army CH-47 Chinook helicopters, which made nine trips from the Game Warden base at My Tho. Naval support sailors, who had volunteered from My Tho, also flew in and worked to paddle the fifty-five gallon fuel drums through neck-high water to set up PBR fueling stations. The large metal shipping containers at the flooded Moc Hoa airstrip became mooring buoys, with the crewmembers living onboard their boats, sleeping on air mattresses and eating C-rats. As the flood waters receded, the PBRs were forced to return to their river bases. But they had proved that they were capable of using any waterway to search out the enemy, and would.

Throughout the remainder of the year, Market Time and Game Warden forces continued to take the fight to the enemy, depriving them of the waterways, lending their fire support to friendly villages, and intercepting enemy re-supply shipments. Inshore coastal patrols during 1965-66 period brought Market Time boats into active contact with hostile forces in more than 200 firefights. Several hundred enemy junks and sampans had been captured or destroyed, more than 450 tons of contraband cargo captured, and more than 1,000 VC suspects seized. The Coast Guard cutters and U.S. Navy Swift boats had ushered in a new concept in modern warfare: the employment of small, high-speed patrol boats to prevent coastal infiltration and the movement of insurgent men and material into South Vietnam. Now, with the smaller river patrol boats of Game Wardens projecting farther up the rivers into long-controlled Viet Cong areas, the enemy began to lose ground fast, but not without a fight. The river and coastal war was beginning to heat up.

RUNG SAT BOILING

By January 1967, keeping the Saigon channel open through the Rung Sat Special Zone dominated the activities of the river force. The clearly stepped-up tempo of enemy activity in the Rung Sat in December had become intense by January, threatening merchant shipping. The Viet Cong waged a relentless campaign on the Long Tau, trying to bottle up the shipping channel. There were twelve mining attempts and automatic weapons attacks against merchant shipping, minesweepers, and river patrol craft during the month. Vietnamese Navy Minesweeper 161 was sunk by a Viet Cong mine, with one U.S. advisor lost. Also in the Rung Sat, the black berets of Operation Game Warden river patrol interdicted a Viet Cong ammunitions resupply junk, killing three insurgents.

Off the coast of South Vietnam in Operation Market Time, Swift boat 71 intercepted a steel-hulled trawler attempting to infiltrate supplies into the Mekong Delta by sea. It was the first time U.S. Navy Swift boats had engaged a steel hulled trawler since arriving in Vietnam in October 1965. As Swift 71, commanded by Lieutenant Junior Grade Richard W. Dawson, moved in cautiously through torrential rain and three-foot seas, the trawler offered no resistance. But when it got within fifty feet, the trawler opened up on the Swift with machineguns and tried to ram her, looking if it was going to board. The Swift took a hit up forward by a large caliber recoilless rifle or mortar, but the firing was so intense no one could go below to see if the boat was taking on water. The Swift quickly pulled away from the trawler, firing with such accuracy that the men could see their tracers slicing into the trawler's hull and sweeping across her decks. The enemy vessel began zigzagging toward the beach as the Swift radioed PCF 68, which was at the upper end of an adjacent patrol area.

When PCF 68, commanded by Lieutenant Junior Grade Alexander Bass, arrived, the trawler was making fifteen knots, so it fired a burst across the trawler's bow as a warning, and a forty-five minute firefight began. Mortar fire from the 68 boat finally brought the trawler to a dead stop as she began drifting to the beach, firing all the time. Then PCF 68 knocked out the machineguns on the trawler with mortar rounds setting her afire. Tracers spewed out of her hold and from her decks, igniting several small, secondary explosions while PCF 68 kept her under fire as the trawler drifted toward the beach. Then PCF 68 got a call from PCF 71 informing them they had discovered a junk in distress that might have been accompanying the trawler. But as it broke off from the trawler to help the 71 boat, it began receiving heavy weapons fire from the beach. The enemy positions on the beach were immediately taken under fire by additional Market Time units which had arrived. The Swifts returned to help the junk, which was sinking, taking six people aboard, and searched for the trawler, which had sunk with debris showing up on the beach later. Both Swift boats were decorated with bullet dents, but fortunately all the sailors survived.

In the central part of the Mekong Delta, Game Warden forces broke up a number of river crossing attempts on the Mekong and Bassac rivers. A crossing attempt on the Bassac by at least 400 Viet Cong was stopped dead in its tracks by patrol boats and an AC 47 fixed-wing Spooky aircraft, also called Puff the Magic Dragon. The WWII Spooky gunship got its name from the little ghost holding a lighting bolt that had been painted on the noise, and while watching her deliver her deadly fire on the enemy from a distance, we sailors often sang the Peter, Paul and Mary's song "Puff the Magic Dragon," as Spooky circled releasing 6000 rounds per minute from each of her three mini-guns while the PBRs blocked all attempts of the VC to cross the river.

On the Mekong, the combined efforts of patrol boats, Seawolf fire teams, fixed-wing aircraft and Vietnamese Army artillery disrupted a crossing attempt by Viet Cong main force unit. My Tho-based river patrol boats also rescued twenty-two people from the Jamaica Bay dredge, which was mined by the Viet Cong while conducting dredging operations for the new delta base at Dong Tam. Throughout the Mekong Delta, river patrol units were engaged in a series of firefights with the Viet Cong, ranging from minor harassments to attempts to overrun friendly outposts along the rivers and canals. River patrols were in almost daily contact with the enemy during the month.

Task Force 116 support ship USS Jennings County, LST 846, returned to Subic Bay, Philippines for repairs while the second Game Warden landing ship, USS Harnett County, LST 821, arrived in country and was stationed near Dong Tam in support of Operation Rampart, which was to block Viet Cong concentration around elements of the U.S. Army's 9th Infantry Division, who had recently arrived in country and moved to Dong Tam. At Vung Tau anchorage, advance units of the newest member of the Naval Forces Team, the Mobile Riverine Force of Task Force 117 began joint training maneuvers with elements of the 2nd Brigade of the 9th Infantry.

At 1120 hours on January 9th, 1967, the British tanker Haustrum was taken under intense automatic weapons and 57mm recoilless rifle fire from positions on each bank of the Long Tau channel, eleven miles downstream from Nha Be at a section of the river referred to as "Alligator Bravo." (Each bend of the Long Tau had an animal-alpha designation.) A two-boat PBR patrol, along with U.S. and Vietnamese minesweeper craft in the area, were unable to suppress the enemy fire and requested a helicopter fire team for assistance. When the two Seawolf gunships arrived, they were fired upon from a tree line 500 yards behind the west bank of the Long Tau, as well as from four sampans in a nearby creek. Two of the sampans were intercepted by the patrol boats, with nine of the occupants detained. Initial interrogation indicated that at least thirty-five VC were involved in the ambush. During the attack, the tanker's master was wounded and his quartermaster killed when a rocket blew holes through the bridge shield. A Vietnamese sailor and American advisor aboard a Vietnamese minesweeper were also wounded during the fight.

Multiple Viet Cong mines were recovered in the Long Tau channel during the month, with two sailors and the entire crew of an Army helicopter killed during an hour-long firefight southeast of Nha Be. The two crewmen of Minesweeper 16, Engineman First Donald G. Peddicord, and Seaman Terry L. Braden, were killed by the first burst of automatic weapons fire from the west bank. Moments later, four PBRs and a helicopter fire team exchanged heavy fire with the enemy. During a low-level firing run, one of the Army helicopters exploded after taking on heavy ground fire and crashed into the trees in flames. River patrol boats immediately lifted a Vietnamese Regional Force platoon to the area for a rescue. When the troops reached the burning chopper, they noted that the bodies of three crewmembers were still inside the helicopter. A fourth burned body was found near the wreckage on the ground.

Ambushes on the Long Tau continued at a feverish pace, with the enemy standing and fighting in many cases. During another Rung Sat ambush on minesweepers and patrol boats, a C-130 Hercules aircraft was called in and pounded both banks of the Long Tau with seventy-six rounds of 105mm howitzer fire. And on still another attack, a Seawolf fire team was called in and suppressed enemy fire until one of the gunships was struck in the rotor blade and forced down. A fixed-wing air strike was then called in to neutralize the enemy positions.

After serving his first year in River Section 511, in the slowest river patrol boat on the Bassac River, Engineman Second Steve Watson was happy to be reassigned to River Section 533 and given a boat that actually got up and moved. His commanding officer, Lieutenant Commander Steed, had made him boat captain of PBR 152. To Watson, it was like a new boat, and he was overjoyed that the fiberglass PBR could actually get up out of the water and run on step with the rest of the section.

When Watson got to Nha Be, just south of Saigon at the confluence of the Long Tau shipping canal and the Soi Rap Rivers, the MSB minesweepers were catching hell on the shipping channel. On more than one occasion, his patrol boat had to stop and pick up dead minesweeper sailors from the river. Watson's patrol had been assigned to provide escort duties for the sweepers. Sometimes they were in front of the sweeper boats, and at other times they we were behind them, dodging their sweeping floats. On January 20th,

'67, they were on a sweeper patrol about fifteen miles south of Nha Be in a canal off the Vam Co River. The U.S. Army's 199th Light Infantry Brigade was on a forward advance, sweeping toward the canal to trap a Viet Cong element and the river patrol boats were serving as the blocking force.

They entered the canal at around 1000 hours, and everything was way too quiet. Watson had the commanding officer, Lieutenant Marty Mitchell, onboard that day with his PBR the third boat in the procession following Barracuda 30, which was a modified landing craft carrying SEALs, with a smaller boat serving as a minesweeper just ahead. The canal was maybe forty-feet wide with one being able to toss a pineapple grenade across, if one had to.

The patrol had just rounded the second or third bend in the canal when the SEAL boat opened fire. Sitting in the forward .50 cal gun tub of PBR 152 was Quartermaster Seaman Ken Delfino, aiming at a Vietnamese hooch in front of him. When Lieutenant Mitchell gave the order to open fire, he did. Ken fired into the hooch, guessing it was someone's home watching jugs full of water and rice explode, while witnessing what a few .50 cal rounds could do to a pig that got into his line of fire. The forward ammo bins of the twin Browning fifties only held 250 rounds each, and this was Delfino's first firefight with his adrenalin pumping, since he was admittedly a little scared.

Delfino fired bursts of six or seven rounds, with twelve to fourteen rounds going out at a squeeze from the big twin machineguns. He continued firing at this and at that, firing into bushes he thought might be camouflaged VC positions, and whatever else looked suspicious until he heard the "CLICK" of the hammer, becoming aware he had just run out of ammunition. Realizing how long it would take to open up a can of ammo in the middle of a firefight - about as long as opening a sardine can - Delfino did the next best thing. His M16 was loaded, with about fifteen magazines in the tub, so he started firing his "made by Mattel gun" to which he received a response of "RELOAD! RELOAD!"

Not knowing how he could shoot and reload at the same time, Delfino opted to follow his boat commander's orders and went below, grabbing a few cans of ammo. Fortunately, the firefight had died down by this time. The Viet Cong were either on the move or had been killed. So he continued reloading the gun's bins till they overflowed, which still didn't look like enough to him.

All Boat Captain Watson remembered was jumping forward as far as he could toward the gun tub, yelling "RELOAD!" Forward gunner Ken Delfino, who was young and looked to weigh all of one hundred pounds soaking wet, had decided that, after expending the forward gun's ammunition, an M16 was a suitable substitute for twin .50 cal machineguns. The more experienced Watson knew this just wasn't so.

Turns out that the boats behind PBR 152 were ambushed and the Viet Cong had let Watson's boat pass through before springing their trap. A few of River Section 54's boats got hit, as this was a joint-unit operation with many boats involved. Needless to say, it was a short-lived ambush and must have been quite a surprise when the VC had twelve .50 cal Browning's shooting back at them. The patrol boats stayed until the Army secured the operation and then they returned back out on the Vam Co River.

The shakes and heebie-jeebies hit Delfino as he quickly finished off three consecutive cigarettes, chain smoking, trying to calm his nerves. He hadn't noticed earlier, but sometime during the event he had apparently bumped his arm against one of the .50 cal barrels and had a nice burn mark, which he still has to this day and considers a badge of honor. Commanding Officer Mitchell wanted to put Delfino in for a Purple Heart, but Delfino rejected it, although the burn stung like crazy. The only casualty the patrol had suffered was the Vietnamese SEAL liaison who had taken a round while standing on the top deck of the landing craft, during the firing of their 105 Howitzer.

Boat Captain Steve Watson had numerous firefights under his belt, having served in combat before arriving. He was calm and directed everyone as if he were directing a movie, and the only time he got excited was when Delfino started using his M16 instead of reloading the fifties. Members of Watson's crew respected him and considered him a good boat captain and leader who didn't panic under fire. They all learned from him and were bummed to see him leave. In their words: "Watson was transferred way to soon."

Later, due to the lessons learned by those early river patrol crews, they split all the T-triggers on the forward .50s so they could walk rounds back and forth to the target with one of the guns and then turn on both guns when needed. They also modified the forward tubs with sheet metal so they could hold 500 rounds each, totaling over 1,000 rounds. Because of this, future forward gunners would not suffer the same fate as Ken "Reload" Delfino. On PBR 152, the patrolmen tried mounting a spotlight on the aft .50 so they could look over the canal bank, but it did not work well. They also used the wooden M79 ammo boxes to hold over 1,500 rounds of M60 ammo. At the time, they held the M60 by hand, with many preferring to fire the light machinegun from the shoulder or hips during a firefight, using a C-rat can to ease the feeding of ammo to the weapon. They found the weight of the weapon countered the recoil, and they were able to keep the rounds on target a lot easier. Only later did they get mounts for the M60. They also discovered that the first Honeywell Mark 18 hand-operated grenade launcher rounds had bad seals on the shell and could cause problems with several rounds jammed in the barrel at the same time. This did make everyone a bit nervous until they learned to dunk the whole ammo belt into engine oil to keep the powder dry.

On February 1st, 1967, the Mobile Riverine Force of Task Force-117 was activated and joined Task Force's 115 and 116 as the Navy's third in-country afloat asset.

In the first week of February, the Viet Cong launched eleven attacks on the river patrol boats and friendly outposts in the Mekong Delta. The River Patrol Force suffered its highest toll of personnel casualties for any single month since Operation Game Warden had begun. Three U.S. Navy men were lost and twenty-four wounded. The war for control of the Long Tau channel had turned into a series of minings and ambushes, while elements of three Viet Cong battalions were reported to be operating fifty miles south of Saigon with a build-up of communist forces around the new base at Dong Tam.

During the month, there were two sabotage attempts involving the PBR base at My Tho. The first attempt was on the afternoon of February 10th when a U.S. Navy sentry was wounded by the explosion of a fragmentation grenade thrown over the fence by a terrorist. The VC terrorist escaped in a large Vietnamese crowd celebrating Tet, the Chinese lunar New Year, in the street outside the base. The second sabotage attempt was four days later, when an 18x24 inch box was sighted floating upstream on the tide about eighty feet from the PBR pier. The watch fired at the box, triggering an explosion whose shock wave was felt one hundred yards from the pier.

On February 2nd, four SEAL fire teams conducting operations in the lower portion of the Rung Sat found a Viet Cong base camp and destroyed a quantity of miscellaneous equipment. Meanwhile, the SEALs' LCM-3 craft, nicknamed Mighty Moe, engaged four enemy sampans in the river, killing two Viet Cong.

The next night; the first river patrol boat was lost to hostile fire when PBR 113 was gutted by fire, following an explosion caused by a grenade thrown by a Viet Cong assassin. At 2200 hours, a two-boat PBR patrol spotted a sampan in the river and turned toward the craft just before sampan's three occupants jumped into the water. PBR 113 approached one of the men and a crewmember tossed him a life ring. The man reached for the life ring and threw a grenade at the PBR. The grenade struck the engineer in the chest and was deflected toward the aft gun mount. The aft gunner and engineer immediately jumped over the side as the grenade detonated, wounding the forward gunner, but not before he shot the grenade thrower. The other two enemy swimmers were killed by fire from the cover boat, PBR 117.

The grenade's explosion initiated an intense fire in the engine compartment of PBR 113 and cooked off the ammunition stored in the boat's aft section. Boat Captain, Gunner's Mate Second Jimmy R. Brown, tried to fight the fire but was forced to abandon the attempt. Brown then put a life jacket on the wounded forward gunner, helped him over the side, and followed him into the water. PBR 117 picked up all of the crew except Seaman August D. Johnson, the aft gunner, who disappeared and was never found. Scuttlebutt had it that his body later washed ashore near the firefight and was looted by the Viet Cong, who again threw the body back into the river. Or at least that is what a Hoi Chanh returnee told Vietnamese interrogators latter.

On February 4th, PBRs 79 and 84 answered a signal for help from a Vietnamese outpost at the mouth of the Mang Thit River under attack from a nearby tree line. Two Navy Seawolf Det-25 gunships answered the call for assistance and arrived just as the Viet Cong had taken the town and were about to overrun the outpost. The Seawolves had launched from Vinh Long in a series of strikes and were joined on station by two additional Seawolf gunships from Det-29 which were stationed aboard USS Harnett County, LST 821. After five air strikes, in which the Navy gunships took and returned heavy fire, in addition to continuous PBR fifty-caliber suppressing fire, the estimated two Viet Cong companies were driven off and retreated back into their jungle sanctuaries. Game Warden units also supported Vietnamese outposts on four other occasions, driving off enemy forces.

On February 8th, a twenty-four-inch spherical mine was discovered in the Long Tau River by units of River Assault Group Twenty-two, after it had been swept by Minesweeper 16. The mine, a controlled type weighing approximately fifty pounds, was recovered and taken to Nha Be, where an ordnance team disarmed it. The PBRs continued to break up Viet Cong river crossings along the upper Mekong and Bassac as insurgents continued to cross into Vietnam from Cambodia.

On February 15th, the Viet Cong ended the post lunar New Year with a series of attacks in the Saigon channel, sinking one U.S. minesweeper and damaging two others. The first attack occurred at 0655 hours, when the Viet Cong sprang an ambush five miles downstream from Nha Be. The enemy employed heavy automatic weapons and 75mm recoilless rifles from well-fortified positions on both banks of the Long Tau channel. Minesweeper 49 received three recoilless hits in her port side, one of which set her fuel tanks on fire. River patrol boats in the area, and Minesweeper 51, returned the enemy outburst and, under heavy fire, assisted the stricken sweeper in beaching, evacuating the wounded and stripping the armament. The patrol boats kept the enemy pinned down until 0710 hours, when Navy Seawolf gunships from Det-27 arrived and delivered an air strike. The Seawolf copters sustained five hits from heavy fire while striking enemy positions, which stretched for half a mile along each bank.

At 0750 hours, a fixed-wing aircraft also struck the enemy positions, followed by a four-company Regional Reaction Force which landed and sweep the area. Two landing crafts from Naval Support Activity, Saigon's Nha Be detachment, towed Minesweeper 49 back to Nha Be. Seaman Rodney H. Rickli was lost on the 49 boat during the action, with seven others wounded. Two VC were known killed.

The enemy struck again at 1020 hours, when a controlled mine sank Minesweeper 45 near the west bank of the river, fifteen miles southeast of Nha Be. Following the violent explosion, the companion boat, Minesweeper 22, picked up five survivors from the water, four of whom were wounded. The injured were evacuated to Nha Be by copters, and a search was begun for the missing crewman, Damage Control Man Third Gary C. Paddock, whose body was found three days later. The armament of the 45 boat was then stripped by divers, and the hulk destroyed by explosives.

At 1428 hours, on the same day, Minesweepers 51 and 32 came under fire from a heavy weapon on the west bank of the Long Tau eleven miles southeast of Nha Be. MSB 51 received two hits, one in the stack and one in the sweep winch. The minesweepers and their PBR escorts then reversed course and headed north. At 1440 hours, the boats came under automatic weapons and small-arms fire from positions two miles upstream from the first ambush. Four additional PBRs joined the action, and a helicopter fire team was dispatched to strike the area. The helicopter strike was followed by a fixed-wing air strike and a sweep of the area by two Regional Force companies, who did not make contact with the enemy. Four U.S. sailors were wounded during the action. On one of the attacks on the minesweeper boats, Gunner's Mate Third Ricky Torres from River Section 533 jumped off of his patrol boat and climbed up to the .50 cal machinegun on one of the MSBs and started firing back in defense of the wounded crew.

The next day, the Commander of U. S. Naval Forces Vietnam, Rear Admiral Ward, sent the following message to the officer-in-charge of Mine Squadron 11, Detachment Alpha:

The courageous action, bulldog tenacity and personal heroism that the men of Detachment Alpha have demonstrated under fire are in keeping with the highest traditions of the Navy. It is singularly significant that in spite of yesterday's efforts by the Viet Cong, the river remains open and unblocked. Your resolution in continuing maximum coverage of the Long Tau with available assets is highly gratifying. To the gallant officers and men on Mine Squadron Eleven, Detachment Alpha, I express my gratitude for your thoroughly outstanding performance of duty and tireless efforts.

At 0820 hours February 16th, Minesweepers 16 and 52 were attacked three and one-half miles downstream from Nha Be by enemy forces on the east bank using automatic weapons and small arms. The minesweepers and their PBR escorts returned the enemy fire, and within an hour, two SEAL fire teams were landed in the area by LCM-3, Mighty Moe. The SEALs killed one Viet Cong while pursuing four others without success, but they did capture two Chinese carbines and discovered a number of observation posts and bunkers. Also that day, elements of the U.S. Army 9th Infantry Division were deployed to the Rung Sat to help secure the river banks. And Regional Force ambush sweep operations were increased and augmented with PBR support provided by River Section 533 while operating on the lower Long Tau based at Cat Lo.

On the evening of February 21st, a PBR patrol in the central Long Tau detected a number of sampans through special night-observation glasses. The area was taken under U.S. Army mortar fire, and a U.S. infantry reaction force was landed, which captured five sampans, a large quantity of rice, weapons, ammunition and documents.

Five days later, a Viet Cong company attempted to overrun an outpost twenty-five miles from Vinh Long on the Mekong River. Two PBRs accompanied by Army and Navy helicopters delivered heavy automatic weapons, grenade and rocket fire into the enemy positions forcing the Viet Cong to withdraw. On the next night, a B-52 strike was delivered in the suspected headquarters area of the Viet Cong commander of the Rung Sat Special Zone.

By March 1967, the Navy had awarded a second contract to United Boatbuilders for construction of 130, new and improved, Mark II river patrol boats. Before the end of U.S. involvement in Vietnam, United had built 294 PBRs.

Although Task Force 115 and 116 forces were holding their own, it was recognized by higher ups that help was needed. The new Mobile River Force of Task Force 117, and the Second Brigade of the 9th Infantry Division, were being brought up to speed quickly, as the simmering river and coastal war was beginning to boil.

THE NINTH INFANTRY

The U.S. Army's 9th Infantry Division, "Old Reliables," was a highly accomplished Army division that had fought across Africa and Italy, landed at Normandy, and swept across France in World War II, as it helped put an end to Hitler's Nazi war machine. On February 1st, 1966, the Old Reliables were once again activated at Fort Riley, Kansas, under the command of Major General George S. Eckhardt, to train for combat in the hostile environment of the Republic of Vietnam. One brigade of the 9th Infantry, the 2nd Brigade, was selected to be the Army component of a new riverine force that would be integrated with Navy Task Force 117, the River Assault Squadrons of the Brown Water Navy. The 3rd and 4th Battalions, 47th Infantry, along with the 3rd Battalion, 60th Infantry, were designated the Riverine battalions of 2nd Brigade.

For the first time since the Union Army operated on the Mississippi and Cumberland, the U.S. Army was utilizing an amphibious force operating afloat. The troops were to live on mobile barracks ships and embark aboard Navy armored troop carrier boats, preceded by minesweeping craft and escorted by heavily armed and armored assault craft, for operations throughout the wetlands of the Mekong Delta. Colonel William B. Fulton, Commanding Officer, 2nd Brigade, had been given latitude to make innovations and to modify training in order to prepare his men for the physical conditions and the tactics of the enemy in Vietnam. Because the training period was short, Fulton elected to stick to normal basic training to prepare his unit for operations in any part of Vietnam.

The newly arrived recruits of the brigade had traveled directly from their reception station to Fort Riley, Kansas, where they were put through eight weeks of basic combat training. For those that were going to be assigned to the infantry, an additional eight weeks of advance individual training was received, followed by eight weeks of basic and advanced unit training. Although it was not generally known in the division, the training had been reduced in order to conclude at the time of the beginning of the Vietnam dry season in December 1966, when the MACV plan called for the introduction of U.S. ground forces into the Mekong Delta.

Battalion strength was 850 men, including officers and non-commissioned officers, with almost 800 draftees mixed in with a small percent of volunteers who had enlisted. Commanding officers were given a few seasoned officers and non-commissioned veterans. West Point class of '66 graduates, along with regular Army officers and reserve officers which had either received direct commissions or graduated officers' candidate school, made up the command structure of the brigade. The draftees had been hand picked by non-commissioned officers sent over from brigade to pick the best from that week's take, filling the division one battalion a week. Still, the men grew into cohesive teams, ready to face the communists in the wetlands and mangrove swamps of South Vietnam.

Upon completion of training at Fort Riley, key officers and non-commissioned officers of the brigade received ten days of special amphibious training from U.S. Navy and Marine riverine warfare specialist at the Navy amphibious training school in Coronado, California, en route to Vietnam. The ten days gave the commanders and staff of the brigade the opportunity to concentrate on purely riverine problems for the first time as they listened to information on operations of the Vietnamese RAGs, U.S. Navy SEAL Teams, Viet Cong intelligence reports, and the riverine environment they would be stepping into.

The 15th Engineering Battalion, 9th Infantry, began arriving in the Republic of Vietnam in October 1966. Lead elements of the 9th Infantry, Headquarters, Signal and Administrative Battalions, landed on the beaches of Vinh Long in the Mekong Delta in December 1966. The 2nd and 3rd Battalions, along with the 5th Battalion Mechanized of the 60th Infantry, 3rd Brigade, were the first combat battalions to arrive. They were transported north of the Rung Sat Special Zone to the 9th Infantry Division headquarters at base camp Bearcat, twenty miles northeast of Saigon. Later they would be moved five miles south of My Tho to Dong Tam, a division-size base, dredged from river sand, that had been selected by General Westmoreland from four sites submitted by the engineers as suitable for building by dredging.

It had been decided initially that the base would be called base camp Whisky, so General Westmoreland asked the official MACV translator to give him several possible Vietnamese names for the base in keeping with its role as the first American firebase in the Mekong Delta. The translator's list included the Vietnamese term "Dong Tam," which literally meant "united hearts and minds." General Westmoreland selected this name because it signified the bond between the American and Vietnamese people, and it was easy for the Americans to pronounce and remember. General Westmoreland felt that the delta might well be a source of stabilization for the Vietnamese economy and, if protected, could produce enough rice for the entire country. The presences of the U.S. division would aid in this acceleration of the region and help protect rice farmers and their crops, ensuring they reached the market places of South Vietnam.

Also among the first 9th Infantry Divisions to arrive in the Republic of Vietnam was the 3rd Battalion, 34th Artillery Division. It was a unique battalion in that its men placed two 105mm Howitzers on each of six custom-built barges, which were used as floating firing platforms, being towed up and down the rivers by Mike-8 landing craft to provide direct artillery support for Mobile Riverine Force operations. In addition, they had two mortar tubes mounted on each of two smaller barges.

Artillery was very important to the infantry, and there were many different artillery battalions within the 9th Infantry Division. In those days, 105mm artillery Howitzers had a maximum effective range of seven to eight miles, so the trick was to position the big guns close to the operations. Artillery battalions in direct support of infantry usually sent over a liaison party to the supported outfit with an artillery captain as liaison officer, serving as fire support coordinator at the infantry battalion level. Artillery lieutenants were also sent as forward observers, serving at the company level, along with the appropriate communications people to tie it all together. Artillery fire support bases were established in operational areas with as many as three separate artillery batteries employed at the same time from different locations. Air mobility was essential to effective riverine operations. It was necessary to have a command helicopter capable of carrying a commander, a fire support co-coordinator, intelligence officer and the necessary radio communications. Long associations between artillery and infantry units helped build teamwork, but random associations between such partners were also effective.

On January 10th, 1967, the 2nd Brigade departed Oakland, California, aboard USS General John Pope and steamed across the Pacific Ocean en route to sunny Southeast Asia. The 2nd Brigade arrived at Vung Tau anchorage on January 28th. In February, after the men had one day of Army and Navy shakedown training, increased activity by enemy forces in the Rung Sat Special Zone demanded immediate deployment of an infantry battalion. The order was prompted by a Viet Cong attack on a freighter steaming down the channel. This brought an abrupt halt to the 3/47 Infantry's training when its men were designated and immediately began conducting combat operations in the Rung Sat. The 3/47th Infantry's mission was to search out the Viet Cong guerrillas and main force elements in the Rung Sat and, once contact was made, continue attacking until the enemy was destroyed.

Operation River Raider I got underway with 2nd Brigade deploying the 3rd Battalion 47th Infantry, commanded by Lieutenant Colonel Lucien E. Bolduc Jr., to the Rung Sat Special Zone, where the Viet Cong had increased the tempo of attacks on merchant shipping on the Long Tau channel winding its way from Saigon to the sea. The 3/47th Infantry was transported by an advance party from River Assault Division 91 of River Assault Squadron 9, commanded by Lieutenant Charles H. Sibley. It was the first joint operation by U.S. Army and U.S. Navy units, who operated old Mike-6 French RAG boats on loan from the South Vietnamese Navy. The Navy's first increment of riverine assault craft were not due to arrive in Vietnam until March 1967. It had been planned for the men to arrive before their boats, so that the Army and Navy units could get accustomed to working together, becoming a team.

This was stepped up to protect shipping. Mine-sweeping support and escorts for movement were provided by Vietnamese Navy River Assault Group 26.

The American-crewed Vietnamese Tango boats, whose radio call sign was "Hogback," therefore became Hogback One, Hogback Two, and so on, all the way up to Hogback Seven. It was an appropriate name for the Vietnamese boats, which were just pigs, the Americans said. The Vietnamese had no parts for repairs and the forward ramps rarely worked. The Army always referred to them as Hogbacks, calling the sailors on the radio saying, "We need a Hogback over here to lift us across the stream."

En route to the area of operations, the Hogbacks provided protection from enemy snipers and ambushes. After arriving at their destination, troops stormed ashore under cover of automatic weapons and mortar fire provided by the sailors of assault division 91 from their Hogback assault craft. The boats then backed off and took up flanking and blocking water ambush positions, preventing Viet Cong cross-river movement and evasion. Because of the lack of firm ground in the Rung Sat, two 81mm mortars were installed in the forward portion of a landing craft to provide mobile fire support on the bank.

Riverine troops were stationed in Vung Tau aboard LST 1169, USS Whitfield County, and on USS Henrico, APA 45, an old World War II attack transport ship with accommodations for a division staff, which served as one of the mobile joint operations centers for Commander River Flotilla One during the first few operations. Day or night, Hogbacks rotated them up and down the main shipping channel to friendly ambush sites or the battalion command post, which stayed in the gluck for about a month. Following arrival at the battalion command post, troops moved out, usually after dark, to their operation areas or base camps set up in the Rung Sat, which was flooded at high tide. The Hogbacks continued to patrol the waterways, and one boat usually stayed in standby range of the Army platoon-size ground force, in case they needed to extract in a hurry.

Fire support for the operation was diverse and highly effective. Naval gunfire was used continuously throughout the operation, including indirect fire originating from several destroyers and direct and indirect fire of weapons from the boats of U.S. Navy Division 91, and River Assault Group 26. Additional fire support was provided by tactical air, and by U.S. Air Force, Army, and Navy fixed-wing and helicopter gunships. Because of daylight traffic in shipping and the channel being patrolled constantly by U.S. Navy patrol boats, minesweepers, and aircraft, extra precautions had to be taken to co-ordinate fire support to protect allied forces. Initially problems occurred in acquiring clearance from the government of Vietnam for fire missions, but this was resolved after a new zonal clearance system was set into play.

Opposition throughout River Raider I was light, consisting mainly of sporadic sniper fire from the sparsely populated Rung Sat. The Viet Cong moved mostly by sampan. On one occasion, an ambush was tripped three times in one night, resulting in seven enemy killed and three sampans with weapons captured. On another night, five sampans were captured with documents and maps revealing the Viet Cong regional headquarters and compromising the enemy's signal system. But the major operational success of River Raider I was the capture of substantial stores of water mines and the destruction of the C909 Work Shop Company's facilities for constructing mines. The Viet Cong C702 local force company was charged with protecting the workshops, and the C2 Engineer Company charged with interdicting shipping along the Long Tau Channel, utilizing the bombs. This proved important in coming months with the limited use of water mines being employed by the enemy. When the 3/47th Infantry did catch sight of Viet Cong groups, the enemy faded before the swift striking power of the riverine force, refusing to engage in any kind of open combat. War in the swampy mudflats deteriorated into long days and nights of stifling heat and humidity while battling swarming insects and fighting the salty water, which rose and fell with the tides, leaving sucking mud with the consistency of toothpaste.

The Rung Sat was a swampy wetland where the water level changed several times a day, depending on the tides and time of year. The troops would depart the boats in waist high water and a few hours later, be in knee high mud, trudging close to the roots of the trees, so as to stay afloat and out of the mud pits. The companies would be sweeping through an open area close to the channel in butt-high water and watch a ship pass by in the distance, leaving waves from the wake of vessel's screws, as the waves rippled approaching, and eventually washed out the men, soaking them and their gear.

Troops on combat operations in the Rung Sat Special Zone were continually in mud, and the salty, dirty water could not be used for bathing. Therefore, certain measures were taken to safeguard the health of the men. After several days of combat operations, soldiers were rotated back to the troopships or Vung Tau for a drying-out period, where they were provided a shower, hot meal, and bunk for the night. All companies received instructions on the care of their feet, which included daily inspections by medics. Army battalion surgeon, Captain Horst Filtzer, worked tirelessly, and effectively, to combat environmental hazards, including long-term water immersion of feet, and measures to limit chafing by soldier's clothing. He recommended getting rid of underwear to minimize chaffing with Lieutenant Colonel Bolduc agreeing and issuing the order. The medical staff worked to insure the troops remained in top physical condition for the demanding job at hand. From February through mid May, the 2nd Brigade kept one battalion operating in the Rung Sat in conjunction with Naval forces. This first joint action of Army and Navy forces, called River Raider I, was later adopted by the 2nd Brigade becoming their nickname, the "River Raiders."

While the Mobile Riverine Force operated off ships in Vung Tau Harbor, it did not have the pontoons alongside the ships as of yet, so access to the boats was via cargo nets, just as the Marines did for amphibious landings. The proper protocol was for all rifles to be unloaded while climbing the nets. One night that did not happen, and a soldier accidentally fired his M16, putting a hole through the bottom of the one of the Hogbacks. On a different day, a soldier's round accidentally found its way into a box of 81mm mortar shells. When the box started smoking, it was quickly tossed over the side.

River Assault Squadron 9 was formed on October 3rd, 1966, when members reported to Naval Amphibious Base, Coronado, California, to commence training. After weeks of introducing the sailors to the Mobile Riverine concept, counter insurgency tactics, and intense survival, escape, and evasion training at Whidbey Island, Washington, and Warner Springs, California, River Assault Squadron 9 was commissioned with Lieutenant Commander C.L. Horowitz as Squadron Commander. River Assault Division 91, commanded by Lieutenant C.H. Sibley II, and River Assault Division 92, commanded by Lieutenant A.H. Binge, had eight officers and 355 men assigned to fifty assault craft.

After Coronado, the squadron proceeded to Mare Island, Vallejo, California, for small boat training. River Assault Division 91 deployed early for combat operations in the Republic of Vietnam on January 4th, 1967, where it operated with 135 enlisted men, conducting operations in Vietnamese River Assault Group boats, until their complement of twenty-five assault craft arrived in-country. River Assault Division 92 arrived two months later, bringing the squadron up to full strength.

On March 10th, 1967, the commanding officer of the 2nd Brigade, Colonel William B. Fulton, moved to Dong Tam and took command of the base with two battalions, the 3/60th Infantry and the 5/60th Mechanized. Eight days later, River Assault Squadron 9 participated in its first combat operation after receiving the first shipment of assault craft, which proved to be better armed and armored. They also had a wider assortment of weapons, and the ramps worked.

On March 20th, the 3/47th Infantry arrived at Dong Tam after being relieved on station by its sister battalion, the 4/47th Infantry, with Lieutenant Colonel Guy I. Tutwiler commanding, which began patrolling the Rung Sat under operations with the 5th Battalion Mechanized, 60th Infantry of the 3rd Brigade. The 3rd Brigade had been moved north to Tan An, the capital of Long An Province in III Corps Tactical Zone, to assist in pacification programs. There were many 9th Infantry line units that rode the boats, but they were not considered riverine. The 4/47th Infantry continued sweeps through the mangrove swamps of the Rung Sat. By the end of the operation, the force had killed some forty Viet Cong insurgents, destroying numerous enemy bunkers and base camps, capturing large quantities of weapons, ammunition, mines, and junks.

By early April 1967, as new boats arrived from the States, Task Force 117 sent over ten river assault craft to commence riverine operations in the Dong Tam area in defense of the base that was still under construction. Within a month, this had build up to a full river assault squadron at Dong Tam conducting offensive operations against the Viet Cong 514th Provincial Battalion, the 263rd Main Force Battalion, and local force sapper and guerrillas who posed a threat to Dong Tam. Initial operations from base were primarily of the quick reaction type. Taking advantage of hard intelligence gained from agent reports, elements of the squadron embarked company-size reaction forces at Dong Tam and transferred them to various locations along the rivers and connecting waterways. The assault craft conducting these operations provided resupply and both direct and indirect fire support to the infantry.

On April 1st, second brigade forces made a raid into northern Kien Hoa Province on the My Tho River south of Dong Tam, using barge-mounted artillery. In darkness, one battery was moved west on the river, followed closely by infantry mounted in assault boats. Once opposite of a manned station of Viet Cong, the artillery poured surprise direct fire into the target area. In order to protect a Ham Long District company, which had set up blocking positions south of the target, time fuses were used on these rounds. After the artillery ceased fire, infantry troops landed and swept through the area, capturing enemy ammunitions and a portion of a labor force of an enemy communication-liaison platoon.

May 2nd marked the beginning of the battle that took place in the Ap Bac II area. This was not a riverine operation, but was a significant battle fought by the 2nd Brigade, which nearly wiped out the 514th Main Force Viet Cong Battalion, a provincial force of excellent reputation. It was the intelligence officer of the 3rd Battalion 47th Infantry, Lieutenant Harold C. Minter, who did the original pattern analysis and had predicted that the Viet Cong 514th Main Force Battalion would be in Ap Bac Hamlet that day. Second

Brigade accepted the analysis, passed it to division, and mounted the operation.

AP BAC

"**A**p" roughly translated means "hamlet" in Vietnamese, and there were many Ap Bacs in Vietnam. Ap Bac II was located in northern Dinh Tuong Province southwest of Saigon, which was described as a normal operating area for the Viet Cong by the commanding general of the 7th Vietnam Army Division. Originally 2nd Brigade command had laid out a beautiful plan with two battalions advancing abreast with the 3rd Battalion: 60th Infantry "Wild Ones," on the west, and the 3rd Battalion, 47th Infantry "Tigers," on the east advancing north from Highway 4, which was its line of departure. In order to establish a blocking force to prevent the enemy from escaping, it was decided that Alpha Company 3/60th would be airlifted at 0700 hours and dropped in by Army copter Slicks on an airmobile assault to secure a blocking position astride the most likely route of enemy withdrawal. Then the helicopters would return and pickup members of the 3/47th Infantry and drop them into position. The rest of the troops would be moved by two and a half ton trucks to their drop off points north of Highway 4, with the 3/60th departing first because it had the farthest to go. The attack was to begin at 0800 hours. This was the initial plan drawn up on May 1st, 1967, by command.

Early on May 2nd, elements of the 3/60th Infantry composed of Bravo and Charlie Companies, plus battalion command post and a combat support company, moved out and arrived at their attack jumping off position without incident. The 3/47th Infantry departure was delayed because of a shortage of transportation, and Alpha Company 3/60th were formed up and patiently waiting for their air assault, but were notified that the helicopters had been diverted because of a tactical emergency. By now the 2nd Brigade commander was understandably a little unhappy. Recognizing the plan had gone to hell, Colonel William B. Fulton tried to figure out the confusion. After discussing the pros and cons with the commander of the 3/60th Infantry, Lieutenant Colonel Edwin W. "Skip" Chamberlain, and the commander of the 3/47th Infantry, Lieutenant Colonel Lucien E. "Blackie" Bolduc Jr., only then did Colonel Fulton decided to continue the operation moving the troops by truck, a move that would take almost two hours.

Alpha Company 3/60th was also to be moved by truck and would go into battalion reserve after arriving. Bravo and Charlie companies of the 3/60th after arriving to the line of departure would begin operations by advancing to a series of objectives to the north of Highway 4. The 3/47th Infantry would also advance to the north, as soon as it arrived by truck that is. Charlie Company 5th Battalion, 60th Infantry Mechanized, was given the deeper objectives because its mobility and speed would allow them to quickly search out the enemy and hopefully compensate for the lack of a blocking force. At the same time, the brigade forward command post elements moved north by Tango boats on the Kinh Xang Canal to set up a post at Long Binh.

The terrain in the area of operations consisted of rice paddies surrounded on four sides by narrow earthen dikes. The paddies were mostly dry and could easily support the weight of an armored personnel carrier. Throughout the area, clusters of coconut trees and mangrove clumps straddled the many small streams, which could only be crossed at certain points and were perfect cover for enemy thick-walled fighting bunkers and spider holes hidden in the heavy undergrowth. There were many thatched hooches made of mud and palm branches in densely vegetated areas, but few people were seen. In addition, farmhouses were scattered throughout the rice paddy terrain with large haystacks, many of which concealed enemy bunkers.

It was another hot clear day by noontime when troops of the 3/60th Infantry had reached and searched as far north as their objective, code named Queen, without making contact with the enemy. But shortly after arriving they found rice caches while searching and knew the Viet Cong were close by. No mines or booby traps had been encountered, which was usually a pretty good sign that it was an area where many Viet Cong frequented.

For them it looked like another dry hole at first. But for the 3/47th Infantry, and especially for their lead element, Alpha Company, what had seemed like a routine day walking in the sun was rapidly becoming a bad one. Almost from the moment they crossed the line of departure moving forward, they had begun to drawn enemy fire from communist weapons. At first it was only sporadic sniper fire that did not slow the aggressive sweep of the troops as they closed in and killed several of the enemy fighters, forcing the rest to flee north. Continuing its advance, Alpha Company 3/47th began to meet more and more fire as its troops cautiously crossed open rice paddies opposite a build-up area of thatched huts along a deep stream that ran across their front.

Meanwhile, 3/47th commander, Lieutenant Colonel Bolduc, had committed his Bravo Company to the right of his Alpha Company for support. Soon Bravo Company was also stopped by heavy fire originating from the enemy hidden in heavy undergrowth inside a wooded area. By 1250 hours, both Alpha and Bravo Companies had encountered the enemy. Charlie Company 3/47th, which was last to arrive in the convoy, had been moving along a canal that flowed north to south farther to the east when troops noticed Vietnamese civilians moving south along the same canal, pulling sampans loaded to the point of sinking. Charlie Company commander, Captain Ronald Menner, did not like the looks of it and radioed the Alpha Company commander informing him of the civilian activity in his area, warning him to watch himself as the civilians seemed to know something they didn't. Shortly thereafter, Charlie Company arrived at a tree line and, after crossing an east-to-west stream, began pushing to the west where troops immediately made contact with the enemy, sustaining one causality. Bravo and Charlie Companies were then ordered to block on the east and northeast of the position of Alpha Company 3/47th, which had come under heavy fire after emerging from a wood line and was deploying against the enemy. But Alpha Company was hampered by heavy undergrowth that made it difficult to see the enemy firing positions and came upon a stream that had to be crossed.

Calling for artillery and air support to improve their position, members of Alpha Company's first platoon moved a squad across the stream under cover of heavy supporting fire as artillery rounds of high explosive and white phosphorous thundered overhead and crashed into the woods, sending earth and trees flying. Keeping low, the squad was moving across an open rice paddy when a concealed communist automatic weapon suddenly opened fire from close range, wounding most of the soldiers and completely pinning them down. The squad immediately returned fire, killing the enemy gunner, but another gunner quickly manned the gun and continued to fire on the exposed squad, as the big gun's rounds pierced the mud dike. Within minutes, the entire squad had become casualties.

By now, fire from all sides was intense, but despite this, several men of the platoon crawled forward to aid the wounded, only to be killed themselves. In a short time, the first platoon riflemen that had crossed the stream lay motionless from multiple wounds and the remainder of the platoon was temporarily wrecked as a fighting force. Reorganizing, the rest of the platoon pushed across the stream under heavy fire and took up positions, pouring in small-arms fire while calling for artillery support, gunships, and air strikes on the enemy's position. Alpha Company's first platoon was led by Second Lieutenant Terry Stull, who made it to the dike in the middle of the field with his radioman, which was as far as any of the platoon was able to advance. Alpha Company third platoon, led by Second Lieutenant Randy B. Bartley, was fighting its way through a wooded area to the right of first platoon, while another squad came up on first platoon's left fighting through a heavy vegetated area at a right angle to the dike.

Learning that elements of the 3/47th Infantry were in contact with the enemy, and anticipating that his battalion would soon become involved, the commanding officer of the 3/60th, Lieutenant Colonel Chamberlain, ordered his Bravo Company forward to the contact area with his Alpha Company following. Chamberlain then recalled the personnel carriers of Charlie Company 5/60th Mechanized from its barren search farther to the west, far north of the point of contact with the enemy, and directed them to turn and advance toward the contact area. This placed the battalion in a perfect position to attack the flank of the enemy, which was engaging the 3/47th Infantry. Colonel Fulton quickly approved of this action and directed that Bravo Company 3/60th, which was closest to the scene of contact, be placed under the operational control of Lieutenant Colonel Bolduc and the 3/47th Infantry, blocking the enemy's escape to the north.

Bravo Company 3/60th quickly occupied its assigned blocking position, without enemy contact, and in doing so, indicated the limits of the enemy's position to the north. But it didn't take long after moving into position that Bravo Company engaged a six-man Viet Cong force, killing three with the other three fleeing to the south. Alpha Company 3/60th, which had been behind Bravo Company, continued advancing along the stream that formed the line of contact farthest to the west. While doing so, it captured a Viet youth riding a water buffalo who confessed to belonging to the Viet Cong 514th Battalion, saying he had been sent ahead to watch for the Americans' approach from the west. By 1500 hours, Alpha Company 3/60th had reached the restraining line designated by Colonel Fulton and was deployed along it in assault formation, with three platoons abreast, with the southern most platoon drawing small-arms fire as it advanced along the stream. The enemy quickly withdrew to the woods when its fire was returned.

By 1530 hours, after traveling a long distance through swampy, marshy areas thought impassable, and crossing two fairly deep streams, the armored personnel carriers closed on Alpha Company 3/60th, with the eleven carriers quickly deploying in a line to the north of them. This was done so that the battalion was deployed on an assault line over a thousand yards facing east. In front of the carriers stretched some 1,500 yards of open rice paddies, cut at five-hundred-yard intervals by two irrigation ditches, with the last being only five hundred yards from the enemy's camouflaged fighting positions. On the north and south of the rice paddies were dense tree lines, with the north end having been swept by Bravo Company 3/60th earlier and known to be free of enemy troops. The south end was believed to harbor Viet Cong, with the southern platoon of Alpha Company 3/60th advancing through to that area.

While the scorching sun beat down and soldiers drained their canteens, the 3/47th Infantry continued to call in alternate artillery fire and eventually three Air Force air strikes into the enemy's positions, effectively bottling up and preventing the Viet Cong from escaping. With Alpha Company 3/47th in the rice paddy south and her Bravo and Charlie Companies dispersed to the east and northeast of the enemy, the battalion slowly applied pressure, chipping away at the enemy's defenses. While this was being carried out, first platoon Sergeant James Pelfrey of Charlie Company, who was with the most northern platoon, saw a company of VC moving 600 yards to the northeast and requested a major shift in artillery fire. Captain Ron Menner would not honor this request as he knew that a company from the 3/60th Infantry was to the north and moving south. Luckily a gunship, which had been constantly circling the area, also reported sighting the Viet Cong force and immediately attacked the group, killing forty. The Viet Cong were slowly being pinned in their bunkers and surrounded, but they stubbornly resisted with heavy rifle and automatic weapons return fire.

By 1600 hours, everything was ready for a coordinated assault, with the 3/47th Infantry closing from the south and east on the enemy and the 3/60th Infantry and track vehicles closing from the west and north on the enemy. Lieutenant Colonel Chamberlain intended to move the 3/60th Infantry forward by stages, getting them as close as possible before making the final assault. The tracked vehicles would advance and recon by fire, destroying individual enemy positions as they were discovered. Although the general location of the Viet Cong was known, it was impossible to spot them in their camouflaged fighting positions until the soldiers were almost on top of them. To further complicate matters, the entire area was honeycombed with small fortified fighting positions that had to be searched and cleared.

Colonel Fulton suggested, and it was decided, to lay a heavy volume of smoke on the suspected area, using a battery of 155mm Howitzers to screen the battalion's approach. It was also planned to place a battery of 105mm Howitzers in direct support of each assaulting company, with each commander concerned directing artillery fire on the enemy's positions so the infantry could move forward as close as possible, crawling the last few yards in the case of Alpha Company 3/60th. Then when the fire was lifted and directed to the rear of the enemy to block his escape, the Americans would attack before the enemy could recover. Each battalion commander used an observation helicopter to coordinate fire in close support of his unit.

At first there were a few problems coordinating the two battalions, causing some delay. Colonel Fulton became concerned that the gradual tightening of friendly troops around the enemy force had brought them dangerously close to each other's fire power. The fear of the armored carriers' .50 cal fire hitting elements of the 3/47th Infantry, even as far back as the fire support base, was great. When they did start their assault from the west side of the enemy, their suppressive fire impacted all around the 3/47th Infantry on the east, resulting in one minor casualty due to .50 cal fire.

For the artillery, it was becoming especially difficult. The tubes were so hot from continuous firing that some of the rounds were beginning to becoming erratic. Still, the unyielding Viet Cong were getting pounded from the shelling and air strikes, with their safe haven in the trees getting smaller and smaller. Although all companies had closed in, they were still being met by heavy enemy fire on all points. When enemy recoilless rounds began hitting the armored vehicles, and a U.S. strafing aircraft wobbled and sprayed the line of tracked vehicles with 20mm mini-guns, Colonel Fulton called off the air strike and ordered the assault to stop.

A few personnel carriers had been hit, wounding several men and killing one. Now in a state of chaos, the tracked vehicles' company commander reported that he was extremely pessimistic about their ability to attack. Meanwhile, Lieutenant Colonel Chamberlain was having problems getting artillery fire support needed for his assaulting companies due to the fact the artillery battalion commander refused to relinquish control of his batteries to the forward observers near contact. The artillery continued firing white phosphorus rounds that were hitting dangerously close to Alpha Company 3/60th Infantry.

Elsewhere, a Viet Cong attack was being launched on the command post of the 3/60th Infantry just south of Highway 4. This force appeared to be the rest of the 514th Viet Cong Battalion trying to relieve pressure on its units north of Highway 4, which were being pinned and slowly strangled.

As darkness approached, Colonel Fulton called another conference together that included battalion commanders Chamberlain and Bolduc, to decide whether to terminate the operation in light of the growing difficulties, or to continue the fight into the night, which appeared to be even more hazardous. Faced with that question, both infantry battalion commanders urged continuing the fight. "Let's turn on the lights and go," they replied, referring to artillery illuminating shells.

Colonel Fulton, satisfied with the response, smiled and said, "Okay, let's go."

Time was becoming a concern, darkness was approaching rapidly as the track vehicles turned on their lights and without further delay, Chamberlain ordered the attack to go forward without artillery support. The armored track vehicles, including the damaged ones, tracked forward firing their .50s as they went. What followed next was more like what one might see at the movie theater on the big screen, or on a blackboard in a training exercise, but rarely in combat. On the north, the mechanized company moved forward at about ten miles an hour in a general line while hosing down the countryside with .50 cal fire, advancing without halting, rapidly closing in to a wooded area. As soon as they reached the woods, the track vehicles dismounted their infantrymen and both track vehicles and supporting infantry began a rapid assault, running down the enemy as they dragged them out of their fighting holes where they had been trapped by the heavy volume of fire.

Alpha Company 3/60th Infantry, west of the contact area, was exchanging fire with the enemy defenders while two platoons in the rice paddies gained fire superiority and began to move again after being momentarily stopped. Within a half-hour, they had advanced to within a hundred yards of the main enemy line, where they were being held off by intense small-arms fire and mortars. Because of the enormous fire being exchanged from both sides, ammunition was rapidly dwindling and some of the soldiers were having trouble with their rifles jamming. Temporarily stalled, with the battle very much in the balance, the company commander requested the support of the empty track vehicles he could see to his north. This was immediately done as the armored vehicles rushed forward into the battle adding their .50 cal machineguns to the furious firefight. So far as Chamberlain was concerned, all of his chips were in the pot. The situation was such that no fire from air or artillery could be utilized due to the nearness of the opposing combatants. Chamberlain's Bravo Company was still on the north, blocking any enemy retreat and in pretty good shape, prepared to prevent any unseen disasters if necessary. But its chances of attacking south along the stream were considered slim. Thus the units in contact would have to finish the job as they continued to slug it out in the fading light.

Darkness was upon them as they fought on savagely in the light of illumination shells and aerial flares, pouring fire into the enemy, hoping the VC would break and run as they inched forward, taking advantage of cover the best they could. Finally, the break they were all looking for came on the southwest flank where one of Alpha Company 3/60th platoons was coming along the stream line. After fighting its way from house to house along the stream, the platoon arrived at a position just short of the enemy's main defense's line. In front of the platoon to their right was the rice paddy where the lead squad of Alpha Company 3/47th Infantry's first platoon had been badly hit earlier in the day. The remaining riflemen of the platoon were dug in along the small dike perpendicular to the 3/60th Infantry front line. Farther to the north, about thirty yards, was another dike parallel to the one that the remainder of first platoon was positioned behind.

The air was alive with tracer bullets, making it impossible to advance across open space. Recognizing the danger, Alpha Company 3/60th platoon leader directed his men to quickly divide into two groups and start crawling along the two dikes under cover of the supporting fire from Alpha Company 3/47th. Alpha Company 3/60th suddenly came under intense automatic weapons and small-arms fire from the enemy bunker system that was protected by numerous snipers in nearby trees. As the second group, under the platoon sergeant, began moving down the second dike, the lead man, a popular squad leader, was killed by fire originating from a foxhole along the dike. The two men following the squad leader, Sergeant Leonard B. Keller and Specialist Fourth Raymond R. Wright, became enraged, seeing their buddy killed. Despite heavy enemy fire, they leaped to the top of the dike and began a merciless assault on the enemy.

Armed with a rifle and several grenades, Wright exposed himself to intense fire from the bunkers as he charged the nearest one. Sergeant Keller neutralized the fire from the first bunker with his M60 machinegun while Wright ran forward and threw in a hand grenade, killing its VC occupant. Then Wright charged through a hail of enemy fire to a second bunker while Sergeant Keller covered for him, and again Wright succeeded in killing the enemy occupant by throwing in a grenade. A third bunker contained a VC automatic rifleman who had pinned down much of the friendly forces that afternoon. Again, with utter disregard for the fire being directed at them, the two-man machinegun team continued their miraculous assault, with Keller covering while Wright charged in and killed the enemy rifleman with another grenade. The two soldiers worked their way through the remaining bunkers, knocking out four of them, busting through the enemy's mainline of defense while destroying a light machinegun post and a mortar tube which had been causing trouble for the brigade.

Throughout their furious assault, Specialist Wright and Sergeant Keller had been almost continuously exposed to intense sniper fire from the tree line as the enemy desperately sought to stop their brave attack. Overcoming stubborn resistance from the bunker system, the men advanced into the tree line, forcing the enemy to run as the two soldiers gave immediate chase, driving the VC back into the trees. The ferocity of their glorious assault had carried the two soldiers beyond the line of bunkers, forcing the snipers to flee their positions, accounting for numerous VC dead along the way, allowing their own units to advance across the open rice paddy without further casualty.

Watching these two soldiers and their gallant charge inspired the rest of the riflemen, who then jumped up and went on the attack, assaulting the Viet Cong in close combat. As the fight raged on hand-to-hand, one VC fighter was beaten to death by a steel helmet and another was stabbed to death. The savageness of the final assault broke the enemy's back as Viet Cong fighters began crawling out of their fighting holes and running, trying to escape. But most were shot down as troops from the 9th Infantry seized the moment and pushed in from all directions, overrunning the enemy's positions in one last assault. As the shadows of darkness started to fall, the roar of machinegun fire and exploding grenades started to slowly die off. Night had finally come to Dinh Tuong Province, but it had come too slowly to help the Viet Cong escape.

Frantic Army medics hurried to stop the bleeding and save as many of the wounded as possible. Men revisited the sounds of battle in their heads as it continued ringing in their ears while they spoke in high-pitched voices as if they were still yelling over the guns and shells crashing to earth. Small fires burnt in the underbrush where the shells had hit, as smoke bellowed into the twilight. Groups of soldiers, physically weak and exhausted, moved about the battlefield looking for enemy survivors, collecting weapons with cigarettes hanging out of their mouths as they tried to calm their nerves. The sound of helicopter blades flapping in the distance filled the air as supplies were brought in and the wounded were rushed off to aid stations that stood ready.

When the smoked cleared, 200 Viet Cong from the 514th Regular Force lay dead on the ground. There was little doubt that some had escaped in the fading light, yet no officers were found except the VC battalion surgeon. Some of the officers could have been the Viet Cong that Bravo Company had encountered earlier in the day. One Viet Cong fighter was found sitting in a bunker upright but dead, apparently killed from the effects of a near-miss by Napalm dropped by the Air Force earlier. The blast from the Napalm had evidently sucked the air from the area, causing his lungs to collapse.

Casualties for 3/60th Infantry were considered relatively light, with two killed in the action and fifteen wounded. It was not so for the 3/47th Infantry, which suffered thirteen killed in the little rice paddy and many more wounded.

South Vietnamese General Thanh, commander of the 7th ARVN Division, estimating the area where the remaining units of the 514th Local Force Viet Cong Battalion had fled, sent an ARVN Ranger battalion in on May 3rd to search them out. The Rangers encountered and attacked an estimated company of the 514th Battalion during the afternoon. The casualties inflicted upon the 514th by the U.S. 2nd Brigade, 9th Infantry Division, and the ARVN Rangers, severely reduced its combat effectiveness. Reports received later suggested that the Viet Cong 263rd Main Force Battalion was forced to undertake training of new recruits and operational tasks of the Viet Cong 514th Battalion due to the losses of men and weapons the 514th had suffered during the battle.

When Sergeant Leonard B. Keller and Specialist Fourth Class Raymond R. Wright had exhausted their ammunition, they returned to their platoon to assist in the evacuation of the wounded. This brave two-man assault had driven an enemy platoon from a well-prepared position, accounted for numerous enemy casualties, and averted further friendly casualties. Their extraordinary heroism, courage, and fighting spirit saved the lives of many of their comrades and inflicted serious damage on the enemy. Their acts were in keeping with the highest traditions of the military service and reflected great credit upon themselves and the U.S. Army. Sergeant Leonard B. Keller and Specialist Fourth Class Raymond R. Wright were both awarded the Medal of Honor for their gallant charge on May 2nd, 1967. The 9th Infantry had proven once again that the American fighting man, with the proper training, is the finest in the world.

FORCE AFLOAT

A t first it seemed to be just another uneventful day on May 9th, 1967, patrolling for the elusive Viet Cong in the Rung Sat, when a single shot rang out, hitting Alpha Company 4th Battalion platoon leader First Lieutenant Frank A. Rybicki Jr. from California. The platoon was under the jungle canopy when the medevac chopper extracted Lieutenant Rybicki by cable. His men watched his body go limp as it slowly lifted away into the hot humid air. The 2nd Brigade of the 9th Infantry had lost another patriot from the West Point class of '66, as many of his classmates mourned the lost of their good friend. For a few fleeting moments, his death brought him fame in Newsweek magazine, as Americans quietly read.

A chilling breeze swept in off the Hudson River that day and rustled in the dogwood trees on the plains of West Point. Down Washington Road marched a cadet band in full dress, playing "Lead, Kindly Light," to the cadence of muffled drums. The band and color guard slowly moved in procession to the cemetery, leading the family and the flag-draped coffin. It was a beautiful spring Memorial Day, and Frank Rybicki Jr. had come home.

Lieutenant Rybicki's marching orders came after his buddy and West Point classmate Lieutenant Terry Stull's own platoon was badly hurt in a six-hour battle with two Viet Cong companies at Ap Bac. "We're coming down to help you out," Rybicki had said over the phone. "About time we worked together again."

But they never got the chance.

Moving out on a five-day search-and-destroy mission, Alpha Company had knifed into a steaming mangrove swamp southeast of Saigon known as the Rung Sat "Forest of Assassins," a Viet Cong stronghold and sanctuary for much of the war. The first day out, the march had bogged down in calf-high water and ankle-deep mud. Stuck fast, Rybicki had thrust his rifle toward one of his men for help, stock first. The man had tugged, and the rifle had gone off. Frank Rybicki fell mortally wounded into the mud.

Longtime friend Terry Stull flew home with Rybicki for one last day at the Point. At Holy Trinity Chapel, Father Edwin O'Brien celebrated the mysteries of youth and death at Calvary, and then the Glee Club sang, "They are here in ghostly assemblage. The men of the Corps long dead. And our hearts are standing attention, while we wait for their passing tread."

Then the slow pilgrimage to graveside, Frank Sr. mashing a handkerchief in his aging hands, while mother Cecilia stared blankly into the grass. Sister Annette's dark eyes were filled with sorrow, with ten-year-old brother James trailing, his body tiny and frail. They sat at the edge of the grave. Thrushes sang softly, followed by the ritual words. Rifle volleys echoed in honor, and then the haunting notes of taps as tears were shed. The honor guard lifted the flag from the coffin and neatly folded it, passing it to Lieutenant Stull, who in turn handed it gently to Mrs. Rybicki. Then a light breeze blew across the Hudson plains, scented with lilac, reminding everybody it was another spring day. Frank Anthony Rybicki, Jr. had at last returned home from the war and to the Point, where his body would eternally lie.

Back in South Vietnam, after four months of constant operations, the squadron boats ran into their first real test on May 15th and 16th, 1967, in a multi-battalion operation west of Dong Tam in the Cam Son Secret Zone, near a stretch of the river know as Snoopy's Nose. The Cam Son area was considered one of the four major Viet Cong bases in Dinh Tuong Province, both by the intelligence staffs of the province and 7th Vietnam Army Division. The operation on May 15th relied entirely on intelligence provided by these Vietnamese units. The brigade plan was to search the southern area of Cam Son along the Rach Ba Rai and Rach Tra Tan streams and to capture or destroy the Viet Cong, their supplies, and their equipment. A forward command post was established approximately one mile north of Cai Be, and barge-mounted artillery was anchored on the southern bank of the My Tho River, three miles southeast of the mouth of the Rach Ba Rai. The two 2nd Brigade battalions were supported by twenty-two Tangos, two heavily armed Monitors, and two command communication boats of River Assault Flotilla One. Naval Commander Charles H. Black, the operational officer of River Assault Flotilla One, joined the brigade command group and coordinated the support of the assault craft.

The operation began at 0815 hours, when the 3rd Battalion 47th Infantry landed from assault craft at the mouth of the Rach Ba Rai and began to search northeast along the stream. At 0830 hours, the 4th Battalion 47th Infantry landed two rifle companies from assault craft on the north bank of the My Tho River, approximately halfway between the mouths of the Rach Ba Rai and the Rach Tra Tan. At 1200 hours, Alpha Company 4/47th was airlifted from Dong Tam, where it had been in readiness in reserve, and was landed a little under two miles north of the My Tho River on the west side of the Rach Tra Tan to act as a blocking force. After landing the troops, the boats of the task force proceeded to blocking stations along the waterways.

At 1400 hours, Bravo and Charlie Companies 4/47th met a Viet Cong force equipped with small arms, machineguns and rocket launchers. Alpha Company 3/47th maneuvered south and met the enemy within one mile of the My Tho River. Although Bravo and Charlie Companies 4/47th made little progress in moving against the enemy fire, artillery and close air support had maintained pressure on the Viet Cong. In an effort to move more troops to the northeast and rear of the Viet Cong, the 3/47th reconnaissance platoon was moved by Tangos into the Rach Tra Tan. But when the low tide and enemy antitank rockets prevented the assault craft from penetrating upriver, the platoon was withdrawn.

By 1630 hours, it became apparent that some enemy forces were escaping by moving to the northeast, away from both Bravo and Charlie Companies 4/47th, which were moving from the south, and from their Alpha Company, which was moving from the northwest. At this point, 2nd Brigade Commander, Colonel William B. Fulton, directed Lieutenant Colonel Lucien E. Bolduc Jr., 3rd Battalion Commander, to move one of his companies by helicopter to establish a blocking position northeast of the battle. This was accomplished by 1700 hours, but the company failed to find the enemy. By 2000 hours, all contact with the Viet Cong had been lost.

The enemy contact had lasted over eight hours with a large enemy company supported by VC rocket squads in concealed fortified positions. River Assault Squadron Nine craft, in support of the 9th Infantry, had five boats hit with fifteen rocket-propelled grenades, suffering fourteen sailors wounded, including River Assault Division 92 Commander, Lieutenant Albert Benge. The fight called attention to the limitations imposed upon maneuvering the assault craft during low tide and the importance of artillery and close air support against an enemy in well-prepared bunkers and firing positions.

The Army had employed search-and-destroy drives toward the Viet Cong positions, while the Navy deprived the enemy the use of the narrow waterways of the backwaters and streams. The continuous assault craft patrols instigated by the boats along strategic streams proved to be the great undoing of the Viet Cong, but the Navy had paid a toll for such success. To regain control of the streams and canals, the Viet Cong launched a series of rocket attacks against the assault craft led by trained rocket teams with orders to take out the river craft. Squadron Nine withstood each attack and in each instance had suppressed enemy fire. But both Army and Navy were concerned by the vulnerability of men aboard the assault craft to rocket fragments. The Mobile Riverine Force was to find vulnerability of troops aboard assault craft one of its continuing problems.

On May 18th and 19th , the 2nd Brigade moved a forward command post by motor convoy north of Cai Ba into western Dinh Tuong Province to control the operations of the 3/47th and 3/60th Infantry Battalions. To reduce the distance the supporting helicopters would have to fly, River Assault Flotilla One assault craft moved both battalions by water roughly twenty miles west of Dong Tam to landing sites on the north bank of the My Tho River. With the infantry battalions positioned within four miles of the center of the target area, one airmobile company was able to insert each battalion rapidly into the area. In the event of substantial fighting, the helicopters could turn around quickly in building up forces.

During this operation, the battalions of the 2nd Brigade met few of the Viet Cong, but the brigade command post was attacked by mortar, recoilless rifle, and machinegun fire during the early hours of May 19th. A Viet Cong ground attack was thwarted when the reconnaissance platoon of the 3rd Battalion, led by Second Lieutenant Howard C. Kirk III, intercepted enemy movement toward the western perimeter of the position. Assisted by artillery, gunships, and an armed illumination aircraft, the reconnaissance platoon broke up the attack and sent the enemy retreating in a different direction.

Throughout the month, a maximum effort was made to establish procedures for close cooperation between Army and Navy elements. Colonel Fulton, commanding the 2nd Brigade, and Captain Wade C. Wells, commander of River Assault Flotilla One, agreed that the helicopter was invaluable for command and control of riverine operations. Finding important terrain features was a very difficult task for the commanders on the ground, but a simpler task for the airborne commander. Foot troop and assault craft maneuver were facilitated by information furnished by the airborne command group. During darkness and in marginal flying weather, the command communication boats were valuable to brigade and battalion commanders in their forward positions. The combined use of command helicopters and command boats by brigade and battalion commanders permitted close supervision and control of the Mobile Riverine Force in combat.

By late May, all of the 2nd Brigade units of the 9th Infantry Division had met and withstood the enemy, thus instilling a feeling of confidence in the commanders and men, providing invaluable operational experience. Of even greater importance was the displacement of Viet Cong units from the Dong Tam area to the western portion of Dinh Tuong Province, from which the enemy could not readily launch a large ground attack on the unfinished base. By this time, the brigade had found enemy troops in three of the four Dinh Tuong base areas and whipped them on several occasions, which had contributed to a period of relative security for the engineers trying to complete the construction of Dong Tam Base, as well as for the province itself.

By the end of May, the mobile riverine base started to come together with the arrival of two self-propelled auxiliary personnel barrack ships, the USS Benewah, APB 35, and USS Colleton, APB 30. They were joined by a landing craft repair ship, USS Askarii, ARL 30. Since only two APB's were available, it was recommended that a non-propelled auxiliary personnel light barracks ship be made available for additional berthing in the combat role. This was approved and APL 26 was diverted and towed to Dong Tam by two seagoing tug boats. A large logistics-support LST landing ship was also assigned and helicopter landing barges joined the force, providing additional flight deck space for the brigade aviation section that included four OH-23 Raven light observation helicopters. These five ships provided repair and logistic support, including messing and berthing for the 2nd Brigade 9th Infantry Division, which began to embark troops on May 31st aboard the mobile afloat base. At first, USS Benewah served as the Mobile Riverine Force flagship as the Riverine Force was finally allowed to begin planning for its first independent operation, code-named Concordia I. Choosing a location that both accomplished a ground tactical mission and was suitable for river assault vessels required close operation between the Army and the Navy

The Army was amazed by shipboard life on the grey 7th Fleet ships, what with all the cleaning and constant painting that went on daily by the young sailors. While trying to find their way around their new Navy homes, Army personnel would constantly be confronted by blocked, freshly painted passageways, leading them to walk around in circles until a sailor pointed out the correct route. The fleet sailors had a standing order: if it doesn't move, paint it.

Then there was the ship's announcement speakers going off all times day and night, with whistles blowing: "sweepers man your brooms" or "reveille, reveille, drop your cocks and grab your socks." The Army was used to long chow lines, but no one had ever seen anything like this. Some said the chow line was so long that, after they finished breakfast, they would get back in line for lunch, waiting several hours before making it back to the food servers and chow. Trying to eat or take a shower while underway, rocking back and forth in rough waters, could be difficult and ruin one's appetite. Because of lack of berthing space in the early days of the mission, Charlie Company of the 3rd Battalion had to set up house and bed down in the forward well deck of a LST landing ship. Bet that was a lot of fun.

After several months in Vietnam, the army battalions that had trained and deployed together started to be reassigned, with men being transferred. This was intentional and in the minds of the military planners as a good thing to do, but had an adverse effect on the men, since many had trained together and had become buddies. Men that had been inducted into military service just a short time ago had to step up and look out for the new guys and rebuild teams.

Most of them had reported for duty thinking it was their turn to serve their country like their fathers and grandfathers had done before them. They came from the small towns and cities across America, and most knew very little about politics or Southeast Asia when they joined. After being drafted, they began to look into the benefits that would pay for their education after service, or the GI Bill, which would help them buy a home. They did not fight for politicians or lawmakers, nor Mom and apple pie. When it came down to it, they fought for each other and the right to return home someday and pick up their lives where they had left off. There was little time for debating on the philosophies of life. Just a few beers with your friends and stay alive, try to survive so you could return home to the world, which is what the States was called in that forgotten place. Letters from home were usually all you had to look forward to, and could often make the difference if you had a good week or bad. Hot showers and food with a bunk to sleep in was your reward after several days slogging through the worst conditions imaginable, in the blistering sun and insufferable heat, loaded down with gear and weapons. Friends were quickly made, and just as quickly they could be gone or worse, with only memories to remind you that they were ever there. They didn't all get to serve a full tour.

THEY PROVED
THEY COULD FIGHT

In early 1967, the 5th Nha Be Main Force Viet Cong Battalion was operating around Saigon. In a series of battles during the spring of '67, the battalion was severely mauled by the 199th Infantry Brigade and chose to retreat to a safe haven in Long An Province, to refit and rebuild. The province was a major rice-growing area and very large. Although the ARVN 46th Infantry Regiment maintained a watchful eye over the district, it never seriously tried to exercise control. That standoff allowed the remnants of the 5th Nha Be Battalion to construct a series of reinforced, well-camouflaged bunkers in a bend of the Rach Nui River, where they began to reorganize and set up house.

By early June, the Mobile Riverine Force had gathered the necessary assault craft to move, land, and support troops, with additional boats arriving every few days. Since the Alpha patrol boats that were scheduled to join the force were delayed, Tango troop carriers continued to perform minesweeping and security duties. The Mobile Riverine Force returned to the Vietnamese Navy the borrowed craft it had used since February. With the new assault craft, the flotilla had fifty-two Tangos, ten Monitors, four command-control boats and two refuelers. After conducting Operation "Great Bend" in the Rung Sat Special Zone from June 13th through 17th, the 9th Infantry Division had been successful in delivering greater security to the Long Tau shipping channel by busting up the headquarters controlling Viet Cong actions, but little contact was made with the enemy.

On June 18th, acting on agent reports, the Mobile Riverine Force moved from Dong Tam to the junction of the Soi Rap and Vam Co Rivers, with USS Colleton remaining its base of operations. One land-based battery of 155mm, self-propelled howitzers from the 2nd Battalion, 35th Artillery, was moved by utility landing craft to the west bank of the Soi Rap at the confluence, adjacent to the mobile riverine base. Ammunition supply for the battery was transported from Vung Tau by Army Mike-8 landing craft from the 1097th Boat unit.

Secured to the shore next to them were two, 3rd Battalion, 34th Artillery batteries, with six 105mm barge-mounted artillery platforms with two howitzers mounted on each of the barges. These units received ammunition support from an LST positioned with the mobile base. River Assault Squadron Nine, operating in conjunction with additional elements of River Division 111 and Game Wardens' PBRs, was to commence operations in the Can Giuoc District of eastern Long An Province. It was the first major riverine campaign, and it was to be centered on destroying the enemy sanctuary occupied by the 5th Nha Be Viet Cong Battalion. The brigade and flotilla commanders, Colonel Fulton and Captain Wells, hoped that Operation Concordia I forces would surround suspected enemy units and destroy them. The only problem was finding exactly where the Viet Cong were. At the time there was no hard intelligence, and although the general area was suspected, the specific location of the Viet Cong was not known.

Can Giuoc District contained a good network of navigable waterways, permitting the assault craft to enter an area that intelligence reports had indicated was used extensively by Viet Cong forces for rest and training. Civilian travel in the district was chiefly done by water, since most bridges - and the one ferry - were no longer serviceable. Previous military actions in this area had depended on movement by boats or aircraft. So advance, flank, and rear security on the rivers, canals, and streams of the region was to be provided by river assault craft. Game Warden patrol units would provide intelligence and recon the route that the force would take. The fact that the Mobile Riverine Force could move its afloat base permitted the establishment of a brigade base within a few miles of the location that had been reported as a remote Viet Cong base area enjoying considerable security.

The mobile base was moved into its anchorage on the evening before operations, with the risk of disclosure accepted because it was believed that the Viet Cong were not familiar with the capabilities of the ships and assault craft. To attack the area, Colonel Fulton and Captain Wells had agreed to anchor the riverine ships as close as possible to the area of operations. The time needed by assault craft to enter the area, and the turnaround time of both helicopters and water craft conducting resupply and medical evacuation, would be greatly reduced because of this move. The two commanders agreed that assault craft would go up only those streams wide enough to permit them to make 180-degree turns. Colonel Fulton and Captain Wells also agreed to use a portion of the assault craft as a blocking force once Army troops had landed and gone ashore. The boats were to enter the waterways as the tide was rising, permitting greater speed and a long period of high tide level immediately following their entry.

The initial plan was to transport five rifle companies of the 3rd and 4th Battalions, 47th Infantry, into the operations area by assault craft and the sixth company, Charlie Company 3/47th, would be moved by water to an air pickup zone, to stand in reserve. But after intelligence indicated there were a greater number of Viet Cong companies, it was decided that Charlie Company would immediately be flown in by copters in an air assault close to the suspected enemy location and sweep north attacking. The ARVN 2nd Battalion 46th Infantry, which was under American operational control, was moved in the early morning hours of darkness to establish a blocking force just west of Ap Bac Hamlet.

At 0500 hours, June 19, 1967, the 3rd and 4th Battalions began transferring from the safety of their barracks ships to the Tango troop carriers alongside. Each rifle company boarded a section of three Tangos from River Squadron 9, which consisted of twenty-six Tangos, five Monitors, two command communication boats and a refueler, as they pushed off, steaming nosily up the Soi Rap River. The heavily armed Monitors followed the Tangos, which were dragging cables and chains along the bottom of the river to cut the electrical wire to any mines. The Navy crewmen stood alert while their Army passengers tried to rest in the gathering light. The Mobile Riverine Force proceeded cautiously up river in a column, turning into the Vang River as the Monitor began firing machineguns and their heavier cannons on the landing sites, seeking to discourage any local defenses and recon the foliage along the river's banks. The Tangos then dropped their bow ramps at 0700 hours, beaching within twenty yards of each other, disembarking five rifle companies north of Ap Bac.

Alpha, Bravo, and Charlie Companies 4/47th Infantry were landed on the banks of Van Creek, two and one-half miles southwest of Can Giouc. At the same time, Alpha and Bravo Companies 3/47th were landed one mile south of Can Giouc on a creek off the Rach Cac River. With the Vietnamese ARVN battalion three and one-half miles southwest of the 4/47th units, the three forces in effect, formed a triangle around the suspected enemy location. The soldiers began trudging through mud flats and swampy areas that progressed into open rice paddies, as they swept south. Alpha and Bravo Companies 3/47th Infantry were covering the right flank with the companies widely scattered in order to cover a large area. The assault craft then backed off, catching sniper fire and returning fire, as they took up blocking positions, surrounding and boxing in the enemy.

Colonel Fulton's plan was to sweep the American companies south toward the ARVN battalion, hoping to crush any enemy forces in between. Fulton and his battalion commanders would be flying overhead in observation copters, from which they could easily move and direct units. For the next few hours, the companies patrolled through rice paddies and occasional dense thickets of banana trees and nipa palm without incident, but while approaching a small village, suspicions were raised. The province was like most in the Mekong Delta: crisscrossed by dozens of small canals and streams. Some could be jumped across. Others required units to swim across, with their equipment floating on air mattresses. Meanwhile, the Viet Cong patiently waited in their hidden fighting positions just ahead, maintaining discipline, watching the Americans approach.

At 0900 hours, Colonel Fulton received intelligence, obtained from a captured Viet Cong village chief, indicating that a Viet

Cong battalion-size force was deployed near the base of the triangle, due east of the ARVN position. The mobile intelligence team at Can Giuoc District headquarters believed that three Viet Cong companies were approximately midway between the 4/47th and ARVN positions. Fulton then issued orders to his battalion commanders, and the U.S. adviser to the ARVN, informing all of the new reported enemy's location and suspected strength. The brigade adjusted and continued to sweep south, humping across dry paddies with trees along the streams, using assault craft to provide communications.

Colonel Fulton radioed Lieutenant Colonel Guy I. Tutwiler, commanding officer of the 4th Battalion, a veteran combat infantryman who had received the Combat Infantry Badge for three wars. Fulton told him to prepare to assume control of Charlie Company 3/47th Infantry and to deploy the company by helicopter south of the reported enemy location. By 1105 hours, Colonel Tutwiler had moved the company in an air assault south, landing them near Route 230 with the mission of patrolling north to search out and destroy the enemy.

Tutwiler then radioed Captain Herb Lind, commanding officer of Charlie Company 4/47th, ordering him to move his company to the river and meet up with the Tangos to re-embark and be transported to the junction of Rach Nui and Ben Via creek, which they did. After being transported south, they disembarked on the bank of the Rach Nui and began sweeping west through an open rice paddy approaching a small stream.

Charlie Company 3/47th, after making the copter assault, became suspicious, seeing the road had been piano-keyed. The VC did this by trenching thirty or forty yards halfway across the road, and then farther down, trenching thirty or forty yards on the other side. This technique made it difficult for vehicle traffic to use the road but did not stop foot or bicycle traffic.

After crossing the road, they patrolled north over rough terrain, making a reconnaissance to locate the enemy. All went well at first, with the plan being executed in a relatively short period of time, but the ARVN had crossed Route 230, which was to be their right boundary, and was moving toward the company. Colonel

Fulton immediately landed his command helicopter and ordered the Vietnamese battalion back across their boundary. Fulton had decided that maneuvering the battalion to the east would be dangerous by the presence of U.S. companies between the ARVN battalion and the VC.

To the north, troops of Alpha Company 4/47th Infantry began bunching up, walking along the berms of the rice paddies, sweeping three platoons abreast with their left anchored against the narrow Rach Nui. Disregarding Fulton's instructions, the new inexperienced company commander allowed his men to mass too closely together, with little security to their front or flanks. Sailing in the Rach Nui, River Squadron Commander, Lieutenant Commander Charles Horowitz, moved slowly back and forth, passing the slow dismounted advance several times. Still, the Viet Cong waited patiently in their bunkers, watching the advance, holding their fire.

Colonel Tutwiler radioed the commanding officer of Charlie Company 3/47th, Captain Ronald Menner, ordering him to sweep northeast through a line of nipa palm that he was sure was the enemy hideout. By 1150 hours, Charlie Company had swept the suspected tree line without finding the Viet Cong, stopping just short of a stream that ran east to west. To the north, Charlie Company 4/47th was sweeping west when all of a sudden heavy automatic weapons, mortar and recoilless rifle fire shot against them from across the stream, where muzzle flashes and tracers lit up the tree line, exposing enemy positions.

Eight hundred yards north, walking toward a small group of huts in a bend in the river, Alpha Company 4/47th ran into a murderous wall of fire from its front and right flank. The enemy bunkers were so well hidden, Alpha Company troops walked to within forty feet of them before triggering fire. The enemy complex stretched for hundreds of yards along a wood line with numerous bunkers hidden in clumps of trees.

And then, the whole world seemed to go crazy. A battalion of hard-core Viet Cong opened up with pinpoint accurate machinegun, rocket, recoilless rifle, and mortar fire from close range. Troops were diving to the earth for their lives, crawling to small mounds of dirt berms in the middle of the kill zone, completely exposed. Alpha Company was locked in brutal, bitter combat, being cut down like weeds. No one had ever seen anything like it; the fighting was described by some as "unreal."

Charlie Company 4/47th second platoon point man, Specialist Bill Reynolds, was out front in lead and hit the ground, hearing the deafening sound of weapons fire. Then realizing he was out in the open, he sprang up, dashing back fifty yards through enemy fire to the last rice paddy, where everyone was grabbing cover behind a small berm. His second platoon leader, Lieutenant Jack Benedick, was following Reynolds with the platoon and was near the stream. The mortar squad was quickly loading its equipment into two small plastic boats, when the Viet Cong sprung up firing, catching them in the open. Both boats were immediately sunk, killing six soldiers, leaving several others wounded but able to reach the shoreline. Lieutenant Sheldon Schulman, the mortar squad leader, was next to the stream and quickly became distraught as he stood in the open watching his men being cut to pieces. Failing to take cover, a moment later his shirt had turned red and he fell to the ground dead.

Second platoon quickly formed a line five feet apart along the berm, which was at the water's edge, with the stream about five feet below. Lieutenant Jack Benedick, Jimmie Salazar and several others had been hit but were still returning fire. The intense firefight stretched for quite a ways, with contact being made at several points on the line, employing hundreds of men in the battle. The Viet Cong had moved additional fighters into the complex the night before and were ready.

Communist recoilless rounds, mortars and screaming rockets were blazing and hitting all around them. They could see the Viet Cong - they were close. But there was little they could do but hunker down and return fire, emptying clip after clip, as M16 rifles jammed and misfired. Alpha Company had so many men hit in the first few minutes that their commander had lost sense of where his platoons were and was screaming over the radio that he needed help. But no one dared to call in artillery, not knowing the disposition of the men trapped in the rice paddy.

Overhead, the brigade and battalion commanders watched from command helicopters while artillery observers and Air Force forward air controllers surveyed the battlefield, waiting to bring in supporting fire. Lieutenant Colonel Tutwiler ordered his Bravo Company, which had been moving on the right flank, to move forward quickly, to add its firepower. He held his besieged Charlie Company on the south side of a stream, which was locked in heavy combat. Captain Ron Menner of Charlie Company 3/47th could plainly see the company pinned down under heavy VC fire and suggested to Tutwiler that he move his men across the stream in an effort to relieve pressure, which Tutwiler agreed to by replying "Roger out." Captain Menner then directed his first platoon to move north across the stream while he and his command group followed.

At 1200 hours, the first artillery rounds were fired at the request of air and ground forward observers, and the rounds soon whistled overhead, slamming into the enemy complex, sending debris flying over the battlefield. Bravo Company 4/47th commander, Captain Engeldinger, called his platoon leaders, Lieutenants Heller, Jenkins, and Bateman, to his location and ordered the company forward, with Phil Bateman and his third platoon leading the way. With nerves on fire, they quickly moved out through dangerous terrain of huge open areas, rushing to aid their comrades while listening to battalion radio traffic.

Back on the small stream, a VC sniper in a tree line to the left of Charlie Company 4/47th was picking people off when he fired and hit RTO Bob French in the lower back, below his radio. French let out a blood-curdling scream and was writhing in serious pain as the yell "medic!" sang out. Army medic Bill Geier bravely came hustling up to the berm with no cover and began performing first aid. Geier bandaged Bob French and had moved on to Ronnie Bryan, bandaging his wound. The medic then gave him a shot of morphine. Suddenly, Geier criedout, mortally wounded. Bill Reynolds made his way to Geier, bandaging his wound, trying to keep him talking. And for a short time, Geier even coached Reynolds with the bandaging. But eventually, Geier's breathing slowed, and he slipped away while his friend watched helplessly, knowing there was little he could do.

After troops called for another medic, Elijah "Doc" Taylor from third platoon made his way up, just as Bill Geier passed away. Eventually all of third platoon was moving forward and joining second platoon, when Riflemen Wes Ostrem was hit by rocket fragments.

Lieutenant Jack Benedick looked over and hollered, "Reynolds, get some grenades out there." Reynolds had been firing his over and under M16 and switched to the under M-79 grenade launcher, firing a few rounds across into the VC bunkers. While Reynolds was reloading, an enemy bullet shot right through his M-79 barrel, narrowly missing him. Lieutenant Benedick yelled, "Reynolds, are you okay?" Reynolds checked himself, looking for wounds. Seeing he was all right, Reynolds and the lieutenant both started laughing from adrenaline rush and how Bill had patted himself down.

Fifty yards back with command, Army Chaplain Windmiller had watched a wounded man struggling in the middle of the rice paddy and just couldn't stand to watch any longer. Windmiller looked to a machinegunner yelling "cover," and took off running like a crazy man across the open rice paddy, diving behind dikes, crawling through enemy fire to get to the man. The machinegunner provided cover the best he could, as Chaplain Windmiller laid down beside the man shielding him with his body while bandaging his wounds and comforting him.

Another who displayed courage was Gary "Doc" Maibach, who was also seen running in the open like a man possessed, going from soldier to soldier, patching up Charlie Company as he performed life-saving first aid, treating the wounded.

Colonel Tutwiler got a call from the commanding officer of Alpha Company 4/47th, who was beside himself, shouting he had walked into an L-shaped ambush and had no idea how many of his men were still alive, other than the handful right around him, and that he had no contact with the rest of his company. Soldiers were scattered all over hell and back, returning fire, hopelessly outnumbered, with wounded and dead lying everywhere. The Viet Cong were well-hidden, with crack-shot snipers in the trees, laying down a murderous volume of weapons fire into the crippled company struggling to survive.

First platoon leader Lieutenant Phillip O. ZumMallen was near the front of Alpha Company, under heavy fire, trying to regroup his platoon, when he was killed. Lieutenant Fred Gordon Bertolino of second platoon, West Point Class of '66, was shot and bled to death slowly on the battlefield, since nobody was able to get to him and his men. Bertolino radioed at first saying, "I have wounded men I must get out of here, including me." As the day wore on, he had lost so much blood that he began babbling and mumbled over the air, while his friends helplessly listened in. In the initial onslaught, the company had lost all of its leaders, machinegunners, radio operators and medics that were down and out of action.

Medic Michael A. Snider saw several of his comrades fall and dashed across the bullet-swept battlefield to them and began administering first aid. He then helped carry the wounded back to a position of relative safety.

Specialist Four Noel T. West, in complete disregard for his own safety, ran forward to treat the wounded as bullets pounded the ground and filled the air around him. He went from casualty to casualty, rendering aid that in several cases proved to be of a life-saving nature. Hostile machinegun fire sprayed the rice paddy, and West, while aiding yet another soldier, was hit and mortally wounded. It was said that West gave his life that day in order that others might live, an inspiration to the men around him.

Colonel Tutwiler requested Tangos to move south on the Rock Nui blocking while utilizing their weapons to provide fire supremacy for his Alpha and Charlie Companies, who were under a murderous crossfire. Choppers and jets were screaming overhead, slamming the entrenched enemy with 500-pound bombs and rockets, when a couple went astray, wounding several soldiers with friendly fire.

By now, all knew that Alpha Company was in serious trouble, as the rest of the brigade advanced on the enemy, attacking, trying to relieve pressure. But the movement of several hundred riflemen was slow due to the type of terrain. It also took a considerable amount of time to get the Tangos in their positions, while they were in a heated exchange of heavy weapons fire with the enemy, with both sides trying desperately to put an end to the other's existence. With limited movement on the left flank, assault craft moved up dangerously close to enemy emplacements in the tree lines flanking the paddies, and began pouring accurate 20mm, 40mm, and machinegun fire together with 81mm mortar rounds into the enemy, pounding troublesome bunkers. Naval gunfire and movements of naval units was coordinated by both Army and Navy officers embarked in River Division 92's command control boat.

The first immediate support came from Navy Lieutenant Commander C.L. Horowitz, who stood completely exposed on top of his command boat, directing fire of his gunboats. Yet even 40mm automatic cannons and 81mm mortars had little affect unless they scored multiple hits. Violating standing Navy orders against entering canals, Horowitz ordered his command boat captain to push forward into a narrow inlet and ran up on the bank. While Colonel Tutwiler's command copter hovered overhead directing fire, the bow 40mm gun pumped several clips into an enemy bunker, blowing the machinegun one way and the gunner another. Then the boat backed out into the main stream, where Navy Lieutenant "Augie" C. Marano and his assault boats continued to hose down the shoreline.

Lieutenant Jack Benedick requested gunboat support and received a call from Navy Lieutenant Commander Francis E. "Dusty" Rhoads, asking him where he wanted it. After Benedick described his location, Dusty also disregarded orders, guiding his Monitor into a small stream and working his way forward until they arrived, running aground. The Monitor delivered devastating 40mm fire, knocking out several bunkers, while Dusty stood out on deck, directing fire.

The sky was clouded with smoke when Navy Chaplain Raymond "Padre" "Doc" Johnson looked out over the battlefield at the gruesome sight of his wounded comrades pinned down in the rice paddy. Because of his previous and extensive emergency training, Padre served every riverine operation in a key medical capacity for the Mobile Riverine Force during his tour of duty, as well as serving as Navy chaplain. Positioned with the medical aid boat, which was run aground with several other assault craft on the Rach Nui, Padre glanced out to see a wounded radioman trying to make his way toward the medical boat. The Padre saw the helpless look on the man's face when he was hit for a second time. For Padre Johnson, it was simply a matter of reflex, as he left the boat and made his way to the soldier, helping him back to the relative safety of the boat. While administering medical assistance, the radioman informed the Padre that all of his platoon leaders and medics were either dead or seriously wounded. The battle was unmerciful in that way. No one dared to venture out or even move with the tremendous amount of fire being exchanged. But wounded were in desperate need, with many bleeding to death. The radioman went on to identify three major areas where serious casualties were massed. Padre Johnson, realizing something had to be done, said a silent prayer and then asked for volunteers. Boatswain's Mate Third C.O. "Swede" Johnson and Engineman Second M.W. "Red" Dolezal from Tango 92-7 both stepped forward, and off the three went, dashing through enemy fire.

Under heavy cover fire from their shipmates on the boat, the three zigzagged their way toward the mass of wounded and dead on the outskirts of the battle, with continuous enemy fire directed their way. During the first attempt, the team managed to crawl through machinegun fire to a protective dike in the middle of the rice paddy. At that point, Padre Johnson realized that he had been hit in the legs. Compressing the bleeding to his thigh, he decided to continue on, more concerned for the safety of others than his own. While trying to map out a strategy, he felt a thud like the wallop of a baseball bat against his chest. At first, he failed to see the entrance of the missile through the zipper lining of his flak vest. But after closer examination, he found the shrapnel had been stopped by his New Testament, somewhere in the Book of James, which for the first time he had stuffed into his pocket prior to battle. Padre Johnson quickly recovered and led his stretcher-bearers toward a group of wounded huddled behind a mound of dirt.

The volunteers ran sixty yards through open terrain, while dirt kicked up in front of the Padre, and along his side, as the enemy somehow failed to connect. After Padre Johnson tended to the wounded, he decided to carry the two most serious back, drafting a soldier to carry one end of the litter, while he carried the other. Boatswain's Mate Johnson and Engineman Dolezal carried the other litter as the four made a hundred-and-fifty-yard dash-and-carry that seemed to last an eternity. After miraculously making it back, Padre Johnson looked down to see the wounded men's eyes, full of gratitude, believing they had a chance to survive, thanks to the Padre.

Men were shaking with fear, as Padre Johnson alone prepared to return to the kill zone, while several boats released a wall of heavy gunfire support that aided immensely in reducing the Viet Cong's accuracy. Padre scrambled from man to man with his medical bag over his shoulder, ducking bullets and shrapnel, while treating the wounded where they lay, saving many lives. On his way back to the boats carrying a wounded soldier, Padre Johnson noticed another wounded man trying to move and yelled out for him to play dead until he returned, which he did. When Padre Johnson retuned from his fourth trip, he collapsed from exhaustion and threw up. Many deserved much for their bravery that day, but none was more deserving than the Padre.

It didn't take long to fill up the boat with wounded soldiers and sailors, as they started spreading them out over the ground creating a dismal sight, waiting for the evacuation copters to come. Doc Johnson and his volunteers set up a make shift clinic and worked frantically, to save as many lives as possible. Additional rescue parties formed and continued to engage in the daring attempt to clear the battlefield of the seriously wounded, thanks to Padre Johnson's direction and courage under fire, which was said to have inspired many that longest day. Several men noticed Padre's wounds, but Doc Johnson refused to be evacuated, pointing out the short supply of medical assistants, while he continued providing aid and words of encouragement to the many wounded men in agony surrounding him. Although many died in his hands while he cared for them, Padre Johnson helped many more to live.

Commanding Officer Ray Riesco of River Division 111, who was taking continuous bunker fire to his own boat, said that each time he watched Padre Johnson move back to the field, he felt for sure that he would not make it. Yet each time, he did and stayed only long enough to help care for the wounded before returning to the rice paddy again. It seemed impossible to Riesco that Padre Johnson survived the ordeal. "He must have had two angels protecting and guiding him," said Riesco.

Major H. Glenn Penny, executive officer and acting commander of the 3rd Battalion, maneuvered his Alpha and Bravo Companies southeast to link up with his Charlie Company, which had used a sampan to cross the stream. Although there was a bend in the stream with heavy vegetation, the troops were lucky and did not receive any enemy fire while crossing. Captain Menner had directed his second and third platoons, under the control of Lieutenant Kitchens, to move west and cross the stream where the map showed a bridge. His command group and first platoon got across the stream, and had not moved more than twenty-five yards, when they came under VC heavy fire. Linking up, Lieutenant Kitchens and third platoon were also slugging it out.

By 1400 hours, they had fought their way forward, flanking the enemy tree line, cutting off the enemy's escape. They advanced slowly by using fire and maneuvering tactics as the thunderous sound of rounds bellowing overhead, kept heads low, while the artillery units back on the river opened up in a furious display of gun support. Then the artillery held its fire while Air Force jets flew in low, releasing Napalm with its flaming clouds reaching high into the sky. Smoke drifted over the battlefield, with flames burning through the complex of the 5th Nha Be VC Battalion, which were beginning to feel the heat.

At 1430 hours, Commander River Assault Division 92, Lieutenant Marano, reported that his Monitor had been hit by a B40 rocket, damaging the 40mm gun, and that he and three crewmembers were wounded. The command control boat immediately rushed to the aid of the badly damaged boat, which had been supporting soldiers ashore in heavy combat with serious wounded. Tango-92-7 and Tango-112-8 also heard the call for assistance and steamed to the site as they established fire superiority and beached, with sailors scrambling off the boats under heavy fire into the field, to aid and evacuate the wounded.

The commanding officer of Alpha Company 4/47th radioed to indicate that his casualties were at seventy-five percent and, because of the heavy volume of fire from a line of bunkers in front of him, he and his men could not move. Steadily, the brigade kept pressing as the enemy stubbornly stood its ground.

Troops of Bravo Company's third platoon advanced, listening to the sounds of the battle and watching helicopters buzzing in circles over the battlefield. They stopped briefly to look for someway to get to Alpha Company without getting chopped to pieces themselves. Thinking there might be a way around the flank, Lieutenant Bateman had his third platoon push forward through nipa palm, only to stumble upon a deep fast-moving canal. Realizing they would have to swim across, the soldiers began setting up. Just then, they were besieged by rounds coming their way. The fire proved to be scattered and inaccurate, so they began crossing while their two other platoons, with Lieutenant Heller's first platoon in the lead, swung wide to the left and were able to go around the canal. After crossing, Bateman and his platoon fell in behind, and a little to the right of first platoon. It was late afternoon when the three platoons entered the battle area and were immediately pinned down by heavy fire. Tutwiler kept yelling over the radio, telling them to "Move, move!" His voice, frantic, shouting, "We have to take pressure off of Alpha Company," as he watched his men being butchered.

Trying to push forward, several of Heller's men were shot in rapid succession. A short artillery round hit to the rear of Heller's platoon, severely wounding his platoon sergeant and several others. Another short round hit to the right, severely wounding Bateman's platoon sergeant, Jack Kester, and one other of his men. Sergeant Kester radioed Bateman half-delirious asking, "What happened, sir?" over and over. Medics began working on the wounded and were lucky enough to bring in a dust-off copter to rush the men off.

Colonel Fulton directed Major Penny to seal off the south where the fighting had developed. At 1600 hours, Major Penny regained operational control of his Charlie Company and had his Bravo Company advance on its left, attacking east of the line, while his Alpha Company moved into a blocking position six hundred yards on its left flank. After linking up, the companies launched a coordinated attack. Captain Ben Myatt, who led Bravo Company 3/47th, moved his men west of Alpha Company 4/47th, and came under immediate heavy fire. Captain Myatt radioed Menner that he was under devastating enemy fire and could not move. Captain Menner told his friend to hold up, that he would see what he could do.

Captain Menner had advanced his company so close that anytime someone peeked over the dike, it brought enemy fire down on them. There wasn't enough cover for everyone, so they all huddled closely together behind the dike, unable to move, while VC snipers slowly picked them off. Knowing he could not advance until they took out the bunkers, Captain Menner had his heavy weapons platoon move its 90mm recoilless rifle forward. This proved to be quite effective. Each time the recoilless rifle was fired into the enemy bunkers, logs blew sky high. Several VC bunkers were silenced before the platoon ran out of 90mm ammo. Captain Menner immediately radioed requesting more, but it would be after nightfall before it would arrive.

Observation copters and gunships had filled the sky all day, while evacuation helicopters tried to land to bring out the wounded. A chopper landed right next to Charlie Company 4/47th with its front exposed and the pilot sitting quite high. The infantrymen quickly placed five of their wounded on board. But as the copter began to lift off, a VC bullet blew through the glass windshield, hitting the pilot in his left shoulder. The chopper began to spin out of control, slamming to the ground with the rotor lurching, throwing men out the door. Luckily, Chaplain Windmiller ducked just in time, escaping a gruesome decapitation. One of the door gunners jumped out and immediately fell from a shot. The wounded were gathered and placed on the ground, shielded by their comrades, while rounds zipped by.

Shortly after, a second copter landed to the rear of the downed bird, with men piling as many of the wounded aboard as fast as they could. The copter quickly took off, with men yelling "Go! Go! Go!" It was well off the ground, 150 feet or better in the air and turning, when the VC found their mark with a .50 caliber machinegun, knocking the copter out of the sky. It plummeted back to earth, sputtering and lurching, a soldier falling out as it crashed on its side. Many looked down or covered their eyes, unable to watch the chopper crash with their friends aboard. Soldiers scrambled to the chopper and pulled the pilots out, who were badly beaten up but survived. Some of the wounded had been thrown out and killed. One of the copter crewmen had his legs pinned by the damaged craft, but rescuers were able to lift it so he could be pulled free. Another soldier died while pinned under the copter.

The commanding officer then requested that the helicopters stop landings, realizing that they would not survive until the bunkers had been silenced. Still, they got another call from a dust-off copter pilot saying he was coming in. They radioed him that it was just too hot, but the pilot said he was coming in anyway. He didn't make it. By the end of the afternoon, four copters had been shot down, and the rest were being waved off.

Casualties were taken directly to the aid stations aboard the barracks ships USS Benewah and USS Colleton, as well as to the medical facility at Nha Be. Many wounded had to wait hours lying on the battlefield in agony before it was safe to bring them out. Medical teams hearing of the battle stood ready and the short trip between the battlefield and the barracks ships saved many lives.

The infantry was amazed by these chopper pilots, who knew they were going to get shot up but, knowing the wounded needed them, came in anyway. It was a welcome sound when gunships flew overhead firing rockets, or when Air Force air strikes made strafing runs, dropping Napalm and high explosives. At times, the bombs and arty rounds hit so close, the blasts lifted the soldiers off their bellies, raining shrapnel down on the men as they tried to burrow in for safety. Meanwhile, Chaplain Windmiller was seen moving among the wounded, ministering, even though he had been wounded himself.

Bravery was the rule and not the exception that longest day, as many rose to perform feats that they themselves would have thought they were not capable of. But they did them anyway. The saying that there is no greater love than that of a man willing to risk his life for another was certainly true that day. Men commonly risked their lives to help a wounded friend, while soldiers lay wounded and dying next to each other, and snipers picked them off. Although most of the young riflemen had been drafted, one would never have known it. They took on one of the greatest guerrilla armies in the world, the Viet Cong, and took as much as they gave, but never wavered from their duty and took the fight to the enemy, who realized that they were in a serious battle with a determined adversary.

Lieutenant Colonel Carroll S. "Skeeter" Meek, commander of the 3rd Battalion, 34th Field Artillery, had been making low helicopter passes over the enemy bunker complex in a three-seated, piston engine, OH-23 bubble helicopter in order to bring precise artillery fire support to bear. The enemy bunkers were built from huge palm tree trunks, which were stacked and placed overhead with three feet of dirt on top for cover, a difficult fortification to destroy. Even the 155mm rounds seemed to have little effect, except to keep the enemy's heads down.

Major H. Glenn Penny and Lieutenant George A. Crocker, who coordinated tactical air support, had also been overhead in the command control Huey, flying low and taking fire. Several times they were brought down in a hail of gunfire in the area of operations, once hard enough to break the tail boom, and twice when all the cockpit warning dials lit up, including the "master caution." Fortunately they were able to hightail it back to the old French Fort, which had turned into a bedlam of activity. At least a half dozen copters circled over the battlefield, or more if gunships were orbiting. The downed army choppers were being slung out by CH-47 Chinooks and moved to the rear.

One of the times we were going down, we were bathed in a mist of JP-4 fuel. I recall looking at the fire support officer, who was Alpha Company's Arty forward observer, and having both of us think "crispy critters." Thank God in those days the pilots were proficient in auto-rotations or we might have burned.

George A. Crocker

Back at the old French Fort where the 34th Artillery platforms were anchored along with "Tiller 9er," which was the 2nd Battalion, 35th Artillery's 155mm guns on the ground next to them, an interesting meeting was taking place. It involved a map huddle by Military Assistance Commander of Vietnam, General William Westmoreland, accompanied by Lieutenant General Frederick C. Weyand, Commander Second Field Force, and Senior Advisor to Forth Tactical zone, Brigadier General William R. Desobry, along with 2nd Brigade Commander Colonel Fulton, and anyone else who could peek over their shoulders, which was difficult, being they were all tall men.

On a map that had been laid out on 105 ammo boxes, no one could seem to estimate the exact disposition of the friendly and enemy forces. It was all very confusing until Lieutenant Colonel Meek broke into the conversation with a complete and accurate layout of all forces, including the Americans killed in action.

General Westmoreland, a artillery officer during World War II and as the chief of staff of the 9th Infantry Division by war's end, displayed his 9th Infantry patch on his fatigues on the off shoulder, which was proper, having served in combat with the unit. Westmoreland was a man of great integrity who cared strongly about his men and spent a lot of time talking to them, of all ranks, listening to what they had to say. He counseled the generals proposing to them that it might be time to saddle up the 25th Infantry, which they eventually decided against.

By late in the day, most of the VC's big guns had been silenced. Lieutenant Colonel Tutwiler directed Captain Lind to leave one platoon of riflemen on the south bank as security for the downed helicopters and move the remainder of his company to the north side of the stream and attack the bunkers in an effort to relieve enemy pressure. Knowing they could not cross the stream without taking heavy losses, Captain Lind's men joined back up with the Tangos who were happy to give them a lift.

At first the riflemen thought, thank God, we're leaving. But then one of their leaders informed them that they were going across the stream to assault the VC bunkers. Although the Viet Cong had been severely hurt, they still had a lot of fight left. The Tangos landed with ramps dropping and guns blazing, as the riflemen ran, shooting at any and everything in their way. The VC scattered like scared rabbits, running for cover. A number of the riflemen charged along the bunkers, seizing the moment, and overran an enemy position. Then they took out a couple more bunkers, but the Viet Cong were shelling them with mortars and eventually they were ordered to drop back.

Rifleman Bill Reynolds ran along a rice paddy dike and spotted a VC standing out in the open on high ground, so he stopped and kneeled on the dike, taking aim. He was about a hundred yards away firing, but his M16 wasn't accurate, or maybe he wasn't. The rifle was his third weapon of the day. The first one was ruined when a VC bullet blasted through its barrel. So there he was, out in the open, firing one shot at a time and then pulling the spent shell out with his fingernails so he could put another round in to fire. Then the M16 jammed on him again. Meanwhile, the VC just stood there, and Bill was pretty sure he was a forward observer for a mortar team, because rounds were dropping all around.

After Reynolds' forth or fifth attempt at shooting the VC, a mortar exploded nearby, shrapnel tearing into Bill's right hand. He continued to reload, blocking out the pain. The shrapnel had ripped apart his trigger finger. So Bill trudged back down the rice paddy dike, passing Specialist Tom Hogle and several other guys, and plopped down next to another soldier and proceeded to cuss up a blue streak about getting hit. All day long, he had witnessed choppers shot down and guys shot up all over the place, and now he himself had taken shrapnel and was pissed off about the whole thing. About then, the soldier next to him turned. Bill saw the cross on his helmet and thought, "holy shit." It was Chaplain Windmiller, who smiled compassionately and said, "Go down to the boat, son." Bill did.

After boarding a Tango, Bill threw his M16 across the deck, bouncing it off the wall. A medic attended to his wound, and then another boat took him and several of the wounded down river, where they dropped them off, without weapons, and told them to wait for a chopper. After the boat pulled away, the area grew deadly silent, except for the distant sound of battle. After waiting an eternity (probably thirty minutes or less) Reynolds boared a chopper flying in. They were all flown off to the Long Binh hospital ending Reynolds' longest day.

Insuring that all the wounded were removed from the contact area, Lieutenant Commander C.L. Horowitz continued to coordinate Navy units in the battle area, to insure proper utilization of the assault crafts' weapons. At 1800 hours, while scouting the narrow streams for night ambush positions, Horowitz was hit by an AK47 round. He continued to complete his coordination efforts and then turned the squadron over to Lieutenant Marano before allowing himself to be medevaced from the area. Marano took charge, directing the assault squadron boats in fire support.

During the battle, certain Tangos re-supplied the troops and naval units with food, water, and ammunition. In addition, other troop carriers served as medical aid and casualty moving stations. On several occasions a number of craft were hit by recoilless rifle and B40 rocket fire. Tango 112-4 was struck below the waterline by a rocket, forcing the craft to beach. After emergency patching had been completed, the craft returned to the riverine base under its own power. In another instance, Boatswain's Mate Third J.C. Naples and Seaman S.G. Yates, rescued a wounded infantryman after he had jumped into the creek to avoid capture.

With the light fading, the first platoon of Bravo Company 4/47th finally linked up with what was left of Alpha Company as they joined lines. The remainder of Bravo Company was about four hundred yards to the north, under fire. Charlie Company 3/47th continued to push north, with their Alpha and Bravo Companies to the left. But the coming of darkness prompted a halt in maneuvers, placing them some six hundred yards west of Charlie Company 4/47th, where the units set Claymores and took up defensive positions as the tense night vigil began. Artillery and air strikes continued to pound the enemy fortifications as the sky flickered in flashes and the reflections of flares that slowly drifted to earth, lighting the eerie night sky. Viet Cong and U.S. troops had been locked in heavy combat throughout the day and now were heading into the night, with 2nd Brigade slowly tightening the noose.

After dark, the remainding men of Bravo Company 4/47th began moving slowly and quietly across the rice paddies toward Alpha Company. There was little moon, but as they got closer they could see bodies lying in the paddies all around them. Medics began searching and checking, but there was none found alive at first. When they reached Alpha Company's commander, he was hunkered down at the end of a shallow ditch, with only six men around him. Artillery continued to pound the VC bunkers, so close that shrapnel was buzzing by, hitting them, burning holes in the cover of their flak jackets. Bravo Company took cover, strung out along the shallow ditch to escape the artillery, scooping mud out of the bottom of the ditch, piling it along the top to give more cover from the exploding rounds. Yet, soon the tide came in, and the ditch started to fill with water. The troops, forced higher up the sides of the ditch, tried to pile mud ever higher for protection.

Captain Engeldinger asked for volunteers to crawl out into the paddies to find wounded that could be brought back and saved. Armed only with grenades, the volunteers made their way out, and then soon crawled back, one or two at a time, with wounded. The ditch was now full of water, so they inflated air mattresses and placed the wounded on them, floating the groaning survivors from man to man down the length of the company to the very end of the ditch, where Lieutenant Heller and his platoon waited until they got five or six wounded before calling for a medevac chopper. As the choppers came in the dark, Heller would light a flare at his position. The artillery would fire six rounds nearby, and then the copter would land so Heller and his men could load the wounded onboard, before the choppers rushed off into the night. This procedure went on for nearly two hours before a short round hit close to the landing site, badly wounding Heller, who was lifted out.

The rest of the night the remaining men spent sleepless, hunkered down in the ditch as the artillery shrapnel slapped into the mud around them, occasionally landing on exposed skin, burning. Lieutenant Bateman was grateful that only two men of his third platoon had been wounded while trying to get to Alpha

Company, but he knew they were all terribly drained and tired from the long fight to get to the ditch.

I remember feeling pretty helpless, as all we could do was lie there in the muddy water, up to our necks if we tried to stay low in the ditch. The wet flak jackets itched, and none of us had eaten anything since early that morning. As we passed the men down the canal on the air mattresses, I remember how quiet they all were. Most had been wounded early in the fight and had lain out, exposed, in the paddies all afternoon and into the early evening. They were all badly in shock and needed treatment.

Phil Bateman

Colonel Tutwiler had directed what was left of the crippled Alpha Company to move back to the bank of the stream, to establish defensive positions for the night. This was difficult with most of the company dead or wounded, scattered all over the battlefield, calling out for help. Elements of the company gathered who they could in a mass exit, while still under fire, with men dragging their wounded buddies, staying low, crawling at times, to get back near the river. Some of the wounded tried to crawl back on their own, but got confused and crawled the wrong way, being pulled into the enemy bunkers and killed. Volunteers continued crawling out through the night looking for friends, recovering wounded, even though the shelling and enemy fire kept the danger level very high.

Men who had trained together as far back as Fort Riley, Kansas, and had become buddies were lost and feared dead. Alpha Company, as many knew it, ceased to exist as a unit after that day. Charlie Company, pinned at the stream, had suffered thirteen men dead with many more wounded. Every company in the two battalions had taken devastating losses and heavy wounded counts. The tension of hearing about their friends dying all day and the brutal battle to retrieve them had exhausted everyone. But by nightfall, it appeared the Viet Cong had been trapped against the Rach Nui and that their destruction was just a matter of time.

During the night, the battalion command post was located on a command control boat positioned behind Charlie Company 4/47th on the river. Chaplain Windmiller went around to all his battalion positions and spoke to the guys, assuring them of his prayers. One of the boys asked him if he would say a prayer for their squad, and Chaplain Windmiller replied that it would be a privilege.

Fire continued into the night as screams for help glommed over the battlefield. The makeshift field hospital which had been set up around the medical aid boat, with several other assault craft in support, continued working in the dim light while Padre Johnson and a group of volunteers performed life-saving first aid to the men of Alpha Company, who had nearly been wiped out. Padre Johnson was exhausted, but the looks in the men's eyes kept him going. This went on all night, with boats coming and going, carrying the wounded out. There were only a dozen or so who had escaped injury in the entire company, as Riflemen Jim Henke and Tony Spradling, and several of their buddies, rounded up M60 machineguns and formed a barrier halfway between the bunkers and the wounded back at the boats. Exhausted and low on ammunition, soldiers set their perimeter by using helmets to dig foxholes in the ground. They waited and waited for the enemy to come, but none ever did. The men of the brigade were covered in dirt and blood, tired and hungry, but most considered themselves lucky just to be alive.

In the middle of the night, Staff Sergeant Julio Diaz of Puerto Rico led a small team from the 3rd Platoon of Charlie Company 3/47th out to find the bunkers by inching forward and attacking the bottom of the "L" in the enemy complex. This time the enemy fired blindly at the sound of the approaching Americans, revealing their positions with their muzzle flashes. Protected by darkness, Diaz crawled to within a few feet of a bunker when a machinegun opened fire. Diaz threw hand grenades into the bunker, putting it out of commission with several explotions. Then Diaz and others crawled a little further, knocking out another bunker the same way. After receiving support fire from their unit, Sergeant Diaz and his team returned safely back, withdrawing for the night. During the night, 3rd Platoon killed two more VC, using a Claymore mine when they tried to sneak west along the stream.

Back at the old French Fort, the artillery had fired continually throughout the day and into the night. Over 10,000 rounds had been fired, with the expended 105mm brass piled so high, the gun crews could no longer throw the expended shells onto the pile. Twice, the firing barges had to be slighty repositioned so they could resuppy and accommodate the expended shells. It was later found that most of the enemy losses were a result of the pounding they received from these artillery units.

One of the strangest occurrences of the day had been a report by CBS journalist Richard Threlkeld. Although the report was favorable, it was lie and many saw Threlkeld as a jackass. Threlkeld saw a helo land with two ponchos filled with enemy weapons and ran over to photograph it, noticing a very old mama-san being helped off the helo. The crew told everyone that she was put on the copter to get her out of the battle area and that she had not been involved in the fighting. Threlkeld then concocted the notion that the 9th Infantry was doing such a good job, that more and more the enemy was pressing the old and infirmed into service, evidence that we were winning the war in the Mekong Delta. The crew told him it was bullshit and would not participate in the filming. He finally roped some private first class and promised that his mom would see him on TV if he would stand over the squatting old lady and pretend to be guarding her. The soldier complied, and Threlkeld filmed the lie, then demanded the helo fly the footage to Saigon, all the while being an aggressive, pushy, "me, me, me" ass.

This was not unusual, as it became harder and harder to distinguish between the truth and the bullshit concerning the press and what was reported. The press was competing for headlines and trying to please editors and readers. All the while, we who were fighting in Vietnam paid for it, as the truth became more elusive.

Some time during the night, a portion of the Naval craft were withdrawn from the Rack Nui, although several boats remained with the medical aid boat on station and others held their blocking positions elsewhere. It is not known if this was done to replace crews, which had suffered wounded, or re-supply ammo and gun barrels, which were weakened from prolong firing. But when Colonel Fulton found out, he became furious and confronted

Captain Wells placing the blame on Commander Horowitz, who along with fourteen other sailors had been wounded. Captain Wells agreed it was a mistake and promptly ordered the boats back out, promising that the Navy would support the infantry on a twenty-four hour basis. Colonel Fulton had led a platoon in Italy during World War II and was fiercely loyal to his men, who in turn, were fully committed to him.

In truth, the two services had performed remarkably well together, with gunboats providing the best immediate support that was available. For the first time since the Civil War, Army and Navy units had stood side by side in a major riverine operation, deploying troops from assault craft, searching out and hunting down a major enemy force, destroying its base camp. Had all the boats remained in place on the Rach Nui, they might have hampered enemy withdrawal, but night had given the enemy fighters all the opportunity they had ever needed. They were known for these types of guerrilla tactics and were very good at them. Although they were surrounded on three sides and had boats to swim pass, many of the remaining 5th Nha Be Battalion slipped out west between the two battalions, moving south in the safety of darkness. The Americans were sleeping in shifts when the ebb tide came in during the early morning hours, waking many of them with six inches of water, turning everything into a muddy mess.

Air Force air strikes were requested at first light on June 20th, followed by coordinated assaults on the bunkers by the avenging battalions, supported by helicopters and the ARVN. They moved in and attacked, being violently opposed by a small platoon-size VC rear guard. But even in the smallest of battles, the VC fought fiercely and there were American casualties. Almost as soon as they started moving toward the bunkers, Lieutenant Phil Bateman was hit and suffered a concussion, catching shrapnel in his neck from a grenade or rocket. After Captain Engeldinger tried to talk to Phil, he saw Bateman's eyes were not focusing, so he told him to board one of the Navy boats and return to the ship. While walking to the river, Bateman ran into Tutwiler, who came over and shook his hand, saying something. But Bateman was dazed and could not hear what he was saying. The next thing Phil remembered was walking aboard the boat and seeing a dozen body bags lying at the bottom of the boat. He wondered if any of them contained his friends. He didn't remember anything else until he woke up in sickbay aboard the ship, with a corpsman cleaning his neck and telling him to take it very easy because they were not sure how bad his head injury was.

Back at the VC complex, the soldiers eventually overran the last few bunkers and killed or captured the remaining Viet Cong. Then they began setting explosive charges, destroying bunkers so the complex could not be used again. Specialist John Miller had just returned from R and R and was sent into the field on a re-supply chopper, working with the morgue detail. "To this day, I can't forget seeing the body bags on deck," as Miller recalls.

Charlie Company 3/47th Infantry was able to pick up a trail, tracking the enemy across streams, moving south. By early afternoon the troops had once again approached Route 229, which they had used for their landing zone the day before. Major Glenn Penny and Lieutenant George Crocker were again flying overhead in the command copter and saw a lot of bunkers in the woods just to the south, so they radioed Captain Menner, warning him of the danger. As Charlie Company continued to cautiously patrol south, a water buffalo charged one of the riflemen, who fired a quick burst from his M16 to ward off the animal. Seventy-five yards south, the woods opened up with VC gunfire. The road was three to four feet above the rice paddies, so the men of Charlie Company were able to quickly drop behind the road and avoid taking casualties. Captain Menner immediately requested artillery support, and Lieutenant Crocker was able to line up tactical air strikes on the enemy's positions. On the initial run, the planes dropped five hundred pound bombs, and Ron Menner witnessed one VC body flying in the air higher than the trees. The Air Force followed up with Napalm at Menner's request, with fire clouds burning high into the sky. This fire was maintained until 1600 hours, when Alpha and Bravo Companies 3/47th maneuvered into position on Charlie Company's left and right. Air strikes were halted while Alpha Company conducted a probe into the woods, where they were immediately met by a hail of gunfire, causing them to pull back to set up blocking positions from the east. Charlie Company was blocking from the north while Bravo blocked from the west. The ARVN 2nd Battalion maneuvered up and set blocking positions from the south, which pinned the Viet Cong in the woods from all directions. Each unit held its position while Crocker called in artillery and air, which pounded the VC for the rest of the day into the night. There were approximately a hundred yards between Charlie Company's left flank and Alpha Company's position, and this is where the VC, or at least part of them, slipped out during the night.

The next morning, the woods were searched while Charlie Company again picked up the trail and tracked the enemy for a mile or two, until the trail split into small groups of two to three Viet Cong, disbanding and dispersing into different directions. This basically ended operations, with Charlie Company standing down that evening.

At the end of the three-day battle, forty-eight Americans had been lost, with thirty-two from Alpha Company 4/47th Infantry alone, which had also suffered seventy-six wounded. There were over 150 wounded suffered by the two battalions, with casualties being dispersed to different medical facilities throughout South Vietnam. In a search of the Can Giuoc complex, 218 enemy bunkers were discovered, with many of them having been destroyed. Later, 255 VC were reported killed, but the true figure was believed to be much higher. The Viet Cong were very good about policing the battlefield and taking their wounded and dead with them, as U.S. troops would have done also. In addition to a number of weapons and documents, the brigade also captured a Viet Cong commander and several VC fighters of the battle who confirmed their high losses. The Can Giuoc battle had not only shattered the 5th Nha Be Battalion, but seriously disrupted the Viet Cong replacement system for many months to come. Normally, local force units like the 5th Nha Be trained their soldiers prior to their assignment to main force units. But after the June 19th battle, the 5th Nha Be had to train its recruits while operating, reducing its combat efficiency for quite some time.

There was a lot of soul-searching by the top brass afterwards, with Lieutenant Colonel Tutwiler feeling it was his fault, which most doubt to be true. Nobody has really forgotten or gotten over it. It has been said that it was Alpha Company's new commander's fault, that he was a gung-ho type who pushed his men too fast, without proper security out front. He was relieved shortly after June 19th and rumor has it that he volunteered for another tour and was killed, or took his own life.

Despite the heavy losses, the operation was considered an overwhelming success and helped develop the Mobile Riverine Force concept. The soldiers and sailors of the force had taken the battle to the enemy on its own ground, crossing streams and rice paddies in the open, administering the 5th Nha Be Viet Cong Battalion a devastating blow, destroying its sanctuary and ending its dominance of eastern Long An Province. Second Brigade casualties never again approached the terrible losses of June 19th, which for many was the longest day of their lives. Once again, everything that they had accomplished had come at a high price.

Many had distinguished themselves during the battle. One was Private First Class George Daniel Miller from Bravo Company 3/47th, who was described as a hero. As an infantry unit moved across an area of open rice paddies, it suddenly came under a murderous volume of automatic weapons fire from a Viet Cong force. In the initial burst of enemy fire, Private Miller spotted one of his comrades fall, wounded. Without regard for his own personal safety and fully realizing the perils of the situation, Miller immediately dashed across the bullet swept battlefield to aid his companion. Although exposed to a torrent of hostile fire, Miller professionally administered first aid to his wounded friend and carried him to a place of comparative safety. During the ensuing battle, Miller gallantly volunteered to make repeated trips to re-supply a machinegun. It was during one of these trips that Private Miller was mortally wounded, ending the life of an American hero.

They fought for freedom, they fought with honor, but in the end they fought for each other.

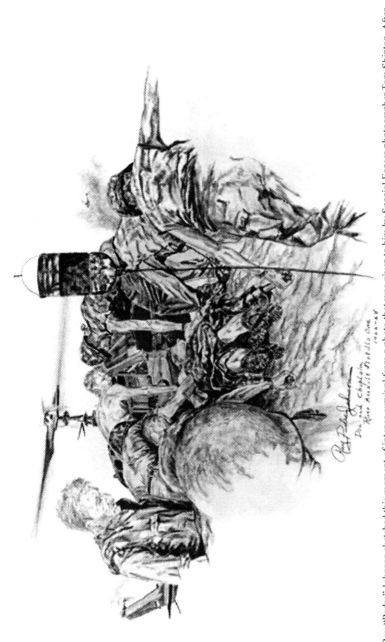

Chaplain Ray "Padre" Johnson sketched this moment of intense survival from a photo that was given to him by Special Forces photographer Tom Shinton. After giving medical assistance to the severely wounded casualty being rushed to the waiting medical evacuation helicopter, his helmeted facial image in the paintings foreground, returns to help another wounded member of their unit. Perhaps the most effective interpretation of his sketch is reflected in the mix of the courage and also the helpless, fatigued "what's it all about" face image of the young man on the left side of the sketch. Both realities say it all.

Ap Bac

Map 3

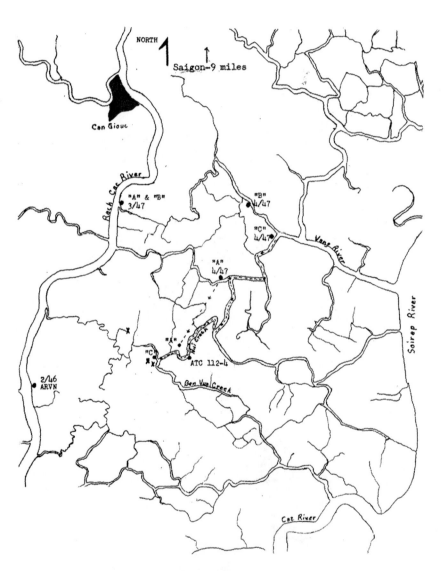

June 19th, 1967

COMPANY COMMANDER

The following is an account of the battle on June 19th, 1967, given by then Captain Ronald Menner, who was an officer of the highest quality, respected by the men who served with him:

I was the company commander of Charlie Company 3rd Battalion, 47th Infantry, and had been since September 1966. The commanders of Alpha and Bravo Companies, MacDonald and Luedke, had been replaced by Captains James McGrail and Ben Myatt, the latter part of May first part of June 1967. On June 19th, the 2nd Brigade was conducting a riverine operation in eastern Long An Province. My company was designated as the brigade reserve and was located at an old French Fort along the Saigon River. I was pretty happy we would be in reserve that day, since we had been conducting a lot of operations and I figured that my company could use a little rest.

Around 0900 hours, Colonel Fulton sent a helicopter to fly me to his command control boat. I was briefed on the situation and told that I would be under the operational control of Lieutenant Colonel Tutwiler, commanding officer of the 4th Battalion, 47th Infantry. I was to move Charlie Company by helicopter to a designated landing zone and search a tree line to the north. Brigade had received information of a Viet Cong battalion in this tree line. One of the companies of the 4th battalion was to be moved by boat and disembark, setting blocking positions which my company and I were suppose to move toward. The tree line was not very wide, so I ordered one platoon to sweep through the tree line while the remainder of the company and I moved slightly behind and to the west. We were deployed along a wide front, out in the open.

My company arrived where members of the 4th battalion was to set up a blocking position before the 4th battalion had arrived. There was a small Vietnamese day hooch out in the open, with an old man in it. The old man was shaking so bad, I knew immediately that something was up. About this time, Lieutenant Colonel Tutwiler called me up and accused me of not checking the tree line and wanted me to go back and do it again. I guess he saw the main part of my company out in the open west of the tree line, when in fact, I had already had one platoon move through the woods and had reached the northern edge. When I tried to explain it to him, he would not hear of it and wanted me to move back to the south and sweep the tree line again.

It was about this time that the company from the 4th battalion was conducting its boat landing and was moving west from the landing beach site. The 4th battalion company was just south of a stream that flowed east to west when it turned out the Viet Cong had taken up positions on the north bank. The Viet Cong opened fire on the 4th battalion company, which was out in the open on the south side of the stream, with little or no cover. At the same time, Alpha Company of the 4th battalion was moving south and had walked into the Viet Cong battalion ambush. Alpha Company 4/47th Infantry had stumbled into a triangle of Viet Cong-fortified positions, with a heavy machinegun set up at each point. In just a matter of a few minutes, most of Alpha Company was dead or wounded.

The commanding officer of Alpha Company 4/47th had been the assistant brigade S-2 intelligence officer and had not had the company but a few days, maybe a week. While still at Dong Tam, he had come to my company area one evening and was asking me a lot of questions about my methods of operation and maneuver. At the time, I did not know he was getting a company or what he was up to, so thinking that he was on some sort of snoop mission, I did not tell him very much. Also, a couple of weeks prior to this operation, we had been in the same area, and I had had the mission of moving into the same area as Alpha Company 4/47th did on June 19th. I feel certain that if I had been in his place I would not have gotten caught like he did. When I moved into this area previously, I had my company deployed across a front of six to seven hundred yards, and we would have bumped the Viet Cong without walking into its midsts.

Anyway, Alpha Company was getting hammered, as was the company moving into the blocking position. I was still in the same position when I realized why the old Vietnamese man had been so scared. I radioed Tutwiler and recommended that I move north, just west of where it appeared that the Viet Cong were located, and cross the east-west stream so as to put pressure on the western side of the Viet Cong's positions. Lieutenant Colonel Tutwiler, with his voice breaking up (I'm sure he was beside himself and still trying to get a handle on the dire situation), said "Roger."

To this day I have my doubts if he understood what I meant. At that time, I directed my second platoon leader, Lieutenant Kitchens, to take his platoon, the third, along with the weapons platoon, and move to the west about four hundred yards and cross the east-west stream. My map had showed a bridge across the stream at that point, which was by a village. I then directed Lieutenant Gatsey, my first platoon leader, to move north across the stream and then turn east toward the Viet Cong. I went with Lieutenant Gatsey, and, when we got to the stream, there was a small sampan on the north bank. We retrieved the sampan and put our gear in it, shuttled it back and forth, and swam the stream until we got the first platoon and my company command group across. This consisted of about thirty-five or so personnel.

Looking back, I can see that where we crossed was fairly close to the Viet Cong positions, within one hundred yards or less, but thankfully, there was a bend in the stream with vegetation along the banks, so apparently we went unobserved. Once across, Lieutenant Gatsey had moved his platoon approximately fifty yards north of the stream and was aggressively engaging the Viet Cong units. During this time, Lieutenant Gatsey had received a crease wound along his chin while looking over a paddy dike. I had moved my company command group, myself, my two radio operators, the artillery forward observer, his radio operator and his recon sergeant, to the east, where there was what I had termed a day hooch.

The day hooch had a nipa palm roof, with a wooden bed and bunker. I think this is where the rice farmers spent mid-afternoon for their siesta. When we got to the day hooch, there were two

Army engineers from Lieutenant Gatsey's platoon inside. Each company had engineers who would take care of booby traps or tunnels we might encounter and blow them in place. I stood just to the north side of the hooch where the doorway was and pulled out my map to make sure I knew where we were. About this time, Gatsey got hit in the arm. I moved inside the day hooch, taking cover behind the bunker. The bunker was about thirty inches tall without a roof. The two engineers were looking through the nipa palm sides. My radio operator, Thomas Gordon, had moved to where I had been standing and was squatting down. I told Gordon that he better get inside the hooch, that there was a VC sniper near with what I figured was an M-I rifle and he knew how to use it. Lieutenant Gatsey had already been hit twice. At about the same instant, there was a loud crack. Gordon reeled back, muttering, "Oh, God damn." I grabbed him by the radio strap and pulled him inside the hooch behind the bunker, telling him he was going to be okay. His eyes immediately rolled back, and I knew that he had died almost instantly. I think the bullet went into his right upper chest and came out near his left kidney, probably passing through his heart. About this time, one of the engineers said something about seeing the Viet Cong sniper and started firing. Then another crack, and one of the engineers was hit in the chest, by what I was sure would be a fatal wound.

Lieutenant Kitchen's second platoon and third platoon, led by Platoon Sergeant First Saavedra, had crossed the bridge and kept going north. It took me a while to get them turned around, moving back to the south, and then east to join up with me. I saw them approaching from the west crossing a log foot bridge over another small stream. I told them to be careful as there was what I thought to be a VC sniper in the area and he knew what he was doing. About this time, I heard another rifle shot and saw dust kick up off of the log. They were about one-hundred yards or so behind me. The guys on the foot bridge jumped into the water, one of them losing his rifle, which we never did find. They closed with me, and I deployed third platoon to the east of the hooch. They were along a paddy dike engaged with the enemy. During this time, I had reverted back to my parent battalion, 3/47th Infantry, under the control and command of Major Glenn Penny, while Commanding Officer Lieutenant Colonel Bolduc was away.

Bravo Company 3/47th had also closed on my north flank. We were directed by Major Penny to conduct a coordinated attack against the Viet Cong positions. Immediately we came under intense fire. Lieutenant Gatsey had been wounded in his legs and was out of it for good. Captain Myatt of Bravo Company said that he was stalled and could not proceed forward. During this time, Major Penny, in his command helicopter, along with the battalion command group, had been shot down twice. (I would not know this until several years later when Lieutenant General George A. Crocker, West Point class of '66, told me. Crocker had been my third platoon leader until his transfer to battalion, where he was the S-3 Officer who requested and coordinated Tactical Air Support, usually from the U.S. Air Force.)

I told Captain Myatt to hold fast and I would see what I could do. Platoon Sergeant Saavedra was saying the same thing and also recommended Myatt hold up. Sergeant Saavedra then asked for the 90mm recoilless rifle. The men of my weapons platoon had an extra machinegun that we had come up with from somewhere. I also had them pack a 90mm recoilless rifle along with three beehive flechette rounds and five rounds of high-explosive, anti-tank HEAT rounds. This weapon really paid off. If I ever received any type of harassing fire, I would bring the 90mm forward and have them fire a HEAT round where I thought we had received the fire, then follow up with a beehive round. Normally, we never heard from that guy again.

I got the 90mm recoilless moved up with third platoon, which laid down a base of fire, and then Sergeant Saavedra directed the 90mm recoilless toward a bunker. They fired the five HEAT rounds and, as I recall, knocked out three enemy bunkers. I requested additional 90mm ammo as that seemed to be getting the best results. Throughout the afternoon, we had artillery and helicopter gunships firing on the enemy. During this time, one of the new third platoon members, by the name of John Donald St. Peters, was killed in action. Several of the riflemen were pinned behind a dike and taking heavy fire, with St. Peters right next to Sergeant

Saavedra, who had joked saying he was going to keep St. Peters with him, thinking that with a name like that, he could not go wrong. The bullet passed completely through the paddy dike and hit St. Peters in the head, killing him instantly. Another round landed in the chest of Specialist Michael Richey, who was standing next to St. Peters and who also thought it was safe. That was not the case.

The wounded and killed in action were moved to the west side of the hooch, which sat on a mound about three feet high, providing good cover and some camouflage to the area. During the afternoon, the blocking company from the 4/47th, Charlie Company, had basically been pinned down out in the open. The men had requested a medevac. When the helicopter landed to pick up their causalities, the enemy placed a lot of fire into the area. The helicopter took off for a short distance and started lifting up, until it ran out of thrust and fell back onto its tail, rolling on its side.

By the time it had gotten dark, helicopters started bringing in the 90mm recoilless ammo with other supplies. I was putting my causalities on the outgoing craft. Now that it was night, I guess the Viet Cong were involved in trying to escape. We had elements of the 3rd and 4th battalions to their north, heavily armed Navy craft on the stream to their east, the blocking company to their south and my company and I on the enemy's west. The mode of operation for the Viet Cong under these circumstances was to send out two-man patrols after dark in various directions. If one of the patrols was able to get out of the encirclement, it would return to guide out the main body in small groups.

One patrol tried to sneak past third platoon's right flank along the stream that I had initially crossed around 1100 hours. They were quickly dispatched by a Claymore mine from the third platoon. Throughout the night, a U.S. Air Force plane overhead dropped flares, along with artillery flares and fire. Just after dusk, one or two Tangos had moved along the east-west stream to my south flank. I put some of the lightly wounded on them, and they ran back past the Viet Cong under a hail of fire. I don't know if they picked up any wounded from the blocking company or not, but they probably did, as the boats would have still been in the general area where they dropped the troops.

The next morning, I was directed to sweep the area. We found one bunker that had been hit by the 90mm recoilless rifle. A lone rifle was sticking out of it. I assume that the shooter on the other end, was dead. All in all, we counted about a dozen dead Viet Cong with weapons.

The brigade had counted over 250 dead Viet Cong, and around September time frame, a 9th Division unit ambush of a Viet Cong unit in Long An Province had captured several documents. One of the documents was the after-action report of the June 19th battle, and according to their own accounts, our brigade figure of their killed was correct. I also saw that it had looked as if a herd of cattle had stampeded to the south across the east-west stream and had slipped out to the west of the blocking company. I was directed to proceed south after them. As we were preceding south, Major Penny, who was flying overhead, told me that the woods to my south were full of foxholes. As we approached the road bed that we had used as a landing zone the previous day, a water buffalo appeared, acting as though he was going to charge one of the guys. A burst of automatic rifle fire into the ground in front of him stopped that. However, it did trigger a barrage of fire from the woods that Major Penny had told me about, which was just over fifty yards south of the road bed. We had found them again. We bellied down behind the road bed, which had good cover.

I got the artillery firing, which included 155mm in addition to the normally used 105mm Howitzers guns. The 155mm guns were firing from the old French Fort. Lieutenant Crocker radioed for tactical air support to drop five-hundred-pound bombs on the enemy's location. I instructed that if there was to be additional Tac Air, I wanted Napalm. The initial bomb drop did propel a VC body above the tree tops.

My experience with artillery and bombs was that where they would hit it proved deadly to the enemy; however, a few feet away, they did little damage. In the delta, the shells penetrated the soft ground and made a nice hole, blowing up and out with not a whole lot of residual damage. However, Napalm would tumble, scoot, and cover a much larger area, with not only injuries, but also psychological impact. Throughout the afternoon, I directed seven

Air Force sorties of two aircraft each. They were 105 jet fighters as I recall, and 550 rounds of artillery. During this time, a Republic of Vietnam battalion was moved to the south side of the woods. Bravo Company 3/47th Infantry was moved in on my right flank, trying to tie in with the ARVN troops. Alpha Company 3/47th was airlifted, I believe, to east side of the woods. By the time everyone was in position, it was late in the day. Members of Alpha Company moved forward, conducting a probe into the woods, and met heavy rifle fire. They pulled back, and we held our positions throughout the night. There was about one hundred yards of open rice paddies between my company and Alpha Company.

The next morning I could see where the Viet Cong had slipped between us. I again began following the footprints to the northeast. It was not very long until the tracks split off into small groups to the winds, and that basically ended the operation. The 4th Battalion of the 47th Infantry stood down. Its Alpha Company was remanded and spent the next couple of weeks retraining. The captain, who had commanded Alpha Company 4/47th Infantry, was reassigned. I understand that he extended in Vietnam, sought command of another company and got killed. My company had two killed in action and four wounded in the battle.

The 3/47th Infantry was on the barracks boat that was moved around by tug boats. The barracks boat could not hold the entire battalion, so my company was housed afloat with the flotilla's tank landing ship. The LST served as the re-supply ship for the Mobile Riverine Force and also held the brigade aviation section. When we first went on the LST, there was some tension between the Navy and Army troops. To start with, on their first day aboard, my guys while standing in the mess line, ground out their cigarettes on the deck. The captain of the ship straightened me out in a hurry. I do have to say, that after the battle on June 19th, we became one and I think that's when the Navy folks really started bending over backwards for us. My relationship with the ship captain was really strengthened.

As it turned out, the engineer that was hit in the day hooch survived. I ran into him about a month later while on R and R in Camp Zama Japan. He was coming out of the USO club as I was going in, and he recognized me. He was as white as a bed sheet but, other than that, seemed to be doing well.

Operation Concordia I had succeeded, but at a high cost, with Alpha Company 4/47th Infantry taking severe casualties. The repair teams on USS Askarii were busy for some time welding holes from the many rocket hits the river assault craft had taken during the exchange. The 2nd Brigade and River Assault Squadron Nine were hurt, but the Viet Cong sanctuary was destroyed. The Mobile Riverine Force had met an enemy Main Force Battalion in fortified positions, disembarked from river boats, and annihilated them.

On June 22nd Commander U.S. Naval Forces, Vietnam, sent this message to Commander Task Force 117 and the Commanding Officer Second Brigade U.S. Ninth Infantry Division.

The performance and gallantry of your men during Operation Concordia I were a source of pride and gratification to all of us. Your achievements have been made possible by the aggressiveness, alacrity and boldness consistently displayed by you, your officers and men. The Mobile Riverine Force has proved to be the potent flexible fighting team so vital to the success of the campaign in the Mekong Delta. Please pass a well done to all hands for the success of Concordia I and may you have continued good hunting.

Rear Admiral Veth Sends

It has been said that the West Point class of '50 was the hardest-hit class in the school's history, cadets being deployed directly to the Korean Conflict after graduation. It is believed that the cadets of West Point class of '66 eclipsed them while serving in South Vietnam.

I fought in World War Two, but I never saw braver men in my life. They went into action without a whimper, never batted an eye, off they went, never knowing what was going to happen. They went and did their job.

William B. Fulton

A SOLDIERS STORY

*T*he *following is a personal account of a young soldier who was drafted and served honorably with the 3rd Battalion 47th Infantry, 9th Infantry Division, in the Republic of Vietnam. Specialist Michael Richey's story is an important and revealing account that gives great insight to what it was like to serve as a rifleman in the 2nd Brigade of the Mobile Riverine Force. For two-thousand years, the Chinese, French, Japanese and Republic of Vietnam forces had tried to pacify the Mekong Delta and failed. The United States Ninth Infantry Division, and Naval Forces of Vietnam, did it in a little over three years, but at a high cost.*

I was working at General Motors and taking classes toward my apprenticeship at a building built some time in the early 1900s, near my high school. I thought I had a plan, and the plan was, after I got a thousand hours, I'd have a deferment. And this would carry me through my apprenticeship for four years. And hopefully by that time, the Vietnam War would be over.

I had already taken a physical for the draft board, but I really wasn't too worried. I'd known several guys who were close to twenty years old who hadn't been drafted. So I thought I had plenty of time.

I was nineteen years old and two months when I got my draft papers. I was shocked. I remember being in my parents' garage, working on my car. My younger brother Jim brought my papers and said, "I think you got drafted."

I said, "Naw, they probably want me to go for another physical. No big deal." I opened it up and there were "greetings" from my "friends and neighbors." By the time I got in the house, my mother was somewhat hysterical. Jim had already told her.

In one of my classes, I had a finals test due after the date I was to report for duty. So I went to the instructor and told him I would not be there for the final and wanted to know if I could take the test early. He said fine. While I was standing there, a guy named Rodney Compton came up. He was in the same predicament. He and I worked at the same Guide Lamp plant, part of General Motors. But Rodney worked at a different end. We didn't know each other.

On May 18th, 1966, ninety-four of us from my county met at the post office to be inducted. We spent the greater part of the day filling out paperwork, and then we took the oath and stepped forward. After we said our goodbyes to our families, friends, and lovers, we were loaded on buses headed to Indianapolis. From that day on, I was in the Army. From there, we went to Fort Knox, Kentucky, and spent the greater part of the night doing more paperwork and getting shots. The next seven or eight days we spent getting our uniforms, a little physical training, and more shots. At the end of the eight days, after falling out in formation, we were told, "If your name's called, go in and get your stuff and report back outside." Well, my name was called, as were the names of a lot of the guys from my small county, including Rodney.

We were loaded on buses and were told we were on our way to Fort Riley, Kansas. It was a long, seven-hundred-mile bus ride with us arriving in the middle of the night. We were told that we would be part of the 9th Infantry Division, would be training while there, and would definitely be going to Vietnam in the near future. But we all took that with a grain of salt. My unit was an artillery unit, so I really wasn't too shocked. I thought, although artillery units are in great danger, at least they don't have to hump. So this couldn't be that bad, firing big guns and pulling perimeter guard once in a while.

After eight weeks of initial basic training, we were again called to fall out. They said, "If your name is called, get on the truck," a deuce and a half, which is a two-and-a-half-ton truck. They told us we would be going to Custer Hill, which was an infantry camp located at a different part of Fort Riley. To be in any part of this was pretty much bad news, going to Vietnam. Sure enough, my name was called, and I remember thinking, "Well, I'm probably going to die in Vietnam. I'm going to be in the infantry."

At the time, I believe the odds were that one in ten soldiers would be in the infantry in some type of combat. So, as the odds narrowed, things got a little bit tougher to deal with. Anyhow, we went to Custer Hill: Rodney Compton, the guy I met in the classroom; Bill Imel from Madison County; Larry Garner; Lanny Garner; and Steve Lawyer, to name several guys from Indianapolis. At Custer Hill we were directed to Delta Company, 3rd Battalion, 47th Infantry. Delta Company was a newly-formed company commanded by Captain Ronald Menner from Boonville, Indiana. That made us all feel a little better, knowing we had a fellow Hoosier in control.

We went through AIT, Advanced Individual Training, and I met a lot of guys from Indianapolis, as well as from other parts of the country, and we all became friends. We were a tight-knit group and felt pretty good camaraderie, making up for lost time, having gotten a slow start. The company was formed about a week after everybody else's. After several weeks of AIT, we were again told to fall out and bring our stuff. They had disbanded Delta Company for lack of troop strength; we didn't have enough people to fill the slots. I was transferred to Charlie Company, along with Larry Garner and Lanny Garner. Bill Imel and Rodney Compton went to Bravo Company, and Steve Lawyer went to Alpha Company, along with some of the other guys from Indianapolis.

Again, as I say, we had become friends with all these guys, and now we were being spread around and diluted. Going to Charlie Company was a completely new experience; I was, all of sudden, without anybody that I knew. Of course, it didn't take long to make friends, and within a week or two, we found out our new commanding officer was coming in. When it was announced that Captain Ronald Menner from Delta Company would become our company commander, I was ecstatic. I really liked the man, and I'd already heard about his predecessor being pretty strict. Ron was strict, but at least he was fair. The first thing Ron did was issue three-day passes for everyone who was eligible. From that day on, everything was kind of looking up.

We spent the next several months training. It was hard work, but we got through it. I came home for Christmas in the middle of

December 1966. Christmas that year was bizarre, to say the least. I remember my mother and father giving me money for Christmas. What else are you going to give a person who's going overseas? My mother was crying and left the room. I think she was aware, and so was everybody else, that that could very well be my last Christmas.

I left for Vietnam on December 27th, two days after Christmas, despite a large ice storm that day. We flew back to Fort Riley and proceeded to gather our gear. I don't remember the exact date we left for Vietnam, but it was within a few days. We boarded planes in Manhattan, Kansas, and flew to San Francisco Bay. There we boarded buses and headed for the harbor. I remember that it was the middle of the night. The next morning we were out to sea aboard the USS General John Pope, AP-110. I remember running upstairs to the deck and getting a glimpse of the United States, thinking I might never see her again.

The trip itself was uneventful. We played a lot of cards, ate, played more cards, wrote letters home, and pretty much killed time. We got close enough to Hawaii to hear the radio station, but we didn't land until we saw Okinawa, Japan. There we had a twelve-hour pass. We landed and went into town to explore the sights. Never having been outside the United States, this was very interesting to me, and we all had a good time. We ended back on the ship that evening and sailed the next morning. We then headed for Vung Tau Harbor and were told there could be hostile action right away, so before landing, we were briefed and issued live ammo. When the gate of the landing craft dropped at Vung Tau, a band started playing. So much for the briefing.

We left on trucks and went to firebase Bearcat. We stayed there a brief time and did a few missions, just to get our feet wet. Then we left and went to the Rung Sat Special Zone on the river. It was actually part of the shipping lanes for Saigon Harbor. The mud was waist-deep, mixed with salt water. The terrain was unbelievably bad. In the evening, we would situate ourselves close to a tree so we could hang our packs and lean back on them to sleep. With the elevation being below sea level, we knew that when the tide came in that evening, we'd get soaking wet if we were lying on the ground.

Water would absolutely flood the whole area. But we did the best we could and got through it. We spent a month there and had a few light casualties, but nothing to speak of. It was terrible conditions, a little bit of action here and there, but we didn't see too much.

Our first replacement that February was a young guy named John St. Peters of Brighton, Illinois. He was a special guy to all of us, very happy and very young. He came by helicopter into the Rung Sat with our food and water. We introduced ourselves and tried to make him feel at home, then spent another day or two out in the field. They brought the boats in from the Navy task force, and we got on. The first thing we always did after boarding was eat and drink water. The Navy always had plenty of water and C-rations, and they were more than happy to share with us. So we'd always get extra C-rations and trade them around. It was almost like a steak dinner to us, to board the Navy boats and be somewhat safe.

What we had learned from our earlier excursions was that if you brought ammo back into the base camp, the higher-ups wanted you to spend time cleaning it, since it had been in salt water. Well, we quickly learned that if you don't bring ammo back, you don't have to clean it. So on the way back someone would issue an order that it was a "free-fire zone," and we'd all get up and burn up all of our ammo, every last drop. Then when we got back to the base camp, we'd have nothing to clean. In our eagerness to welcome St. Peters, we forgot to tell him that this was routine and we'd burn our ammo up on the way back in. We're eating and having a good time, and then the word got passed around that it was a free-fire zone. So we all jumped up and started throwing Claymores and grenades, cleaning our guns out, every clip we had. St. Peters, however, thought we were in a big-time battle and it scared him to death. He thought we were a bunch of John Waynes, because we were all standing up like we were, well, John Wayne, shooting and carrying on. We all got a big laugh later when he told us, "I had no idea what you guys were up to."

We left firebase Bearcat and went by deuce and a half to a place called Dong Tam, which was our new base, home to 2nd Brigade and our Navy task force. When we first got there, we saw that it was pretty much flat, barren land. We set up a perimeter, and within a few months, I remember coming back to the base and seeing two-story barracks, showers, beer halls and NCO clubs. That's how quickly the Vietnam War escalated.

From Dong Tam we operated on boats, helicopters, and, occasionally, by trucks. We'd go out on the boats, come back by helicopter, go out on helicopters and come back on trucks. But most of the time we knew very little of what was going on and where we were at. Occasionally, we would see a landmark or something to tell us where we were. We had no access to maps or any of that stuff. The platoon leaders had all of that information, and you'd either follow the guy in front of you or, if you were out on point, you would go left or right, whatever the platoon leader would dictate. Over a period of time, we would hit occasional resistance and had a few casualties here and there. Mostly, early on, it was booby traps and occasional sniper fire.

Our first major confrontation was April 6th and 7th, 1967. We had gone on a long-range brigade operation involving over a thousand troops. We swept southwest of Saigon on the southern edge of the Plain of Reeds, close to the Patriot's Beak of Cambodia. We found very little there, a few pockets of resistance. At the end of the sweep, we were all chowing down and getting ready to board helicopters when a buzz started that something was going to happen. Later on, we found out that out of the thousands of troops that were going to be there, we were among thirty-three guys, plus a platoon leader and a forward observer for the artillery, who were going to stay behind and see what the VC had up their sleeve.

Normally, when you have an operation like that, the Viet Cong, or even North Vietnamese regulars, would come in later and sweep the same area, looking for unused ammo, dropped Claymores, or just gather intelligence to see what we were up to. Our objective was to ambush the party that was coming through and gather intelligence. We had little knowledge at the time what was in store for us. We were supplied with extra ammo, so much, that we could barely walk. We crouched in a ditch and waited for nightfall. It was a disheartening sound listening to the last of the helicopters take off. Then it was quiet, and we knew we were by ourselves.

At the appointed time, we moved into an ambush position not far away, but enough to change our position. We went to a Y in the river, somewhat of a creek. As in a lot of areas in the delta, the creeks were very narrow, but they would be deep from the tide coming in and washing them out. We set up a perimeter, and I remember the first part of the evening was spent fighting off hungry mosquitoes, which were biting us to death. Even the Army-issued insect repellent was doing very little to repel them. But we knew we had bigger fish to fry, so we endured it. There was a sense that something big was going to happen. So we set up our perimeter with Claymore mines and began to wait.

During the night, even when you were not on guard, you'd sleep for an hour and be awake for an hour. With the mosquitoes biting us and the anticipation that something was going to happen, I don't believe anybody got much sleep that night. I remember being along the creek bank and seeing a sampan coming. Because this was a free-fire zone, which means that anybody moving in that area is the enemy, I had my hand on the plunger, ready to blow my Claymore. Just as the boat got to my position, Benny Whitney from Kentucky blew his Claymore and sank the sampan. That was an eerie feeling, hearing the agony of the two or three guys in the sampan as they sank to the bottom of the brown, fast-flowing canal water.

The idea was to use your Claymores and grenades. Explosions could be random. Small-arms fire meant there was someone approaching. Since we were trying to conceal our position, there was no small-arms fire whatsoever. That was our last resort. Next morning, we were on the left flank and there was activity on the right flank. I believe a Sergeant Diaz was involved. He threw his grenades and blew a couple of Claymores at advancing troops. Right away we knew the war was on again. We hunkered down low and waited for the enemy to approach. After they probed with small-arms fire, which we did not return, we knew we were in deep crap. Then here they came, hundreds of them at a time. I believe they estimated close to five hundred troops coming toward our position, and there were only thirty-three of us.

We threw everything we had at them and fought as long as we could with what we had, and then called artillery in real close to our position, trying to ward them off. We had established an extraction point, and luckily, everyone had listened during the briefing. When the order came in the early morning to extract, we moved as quickly as possible. Although we carried light packs, we still had combat boots on, yet we extracted at the speed of light. It was a little bit like cowboys and Indians. As we were running toward the helicopters, the bad guys were coming out of the tree line, shooting at us, kind of like, well, cowboys and Indians. We all jumped on the closest helicopter, grabbed hold, and then we lifted and took off.

When we landed at the base camp at Dong Tam, we were all tired, dirty, hungry, and thirsty. All we wanted to do was grab something to eat and a quick glass of ice tea. But as we got off the helicopter, we noticed there were a lot of guys in formation. We had no idea what this was all about, but supposedly during the night, they had gotten word that we were trapped and that several, if not most, of us would not be coming back. So when we got out of the copters, they told us to fall into formation and count off, which seemed kind of peculiar to us.

Come to find out that the reason we counted off was to find out who had made it back. Much to our surprise, all thirty-three of us made it. Now a few of us had some minor scratches here or there, but it was a miracle that everybody made it back, considering the amount of close combat we'd experienced.

Next combat I remember was when we landed at a hot helicopter LZ, landing zone. We were doing "eagle flights," where two different units, in coordination with each other, would go and land on opposite sides of the rice paddies, in the vegetation that normally surrounded them in the delta. At one flight landing, one company would sweep toward a blocking force of the second company, and whoever was between us, would run into the blocking force. At the end of the operation, usually one or two hours, the helicopters would pick us up, and we would move to another LZ. It was hit-and-miss and we moved quickly, trying to surprise the enemy.

During one landing, we started hearing small-arms fire hit the helicopter. The helicopter pilot kept yelling, "Get out! Get out! Get out!" while we were trying to figure out how far we were off the ground. Most of our packs weighed anywhere from sixty to a hundred pounds, and our body weight was only 140 to 150 pounds, so if you weren't careful when you jumped, you could break your back. As we approached the area, we could see bad guys all around us, shooting toward the helicopter. We were weighing in on when to jump, when the door gunner on my side of the helicopter took a shot in his throat. At the time, I thought it was fatal; I learned later that it may not have been, but to this day, I have no way of knowing. As he took the shot, I jumped. I felt like a Weeble, one of those wobbling little toy characters kids play with. I landed up to my waist in mud and could hardly bend down. What we had done was land in their perimeter. It was a bizarre meeting, to say the least. From that position, we moved forward, mostly by low crawl, and we advanced in opposing directions. Not far from there, my machinegunner, Dan Mosier, took a shot in his leg, and I grabbed the M60 machinegun. He was okay and assured me he would be fine, so I crawled forward with the M60, right into a bed of leeches. I remember at the time – and it still sticks with me to this day – thinking, "You're not having a good day, Richey. You've got leeches all over your body, people shooting at you, and you've already seen many people hurt. This is not a good day."

I remember seeing bad guys get up everywhere; it was almost like a shooting gallery. We'd been in combat several times, but that day, I got my first confirmed kill. I knew I had hit at least one person who did not survive the assault.

After the initial combat had died down, we got up and started moving around. I went up to see how many bodies that I had possibly collected. I saw some vegetation that didn't look quite right. I kicked it open and inside was a sixteen-year-old female Viet Cong carrying an M-1 rifle and explosives. At the time, my Vietnamese was somewhat good, so I told her to get out, and she did. I took her back to our lines, and they called for Intelligence to come interrogate her. They found documents on her showing she was from North Vietnam. I tried to give her some crackers, feeling sorry for her. I assumed they were probably going to kill her after they had extracted all the information out of her. But she didn't want any part of it. I even ate a couple cheese and crackers from my C-rations, to show her that they were okay. I felt bad about that incident, because to this day, I have no idea what happened to her. That skirmish lasted only a few hours, with one 2nd Brigade radioman killed, and Dan Mosier and the copter door gunner wounded. The Viet Cong lost thirty-one, with one captured.

Our next skirmish was May 2nd, the Battle of Ap Bac. I remember hearing that Alpha Company had gotten hit hard, and we were there to support them, as we moved into position. Myself, I didn't see a lot of combat that day, but still more than I wanted. We kept hearing that Alpha Company was getting hit hard. Alpha Company had consisted of a lot of my friends from Delta Company, so it was a bittersweet day. I came to find out later that Steve Lawyer, who had been drafted the same day as I, had survived only because he had traded off the radio with somebody else. If he hadn't, he would have been in position to be in serious peril. We did lose Harold Mundy, Mike Pugh, and Otto Meyer. These were all guys from my Delta Company experience, and in fact, I had Harold Mundy's fatigues on. I'd gone to the laundry and my fatigues hadn't come back yet, so Harold loaned me a pair of his that day.

The next evening, we went down to Alpha Company to console whoever was left. It was a terrible feeling seeing the empty bunks where they had already gathered up the personal belongings of our friends. They were no longer around. They were gone.

From there, we had several short missions and took a few casualties, mostly from land mines. I remember late one evening when we were moving. We moved quite a bit at night. We hit a land mine, and four guys were injured and required attention. I knew two of them, Dave Mattull, who I believe was from Florida, and James Noble, who I think was from Idaho. I was first to reach Noble, wrapping him with bandages until the helicopters got there for his dust-off. There was blood everywhere, but that was part of war. Luckily, everybody survived that Claymore mine incident. We also had some casualties on the islands off the coast of Dong Tam, but everything got pretty quiet from then on.

Then came June 19th.

We were a reserve unit, kind of resting and recuperating, but it didn't take long for us to get called forward. 4/47th got hit hard. We knew it would be a special day. We moved by helicopter to our new position, after initially setting a blocking force. I remember being on a large dike between rice paddies and seeing guys move forward. One in particular was Chuck Cataldo from Fort Wayne, Indiana, drafted about the same time we all were, but not in my unit, but a guy I had befriended. Chuck got hit with a 40mm shell from the Navy boat, we believe, and it removed his left arm. He stood up with what was left of his arm, and everybody was trying to get him to sit down and protect himself, from the firepower coming in. I know he survived, but I've never seen him since.

About the same time, Captain Menner, who was not far away, lost his RTO, radio telephone operator, Thomas Gordon. We moved up into position to try to alleviate some of the firepower that was being dished out to the 4/47th. On our way toward the front, we came to a small creek, and there again, the creeks were not so wide, but the tide would come in and wash them deep. Several others ahead of us had secured a sampan, and the idea was to put your gear into the sampan and push it across the stream as you were swimming beside it. We couldn't possibly navigate the stream with our packs on.

We got on the other side, and I threw my pack up on the shore and turned around to shove the sampan back, so the next person could use it. Then I noticed that coming over the top of the hill was Rodney Compton, my friend that I'd met in class that day the year before. Bravo Company was to our left flank, and Charlie Company was to my right. So we had kind of bottlenecked in the stream to get across. I let him come across and then lay on the bank briefly and said, "Boy, we're really into it today, Rodney."

He said, "Yeah."

I remember saying something to the effect of "good luck, and see you later." Rodney went to the left, and I went in search of my unit.

At first, I hooked up with the 2nd platoon. In combat, things get somewhat fragmented, and you don't always end up where you're supposed to. I advanced through and found out where 3rd platoon was, met up with my guys, and we started advancing, which was slow. A few guys would lay down a line of fire while a few got up and ran forward, finding cover. Then they laid a volley of fire so the guys behind them could get up and advance.

What we were up against was nothing like what some people might expect about the Vietnam War. These were fortified bunkers with an enemy unit that was dug in, and the VC had everything going for them. Our small arms fire was doing very little to combat their firepower. They had definitely taken the advantage. We had artillery and Navy support, even a little bit of Air Force, but it did little damage to their fortified positions.

We moved as far as we could before, suddenly, we were hit hard and began to take heavy casualties. I remember peeking up a couple of times and seeing the helicopters. They were shooting them down faster than they could land. They were good shots, and they knew where to shoot. We knew going in that this was going to be a bad day. We got as far as we could. My platoon leader at the time was Sergeant Saavedra. He told everyone to hold up, that we were going to take more casualties if we moved forward. He said, "We need to get some of the bunkers knocked out." So he got on the radio and ordered a 90 millimeter recoilless rifle, which is similar to a bazooka.

In the meantime, while we were waiting for the 90mm to come forward, I noticed that I could look up and see the tree lines, so I thought, "I better move forward. I'm still in the line of fire." I was lying prone, and as I turned onto my side to crawl forward, something hit me in my chest like a baseball bat. I stopped and looked around.

I must have had this look on my face, because Sergeant Saavedra was right next to me asking, "Did you get hit?" I started to say yes, but nothing came out. I nodded my head. With that, Saavedra dragged me behind the dike, and then a little further. I lay there, helpless, while he called for a medic.

I was told of the four medics in our company, three had been killed that day. But we had one left, and he came and administered first aid. He did the best he could under terrible conditions. I suffered a sucking chest wound, and he put a plastic wrap from the first aid kit on my chest and wrapped it as best he could. I'm sure he saved my life.

I lay there for a long time, listening to guys screaming and hollering, and I knew something bad had happened. Somebody leaned over and told me that John St. Peter had suffered a fatal wound just a few minutes after my injury and just six to eight feet away. I was hit approximately 1830 hours. John was killed at 1845 hours in the early evening of June 19th. I would later learn that Rodney Compton was wounded within a half hour of my injury. He was right next to George Miller, one of our buddies from Delta Company, who was also killed during the exchange.

As the fire died down over the next two to three hours, I lay there wrapped in a poncho. I had been dragged to the rear by several guys, at great personal danger to themselves. One of the guys who dragged me was Jerry Savarese from New York, and I think Glen Corbett from Ohio also had a hand in it.

As I lay there, the smells and sounds of war were all around me. They're things most people will never experience, fortunately. Napalm, the jungle, gun powder, death, the intense heat and terrible humidity, all types of explosions, jets dropping bombs, artillery, and small arms fire. Each of those has a distinctive smell, and you pretty much knew what each explosion was, after you'd lived through it for a period of time.

We didn't go back very far; the firing had died down considerably. I remember it was quiet while I was lying there; I had this serenity about me. The war was over for me and my friends John St. Peters and George Miller. John and George were dead, and I didn't know if I was going to live or not, but I did know the war was over for us.

At the time, it gave me a lot of relief, that all the misery and suffering was going to be behind me, one way or another. What I didn't know was that later on, down the road, I would suffer from survivor's guilt, knowing that I was safe and everybody else was still in harm's way, with many of my buddies wounded or killed. But that's something we had no way of knowing about; that's just part of combat. We were a small cluster of brothers, doing the best we could, so everybody took John St. Peters' and George Miller's deaths as terrible losses. I knew my condition was failing; I could feel the warm blood flowing from my back wound, which had not been patched. I had the general feeling that things were not going to end well. I lay there for four hours, retaining consciousness.

Colonel Fulton later told us that he had to suspend medevacs because they were shooting the helicopters down so fast. He said it was one of the worst things he ever had to do in his military career. He knew there were people who needed help, but they were unable get us out.

After a while, Captain Menner bent down, and we talked briefly. He said, "I'll get you out on the next chopper." They had suspended medevac choppers earlier in the day, but there were still ammo choppers flying. They would swoop in low, hardly if ever land, except maybe for a second, kick off ammo, food and water, then take off. This was normal procedure; ammo choppers were never around much, as they were in great peril.

At 2230 hours that night, an ammo chopper swooped in to where I was waiting. I'm not sure who had gotten me to that area, but I do remember being thrown on the deck of the chopper and told to hang on. I had to hang on with my right arm; my left arm was immobilized. The bullet had passed through my left lung, rib cage, and muscle tissue. I grabbed hold of something with my right arm – I'm not sure what – and the chopper took off at a great, steep angle forward. As I heard the chopper lift up and move off, I was sure that my time in Vietnam was over. I still had the feeling that I should have been down there with my guys. That's the only thing that had kept us together. We had no support back home, other than our immediate family. Even our indirect families were kind of oblivious to what we were going through. We were our own family, and, over a period of time in the years that followed, we would realize that we were all we had.

After I was picked up by the chopper, there was a short ride, to where, I have no idea. I can only guess that it was the USS Colleton, a Navy ship out in the bay. I remember landing and guys lifting me off the helicopter. They took me down a long gangway for some reason. I don't think the ship was equipped for medevac choppers; they had problems getting me into their sickbay. Nonetheless, I ended up in a canvas bunk, lying there, and I remember they started putting all kind of IV's in me – left arm, right arm, left leg. I remember the urgency. I knew I had lost of lot of blood; they were trying to stick me everywhere to put blood back in me. Somewhere, I heard the words, "We need to hurry." Then I kind I perked up a little bit. Maybe it was the blood going into me, I don't know. I looked around and saw my friend Larry Garner from my hometown, Anderson, Indiana. In my mind, I wondered, "Is this real, or is this a dream?"

We all had nicknames for each other. Mine was "El Rico," pronounced "ricko," and his was "Root." Larry walked up to me and whispered, "El Rico, how you doin'?" With that, I knew it probably wasn't a dream.

I said, "Root, I need a drink of water. I've been laying in that swamp for four hours." The medical staff wouldn't let him give me any water, but he did get a gauze pad and soak it full, as if to cool down my forehead. Instead, he snuck me sips of water as he sat there with me. I would never really know why Larry Garner was there. He would later tell me something about being on sick call. Larry died in a traffic accident in the '70s. I lay there, while they were inserting all these tubes in me, and although it was painful, it wasn't that big a deal. I was already starting to get survivor's guilt. I was in a nice, comfortable, air conditioned ship with clean sheets. And even though my life might have been in jeopardy, I was starting to be concerned about the guys who were still out there fighting. It was 2330 hours at night, and I knew they were in deep, deep combat. And that bothered me more than anything else.

After a period of time, they started working on me, and I remember thrashing around because of a cramp. They said I had to remain still; I was pulling all the IV tubes out. "I can't help it. My back hurts," I said. They turned me over, and there was nothing there but the wound. Maybe it was the loss of blood.

Suddenly I woke up and it was two days later. I guess they had given me something to put me to sleep. I looked around and appeared to be in a Quonset hut of some kind. I looked to each side and across the aisle, trying to raise my head. I was too weak, and to think, just a few days before I was probably in the best physical shape of my life. I saw all the tubes in me – in my nose, in my chest, in my legs. I decided I wasn't ready to face it, so I went back to sleep.

Finally I woke up later, after I don't know how long, and all the tubes were gone, except for the tube in my chest. I felt better about that. I lay there for a while, trying to get my bearings, just looking around. Across the aisle there were several guys looking at me. I'm not sure if they had a pool on whether I'd make it or not, but one of them said, "He's awake." I lay there for another day without saying a word or doing anything, just lying there, glad to be alive.

After a couple more days, they came to tell me they were transferring me to another ward and I still needed to be very careful. They didn't really explain much. The next day I left and went to the new ward. I hadn't eaten in several days; I didn't feel like it and really had no appetite. But after they brought trays around, and I began smelling the food, and it smelled good. I felt hungry. I asked the sergeant, "Can I get a tray?"

He said, "Well, yeah, you can get up and get your own tray." And then he left.

I laid there a little bit, thinking, "Boy, that food really smells good. I'm going to get up and get something to eat." So I got up, rolling around a bit, and got dizzy, barely getting to the tray cart. After retrieving a tray, I got dizzy again making my way back to my bed, laid the tray down and collapsed. I was sick and couldn't eat.

After a long while, the guy in the next bunk said, "Are you done?"

I said, "Yeah, I can't eat."

"I'll take it back for you."

I thanked him. I was completely sick and couldn't function.

The Red Cross had given each of us a little white box with the Red Cross on it. Inside were envelopes, paper, a small shaving kit, soap, and whatever. Mine had been sitting on the end of my bunk for quite a while. Then I looked at myself. I still had dried blood on me from my wounds, which I had gotten at least a week prior. I thought, "I need to clean up and shave." In my own mind, I decided if I could get up and get my own tray, I could get cleaned up. I asked someone where to clean up, and they said to walk outside. There was a small table there with a bucket and running water. There, I could shave and whatever I needed to do. After a while, I finally got out to the table and was doing pretty well. I was almost shaved, and it felt good. I was starting to feel clean. A female captain came out and asked, "Are you Specialist Richey?"

Of course, I tried to stand as best I could. "Yes, ma'am."

"What are you doing out here?"

"Well, I'm trying to clean up. I haven't been clean for at least a week."

"You're not supposed to be out of bed," she said.

"No one told me that. In fact, I figured if I could get up and get my own food tray, I had permission to get up."

"Who told you that?" she asked.

"Well, this sergeant did."

Turns out, she had come to get me for surgery. I had no idea that I hadn't been sewn up from the wound. I was bandaged, but not sewn up. And I was still bleeding and had complications and infections.

"You get on this gurney right here," she demanded.

Then they wheeled me through the ward, and I watched as she commenced to chewing this sergeant up one side and down the other, which I thought was great, since he'd been so nasty to me.

Later, during the surgery, when the pain became too intense, that captain was there stroking my hair to comfort me, all the way through the procedure.

Things went smoothly for a few more days, and then I was transferred to Long Binh Air Force Base. From there, I flew to Tachikawa, Japan, thanks to the U.S. Air Force. It was the first time I'd felt air conditioning in a long time, and it really felt good.

I flew into Tachikawa and was transferred by bus to the 249th General Hospital in Tokyo, where I was stationed for two months with no pay. The one thing I remember about the 249th, was that everyday was the same. You wake up, eat breakfast, lunch and dinner, and the next day you woke up and did the same thing. The only break we had was that we were able to read. I read every paperback in the library and walked all I could. We weren't allowed to wander too far; we only had pajamas on. Life was short and tedious, but it did fill the bill.

Later on, during my stay there, they came around and told me I was going to be sent back to the United States. My injuries dictated that I would not be combat-ready for at least six months. I was put on a helicopter and flown back to the Air Force base and staged to come home. That was September 1967. After a seventeen-hour flight, we landed at Andrews Air Force Base. Our plane taxied to the terminal, and I got off and boarded a bus. We sat there for a while, and this full-bird colonel got on the bus, and the first name he mentioned was mine.

I thought, "What'd I do now?"

He walked back to where I was sitting and thanked me for serving in Vietnam and being a good soldier, just offering appreciation from one fellow American to another. It was kind of nice.

The next couple of days were spent at the hospital at Andrews, and then they flew me in a small plane to Fort Knox, where I spent almost a week. It was at Fort Knox that all of these emotions I was experiencing really set in. I was almost home and angry about the whole situation of what we'd been through, and the fact that nobody cared. I was two hundred miles away from home and didn't care if I got there or not.

After about a week in the hospital at Fort Knox, I called my parents and told them to come get me, but not to bring the girl I had been dating. For some reason, I didn't want to see her, even though I cared about her. I just had too much stuff going on. Saturday morning I was signing out of the hospital and in walks my family, early, and they had brought the young lady. There I was, embarrassed and standing in my pajamas, angry. I got home, and the next day we had a big dinner. I couldn't stand being around all the people, so I went outside to wash my car, just to have something to do. After that, I took the young lady home and never took her out again. To this day, I'm sorry about that, I really cared for her. I just had too many emotions going on at the same time.

I had pretty much an uneventful leave and then returned to Fort Knox. It was there that I had a slight setback, coughing up blood and spending another week in the hospital. I managed to serve the rest of my time, and I was discharged from the military on May 17, 1968, exactly two years to the day.

After about twenty years of trying to forget and get back to living, I decided I wanted to reconnect with some of the guys, especially Captain Menner. I knew he lived in Boonville, Indiana, so once when I was going fishing with some friends, I called him up. I told him who I was, and he said he didn't know that I had survived. He had no idea of my fate, where I had gone, or where I was transferred. We had a really nice visit. He was the first person I had reconnected with, other than the ones I had come home with, and some of them were licking their wounds also.

In the early '90s, there was a Mobile Riverine Force reunion scheduled in Las Vegas. I had started compiling addresses and phone numbers, and I sent everyone the information I had about the event. I wrote one letter to Sam Saavedra, my platoon sergeant, who was next to me when I was wounded. I said in the letter, "I hope to see you at the reunion." I knew he lived in California and thought we could reconnect in Vegas. I didn't receive any kind of response and thought that was odd. But I was assured by others that he was going to be there, so Bill Imel and I went ahead and flew out to Las Vegas. Bill was in Bravo Company and had been wounded on May 2nd, 1967.

When we arrived at the reunion, I went to the hospitality room and there sat Sergeant Saavedra on a barstool. I walked up to him and said, "Sergeant, you don't look much different." He was maybe a little grayer and a little heavier. I then said, "You don't know who I am, do you?"

He said, "No."

I told him that I was Mike Richey. So he kind of looked me up and down and said, "Pull your shirt up." I had to pull my shirt up to show him the wound that he knew I had received on June 19th. Only then did he believe I was still alive. He later said that he hadn't known if someone was playing a cruel joke when he got all the letters from me. "I was pretty sure we put Richey in a body bag," he said.

Over the years, several others would also tell me that they didn't know I survived.

On November 1st, 1999, after getting drafted together, going through basic training together, shipping out together, and getting wounded together, Rodney Compton and I both retired from the Guide Lamp Division of General Motors.

And I'm still glad just to be alive.

The following was written by Carolyn Wininger, the mother of Private First Class George "Danny" Miller of Bravo Company, 3rd Battalion, 47th Infantry Regiment, 9th Infantry Division, who was killed on June 19th, 1967, after saving a buddy's life.

From the muddy fields of Vietnam two years ago today, God reached out and touched our Dan, and took his life away. We don't know if he suffered, we did not see him die, we only know he is gone from us, and we couldn't say goodbye.

This was written by George Daniel Miller's cousin Sandy Weesner and his uncle William Bronner on November 24th, 2004.

Danny, how we wish we could've grown old together, watching our children and grandchildren play and grow. We never got the chance; you were taken from us far too soon. The day you died, saving a buddy's life, made you a hero...but it also broke our hearts. We still talk about you often and you still live within our memories. Even after all these years, we still miss you Danny, and we know someday we will see one another again.

A PCF and two LCM-8 landing crafts escorting a captured enemy trawler.

Secretary of the Navy Paul H.Nitze visiting the Navy in Nam.

On June 15th, 1966, Harbor Clearance One, using two medium craft borrowed from the British, raised the French river steamer Paul Bert.

Coast Guard Cutter Point Slocum on Market Time patrol

4/47th Infantry aboard USS POPE. *Bot Right* Bill Reynolds, Jimmie Salazar, *Top Right* Mario Lopez and Ray Layman *Top*. Idoluis Cesares. *Left Standing* Ron Schworer. USO Show *middle right and Bottom*

Rodney Compton (IN) with Steve Aldrich (CA) behind him on LST.

Benny Whitney (KY) holding the flag with Jack Whitehead (OK) holding the entrenching tool.
Mike Richey (IN) leaning against platoon motto sign.

Top Left Bob Geier.   *Top Right* Bill Reynolds with a Mekong Delta girl.
September '67 survivors of Jack Benedick's 2nd Platoon Charlie 4/47th, and patrol.
Bottom left Idoluis Casares, Willie McTear and Bob Ehlert at Camp Bearcat.

Gregg Ritter with captured prisoner, 2nd Platoon, Charlie Company 3/47th Infantry.
Danny Mosier and Mike Richey with captured Russian Flag. Arms cache.
Copter assault. 3rd Platoon Charlie Company 3/47th Infantry falling out.

NAVAL COMBAT

On March 6th, 1967, PBR 124 of River Section 532 was on patrol on the Mekong River during the early evening hours when Seaman David G. Ouellet observed suspicious activity near the river bank and alerted his boat captain, recommending they move the boat to the area to investigate. While the river patrol boat was making a high-speed run along the river bank, Seaman Ouellet spotted an incoming enemy grenade falling toward the boat. He immediately left his protected position on the forward gun mount and ran aft for the full length of the speeding boat, shouting to his fellow crew members to take cover, pushing his boat captain down to safety. In the split second that followed the grenade's landing, and in the face of certain death, Seaman Ouellet fearlessly placed himself between the deadly missile and his shipmates, courageously absorbing most of the blast fragments with his own body in order to protect his shipmates from injury and death. His heroism and courageous action on behalf of his comrades at the expense of his own life were in the finest tradition of the United States Navy. Seaman David G. Ouellet became the second Game Warden sailor to be presented the Medal of Honor. It was awarded posthumously.

In the early morning hours of March 14th, PCF 78 based at Chu Lai was involved in a two-hour action that blocked an enemy infiltration attempt and netted a large amount of weapons six miles south of the enemy base. When the Swift's crew members approached and were about 100 yards from the enemy trawler, they illuminated the vessel with a search light. Immediately, a big explosion shook the Swift, its port engine suddenly going sluggish. At first, Patrol Officer Lieutenant Junior Grade Kelly McCutchen Jr. thought they had been hit by an enemy mortar round, that was a near miss. When the trawler turned her stern to the Swift, the sailors knew something was up. So the Swift made a sharp right, and then another round went off astern. Shortly after, the enemy started throwing .50 cal at the Swift, so the sailors turned their stern to the trawler and got out as fast as possible.

The Swift boat had been ordered by the on-scene commander, the commanding officer of the destroyer radar picket ship USS Brister, DER 327, to cut off a suspicious contact headed for the beach. The Coast Guard cutter Point Ellis was also ordered to the area. The sailors had gained contact with the trawler by radar, but it was still very dark and they couldn't see her. So they waited around thirty minutes until first light and as soon as they saw the trawler on the beach, they opened fire on her and on the beach, to prevent anyone onboard from leaving or to stop attempts to off-load. But within minutes, the trawler had disintegrated from a violent explosion inside her hull, leaving a tremendous cloud of white smoke. The shock wave of the explosion was so strong that the Brister crew reported feeling it three miles away. After the cloud of smoke cleared, all that could be seen of the trawler was a small portion of her hull, but soon the incoming tide covered it. The Swift was joined by PCF 16, the Brister, and Point Ellis, remaining in the area until late afternoon firing in the tree line to prevent the enemy from recovering anything from the beach and from the submerged trawler hull.

Then USS Brister dispatched a motor whale boat with four sailors to go ashore and see what was scattered on the beach. The four sailors, covered by Coastguardsmen aboard Point Ellis, recovered Claymore mines, cases of blasting caps, cases of rifle ammunition, bolt-action rifles, heavy automatic weapons, packages of spare parts for weapons and plastic explosives. As soon as it was determined - by the Brister shore party and a Navy Underwater Demolition Team which investigated the sunken hull - that salvage would be worthwhile, U.S. Marines were landed by helicopters to set up a defensive perimeter. Salvage crews then went to work. The trawler was the sixth captured or sunk by Operation Market Time units along the northern coast of South Vietnam. There were no friendly casualties, but the Swift sustained moderate damage from the trawler's automatic weapons fire. Enemy casualties were unknown.

On March 15th, a large mine exploded between two speeding river patrol boats on the lower Long Tau, throwing a column of water 150 feet into the air. But the mine, which was evaluated as a command-detonated device, caused no casualties. PBRs of River Section 513 based at Vinh Long killed two Viet Cong and destroyed a sampan later that night. The patrol spotted and illuminated two sampans with three persons aboard, and at the same time, came under small-arms fire from the riverbank. One sampan occupant was seen holding a rifle. The PBRs took the sampans under .50 cal and grenade fire, killing two of the men and destroying one sampan. Machinegun fire also suppressed the small-arms fire from the riverbank.

PBRs from Nha Be were hit by nearly everything in the enemy's armory in the early morning hours of March 16th, while on a routine patrol of the Long Tau in the Rung Sat. The two river patrol boats were illuminated with a flare and then began receiving heavy machinegun, 57mm recoilless rifle and anti-tank rocket fire from the riverbank. The patrol quickly cleared the area, but returned after being reinforced by another patrol, with the four PBRs gaining the advantage and suppressing enemy fire. One boat was damaged by a recoilless rifle hit with one crewman wounded. Seawolves made a strike on the area following the departure of the PBRs.

Later that afternoon, PBRs and an Army helicopter team joined forces to aid a merchant ship, the SS Conqueror, which was under recoilless rifle attack on the Long Tau channel heading into Saigon. The enemy fire was suppressed but not before the ship had been hit six times, wounding three crewmen. Two seriously wounded were transported by PBRs to Nha Be for first aid. Further south, Viet Cong who had opened fire upon a spotter aircraft found themselves on the receiving end of 81mm mortar fire from PCF 11, which was based at An Thoi. The enemy was silenced quickly and withdrew.

On the afternoon of the following day, Game Warden units helped fight off an attack by an estimated 200 Viet Cong on a Vietnamese outpost near Tra On, on the Bassac River. The fire support supplied by the PBRs and Army artillery caused two huge explosions, sending a fireball and smoke seventy feet into the sky. The Vietnamese outpost commander later credited the PBRs with killing sixteen of the enemy.

Off the Cau Mau Peninsula, the southernmost point of land in South Vietnam, on the afternoon of March 19th, PCF 94 crewmen killed all five occupants of a sampan when they ignored a warning shot and attempted to swim to the beach. VC supplies and a M-1 rifle were later recovered from the sampan.

On the next afternoon, approximately twenty-five persons in green uniforms were sighted from the Coast Guard cutter Point League on a beach at the mouth of the Co Chien River. Upon seeing the cutter, the VC ran into bunkers and huts. After the Point League received permission to fire, and calling in PCF 98, the position was blasted with 81mm mortar rounds, producing two secondary expositions. In a similar incident the same day, PCFs 38 and 68 received automatic weapons and small-arms fire after closing the beach to investigate ten men seen running along the dunes. Counter fire from the Swifts destroyed four bunkers and caused two massive explosions.

Also on that day, PCF 65 detained five young men who were later determined to be Viet Cong. The men were taken off several small junks because they weren't carrying draft cards. And in the final action of the 20th, PCF 72 gave gunfire support to a spotter aircraft being fired on by the enemy. The action continued on the following day when PCF 66 fired mortar rounds to neutralize a position near Tuy Hoa that was being used by the enemy to fire on Vietnamese Navy junks. And last but not least, Swifts 38 and 68 started fires in enemy bunkers near the mouth of the Co Chien River, which had been bombarded the proceeding day.

March 22nd was another eventful day for PBR crewmen, with three major firefights reported. In one incident, four of five Viet Cong occupants of a motor-propelled sampan were taken under fire when they beached their craft and attempted to flee into the brush after being approached by Can Tho-based PBRs 31 and 32. As the patrol boats neared, additional VC along the riverbank opened fire on the patrol boats. The PBRs then opened up, killing four of the fleeing men. One PBR received light damage, but there were no friendly casualties. Patrol Officer was Chief Petty Officer Paul J. Hendrix.

The same day, newly-assigned men on a training exercise on PBRs 59 and 60, also based at Can Tho, found their training more realistic than planned when VC gunners opened up on the boats with automatic weapons from three positions along the Bassac River. The PBRs returned fire while moving down river and suffered no casualties.

The third incident of the day occurred when PBRs received small-arms fire on the Long Tau. One boat received light damage, but again there were no casualties. Seawolves and fixed-wing aircraft were called in and delivered strikes on the VC positions.

The next day turned out to be another action-filled day when patrol boats went to the aid of a Vietnamese Navy river convoy that was being fired on by recoilless rifle, mortars and automatic weapons from approximately twenty-five positions. The PBRs provided covering fire for the withdrawal of the convoy, with Patrol Officer Chief Grant E. Fuqua spotting artillery fire directed at the enemy positions.

Other actions included an ambush from the banks of the Bassac in which at least 200 rounds of .50 cal were directed at patrol boats. A helicopter fire team called in by Patrol Officer First Artley Driggers helped suppress enemy fire with no casualties suffered. Also during that day, the PBRs supported a Vietnamese troop landing with fire and blocking support, and, still later in that busy day, PBRs 34 and 36, commanded by Patrol Officer Chief Billy D. Strength, blasted a VC combat hamlet with machinegun, grenade, and automatic rifle fire, while receiving small-arms fire in return. Another relatively routine firefight also took place on the Ham Long, when PBRs found themselves the targets for automatic weapons fire. They responded with machineguns, grenades, and automatic rifles themselves, as well as a call for artillery.

On March 24th, Minesweeper Boat 31, based at Nha Be, was rocked by what was later confirmed to have been a Claymore mine detonated on the west bank of the Long Tau channel. MSB 31, which was conducting a routine sweep at the time with MSB 18, received superficial hull damage, but none of the crew was injured. Immediately after the large explosion, small-arms fire was received. The fire was returned by the MSBs and river patrol boats with helicopter gunships joining in, hitting the enemy positions. It was the third attack of the month on the minesweeper boats and the second utilizing a Claymore mine. No casualties were suffered, a sharp contrast to February, when two sailors were killed and sixteen wounded during numerous attacks on the minesweepers as they battled to keep the vital shipping channel to Saigon open.

The Coast Guard cutter Point Partridge turned its mortar fire on enemy positions near the mouth of the Bassac River on the same day, setting off a brush and petroleum fire besides destroying several VC structures. PCF 89, along with Coast Guard cutter Point Comfort, found themselves called on to hit a somewhat out of ordinary type of target the next day when enemy cave positions were discovered that could only be hit from seaward fire. The Market Time units successfully lobbed mortar rounds into the caves, resulting in three explosions.

An unusual type of attack was made against a Navy Seawolf gunship March 26th. The enemy attempted to down the bird by exploding a charge underneath it as it was gaining altitude during takeoff from the landing ship USS Jennings County. The Viet Cong succeeded in raising a large cloud of dust and debris about 150 feet into the air, but the Seawolf flew off unscathed. Also, a nearly daily occurrence was fire support given to Vietnamese outposts under VC attack. A typical such action happened at the end of the month when enemy forces attempted to overrun a Vietnamese outpost on the Co Chien River, attacking from three sides. Game Warden PBRs patrolling nearby brought their .50 cal machineguns into play and called in Seawolves for additional support. The two-pronged Navy punch was too much for the VC, who broke off the attack and ran.

Also on that day, it was confirmed that forty-four of 197 persons detained by Market Time forces while trying to escape from the area of Operation Pershing were, in fact, Viet Cong.

The Coast Guard cutter Point Cypress had good fortune on the next day when it hit enemy structures alone a beach in a VC controlled area of Vinh Binh Province known as the Long Toan Secret Zone. Eight camouflaged structures were destroyed.

On March 31st, 1967, Captain Paul N. Gray relieved Captain Burton B. Witham as Commander River Patrol Force, Task Force 116, Game Wardens. Before Witham was relieved, Rear Admiral Norvell G. Ward, Commander Naval Forces, Vietnam, commended him for a job well done as the head of operations of the river patrol force.

On April 1st, 1967, Helicopter Combat Support Squadron One was disestablished and commissioned as Helicopter Attack (Light) Squadron Three, HA(L)-3. The Seawolves of Helicopter Combat Squadron One received initial temporary additional duty orders for six months. Around Christmas, they were changed to permanent change-of-station orders. During the changeover all the Helicopter Combat Support Squadron One personnel were absorbed by HA(L)-3 when it was commissioned. The first Naval helo fire teams had done a heck of a job considering the Army had given them only six birds initially. Pilot Frank Koch of Detachment 29 had put one of them in the river off My Tho, and the Army gave them a replacement. Detachment 25 also crashed one, and it was replaced as well.

It was originally understood that the agreement with the Army indicated that Army personnel would perform the maintenance on the helicopters which is why there weren't any Navy maintenance personnel assigned at first, just air crewmen. The Naval aviators thought that when a bird came due for a periodic inspection, every twenty-five hours, they would just fly the bird into the maintenance depot at Vung Tau and pick up a replacement. But it didn't work that way. When the Navy fire teams flew into Vung Tau, the Army expected them to wait their turn until they got around to it. The Seawolves knew if they had done that, the river patrol boats would have been without gunship cover for a week or more, patrolling the many dangerous rivers and canals, and that couldn't happen. Fortunately, someone was thinking ahead. The air crewmen held a variety of aviation rates, so they ended up doing the inspections and basic repairs themselves, which made their turnaround time a day or two at the most, instead of a week or two, and they were able to return to patrolling alongside the PBRs.

One other item of interest concerning those early Seawolf crews was that the decks on the LSTs were so small that only one chopper could engage its rotors at a time, so one helo would take off before the second could engage its rotors to follow. And after returning home, the first helo would have to land and shut down its engine before the second could do likewise. It was said night takeoffs were especially hairy because the helos usually had no visual references and were normally at their max gross weight with all the armor and ammo. For this reason, they took on only enough fuel for about an hour airborne, leaving little room for error. Originally given UH-1B Hueys with the narrow rotor blades, they later retrofitted them with the wider blades to provide more lift.

Lieutenant Commander William A. Rockwell awarded ninety-eight Air Medals to the sixteen Seawolf Detachment 29 personnel in a ceremony onboard USS Hunterdon County. The detachment had flown more than 325 combat missions in support of Operation Game Warden since arriving in Vietnam ten months earlier. Lieutenant Frank Koch with Det-29, the first gunship fire team to arrive in-country, had been awarded fifteen Air Medals and had the privilege of being the first person to detach from HA(L)-3 in May of 1967. By then they did have maintenance personnel assigned, in addition to the air crewmen who could also perform maintenance.

The men who flew in Helicopter Combat Support Squadron One cut a trail for all Seawolves to follow by making the difference in waterborne battles involving Navy patrol boats. Flying in to the rescue, they often stayed aloft of the battle areas all day, and truly earned the reputation of being the Cavalry of the Mekong Delta.

Another first took place during April when the Seventh Fleet tank landing ship, USS Kemper County, LST 854, landed eight tanks at high noon fifty miles south of Chu Lai on a VC-controlled beach. Heavy fire was taken by the 3rd Battalion Seventh Marines, although A4 and F8 jets and Huey copters made strafing runs in what was believed to be the first tank landing since the Korean conflict. An underwater demolition team detachment from UDT-

11 made a preliminary survey of the beach and was in the water three hours prior to the landing. One year earlier, Kemper County and her "Happy Hundred," as the crew was called, had gone to the rescue of the Panamanian tanker, SS Paloma, which lay burning and adrift in the Saigon River after a Viet Cong attack. On reaching the scene, Kemper County shelled the river bank from which the communist attack had been launched, driving off the enemy with cannon fire. Then the LST went alongside to help extinguish fires and render first aid to the Paloma's crew.

And so it went, with firefights a daily routine for the valiant coastal and river patrol crewmen and their Seawolf gunship support. But mercy missions were also numerous, so numerous as to become nearly routine. Some twenty-four wounded Vietnamese Popular Force soldiers and civilians were medically evacuated the morning of April 5th alone. The boats participating in the mission were from River Section 522, based at the new Tan Chau base. And then there was a woman who gave birth to a baby boy on PBR 138 while its crew rushed her to the hospital at Vinh Long. Patrol Officer First Ronald W. Yohe and Boat Captain Second Jerry A. Barlow of River Section 523 were happy to be of assistance.

PCF 92 of Operation Market Time went into action off the coast of An Xuyen Province near Ca Mau Point on April 7th when it was led by two evading sampans to enemy positions on the coast that included a camouflaged metal building. The Swift was taken under fire by four persons in a sampan trying to escape ashore, but they were hit by the Swift's .50 cal fire. The An Thoi-based craft then put twenty-four rounds of 81mm mortar fire on the enemy position.

The Coast Guard cutters Point Grace and Point League were in the spotlight April 8th when Point Grace received heavy automatic weapons and mortar fire while patrolling 2,000 yards off Vinh Binh Province. The Cat Lo-based cutter suppressed the enemy fire. And then Point League, also based at Cat Lo, spotted fifteen persons unloading a sampan near the mouth of the Mekong River. Upon receiving permission to open fire, the cutter caused a large explosion with 81mm mortar rounds.

But one of the most profitable single operations for Market Time forces was on the following afternoon when PCF 15 killed eight VC while supporting Operation Canyon. The Swift crewmen spotted two groups of armed men running from advancing Marines at the mouth of the Cua Dai River, about twenty miles south of Da Nang, when the Swift began receiving small-arms fire. The Swift swept the area with intense fire for five minutes before ceasing to let the Marines advance. The Marines counted eight bodies and recovered several weapons.

Saturday April 9th, was also another eventful day for Game Warden sailors when a supply sampan was destroyed with a large explosion, three ambushes were suppressed, an attack on a friendly outpost was repulsed, and a merchant ship under attack on the Long Tau was aided. The ship's crew said the mere presence of the PBRs caused the VC to cease fire on the ship and run.

On May 24th, two river patrol boats of River Section 531 were on patrol, silently drifting down the Ham Luong in the river's flow with their engines off. The two fiberglass patrol boats had just entered a small canal when several hidden enemy machineguns opened fire from heavy vegetation along the riverbank. A moment later, a 57mm recoilless rifle round soared across the water and hit the lead PBR just as its engines came to life. The forward gunner had swung his twin .50 cal machineguns toward the enemy, just as the round struck his gun mount, killing him. Shrapnel from the recoilless round swept the length of the PBR, hitting the coxswain and a seaman in the face, killing them both. With the radar dome blown off and no one at the helm, the boat began to circle out of control. The aft gunner, who was wounded but not badly, rushed to the coxswain's flat and took control. To do this he had to move the coxswain's body to get at the throttles and steering wheel. A second wounded crewman jumped on the aft .50 and pulled the trigger until the weapon burned off all its ammunition. He then grabbed an M60 and fired off several belts until it, too, was out of ammo.

While getting up to speed, the second PBR had taken a recoilless rifle round amidships, ripping a hole in the armor plate, killing the Vietnamese policeman. The aft gunner was blown off the .50 cal and over the side, dead. The forward twin .50 cal gunner opened fire at the shoreline, which was lit up with muzzle flashes from communist weapons. Then the cover boat erupted in flames as the two patrol boats sped down river trying to recover from the brutal attack and get clear of the onslaught of fire.

The Viet Cong had lined the riverbank and island with three miles of a battalion, armed with automatic weapons and recoilless rifles. The two PBR's expended their remaining ammunition trying to escape the extended ambush as they reloaded again and again. The gunner who had taken the wheel of the cover boat radioed for air support, which didn't arrive until the boat had cleared the long contact area into the main river. Then the cover boat, burning and taking on water, sank until only its Styrofoam-filled bow stuck out of the water. The heavily damaged lead boat, also riddled by bullet holes with chunks missing, returned to pick up the survivors of the cover boat.

The frantic calls for help were heard back at headquarters by Naval officers listening in over the radio. But by the time a second PBR patrol had arrived on the scene, the battle was over and half of the two crews had been lost. The wounded were evacuated by helicopter to hospitals in Saigon. The sailors who were lost were Patrol Officer Lieutenant Charles Donald Witt, Boat Captain Electronics Technician Second Roy Lee Castleberry, Seaman Michael Courtney Quinn, Fireman Terry Franklin Leazer and the Vietnamese policeman. The survivors said Lieutenant Witt was lost while manning the forward fifties, which he loved to do.

Operation Game Warden was highlighted during the first few weeks of the month by firefights initiated by a PBR patrol from the LST USS Garrett County, headed by Quartermaster Chief T.M. Digenan. The fights killed ten of the enemy in two separate encounters on June 24th. In an area near the Bassac River mouth, Chief Digenan's two PBRs were busy inspecting four small sampans on the river when a fifth was seen entering the stream from a canal. Its two occupants turned their small boat back toward the canal after spotting the PBRs in midstream. They ignored warning shots as the Navy boats left the other sampans to give chase. When the PBRs drew closer, both men in black leaped from the sampan to swim for shore. Chief Digenan ordered his crew to open fire with machineguns, destroying the sampan and killing both men in the water.

Four hours later and about fifteen miles up river, the patrol spotted a sixty-foot junk escorted by a sampan coming into the river from a small canal. Sighting the patrol, the huge junk fled back into the canal. The Chief ordered his patrol to pursue the junk. As PBRs 56 and 58 entered the canal to close on the junk and sampan, the enemy opened fire with small-arms from both boats. Answering the fire with .50 cal and 40mm grenades, the PBR crewmen killed three occupants of the motorized sampan and blew up the junk, killing five more.

A U.S. Navy Swift boat was hit by enemy fire and sank in shallow water the next day, near the mouth of the Ganh Hoa River off the Mekong Delta. The Swift was on routine Market Time patrol about 150 miles south of Saigon when at 0730 hours it received recoilless rifle and machinegun fire from enemy positions on the beach. A 57mm recoilless rifle round tore a two-and-a-half-foot hole in the Swift's starboard bow. The Swift returned fire as she turned and headed seaward. Minutes later, the Swift sank in forty feet of water. Arriving on the scene, PCF 26, also based at Cat Lo, picked up the six crewmen and took the sailors to the LST USS Sedgwick County for copter evacuation. Later that day, PCFs 26 and 98 responded to an aircraft report of enemy movement in the same area where the Swift had been sunk earlier. Using mortars and machinegun fire, the Swifties killed twelve VC, destroying four bunkers and two sampans with what the spotters called outstandingly accurate fire. This was the second Swift boat lost to enemy action.

In a fierce battle on the Bassac June 28th, PBRs sank a fifty-foot junk and small sampan, but suffered three sailors wounded. The action began when a PBR patrol sped out after a small sampan which tried to evade back into the canal it had exited. The patrol could not penetrate deep into the canal because of obstructions, but spotted a fifty-foot junk making its way farther up the canal. The PBRs' warning shots were answered by automatic weapons fire from the junk and both sides of the canal, resulting in wounds to three PBR crewmen. A Seawolf fire team scrambled to the scene and began raking the enemy positions as the PBR patrol withdrew to the support ship USS Garrett County with the wounded. Meanwhile, a second PBR patrol arrived and made four firing runs on the junk and enemy shore positions, temporarily suppressing enemy fire. Two PBR crewmen volunteered to enter the water and attached lines to the enemy sampan, which had been beached. As they secured the lines to the sampan, the enemy opened up on the men. While fire was being exchanged by the boats and enemy, the two sailors were recovered unharmed. One PBR left the canal with the sampan in tow, but the enemy craft was so badly damaged that it sank.

The Seawolves again swooped in on the enemy positions as the fighting raged on, and soon the enemy weapons were silenced for a second time. Two more sailors entered the water and attached lines to the fifty-foot junk as enemy weapons again responded. The swimmers returned to their patrol boat under cover of .50 caliber machineguns, which permanently silenced the enemy positions. The junk sank as the PBRs pulled it into deep water.

The following day, four Nha Be-based PBRs came under heavy attack while patrolling the upper Dong Thanh River in the Rung Sat, nineteen miles southeast of Saigon. At 0800 hours, the PBRs of River Section 541 were hit with recoilless rifle rounds and automatic weapons fire from an estimated enemy heavy weapons squad, supported by an infantry platoon. One PBR received three direct hits from a 57mm recoilless rifle, wounding four sailors and the Vietnamese interpreter aboard the boat. Returning fire with their .50 cals and M60 machinegun, along with 40mm grenades, the PBRs fought their way out of the area. Calling in armed helicopters, the PBRs stood by while the gunships saturated the area with rocket and machinegun fire. Shortly thereafter, 105mm artillery from Vietnamese Marines opened up on the area.

On another occasion, the enemy attempted to lure two PBRs into the path of a Claymore mine exposition on June 29th. The PBRs were in pursuit of an evading sampan when the mine was set off as they entered a canal from the Bassac River. About the same time, automatic weapons and small-arms fire was received from both banks of the canal. The PBR patrol, which was from River Section 511 based on the LST Garrett County, was able to suppress the enemy fire with mortars, machineguns, and grenades. One sailor was wounded.

The next day, the enemy engaged Can Tho-based PBRs on the Bassac. The Navy had been alerted that about seventy Viet Cong would attempt to cross the river, so a blockade had been set. The action started when the PBR crews spotted a camouflaged sampan beached on the bank and moved in to investigate. The enemy opened up with intense automatic weapons and small-arms fire from the river bank, wounding two sailors. The PBRs responded with machinegun fire, killing four VC who had been firing from behind the sampan and also destroying the sampan. One patrol boat made a firing run at thirty or so men scurrying along the river bank.

The initial two boat patrol was later relieved by another PBR patrol, supported by a Seawolf fire team, which also encountered heavy enemy fire when it moved in to investigate a second sampan. The Seawolf gunships and PBRs saturated the area with machineguns, grenades and mortar fire, which silenced the enemy.

Two Seawolves hit the enemy hard July 1st, killing ten VC and destroying eleven sampans in the process. In the first action, Seawolves sighted and attacked enemy supply sampans on the Bai Lai River, fifty miles south of Saigon in a curfew area. In the initial attack, seven sampans were destroyed and one damaged, with eight VC killed. Flying a few miles west of the initial contact area, the helos detected and attacked another group of enemy sampans, destroying one, damaging one and killing two more Viet Cong.

On the morning of Sunday, July 2nd, the PBR sailors interrupted a supply mission on the upper Ham Loung River. The two-boat patrol from USS Harnett County surprised VC as they were unloading a large junk and sampan in a zone restricted from civilian traffic. The patrol took the enemy under fire, with the cargo handlers returning fire with automatic weapons and small-arms. The sailors destroyed the junk and sampan, accounting for five VC killed. PBRs returned to the same area the afternoon of Fourth of July and again hit the jackpot. The sailors were firing grenades onto the river bank to harass an enemy heavy weapons company reported in the area.

Suddenly, a gigantic secondary explosion rocked the area, sending flames soaring 500 feet into the air and 150 yards along the river bank. The fire burned for an hour and could be seen ten miles away.

A young sailor on his last combat mission before being rotated Stateside ignored bullets whizzing past his head and dropped from a helicopter into jungles of North Vietnam to rescue an injured Air Force pilot. Aviation Technician Anthony C. Hanson was aboard a Seawolf chopper searching for the downed Air Force pilot in the North Vietnam panhandle. The chopper found the crash site, but there was no sign of the pilot. With bullets flying about him, Hanson was lowered to within fifteen feet of the jungle floor. He let go and jumped into dense foliage to search for the missing pilot. After fifteen minutes, Hanson found the man semi-conscious, propped against a tree with his leg broken. The jungle was too dense for the helicopter hoist to penetrate, so Hanson dragged the pilot some fifty feet to a more accessible spot. There the pilot and Hanson were hoisted to safety, with the pilot later being transferred to a hospital to recover. Hanson resummed his trip home.

Petty Officer First Wayne G. Jones, a Navy SEAL, was manning a .50 cal machinegun aboard a large personnel landing craft supporting a SEAL fire team on a mission in the Rung Sat when a round hit him and knocked him across the back of the boat. It had gone partially through his flak jacket, through his fatigues and his T-shirt, leaving only a small puncture wound, just breaking the skin above his heart. "After my wife and two daughters," Jones said, "my flak jacket is my most prized possession!"

THE SEAMAN

L ate in the spring of 1967, units of River Section 533 were transferred from Nha Be to the support base at My Tho in Dinh Tuong Province. Their job was to patrol the rivers and canals of the area, inspect river craft for possible Viet Cong and North Vietnamese contraband, and seek out and capture or kill the enemy. Dinh Tuong Province, southwest of Saigon, was infested with Viet Cong guerrillas, so much so that Task Force 116 had positioned a Naval support base to support River Sections 531, 532, and 533. These were some of the first Mark I river patrol boats to arrive in South Vietnam. The thirty-one foot speed boats were the first time in which the U.S. Navy had used jet-pump propulsion systems rather than screws. This had made a huge difference in river warfare.

The patrol boats had become a major force protecting the waterways, allowing the locals to move freely and get to the market. And My Tho had a larger-than-average market place. The boats had also become the great nemesis of the Viet Cong, robbing them of the small canals and waterways that they had controlled just months earlier. The enemy was in a battle with the river patrol units to regain access of these waterways and wanted desperately to blow patrol boats out of the water or trap and capture them.

On January 18th, 1968, Seaman Albert "Pancho" O'Canas was checking the guns on PBR 112 of River Section 533, with his "go, no go" gauge, thinking maybe today was his day to get hit, which he always thought when they were about to go out on patrol in the highly contested Mekong Delta. Their call sign was "Hotel Patrol," and members of PBR 112 consisted of Boat Captain Gunner's Mate Second Aubrey "Spiderman" Spell, Seaman Allen Townsend, Fireman Bob Meade, and Seaman O'Canas. The patrol officer for the day was Lieutenant E.R. Dolan, who would be riding in PBR

112. The patrolmen of PBR 153 were Boat Captain Boatswain's Mate First Bill "Boats" Goldman, Seaman Fred Caufield, Gunner's Mate Seaman Duane Pulliam and Fireman Harlan "Mac" McPherson, with a Vietnamese maritime policeman riding on the cover boat as interpreter.

As the men of Hotel Patrol were proceeding on the My Tho River en route to their operations, they stopped to talk to Juliet Patrol for a moment, and then they continued on their way with PBR 112 in the lead and PBR 153 lagging behind. The lead river patrol boat had just passed a canal when two sampans came out into the open so that the cover boat could see them, trying to sucker them into an ambush. The sampans then reversed course, evading as Boat Captain Goldman took the helm, relieving McPherson, and radioed Lieutenant Dolan that they had an evading sampan. Dolan ordered Goldman to intercept, and PBR 112 made a 180-degree turn, closing in fast to support the cover boat. PBR 153 gave chase to the sampans and, as the boat closed on the river bank, cut its engines. With the boat drifting slowly, the crew called out to the sampans. At that, a Viet Cong platoon sprung up out of fighting holes and began firing. Rockets came burning out of the jungle, hitting 153, blowing the patrol boat into pieces.

"Sonofabitch," Pancho shouted, as the crew of PBR 112 opened up and commenced to fire on the enemy's positions the best they could, trying to cover their friends in trouble. The jungle filled with smoke as the sound of automatic weapons and small-arms crackled and rained down on the two fiberglass patrol boats, who were returning fire. Boat Captain Goldman, though seriously wounded, contemptuously defied the fire in the cockpit and looked up to see the Viet Cong laughing as he struggled to remain in control of PBR 153. The patrol boat had received two direct rocket hits: one exploded in the coxswain's flat, setting it on fire, seriously wounding Goldman, and the other impacted the radar dome, sending shrapnel every direction. Two additional B40s had passed through the hull without exploding. Every sailor on the boat suffered multiple wounds from the two blasts. Seaman Caufield was down and out. Mac McPherson alone was able to hold on to the aft .50 cal machinegun returning fire, although the blast blew his helmet into the river and almost knocked him off the boat. Pulliam, severely wounded, his eye hanging out, began to lay on the damaged front .50s, getting off a few bursts. A 57mm recoilless round came out on nowhere and slammed into the portside of the boat, knocking the crew down for a second time.

Smoke began to roll off PBR 153 as it went up in flames and drifted dangerously close to the river bank. Again, Mac was able to recover and man the aft .50, returning fire on the VC, who were dangerously close to swarming the boat. Fearing the worst, Fireman Mac McPherson made his way to the coxswain's flat and hit the throttles, and the boat started inching away from the bank. Then Mac returned to the aft .50 and resumed firing as he stood in the open, bleeding from multiple wounds, boldly resisting the enemy rounds that were zipping by him. The fire and smoke grew as Pulliam crawled off the front .50s, trying to escape the flames and get to safety.

Meanwhile, PBR 112, with Meade on the forward twin .50s, Pancho on the M60 amidships, and Townsend on the aft .50, with all guns in a thunderous return of fire, worked their way between the bank and PBR 153, trying to protect the damaged boat and recover the crew from the burning boat. Taking fire, Boat Captain Spell came alongside a little too hard and, when the two boats collided, knocked fireman Meade over the side into the brown water. Meade swam over and pulled himself up onto the burning 153 boat, to help the crew.

The two-boats of Juliet Patrol, hearing the call on the radio, rushed to the ambush site and commenced suppressive firing runs as they arrived. The jungle lit up with muzzle flashes, smoke and tracers while the crew of PBR 112 worked to save the patrolmen of the 153 boat. Pancho reached over and pulled the wounded Viet interpreter and his weapon aboard. Then Pancho pitched a fire extinguisher to Seaman Pulliam, but Pulliam was in no condition to do anything with it, as he was covered in blood and completely spent. Seeing this, they began concentrating on helping everybody off the burning boat. Meade and Pancho, after looking around, asked where Boat Captain Goldman was and somebody said he was still at the wheel. Meade and Pancho immediately jumped back over under heavy enemy fire and made their way into the burning coxswain flat, where they found Goldman on his knees, still clutching the wheel, semiconscious.

Goldman was a big man, over six-foot tall weighing around 225 pounds, but solid not fat. He was so strong that he had actually bent the wheel, and it took both Pancho and Meade to pry his hands off so they could get him out of the smoldering coxswain's flat. Meade started puking and told Pancho he couldn't take anymore as he jumped back aboard PBR 112, out of the bellowing, stinking, fiberglass smoke. Now Pancho, who was also weak from the fumes, wrapped his arms around Goldman and tried his best to get him out of the burning coxswain's flat and to the back of the boat. This was no small feat when you consider Pancho was a much smaller man. But he had a big heart and wasn't about to leave his big friend to the flames. His determination to save his buddy helped him work the wounded boat captain onto the engine covers, where rounds of small-arms were hitting all around them. Now completely exhausted from the smoke, fumes, and physical exertion, Pancho thought for sure they were both going to be killed.

Seaman Pancho O'Canas then started screaming at Goldman to help him, but was unsure if he could. Then Goldman seemed to come to, putting his arms down, as if to help. Pancho, in a sitting position, again started dragging him, his arms underneath Goldman's arms, while rounds zipped overhead and smoke sucked up the air. Goldman seemed to be coming around; while Pancho pulled, he began pushing with his legs and arms. Suddenly, Goldman's left shoulder popped out of its socket, exposing the bone. Pancho screamed again, but this time for Goldman to stop, as they had somehow managed to clear the smoke. By this time, the two boats of Juliet Patrol had come alongside to assist, and someone jumped aboard to help Pancho get Goldman off the burning boat. Realizing they had got all the patrolmen off, Pancho jumped on the aft .50, returning fire in anger for what the enemy had done to his friends. The crew of PBR 112 brought the boat alongside so Pancho could come back aboard as he jumped off the heavily damaged river patrol boat. Then PBR 112 immediately started heading to Dong Tam at flank speed to evacuate the wounded that were sprawled about the boat. PBR 112 aft .50 cal gunner, Seaman Allen Townsend, had already started attending to the wounded. The ambush had only lasted twenty minutes or so.

After getting underway, Pancho went to the forward deck where Goldman lay and started loosening his belt, applying water so Goldman's clothes wouldn't stick to his wounds. He began to clean off small pieces of Goldman's skull that were splattered all over his friend. Goldman mumbled, "Pancho, where are you?"

"I'm here Goldy," Pancho answered his friend.

Townsend and Meade continued first aid, yet thought to themselves that there was little chance the severely wounded crew was going to make it back.

U.S. Navy Seawolf gunships arrived overhead to cover the burning craft until a patrol from River Section 534 arrived to extinguish the fire. Then an air strike was called in after the Seawolves had expended their ordnance and moved off. Two Vietnamese A-1 Skyraiders conducted the strike, hitting the target with 250-pound bombs, Napalm, and 20mm cannon fire. Numerous VC were seen running from the ambush site during the air attack. The number of enemy casualties was undetermined, but two structures and two bunkers were destroyed and four more structures damaged, with the VC on the run.

When the patrol boats and wounded finally arrived at Dong Tam, there was an ambulance waiting. Everyone helped the wounded transfer over to the litters and medics. Pancho looked at McPherson, standing there with shrapnel wounds all over his body, but Mac didn't seem to want to get into the ambulance. So Pancho yelled at his friend to get his butt in the ambulance, and Mac, rather awkwardly, ran over and climbed in.

Patrol Officer Dolan was off bragging to some of the Army soldiers about all the action they had seen. Pancho got pissed and told him, "You can stay here and bullshit all you want. We are going back after the 153 boat." Then Pancho jumped aboard and told Boat Captain Spell to fire up the engines. Lieutenant Dolan looked at Pancho funny, but got aboard. The tension in the air was thick. When they returned to recover PBR 153, there was a Mike boat and additional PBRs who had already extinguished the fire and had the badly damaged PBR 153 in tow.

When they got back to My Tho, the first person waiting for them was their shipmate Gary Crest, who had been relieved by McPherson. Crest was feeling very bad about not being with his shipmates during the attack, but his tour was over and he was scheduled to return home. Crest was very moved by what he saw that day and later volunteered to go back to Nam for a second tour with the river patrol boats.

Later, Pancho was summoned to headquarters. His commanding officer, Lieutenant Jerry Sapp, reminded him that he was only a seaman and not an officer, and therefore should not be giving orders. Boat Captain Spell then stepped up in Pancho's defense and told Sapp that he never wanted Dolan on their boat again. The crew did not feel Lieutenant Dolan was a coward, but they did feel he was not suited for combat. Pancho just stood there, still soaked in his friend's blood.

Meade and Pancho went back to their room at the carter billet - PBR 112's crew all slept in the same room, as most boat crews did - and commenced to drink themselves silly, trying to drown their sorrows. A quartermaster first class came into their room and asked what happened. They started telling him about the ambush. The quartermaster replied, "You saw your chance for a medal." This had an adverse effect on the guys, as Pancho kicked him in the face and he and Mead started to beat his ass.

The Vietnamese interpreter died that night, becoming the only man lost in the ambush. Boat Captain Goldman lost use of his left arm and sight in one eye; later a plate was put in his head. He told Pancho that he had been ashamed to let his men know he was down. He had hollered for Caufield to take the wheel, but did not know Caufield was hit and down himself. Seaman Pulliam on the front .50s, was also wounded severely and lost one eye. Fireman Harlan McPherson was severely wounded but survived, with many considering him a hero for saving the boat and his shipmates that day. The United States Navy awarded him a Silver Star for bravery. The crew of PBR 153 had withstood heavy small arms fire and was hit by four B40 rockets and a recoilless rifle round and still answered with return fire.

On the night of January 17th, Golf patrol had been firing and calling in air strikes to the same area where the ambush occurred the next morning. Whoever briefed Hotel Patrol either didn't mention this, or the patrol officer chose to ignore it. There was a serious communication or misinformation problem somewhere. They didn't know it at the time, but Hotel Patrol had accidentally stumbled on a major Viet Cong staging area exactly two weeks before the 1968 Tet Offensive.

The following is an account of the battle through the eyes of Gunner's Mate Seaman Duane Pulliam, who survived to tell his story:

As I recall, it was approximately 0900 hours, and we on Hotel patrol were in route to our area of operations. We on the 153 boat were lagging behind 112 when we spotted the sampans. "Boats," called Dolan, saying something about the sampans and that we were intercepting. When we got fairly close to the bank, Goldman slowed 153 to a stop, and we were just sitting there with the engines idling. We did the usual shouting in Vietnamese "Li day," which translates into "you'd better get your sneaky little asses out here before we blow the shit out of you!" We sat there for a few seconds before I heard the first rocket fire. It was just a muffled whoosh. Before I could actually think about it, the rocket hit, and it seemed like the whole freaking world exploded in my face.

I have always believed that the first rocket hit the radar dome. When it hit, it felt like someone had slapped me upside the head with a sledge hammer. Something, I believe part of the radar dome, hit me in my left eye and tore my eyelid, or the blast slammed my face into the guns and that did it. Either way, it knocked me down in the gun tub. When I stood back up, I grabbed the guns but for some reason I couldn't seem to grip them. When I looked down at my hands and arms, I could see they were full of holes. Actually, I couldn't see worth a shit. So I went to feel for my eye and could feel part of it hanging down. I thought, Fuck, they shot my eye out. I was able to push the triggers on the guns and got off about ten to fifteen rounds when another rocket hit somewhere around the coxswain's flat and the boat immediately started burning. I don't remember if the second rocket knocked me down or not. Everything went into slow motion for a few seconds. After the second rocket hit, it was dead silent. I couldn't hear anything but the sound of the engines idling. I thought, Shit, everyone has been killed, and the fucking boat is burning up underneath me.

The interpreter was sitting on the bow beside the gun tub, without a helmet or flak jacket on. Because of the fire I had to crawl out of the gun tub. All of a sudden, it seemed like 10,000 AK47s opened up on us, with bullets hitting everywhere. I don't know if they were hitting the boat, but I could see them hitting the water all around the boat. I looked at the interpreter and thought he was dead because he wasn't moving and his head was all smashed in one side and his eyeball was bugged way out. I remember thinking, You should have worn your helmet and flak jacket, dumb fuck.

I didn't know whether to jump off the boat or not. I just remembered thinking that in Vallejo, during small boat training, they told us take off our flak jackets before jumping in the water because they would make us float. I thought, Shit, if I jump in the water, the bastards will shoot me, and if I stay on the boat, the bastards will capture me and then shoot me because I'm too shot up for them to want to screw with patching me up. I decided my best bet was in the water. I was sitting on the edge of the bow with my flak jacket off, ready to jump, when the interpreter grabbed my arm and was shaking his head no. I guess he was trying to plead with me not to leave him; anyway, I laid back down on the bow. That's when the aft .50 caliber started shooting. I thought, Thank you, God, some of the guys are still alive back there. The shooting went on for a few seconds and then the engines revved up and the boat started out toward the center of the river. I was able to hold onto the side of the canopy enough to make my way to the back of the boat. When I was going down the side is when the flag was blowing in my face and my blood got all over it. When I got to the back of the boat, I could see Mac at the wheel. Caufield was down by the engine covers, and I couldn't see Boats. With blood in my eyes, I couldn't see a hell of a lot of anything. I looked up and saw PBR 112 making a firing run between us and the ambush spot. I motioned with my arm for them to come over to us. I can still hear Pancho shouting over all the noise to the other guys on his boat "I think they need our help." PBR 112 made its firing run, and it seemed to have taken several minutes, but was actually only a few seconds. Then the boat came along side. Pancho had a fire extinguisher in his hands and said, "Here Pulliam, take this." But I couldn't grip anything with my hands so slippery, covered with blood, so I just held out my arms and Pancho laid the fire extinguisher in my arms and then jumped on the 153 boat with us.

Next thing I remember was crawling over the side of 153 onto the 112 boat. I vaguely remember someone throwing ammo from 153 over the side. When they got us all onboard and started back to Dong Tam, I remember lying down on the engine covers, trying to get warm. I was freezing may ass off. I told Dolan to put a poncho over me. I was cold, probably shock or loss of blood, I guess. I know my wounds hurt pretty badly. Felt like someone was poking me, sticking red hot steel rods into my body. I also remember thinking those little bastards really kicked our ass this time. Paybacks are a sonofabitch.

Of the nine sailors on Hotel Patrol involved in the Viet Cong ambush of January 18th, 1968, six were enlisted E3, four seamen and two firemen, with fireman being equal to a seaman, only in engineering. Neither had earned rate yet, but they were the workhorses of the U.S. Navy and proved time and time again that when it comes down to it, they could perform in the highest traditions of the Navy. And, even if they were young at the time and had very little power to command, they were still worth listening to. Thank God for the seaman.

ATTACK ON MY THO

During the Vietnamese Tet holiday period of 1968, a cease-fire truce was drawn up and declared by both North and South Vietnam to begin on January 29th and end on the February 3rd, allowing the Vietnamese time to travel home and be with their families. For a thousand years, the Vietnamese Lunar New Year had been a traditional celebration that had brought the Vietnamese a sense of happiness, hope and peace. Shortly before the truce began, the Mobile Riverine Force had been ordered to western Dinh Tuong Province and the eastern part of Kien Phong Province to prevent the enemy from using communication routes running east and southeast through that area.

There had been continuous credible intelligence reports of enemy activity within these districts. Accordingly, four bases were established, three along the Rach Ruong Canal from the My Tho to an agroville, which was one of the many agricultural resettlement areas established by President Diem early on in the war. Three CH-47 helicopters were used to set down the artillery on the agroville site, and the battery was laid and ready to fire by 1800 hours on January 29th, the beginning of the Tet truce. The fourth base was just off Highway 4, about a mile north of the river. The Mobile Riverine Force elements met only sporadic sniper fire while moving, but the CH-47s were fired upon with .50 caliber machineguns.

Two of the 2nd Brigade's battalions, in addition to defending the fire support bases, actively patrolled the surrounding areas, aided by radar surveillance equipment mounted on the Alpha assault patrol boats. The first violation of the truce occurred just three hours after it began, at 2100 hours on January 29th, when fifteen rounds of 82mm mortar fire fell on one of the riverine fire support bases, but without causing any damage or casualties. No further enemy activity occurred during the remainder of the evening, with the riverine force dispersed to ambush positions to prevent major enemy movement, just in case.

At 1000 hours the next day, the Military Assistance Command, Vietnam, cancelled the Tet truce because of attacks on cities in the III Corps Tactical Zone to the north of Saigon. Because of this, riverine forces were directed to resume offensive operations, with particular attention to defense of headquarters complexes, logistical installations, airfields and population centers and military billets, where troops were lodged. While two companies of the 3/47th Infantry remained to provide security for the fire support base, the rest of the battalion and the 3/60th Infantry conducted patrols east toward Cai Be. At the end of the day, forty suspects had been detained, with forty bunkers destroyed and several caches found. But the enemy's intentions were not fully known until the massive Tet Offensive was launched in the early morning hours of January 31st, against My Tho, Ben Tre, Vinh Long, Sa Dec, Cai Be and Chau Doc cities in the Mekong Delta, as well as Saigon, Da Nang, Hue and just about every other city and military installation throughout the Republic of Vietnam.

Task Force 116 units played a prominent role in the defense of several of these cities that came under attack during the communist offensive. At the one-time quiet provincial city My Tho, SEAL Team Two members and PBR crewmen from River Section 533 augmented the defense of U.S. billeting areas in the city while patrol boats attacked VC units from the waterways adjacent to My Tho and Ben Tre. My Tho was attacked by an estimated 1,200 Viet Cong of the 263rd and 514th Main Force Battalions, and the attack on Ben Tre was launched by Viet Cong forces of the 518th and the 516th Local Force Battalions. Navy Seawolf helicopter fire teams flew in support of My Tho and Ben Tre almost continuously. At Cai Be and Cai Lay, the attack was conducted by the 261st Main Force Battalion, supported by the 504th and 530th District Companies and local force Viet Cong guerrillas. The Mobile Riverine Force had not found any Viet Cong in the populated areas along the Rach Ruong, but when the force tried to move back to the river, to embark on transports to the scene of the major battles, the VC made an effort to delay their movement.

Up river, Vinh Long was the scene of heavy fighting when it was attacked by a force of 1,200 Viet Cong from the 306th, 308th, and 857th Battalions and Local Force guerrillas. During that time, Game Warden river patrol units were confronted by the advancing enemy. The assault on Vinh Long Airfield began when commandos slyly entered the base and started setting off satchel charges on the Army copters. This was quickly followed by a sustained twenty-five minute mortar attack by the 857th VC Battalion, in conjunction with an infantry attack on the MACV bunkers of the Army and Navy as the defenders quickly took up defensive positions on the base. During the chaos of the enemy siege on the airfield, and from two directions on the city, there was talk of possible evacuation. Game Warden river patrol boats bravely fought alongside the ARVN 2nd Armored Calvary and 43rd Rangers on land, plus Vietnamese Navy RAG boats, with all pouring fire into the advancing enemy. One mobile riverine infantry company was airlifted to assist in the defense of the airfield.

Although unable to launch during the dark hours of the main assault, Navy Seawolf gunships flew extensive missions in support of the airfield and surrounding areas of Vinh Long for the next few days. The MACV compound, which was located on the southern edge of the city, had been cut off and was running out of food and water, with SEALs trapped in the compound along with the normal inhabitants. Seawolves flew overhead and escorted vehicles from the airfield through downtown Vinh Long and south to the MACV compound. They did this four times in one day, the vehicles making it through safely without casualties. Additional Seawolf crews had been flown in to augment Det-3, which had been flying nonstop and was exhausted.

In Saigon, Viet Cong elements launched attacks on such key targets as the United States Embassy, the Military Assistance Command headquarters, the Radio Station, and the Embassy Hotel. A thirteen-man Viet Cong Sapper squad also assaulted the Vietnamese Navy headquarters. VC units roamed the streets dressed in black uniforms or in civilian clothes with arm bands designating unit identification. Many also wore yellow handkerchiefs around their necks.

A Seawolf fire team from Det-2 in Nha Be, fifteen miles southeast of Saigon, was in its bunker adjacent to the matted runway, dressed and ready to go. Its members were requested to launch into the direction of Saigon. They were to illuminate the heart of the city to help the Military Police of the 716th Battalion, and other friendly ground forces, who were in battles on the small streets and alleys of the city. The Seawolves from Nha Be succeeded in being one of the first air units to arrive to defend Saigon and, during the following four hours, dropped dozens of high-intensity parachute flares, which slowly floated down from the skies to help identify the Viet Cong attackers. At the U.S. Navy barracks, Annapolis Hotel, the Naval support sailors manned two .50 cal machineguns behind sandbag emplacements on the roof and stubbornly held off the Viet Cong, who were firing a big gun into the building from across the street.

In Chau Doc City on the upper Bassac River, four PBRs from River Section 535, five PBRs from River Section 513, and U.S. Navy SEALs from Detachment Alfa, Eighth Platoon, operated in conjunction with the local Provincial Reconnaissance Unit, which was composed of thirty-six Nung mercenaries led by Staff Sergeant Drew Dix, the Province Senior Advisor. All of these forces contributed significantly to saving the city from seizure by 1,400 communist insurgents from the 313th Main Force Battalion, which happened to be commanded by a woman.

During the heavy fighting that lasted throughout the day, the SEALs and Nungs waged intense combat within the city while river patrol boats attacked enemy positions and evacuated civilians and wounded. During the battle, PBR crews went ashore four times to secure helicopter landing zones and joined the SEALs in defense of the U.S. Special Forces Camp, the home of the B-42 team of the Special Forces Group Airborne, commanded by Lieutenant Colonel William F. "Whiskey Bill" Smith.

One of the civilians rescued by the SEALs was an American civilian nurse. She had barricaded herself in a locker in her quarters with a carbine and was determined to take as many VC with her as possible, while hopefully saving one bullet for herself. She would later marry a Navy lieutenant who was with the river section at Binh Thuy.

Back on the Mekong River at Sa Dec, PBRs maintained a blocking force as ground units counter-attacked the Viet Cong, who had taken control of sections of the city.

In I Corp Tactical Zone, river patrol boats joined the ARVN and U.S. ground forces in a counter-offensive against Viet Cong forces, attacking the Hue landing craft ramp during the early morning offensive. Eight river patrol boats charged up the Hue River and encountered heavy mortar, rocket, and sniper fire when they arrived at the ramp. The enemy appeared to be in control of the northern bank of the Huong River opposite the landing ramp. The river patrol boats made repeated firing runs into the night, until enemy fire was suppressed and the north bank was secured by U.S. Marines. PBRs remained in the area to maintain the security of the ramp. Two river patrolmen received minor wounds in the day-long action.

Back in My Tho City on the morning of January 31st, the usual Viet Cong mortar rounds started to drop, as was customary. The off-duty PBR boat crews got up, dressed, and ran off to disperse the boats at the base, while rounds continued to fall around My Tho. Carter billet, the Navy barracks, and Victory Hotel, where the Navy headquarters had been set up, were located around the corner from each other and about eight blocks from the base, so the boat crews were exposed to enemy fire for quite sometime as they began to scramble to their boats. During the time river patrol units had spent in My Tho, they had been visited by the local VC forces with a weekly mortar attack. The enemy would drop five to eight rounds on various nights, usually between 0300 to 0500 hours in the early morning, and then stop. These were usually just harassing rounds.

Some of the patrolmen, however, were a bit slow waking up that morning. One was patrolman Quartermaster Third Class Kenneth A. Delfino, who was sick and not feeling well, so his crew put two mattresses between him and the street to protect him against shrapnel. They then ran off to do what needed to be done. Ken was half asleep, subconsciously counting the mortars: three...four... five...six....crack-crack-crack, braaaaaaaaaaak... seven!

Ken woke up when he heard the small-arms fire, since he had not heard that in town before and it was very close. His adrenalin kicked in as he jumped up, quickly dressed, armed himself, and hurriedly ran off to report to headquarters for further orders.

No one really knew how large a force was attacking, whether it was a Viet Cong squad, platoon, company, or what. But the patrolmen knew the enemy was wreaking havoc on the city with incoming rounds falling down and exploding. They soon found out that they were being hit by two Viet Cong battalions and that they had penetrated to within three blocks of the Navy base, before the Army of Vietnam's 6th Armored Cavalry and 11th Infantry got their tanks up and shoved the enemy back to a main arterial entrance to the city of My Tho, located on Highway 4, the main road to Saigon.

When Ken got down to the now chaotic streets, he was able to catch a ride with his friend, Engineman Third Jose Garza, who was also a patrolman assigned to River Section 533. Speeding down the road, they received fire from several side streets. Upon reaching the base, Ken asked his commanding officer, Lieutenant Jerry Sapp, that he be allowed to serve as Garza's shotgun rider. Sapp ordered Ken to do so, and Ken spent the morning riding shotgun in a Navy grey pick-up truck, covering Jose as they sped through My Tho, ducking shots and mortar explosions, weaving through the city. Meanwhile, units of River Section 533 had got underway and were running up and down the river in support of the cities, villages, and hamlets that were all under attack from communist forces.

Units of River Section 532 sent to help Ben Tre City were trapped on the Ben Tre Canal, fighting for hours until they battled their way out. YRBM 16 was also stationed at Ben Tre and was shot up pretty bad. Ben Tre City was all but destroyed by the Viet Cong, but newsman Peter Arnett reported that Americans had destroyed Ben Tre, in order to save it. The LST USS Hunterdon County destroyed a brick factory that was at the mouth of the canal with her 40mm guns after the NVA and VC holding up there refused to give up. The

Hunterdon gunners pounded the piss out of the factory for two hours until it was a heap of rocks and no one was left alive.

Back at My Tho, around 1000 hours, Ken asked Jose to stop by the My Tho provincial hospital so he could check up on his friends, the Philippine medical detachment. Upon arrival at the hospital, Ken learned that half the team was still trapped in their quarters back near the main entrance to My Tho, which was under enemy control. Ken, an American of Philippine ancestry, had gotten to know the Filipino detachment quite well, and several of them knew some of Ken's family back in Manila. The two allied forces had become good friends and the medical detachment had had the Navy personnel over to their quarters for dinner on more than one occasion. Due to the fact the Philippines were a neutral country, Jose felt the people didn't deserve to be killed in an unjust manner and was more than willing to go with Ken as they kept moving, returning fire to the sound of gunfire.

Ken and Jose returned to base and obtained permission from the base commander, Commander Sam Steed, to get a team together and get the medical staff out if they were still alive. (Ken also kept River Section 533 Executive Officer, Lieutenant Bob Moir, up to date on all activities.) After receiving permission, Ken and Jose went around the base compound to get a couple of volunteers and better firepower. At the base, they were joined by Gunner's Mate Second Rich Wies, one of their shipmates from River Section 533 who was on medical leave with a nasty ear infection, and Gunner's Mate Third Dennis Keeffe, who was assigned to the Naval support unit but quickly volunteered to accompany the three patrolmen on the rescue mission.

The river patrolmen of Game Warden units relied heavily on the work of the base support personnel at all Navy facilities in South Vietnam. The Naval Support Activity (NSA) sailors assigned to Task Force 116 had to see that the boat's supplies of weapons, ammunition, fuel, spare parts, and water and food provisions were adequate. In addition, they had to protect the base itself from attack from enemy ground forces. The bases were relatively small, so the river patrolmen and support sailors relied on each other to cover each others backs while they slept and ate, recuperating from the long nights on river patrols or base guard duty.

Petty Officer Keeffe had the midnight watch and was making the rounds at Carter Billet checking on the sentrys, one out front, one on the roof, and one roaming. While stopping to shoot the breeze with the sentry on the roof, they began noticing tracers. At once, the sky was filled with red and green tracers. Then mortar rounds started dropping in the street near Carter Billet and the Victory Hotel. Keeffe stayed at his post until relieved, then made his way around the corner to the Victory Hotel, where he joined up with river patrolman Rich Wies and several other NSA sailors. The armed group decided to make their way by foot to the base receiving and returning fire along the way. It was especially hairy near the civilian hospital and from across the base, where they had to fight along the way, but all made it safely. After they arrived, Rich and Keeffe met up with Ken and Jose, to go back out on the streets in vehicles.

They split up into two teams, with two in a jeep that they had requisitioned, and two in the crew shuttle pickup truck, as the four sailors dressed in jungle greens, carrying weapons, took off speeding to the Vietnamese tank perimeter, ducking enemy fire along the way. Much to their dismay, the tanks were three blocks from the medical team's quarters at the main entrance to My Tho and would not position their tanks in the road to give the team covering fire, let alone have any of their troops escort the sailors to help find the Filipino medical team.

Now the four sailors knew for certain that they were on their own as they cautiously proceeded on to the Filipino's villa, encountering Viet bodies in the street. They were amazed as they viewed the beautiful French-styled homes that were riddled with bullets, with sections of walls blown away. The place was a total mess, appearing to have suffered several rocket hits, with enemy bodies strewn over the grounds. Suddenly the shelling stopped, and it became eerily quiet, but the team did not hesitate moving forward. The four sailors, equipped with only small arms, proceeded into the villa compound. There they searched a bunker jammed with scared Vietnamese civilians. But the medical personnel were not there.

Ken approached the Philippine medical detachment living quarters and went up to the window of the building and tapped loudly once...then twice, yelling out the names of a couple of the nurses. At about the same time, Rich Wies saw activity in several second-story windows across the street and began firing twelve-gauge buckshot rounds in the enemy's direction, in order to keep their heads down.

Then the face of Lieutenant Myrna Milan appeared in the window. Ken yelled at her to get the rest of her team, including Captain Norma Gumayagay, Captain Fabros, and the security detachment, so they could move them safely out of the building and back down the street. The sailors then hustled the medical team out of the building and into the truck, with Jose Garza driving and Ken carrying an M-3 Burp gun. Keeffe drove the jeep while Rich Wies, armed with a Winchester pump shotgun, provided cover fire, keeping the enemy at bay. Again they raced back through the streets of My Tho, ducking rounds and swerving around wreckage. U.S. Air Force jets flew unbelievably low-altitude firing runs on the My Tho traffic circle, putting on an awesome display of firepower, sending flames and debris flying into the air. Half a dozen SEAL Team II members held a two-square block area that was under constant attack. The Vietnamese Ranger Battalion was also heavily involved in perimeter security and city clearance.

After reaching the hospital with the medical personnel, the team found out that one of the Filipino sergeants had gone back up to the third floor to destroy the radio equipment, so as not to allow the enemy to gain possession of it. Now the Navy rescue team realized that they had to go back to get the sergeant out. Of course, they did not have to go back or do any of what they had already done - it was not really their job to do so. But these were their friends and allies, and they felt that they could not leave or abandon them to the enemy, even if the South Vietnamese forces seemed unwilling to help. That's why many Americans had volunteered to serve in the Republic of Vietnam in the first place, to fight for their nation and help keep all people safe, no matter what their race or creed.

The team gathered up their weapons and courage and once again returned to the villa, racing through the streets ducking tracers and returning fire. Again, the Vietnamese tank commander would not support them with any forward movement. After giving them permission to re-enter the enemy held area, the commander replied, "You people are crazy for going back in with the chance of being fired upon or caught in a crossfire between our tanks and the enemy." Still the Navy team reentered the kill zone for a second time. It remained eerily quiet, as they searched, eventually finding the sergeant hiding behind a door with a small caliber gun in his trembling hands, saying he was too scared to move with the Viet Cong in the area. Finally, after several minutes of talking to him, they persuaded him to surrender his weapon and return with them. As they left the area, they took fire from the Viet Cong located in a nearby house, but they answered stubbornly with return fire and cleared the area with no one hit, thankful to make it back to the hospital with all safe and sound.

At around 1300 hours the same day, a medevac was called in for a soldier who had been wounded earlier in the day. The dust-off was to pick him up in the soccer stadium in the middle of town. The impromptu Navy team, which had stayed together and was now running patrols through the city, heard of the medevac about to take place and proceeded to the soccer field, arriving as the dust-off helicopter was circling. The stadium was surrounded by a school on one end, as well as another three-story building on the other end. As the dust-off helicopter was coming in to land, a window swung open and a black-clad armed figure appeared in the window ready to fire. The sailors immediately took the building under fire while waving off the medevac helicopter. After receiving fire from the announcer's booth across the field, they also took it under fire as well. The ARVN did finally go into the building to find the enemy, and the sailors provided escort for the American wounded in action back to their base for transfer by boat to Dong Tam Army hospital, four miles up river.

That night at the chow hall, Ken Delfino met up with another group of friends, and together they decided to camp out on a roof of a building across the street from the Victory Hotel as a lookout position, taking along a good supply of ammo and grenades just in case Charlie was still in the vicinity and had zeroed in on Carter Billet. From there, they had a pretty good view overlooking the city to the west and in the immediate foreground was the Vietnam 7th Army Division complex. They picked the spot because it was above a busy intersection. On that first night, they were taken under fire from the direction of one of the ARVN headquarters buildings. Rather than shoot back, they stayed down until someone got a call over to the ARVN to verify if the Viet Cong had taken over their building. They had arrived at this decision because the weapons used were not AK47s and there were no green enemy tracers coming at them, but it did sound like M-1 carbines, which were commonly carried by the ARVN soldiers. Turned out they were right in their assumptions; it was just nervous ARVNs, as they suspected.

Also on that first night, Rich Wies and Dennis Keeffe stayed at the base and took a lot of enemy fire from several places outside the base as they stood their ground and returned fire. The next morning, they brought the doctors and nurses back to the base, feeling it was safer than the hotels. Most of the active fighting in defense of My Tho that first day had been done by the 32nd Vietnamese Ranger Battalion. Unbeknownst to the U.S. Navy, South Vietnam President Thieu was visiting his daughter in My Tho that evening.

Elements of two 9th Infantry battalions were landed by water craft in My Tho at 1520 hours, February 1st. The five major ships of the Mobile Riverine Base moved from Vinh Long to Dong Tam, to be in a better position to support operations. After landing unopposed in My Tho, Bravo Company, 3/47 Infantry, secured landing sites on the southwestern edge of the city for its parent battalion and was joined by Alpha and Charlie Companies. As the troops began to move north into the city, they met heavy fire. With the 3/60th Infantry moving on the west, both battalions advanced north through the western portion of the city, receiving small arms, automatic rifle, and rocket fire. Fighting was intense and continuous, and of a kind new to the riverine battalion. The city had to be cleared slowly and systematically; pockets of enemy resistance had to be wiped out to prevent the Viet Cong from closing in behind troops.

While advancing through the city, Alpha Company 3/47th Infantry met heavy fire at 1615 hours, and Echo Company was ordered to reinforce. On the way, the lead elements of Echo Company also met intense fire and were eventually pinned down at the western edge of My Tho. By this time, both battalions were involved in pitched battles and were taking casualties. The 3/60th continued its movement north, advancing under heavy enemy fire, and air strikes were requested at 1740 hours to assist the battalion's forward elements. Troops moved in and out the doorways, from house to house, and from street to street. Artillery was employed against enemy troops who were fleeing the city, running for their lives. At 1955 hours, a group of Viet Cong who had been in a previous engagement with troops of the Vietnam 7th Division attempted to enter the streets where Bravo Company 3/47th was fighting, but by 2100 hours Bravo Company had eliminated them.

Alpha Company, 3/47th Infantry requested a helo fire team to support its point element, which had met intense resistance from small-arms and rocket fire and had suffered several casualties. The light fire team arrived and was used to relieve the pressure on Alpha and Echo Companies by firing on Viet Cong positions. The team made runs directly over Alpha Company and placed fire within twenty-five yards of the company's lead elements. To evacuate the wounded, a platoon leader sprinted through enemy fire, jumped into a Vietnam Army jeep parked in the street, and drove to the wounded. Ignoring the fire directed against him, he helped the wounded men aboard the jeep and drove back to his company lines. By 2100 hours, most of the firing had ceased and the enemy had begun to withdraw under cover of darkness. Throughout the night, sporadic sniper fire and occasional grenade attacks were directed against the Americans and South Vietnamese, but no large major engagements developed.

The next morning, the 2nd Brigade continued to attack strongholds within the city, which was encircled by friendly units. At 0630 hours, both U.S. battalions continued a sweep to the north in the western portion of the city, encountering only light resistance. At 0915 hours, a Viet Cong force was engaged on the northern edge of the city. Tactical air strikes with Napalm were called in and dislodged Viet Cong troops holding a guard tower near a highway bridge. The damage to the bridge was repaired under fire by the Mobile Riverine Force's supporting engineer platoon. Upon completion of the sweep, the city was somewhat cleared of enemy units, and the Mobile Riverine Force battalions loaded back onto armored troop carriers for redeployment to the Cai Lay District. The Riverine force moved from My Tho to the Cai Lay area to cut off enemy escape routes, but there were no significant engagements with the Viet Cong remaining close to My Tho. On February 4th, at the direction of the senior advisor of IV Corps Tactical Zone, the 3/60th and 3/47th Infantries moved to Vinh Long to relieve continued Viet Cong pressure on South Vietnamese units there. The Mobile Riverine Force with 2nd Brigade, 9th Infantry, and ARVN and Regional Forces by its side, continued to pursue Viet Cong forces through the wetlands and rice paddies in heavy combat, receiving recoilless rifle, rockets, 60mm mortar and automatic weapons fire for the next few days, until they broke the communists' backs and the enemy broke off, retreating into the wilderness. Back in My Tho, they found fresh graves where the Viet Cong had gathered people and buried them alive, while their families watched.

For the Navy in My Tho, the next few days were spent patrolling the city by day and setting up ambush and lookout posts at night. The attack on My Tho officially ended on February 7th, 1968, and then the Navy teams all went back to their respective duties. Two weeks after the attack, Philippine Brigadier General Gaudencio Tobias visited My Tho with his staff and a television reporter named Max Soliven and his cameraman. Soliven asked many questions, and sensing where he was going, Ken Delfino and the sailors were pretty guarded in their comments of political nature and outspoken on the military questions and how well the military had responded.

About a month later, there was a small ceremony at the Navy support base where Petty Officer Kenneth Delfino was honored by General Tobias, with a letter of appreciation for leading the rescue squad. While Ken was not expecting anything for doing what he considered his job, he did appreciate the nice thank you from General Tobias. He was not aware that Garza, Keeffe, and Wies had not received any recognition for their bravery that day, a day in which these four sailors distinguished themselves by unselfishly putting the safety of the Philippine medical detachment ahead of their own. Ken knew that, without Jose, Dennis, and Rich, he could not have accomplished this feat, and that the medical team probably would not have survived. For this, Ken has always been especially grateful to the other three sailors who rose to the occasion and came to his aide and supported his actions during the attack on My Tho. Although Jose Garza, Dennis Keeffe, and Rich Wies have never officially been recognized for their actions during the 1968 Tet Offensive attack on My Tho, they have all earned the respect of their fellow Black Beret brothers who learnt of their bravery through Ken Delfino and their many friends.

Task Force 116's efforts during Tet were recognized on February 12th, 1968, when they received the following message from U.S. Major General George Eckhardt:

Since the Tet Offensive started January 31st, 1968, I have received many reports from the advisors throughout IV Corps of the effectiveness of your command in coming to their assistance during these crucial times. I know you have suffered grievous losses but your brave men covered themselves with glory because of their courage and dedication. You have dealt the aggressors a heavy blow which speaks well for the professionalism and capability of your organization. Please pass my deepest appreciation to all concerned and best wishes for continued success.

George Eckhardt

To this day, if you ask most Vietnam veterans that were in-country in early '68 what they remember most about their tour of duty in South Vietnam, they will reply "Tet."

SNOOPY'S NOSE

On July 29th, 1967, Monitor-91-2 was lead Monitor with two Tangos equipped with drag chains serving as minesweepers just ahead, as they cleared Snoopy's Nose, leading a column of Tango transports down the Rach Ba Rai, which branched north off the My Tho River into Dinh Tuong Province. The Monitor assault boat had just cleared the nose area when it took multiple rocket hits. Of the thirteen crewmembers onboard, eleven were wounded before it was over, and Monitor-91-2 had taken seven hits. The Monitor's crew had additional Riverine sailors riding along, helping out. The boat coxswain and Patrol Officer Lieutenant Junior Grade Al Breininger were the only two sailors that weren't hit in the exchange. There was blood from one end of the boat to the other, they said. But luckily, all of the wounded but one were not serious. The one was Boatswain's Mate Second Pruitt, whose head was covered with blood, leaving him looking like he was not going to make it. Then they dumped twenty gallons of oil into the last operating diesel engine in order to keep it running, so they could rush the wounded back to the medevac location. Most of the gunners never saw the enemy. All they heard was Engineman Second Joseph in the aft gun mount yelling, "I got a guy taking a bead on us" just before the first rocket hit. At that, the Mobile Riverine crew cut loose, returning fire in all directions, while being pounded by rockets from killer rocket squad teams, who had been trained to zero in on the badly hit Monitor assault boat.

Afterwards, on August 1st, the troops were extracted from Snoopy's Nose and the stream adjacent to it. The assault boats had taken twenty-five RPG hits during the operation that lasted three days. After returning to the mobile base, they were all presently surprised to see Pruitt back at the ship with a bandage wrapped around his head above his eye. The morale of the men was high, and they were a great bunch of guys who had become a well-oiled team of fighters determined to defeat the enemy.

On September 15th, there was another operation at Snoopy's Nose. Eighteen boats were hit with fifty-five sailors wounded and three dead. River Assault Squadron 11 saw most of the action in what the Associated Press called the worst Navy battle of the year.

As Commander of River Assault Squadron 11 that day, Lieutenant Commander Francis E. "Dusty" Rhodes Jr. was in command of twenty-three riverine assault craft, with elements of the 9th Infantry's 2nd Brigade embarked. While transiting the Rach Ba Rai River during combat riverine search-and-destroy operations in the Cam Son Secret Zone, the entire task group came under heavy VC fire from fortified bunkers on both banks of the river, sustaining numerous personnel casualties and damage to several boats. Although momentarily stunned when two rockets knocked Dusty and his crew to the deck, Lieutenant Commander Rhodes stationed himself in an exposed position on his command boat in the face of heavy, direct enemy fire from close range. He quickly noted the condition and disposition of his units, taking command by radio, ordering them to regroup and return downstream out of the enemy's fortified area. After transferring casualties and reassigning personnel so that all boats were manned, Lieutenant Commander Rhodes again took his task group up the river and was subjected once more to heavy enemy fire. Despite a large number of casualties, Dusty nevertheless successfully landed and disembarked units ashore in the assigned objective area and set up a Naval blockade on the river.

Boatswain's Mate First Carroll E. Dutterer Jr., Boat Captain of Tango-111-6, also came under intense automatic-weapons, recoilless rifle, and rocket fire from enemy positions on both banks of the narrow stream. Petty Officer Dutterer's boat, one of the lead units in the formation, was returning maximum fire when it was hit simultaneously by two enemy rockets, wounding Dutterer and four other crewmen, destroying all their communications equipment. Unable to receive instructions by radio, or to observe movements of the other craft through the dense pale smoke, he was unaware that other units had been ordered to reverse course and retire to a safe area for casualty evacuation. Determined to carry out his assigned mission, Petty Officer Dutterer, alone and with no fire support, directed his craft through the entire 1,800-meter enemy barrage and landed his troops. When the troops were pinned down by enemy fire, he directed fire from his exposed position topside and rebeached his boat to pick up the troops. During the re-embarkation, Dutterer was seriously wounded when his boat was again hit by an enemy rocket. Despite his wounds, he maintained control of his craft until re-embarkation was completed.

Their heroic conduct and inspiring devotion to duty in the face of intense enemy opposition were in keeping with the highest traditions of the United States Navy, resulting in Lieutenant Commander Francis E. Rhodes Jr. and Boatswain's Mate First Carroll E. Dutterer Jr. both being awarded the Navy Cross for their parts in the battle.

Meanwhile, a group of reporters had been flown to the firebase earlier in the day and were preparing to be taken up to the battle site by boat to witness the aftermath. They were so eager to report the story that, back at the makeshift artillery firebase, Lieutenant Junior Grade Al Breininger asked the reporters to calm down and respect the wounded and killed in action from the battle. It seemed to have little impact on the shark-like reporters, who seemed to be interested in stories and headlines and not in the men who had paid the price for that day's battle.

Snoopy's Nose was located on the lower part of the Roch Ba Rai, and one of the worst spots in the Mekong Delta. It ran north to south from the My Tho River into Dinh Tuong Province and was a favorite ambush sight of the Viet Cong. The U shape of the river made it difficult to fire into the heavy foliated banks, without risk of hitting the lead assault craft on the opposite side of the peninsula. On more than one occasion, the enemy had waited until the forward minesweeper turned the bend in the river, leading the column of Tangos, and then initiated a firefight by firing at the forward and rear boats, who would return the fire with their rounds passing over the enemy position, hitting their own boats on the other side of the dense peninsula. These boats, in turn, returned the fire, resulting in a full-out battle between the forward and rear assault craft. The heavily armed boats continued firing until someone would figure out they were firing on each other. At the mere mention of Snoopy's Nose, sphincter muscles would tighten on men who went back time and time again. Snoopy's Nose continued to be a thorn in the side of the Mobile Riverine Force for many years to come.

The topography of Snoopy's Nose was as the name implied. The curvature of the river was such that it created a peninsula that looked like the nose of the Charles Schulz cartoon character, Snoopy the dog. Although we were in Vietnam, it was Snoopy that everybody read about, flying his dog house biplane against the Red Baron in deadly aerial dog fights. In an attempt to find a little humor in almost anything and everything, sailors would come up with appropriate titles for scary ambush sites on the rivers and canals. It seemed sailors in the Mekong Delta were very good at this, to help relieve the anxiety of what was to come. They had dubbed many names of unique places where similar tactics were used. "The Mouse Ears," "Four Corners," "Rocket Alley," "Route 66" were just a few of the many titles given to bends in the rivers. The enemy was clever, choosing its fighting ground well. The Viet Cong would use the peninsulas created by the river and employ simple tactics. They knew when the boats were about to navigate around Snoopy's Nose, simply by the sound of engines in the column approaching. Even with the engines muffled, the enemy could hear the boats coming a mile away, allowing plenty of time to prepare for their plan of attack on the vulnerable but determined Mobile Riverine Force.

On July 13th, 1968, while transiting the Rach Ba Rai River, two Tango boats of River Assault Squadron 13, Tango-131-8 and Tango-131-13, were sunk at the mouth of Snoopy's Nose, on the southwest corner of the entrance. Tango 8 was lead minesweeper boat, leading the column of assault craft to pick up elements of the 4/39th Infantry, with the intentions of delivering them to a pickup zone, where the troops would be air lifted back to base camp. The column of troop transports loaded the soldiers with no problem, but when they returned past Snoopy's Nose, they received enemy fire from both banks. River assault craft quickly returned fire and suppressed the enemy. They had learned long ago not to steam as a full column, for fear that the Viet Cong would fire B40 rockets at the lead boats, who would intern return fire, with rounds passing over the enemy positions, hitting the trailing boats of the column. To avoid this, they would steam around the nose, five boats at a time. After the lead boat made it through, they would beach at the mouth and provide cover fire while the rest of the boats transited through and cleared the nose.

The decision was made by command to land the 4/39th Infantry on both sides of the entrance of the Rach Ba Rai, to recon the area and search out the enemy. After prepping the beach with reconnaissance fire, Charlie Company of the 4/39th Infantry was disembarked to seek out the enemy. While Tango-131-8 was beached, she went to adjust her position and set off an underwater explosion that blew a hole in the Tango's hull, under the starboard fuel tank, which flooded the engine compartment. As Tango-131-5 made its beach approach with Alpha Company, it was greeted by enemy automatic weapons fire and took a heat round through the Mark 19 automatic grenade launcher mount, wounding the gunner and damaging the weapon beyond repair. The wounded Tango fought back as it took a second round on the starboard side below the 20mm gun, damaging the bar armor and leaving a hole in the armor plate at the base of the 20mm mount. Tango-131-13, after offloading its troops, came along the left side of Tango 8 to help take on guns and equipment, when it also hit a mine, sinking right next to Tango 8. There were no casualties from either explosion, but Tango 13 now had an eighteen-inch hole in the port shaft tunnel storage area, and both Tangos were disabled and unable to get underway. The two Tangos remained beached while several river assault craft went to their aid and beached alongside, setting up a perimeter to protect the disabled boats and their crews.

Zippo Monitor-111-3 immediately sprayed the area of contact with a flamethrower until all fuel was expended. It was relieved on station by Monitor-91-2, which arrived with Alpha-92-6 from Mobile Riverine Group Alpha. Tango-131-1, with an Army flame unit aboard, escorted Zippo Monitor-111-3 back to USS Windham

County, LST 1170, which remained on the My Tho River in support, refueling assault crafts in relays during extended operations that lasted all day. Several boats remained beached in the vicinity of the damaged Tangos throughout the night, while salvage operations continued. Windham County had provided outstanding service to river assault boats with chow, Cokes, fuel, and water, supplying damage control equipment and ship-fitters who reported with their welding torches and worked into the night, shoring up the damage in a short period of time. In addition, Windham County shifted anchorage in a defensive measure moving closer to the ambush site, and expended forty rounds from her three inch gun mount in support of Mobile Riverine Forces.

That night, two sailors with small-arms and hand grenades were left behind on each of the two damaged boats, to protect them from enemy sappers who would have blown the Tangos to smithereens, removing them both from any further service. Late that night, movement was heard out in front of the boats as Ralph Bigelow and Bobby Dean Dawson called out but received no answer. Then the shit hit the fan, as both the enemy and the sailors opened up with heavy fire, for an interminable hour, before it quieted down. The next morning, the 9th Infantry soldiers did a sweep in front of the boats and found a blood-soaked backpack and a lot of blood, but no bodies. The two Tangos were then backed off the beach, one at a time, and secured to two additional Tangos, one on each side, and returned to base for repairs. Once the transports were out of the water to be repaired, wire was found wrapped around the screws and shafts. The mines had been connected by wire underwater and sucked into the screws, causing the explosions that sunk the boats.

During the morning action the day before, seven 9th Infantry soldiers were wounded, with two requiring a medical dust-off, and nine American sailors were wounded, with one remaining in Dong Tam while the others were medevaced to Long Binh. The Army found one Viet Cong floating in the water and one in a bunker, crediting both kills to the Navy. After Tangos 8 and 13 were patched, pumped, and floated, they returned to Dong Tam, escorted by Alpha-111-3 and Monitor-91-2. River Assault Squadron 13 units remained at the mouth of the Rach Ba Rai with 4/39th Battalion units aboard, until the two Tangos were salvaged and underway. After all the infantry and craft had returned to Windham County, there was a stand-down, and the Mobile Riverine Force returned to Dong Tam.

The following are a series of diary entries recorded by twenty-year-old Seaman Terry Sater from St. Louis, Missouri.

July 13th, 1968: *We're on an operation at "Snoopy's Nose," in the Mekong Delta. On the tenth, we were on basic interior defense patrol and the next morning, we all volunteered and left for the operation. Last night the boats took sniper fire. This morning it "hit the fan." We were on our way out of Snoopy's Nose and started taking automatic weapons fire. We had the Monitor and two Alpha boats ahead of us. Then RPG-7 rockets started flying. One fell just short of our stern, and we took heavy shrapnel. The end of the .30 cal barrel was shot off and five straight legs took shrapnel here in the well deck. One guy, who had the .30 cal machine gun right next to me, fell from getting it in the ear. Tango 5 is now operating on half their crew. They took two rockets, one at the water line, and one in the Mark 19 mount. You can't recognize the Mark 19 gunner; he got it in the face so bad. The 20mm gunner got it in his leg and side.*

Diary entry: *We are back at the ship now. We are refueled and are getting our port 20mm and Mark 19 repaired before going back on the line. I remember seeing the Mark 19 gunner on Tango 5, now. He is a tall blond guy. Good looking. Has a girl stateside. Now they say he's not expected to live. Cooper, who is on the same boat, went into shock, but he's okay now. Tangos 8 and 13 hit mines, and have holes in their well decks. Everyone is on edge, unnerved. Everybody knows it could be his turn next time. A black sailor on Tango 5 refused to go out on the boats again. The sky is gray, overcast. There is a cool wind blowing. It fits the mood after a battle. Charlie knew we were coming. We got hit just as we were getting to the exit. He had two days to get ready for us. I can still remember it like it was seconds ago, the sound of Charlie's AK47 Chicom rifle.*

July 13th, *a bleak day for River Assault Squadron 13.*

Snoopy's Nose was a popular ambush site for the Viet Cong because of its shape. We were always at our guns and alert when we went through the area. On July 13th, the Viet Cong waited until we were leaving the nose and started relaxing, taking off our flak jackets and helmets, not alert. That's when they hit us.

Diary entry Sunday, July 14th: *Squadron 13 is mending their wounds. Tex Frank, the Mark 19 gunner on Tango 5, is going to be okay. We were sure he was going to be missing one eye, but now he's not. Tango 3 took .50 cal fire but no injuries. We had beer call, and I got two letters from Judi. That's all I needed. When I heard about Tex, and it sounded like he was going to be blind, I thought of the life he would lead, how I would take it. I would have to find the courage to break with Judi.*

Diary entry, July 17th: *We're on basic interior defense patrol again. As it turns out, Tex Frank will be losing one eye, and the 20mm gunner will be a cripple. Our starboard 20mm gunner left for Saigon this morning for a hernia operation. I'll take his place on the 20.*

Terry Sater added the following so his kids would understand:

The reason the black sailor on Tango 5 refused to go out, is that a rocket grenade hit his boat in the coxswain's flat. He was below in the well deck. The rocket grenade burned through the armor plating of the coxswain's flat, hit the opposite bulkhead, and dropped through a hatch, hitting him on the top of his helmet, landing at his feet. It was a dud. He felt that he had used up all of his good luck at that moment. He would never go into combat again. Our lieutenant begged him to go back out, because if he didn't, he would face court-martial charges. He steadfastly refused to get back on the boat. He was taken away and I never saw him again.

When we returned to the ships for repairs, I recall sailors coming down to the boats with their cameras. The boat captain of Tango 5 was a short, fat guy, who was enraged by the cameras. He screamed at all of them to get away from his boat. Nobody argued with him.

A couple of weeks later, river craft of River Assault Divisions 91 and 131, with embarked ARVN troops, were ambushed near the intersection of the Cai Nhut Stream and Cai Tu River south of Can Tho in Choung Thien Province. Before Tango-131-9 left for the operation, a friend walked Boatswain's Mate Second William R.

Taylor down to the dock to see him off. He told Bill Taylor that he would see him when he got back. Taylor replied that he would not be coming back. He had never made that statement before. When Tango 9 was ambushed, Taylor was stationed in the well deck. He jumped on a .50 cal and pulled the handle back to jack a round into the chamber. Before he got a shot off, a rocket grenade hit the boat in the side. Another hit the ceiling under the helo deck, spraying shrapnel and hitting Taylor in the head and neck. Boatswain's Mate Second William R. Taylor was killed and eleven other sailors were wounded by the rocket and automatic weapons fire that day, while ARVN casualties amounted to two killed and nineteen wounded. Four Tangoes were damaged in the attack. James Bowen, who was manning the .50 cal opposite from Taylor, actually had to be pulled from his gun. His flak jacket looked like a screen door. Last they heard he was on his way to Japan. Gunner's Mate Third William Hodges took control of the boat, as everyone was wounded and in shock, including the boat captain. Hodges called in the dust-offs and ordered Frank Springer back to his gun mount to keep him from seeing the horror of what had happened to his shipmates in the well deck, as well as to cover the river bank. They later found out that William Taylor was younger than he had claimed, and had lied about his age to join the Navy.

William R. Taylor's good friend, Frank "Little One" Springer, was also wounded on Tango-131-9 that day. His citation reads.

Fireman Springer participated in operations involving numerous combat missions which struck deep into the enemy infested waters of the Mekong Delta and inflicted heavy losses to the enemy. In each instance, he reacted quickly and courageously. Despite exceedingly long operational periods, he unfailingly met the requirements of the combat situation with enthusiasm and determination.

Radioman Third Glenn H. Ledford, who was on Tango 9's 20mm gun, was also wounded. His citation reads.

While serving with River Assault Squadron 9, Petty Officer Ledford's boat was attacked with rockets and automatic weapons fire. Although knocked from his firing position twice by direct rocket hits, bleeding and dazed from shrapnel wounds, Petty Officer

Ledford courageously re-manned his gun and returned the enemy fire until he was finally overcome by his wounds.

There are many memories etched into the minds of the sailors who steamed down the Mekong Delta's rivers, streams, and canals, and still they went. In Terry Sater's case, he had arrived in Vietnam on March 19th, 1968, one of a group of seventy-two sailors from Mare Island's River Warfare School. The new riverine sailors were split between River Assault Squadrons 11 and 13, divided up into four river assault divisions. Originally, Sater was assigned Tango-131-3, in the first batch of squadron 13 boats that arrived in-country. After a while, they split the crew up and reassigned Sater to Tango-131-6. That is the boat he was on at Snoopy's Nose on July 13th. Not long after the operation, Tango 6's boat captain told Sater that he had volunteered to send him to Tango-131-9 to replace Bill Taylor, who had been killed. Tango 9 had taken several rockets and had crewmen in the hospital as well as losing Taylor, so they needed someone with experience. While Sater was on Tango 6, his battle station was in the well deck along with an engineman by the name of Tiny. The two of them manned two .50 cal and four .30 cal machineguns, receiving help from the Army troops when they were aboard. When Terry transferred to Tango 9, he began manning the 20mm cannon:

During my time on Tango 9, Glenn Leford had the port 20mm cannon while I had the starboard 20mm cannon. We literally fought back to back, and, we were close friends. I found Frank Springer to be a profound example of quiet courage, in intense combat conditions, courage comes in all sizes. "Little One" may not have been the largest man in the River Assault Group, but he took a back seat to no man, in knowing that you could count on him.

My boat captain on Tango 6, "Mac" came to me after a staff meeting and told me that it was discussed at the meeting that Tango 9 was hurt badly and needed new personnel. Mac told me that the boat captains were asked to volunteer a good man to go to Tango 9. Mac told me that I had experience and wanted me to go. I didn't want to go to a third boat after making friends on Tango 6, but I knew I had to. I know I should have taken Mac's gesture as a compliment. He had tears in his eyes when he did it.

This is the last entry Terry Sater would make into his diary on September 2nd, 1968: *We are on an op. They have put me on Tango 9, which had only a five man crew. This is the boat that Taylor was killed on. Another guy is in the hospital. I man both 20s, right now. It's going to be interesting in a firefight. The crew seems to be okay.*

The following was written in 1985 by Terry Sater who was upset after calling one of his shipmates from Tango 6 who had not fared well. His wife suggested that he should forget it, so he stayed up late that night trying to figure out how to explain it all to her. The next morning he gave her this poem.

> *She said, "Why not forget it? It happened long ago."*
> *The deepest wounds, cut to the heart, Will always heal slow.*
> *The nightmare of the Mekong, of death, despair and fear,*
> *could not be left in Vietnam, it's fresh, it's crisp, it's here.*
> *My body's strong. My mind is sound. I suffer from no pain.*
> *But once a man has been to war, he's never quite the same.*
> *For I know war for what it is, no glory in the fight.*
> *It's friends who die, and crippled kids, and voices crying in the*
> *night. I know the chill of monsoon rain, the heat of tropic sun.*
> *For some it never happened, and most will never know,*
> *except for those who fought the war. It happened long ago.*

When Third Class Petty Officer Terry Sater returned home after serving in Vietnam, he took his girlfriend of four years, Judi, into his Mom and Dad's bedroom, kissed her, and asked her to marry him. They were married six months later and then twenty-one-year old Terry carried Judi across the threshold of their mobile home in Summerville, South Carolina, where Terry was stationed aboard USS Hunley in Charleston, South Carolina.

Judi immediately started crying, missing her Mom and Dad, but they weathered the low pay and living far away from where they had been raised. Judi learned how to fry an egg and be a wife, and she stroked Terry's back when the nightmares came, helping them to go away. She gradually rubbed away the calluses that had built up from when he had to learn how to deal with death.

Since Terry was released from service in August 1970, they have lived well, laughing often and loving each other through the years as they moved on with their lives, not accepting the Hollywood version of the Vietnam war and the thought that we Vietnam veterans should be ashamed of our service. We will always be proud of our units, our brothers in arms, and what we accomplished and went through together.

Terry and Judi are still married, and Judi still complains that Terry tells the same joke about them being happily married for twelve years out of the thirty-eight they have been together, but she still puts up with him. Secretly, Terry still cherishes Judi as much as the day he married her, even though she may not realize it. Terry has gone on to have a good career in the electrical industry and has enjoyed life to the fullest, scuba diving in Cabo, hot ballooning, birding a few holes at Pebble, following the greats at the Masters, and fishing in the Gulf of Mexico. But best of all was when he held his first-born son, Chris, thirty-five years ago. Thirty-one years ago, he was blessed again and gazed upon one of the most beautiful baby girls ever born, Dina. Both Chris and Dina have grown to be the kind of adults that make their parents proud.

The day Terry was married, he thought of his friends who died in the Mekong Delta and what they were missing. On the days that his children were born, or when he had a taste of good wine, sat by a fall campfire or watched a Caribbean sunset, he again thought back to his friends and what they were missing.

For some, we will never forget these silent heroes of our past, and we hope that somehow they know that we did not forget them and will never forget until the day we die. In some small way, this means something to us that served in that forgotten place and survived, and it always will.

SWAMP RATS

River Assault Squadron 15, nicknamed the "Swamp Rats" with the unofficial motto of "you call, we haul," was the last of the four Navy squadrons formed to serve with the Mobile Riverine Force. The assault squadron was commissioned with a modest ceremony in San Diego, California, on May 11th, 1968, with Navy Commander Walter C. Deal Jr. as commanding officer. Most of the officers and enlisted men assigned to the newly formed squadron were still undergoing training at the U.S. Naval Inshore Operations Training Center at Mare Island, Vallejo, California. The squadron's river assault craft were still being built at various locations and would catch up to the sailors in Vietnam. On June 4th, 1968, Commander Deal commissioned River Assault Division 151, with Lieutenant Joseph Philip Ferrara Jr. in command, and River Assault Division 152, with Lieutenant Donald M. Tobolski in command.

By June 24th, the first sailors of River Assault Division 151 had completed training and reported in-country Vietnam for duty. The division was first stationed at Vung Tau on the coast aboard USS Bexar, USS Indra, and USS Okanagan, but no assault boats were available at first, so they undertook a routine of tactical training exercises, using regular weapons. By August 7th, the squadron's first boats arrived for activation, with the sailors beginning to outfit the craft, preparing them for combat. Preparing a boat and its crew for operations averaged ten days as crews worked together in the blistering sun, becoming teams. As boats became operational, they were sent to assist units already operating on the Vam Co and Soi Rap Rivers. River Assault Division's 151 and 152 craft also began participating in riverine operations in the arduous Rung Sat and in areas southwest of Saigon, which were all Viet Cong strongholds.

For a ten-day period in late July and early August, 1968, Mobile Riverine Task Groups Alpha and Bravo were operating on the opposite extremities of the Mekong Delta, more than one hundred miles apart. Task Group Bravo was conducting missions against Viet Cong elements in the area around Nha Be. Meanwhile, Task Group Alpha was making the southernmost penetration into the U Minh Forest, which had been a communist base area for at least a decade and perhaps as long as twenty-five years. More than 250 Viet Cong soldiers were killed and huge weapons caches were captured in this operation south of Can Tho, where the trees were so thick at points that the Viet Cong were rumored to live in them. The boats, with their arsenal of heavy weapons, played a significant role, as did the Vietnamese 5th Marine Battalion, which was operating with the Mobil Riverine Force for a nine-day period. In the past, the Mobile Riverine Force had participated in many productive battles in which it operated with the Viet Marines, specifically December 4th – 6th, 1967, when 266 Viet Cong were killed in the U Minh, producing large stock piles of captured weapons. Both operations into the Cau Mau Peninsula were very successful endeavors, but the area remained a VC stronghold for much of the war.

On September 15th, 1968, the river patrol force administrative title changed from River Squadron Five to River Patrol Flotilla Five. Simultaneously, the force's River Divisions and River Sections became River Squadrons and River Divisions, respectively. It was also in September that units of River Assault Division 151 participated in their first independent operations with two ops between September 19th and October 1st, 1968. They were also active on October 5th and 7th, in support of the ARVN and local Regional and Popular Forces. The highlight of the operation was the successful defoliation of an area used by the Viet Cong for storage and regrouping, but contact with the enemy was sparse.

River Assault Division 152 was completing outfitting on October 9th, while River Assault Division 151 was participating in a landing on the Vam Co Tay River in the Plain of Reeds in support of the 7th ARVN Division.

On October 10th, River Assault Division 151 Commander Lieutenant Phil Ferrara and his river assault craft were detached for independent duty in the Saigon "Rocket Belt" area. Lieutenant Ferrara, in conjunction with the 3rd Battalion 39th Infantry, operated from Nha Be, and in the area of Can Giouc. The division also operated with local Regional Forces participating in troop insertions and reconnaissance in force patrols. Throughout the month, several river assault craft of Assault Division 151 were continually engaged in some form of operation and combat.

On October 16th, the division was supporting a thirty-six-person MEDCAP (Medical Civil Action Program) team in eastern Long An Province, when they were asked to quickly move south to ambush the Viet Cong, who had been spotted. Their rapid response resulted in them killing two VC and capturing one deserter, who wisely switched sides. A few days later, Tango-151-1 captured a Viet Cong prisoner, the first of the new division's boats to do so. The division continued to engage in search and destroy missions throughout Long An Province for most of the month and on the 27th, River Assault Division 151 began conducting night ambushes. The Swamp Rats, and their embarked troops, were credited with high numbers of enemy killed, prisoners captured, bunkers destroyed and weapons seized, but on Halloween '68, the enemy retaliated by ambushing the river assault craft with rockets south of Can Giouc. Tango-151-13 took four rocket hits, wounding two sailors and fourteen U.S. soldiers before they gained the upper hand and suppressed fire.

River Assault Division 152 was initiated into battle on October 13th, supporting the 6th Battalion 31st Infantry and Regional Forces, in an attempt to capture a Viet Cong Province Chief in Dinh Tuong Province. Although the Province Chief slipped away, four Viet Cong were killed. October 22nd found Division 152 again in support of the Vietnamese 4th Marine Corps Battalion in western Dinh Tuong Province, conducting search and destroy missions. During the mission, a VC district leader, a squad leader, and a tax collector were captured.

On November 1st, River Assault Squadron 15 units began participating in Operation SEA LORDS (Southeast Asia Lake, Ocean, River and Delta Strategy) with Task Forces 115 and 116 units, in the first combined operations in the Mekong Delta. Assault operations were launched to stop the flow of insurgents and equipment across the Cambodian border southeastward into

South Vietnam. That night, the river assault craft of River Assault Division 151 were on night ambush stations when they caught and engaged the enemy, killing fifteen Viet Cong before it was over. Charlie got his dander up and retaliated by ambushing the boats on six occasions after that night, wounding two soldiers and eight sailors in the next few days, while losing twenty Viet Cong fighters in the process.

Around the same time, other elements of the division were providing boat support to explosive ordnance and harbor clearance teams for salvage clearance operations. Four sunken barges had been positioned by the enemy to partially block a key canal. During the operation, 1,520 pounds of explosives were used in twelve detonations. A survey following the successful operation indicated a minimum of six feet clearance over the former obstruction.

The USS Westchester County, LST 1167, Wesco, as she was called, was anchored on the My Tho River with several other support ships of River Assault Flotilla One. The tank landing ship was acting as a troop carrier and supply ship for a large number of assault boats being used by the Army's 9th Infantry Division, and the sailors of the Mobile Riverine Force. Wesco provided berthing for approximately 250 U.S. Army personnel, in addition to her 140 crew and officers. In her belly, she maintained a massive amount of supplies for the flotilla. Among the cargo on her tank deck were 350 tons of ammunition and explosives. All guard stations were manned with picket boats circling the ship and dropping concussion grenades at random intervals to ward off swimmers. Still, the riverine ships were never really safe from the Viet Cong sapper swimmers.

At 0322 hours, on the morning of November 1st, 1968, while all the men were asleep in their racks, two giant underwater explosions were detonated on the starboard side of Westchester County. The two mines had been attached directly under the fuel and berthing compartments of Wesco. In the confusion that followed, crewmen tried desperately to find their way to their battle stations through the dark, steam-filled, diesel-soaked wreckage. Unable to locate personal items in the pitch-black compartments, crewmen showed up to their battle stations in their underwear and less, with many of them wounded and bleeding. Five of the ship's first class petty officer department heads were among those killed instantly in the blast that rocked the ship and woke up the flotilla. In many cases, much lower-ranked sailors took the initiative, manning damage control stations without hesitation, assuming responsibilities of their missing department heads.

The ship's commanding officer, Lieutenant Commander John W. Branin, immediately tried to stabilize the severely damaged ship, which was starting to list to the starboard side due to the massive flooding of her lower decks. The danger of flash fires igniting the more than 350 tons of explosives and ammunition on the ship's forward tank deck, was of great concern to Captain Branin. The entire ship was engulfed in an atomized cloud of diesel fuel, which lingered in the air surrounding the ship, as damage control teams quickly rushed in with fire hoses and suppressed the flames. The captain had no doubt that any miscalculation at that point would have resulted in a catastrophic explosion, causing not only the loss of the ship and all hands aboard, but also resulting in death and destruction to anyone within a very large radius of the ship, which had become ground zero, with many rushing to her aid.

Battle stations remained at the ready, as it was not known if this was the beginning of a much larger attack or if more unexploded charges were still attached to the ship's hull, waiting to be ignited by the enemy sappers. Damage control teams worked frantically to suppress and control the flooding, while attempts were made to free Navy crewmen and Army personnel trapped in the mangled wreckage. Many of the killed and wounded were crushed and pinned between the deck and overhead while still in their racks, making rescue very difficult at best. All teams were instructed to conduct their rescues and repairs without the use of cutting torches or welding equipment.

At one point, the ship's corpsman, Hospital Corpsman First John Sullivan, clambered down into the wreckage to locate two men pinned in the lower compartments. He remained at their sides for more than an hour until both severely wounded men were freed.

As damage reports made their way to the bridge, the names of the lost and missing began to add up. By daylight, the numbers were in, with seventeen sailors from the ship's company killed or missing. Five U.S. Army soldiers and one sailor from the riverine assault force were also lost, with one Vietnamese sailor and one Vietnamese Tiger Scout killed as well. There were also twenty-seven wounded, seven of which required medical evacuation.

Lieutenant Commander Branin and the rest of the crew knew there was no time for emotions over their losses, as the ship and crew remained in grave danger for many hours to come, with Captain Branin and Executive Officer Richard Jensen wondering why the ship hadn't gone up. The crew members continued to work with no consideration for their own safety, as all did their best to save the ship and their wounded shipmates.

Many of the crew and Army personnel onboard USS Westchester County that day, received citations and awards for the part they played during the rescue attempts and in keeping the ship afloat and from going up in flames. The twenty-five men lost in the explosion that tragic morning came to represent the U.S. Navy's greatest loss of life in a single incident as the result of enemy action during the entire war.

After offloading all Army troops and Navy assault squadron personnel, and their equipment, the Westchester County was beached on November 4th, in order to accomplish temporary repairs to make her seaworthy. Just ten days later, the ship got underway, testimony to the professionalism and hard work of the sailors from several units who cooperated in getting the repairs completed quickly. Wesco arrived at Yokosuka, Japan, her home port, on November 26th, 1968. The Mobile Riverine Force had withstood a severe blow, but would bounce back to deliver devastating assaults on enemy strongholds, with the memory of the Westchester County and their lost shipmates as an incentive to spur them on.

On November 2nd, 1968, the same day Operation SEA LORDS commenced, the commander of U.S. Military Assistance Command, Vietnam, by presidential directive, commenced the accelerated turn over to the Vietnamese, by which U.S. forces in time would transfer over their equipment and combat responsibilities to the Republic of South Vietnam. For the next two years, the River Patrol Force, in combination with the Coastal Surveillance and Mobile Riverine Forces, would see action in SEA LORDS, while simultaneously transferring assets to the Vietnamese Navy.

On November 6th, River Assault Division 151 operated out of Nha Be with the 9th Infantry's 3rd Battalion 39th Infantry. This was followed by operations in the "Three Sisters" area, about ten miles northwest of Rach Gia. By the 16th, the river assault craft had moved west where Vietnamese Marines accounted for eight VC killed and two captured. The river assault craft maintained blocking and interdiction stations and were credited with ten sampans destroyed. Afterwards, the Viet Cong said goodbye to the division with an eight-round mortar attack that resulted in no casualties or hits on the departing river craft. The division then moved back to Nha Be to support the 9th Infantry.

Enemy swimmer sappers again struck the Mobile Riverine Force the night of November 15th when Light Lift Craft Four, a landing craft converted to salvage work by the addition of a large boom and salvage and diving equipment, was mined and sunk while at anchor on the Ham Luong near the entrance to Ben Tre. Two explosions within seconds of each other were observed, with the craft sinking almost immediately. Two sailors were lost and thirteen wounded, including four crewmen of an assault craft which was moored alongside.

For the next week, river assault craft shifted their area of operations twenty-five miles south southwest of Rach Gia. After landing the 4th Vietnamese Marines, the craft set up interdiction patrols in the surrounding waterways. River Assault Division 151 then concluded operations at Nha Be by the end of the month.

In December, mobile riverine assault operations were strung out from one end of the Mekong Delta to the other. Riverine warfare was characterized by interdiction, escort, and patrol, with base security and pacification operations. For most of the month, Mobile Riverine Group Bravo operations consisted largely of a variety of special operations in the vicinity of Can Tho and in the southern Mekong Delta in coordination with units of the 2nd, 3rd, and 4th Vietnamese Marines. Most of Riverine Group Alpha had spent that same period of time conducting operations around Dong Tam and Ben Tre City. Several battalions of the 2nd Brigade of the 9th Infantry were involved in vigorous pacification efforts in Kien Hoa Province, of which Ben Tre City was the provincial capital. Small unit actions over wide areas in four provinces accounted for 454 Viet Cong killed.

Mobile Riverine Group Alpha engaged in a series of operations, designated Operation Kidney Flush, which were designed to keep constant pressure on the Viet Cong. With frequent insertions in Kien Hoa Province, Army ground elements continued to seek out and destroy the enemy with a vengeance. These operations, which employed riverine, air and ground assets, continued to gradually wear down enemy units. The toll to the Viet Cong had been ten dead, coupled with loss of supplies and equipment. Of the many detainees taken during these actions, about twenty percent were classified as VC with the remainder determined to be innocent civilians.

About this time, night ambush patrols began being incorporated into the operations of the 3/60th Infantry. This was a clearly defined change in riverine force procedure, as night landings were previously avoided as too dangerous. The procedure was changed so as to rest the troops during the day, land them after dark, and extract them the following morning. This was the same method successfully employed by units of the 9th Infantry in Long An Province, which kept the VC on the run.

On December 5th, River Assault Division 152 got underway from the riverine base at Can Tho, with thirty assault craft for operations in southern Chung Thien Province. Three companies of the 4th Vietnam Marines came aboard the next day, and the task unit proceeded to begin operations. Throughout this period, the Vietnamese Marines conducted ground sweeps in selected locations, and the assault craft patrolled in the general area within a ten-mile radius to the south and southwest. Enemy reaction to the riverine force presence came in the form of fourteen separate B40 rocket ambushes in a six-day time period, where seventy-five B40 rockets were fired at the riverine force. Enemy fire was returned and suppressed in all but one instance, in which friendly troops were in the area making it too dangerous. Two assault craft were damaged as a result of these actions, with four U.S. sailors wounded. On two separate occasions, B40 rockets became lodged in the Styrofoam on a Tango and a Zippo, failing to detonate. This operation turned out to be one of the most successful to date and resulted in fifty-five Viet Cong killed, while only one Marine was lost. In addition to the large body count, a VC prison camp was discovered by the Marines, resulting in the release of ten Vietnamese prisoners. Several tons of weapons, ammunitions, and military supplies were captured or destroyed as well.

The Mobile Riverine Force concept was projected into the open sea for the first time when boats accompanied units to conduct operations in the western end of Cua Lon River. Operating as units of SEA LORDS, Monitors, Alphas and Tangos, with one Mobile Strike Force Company embarked, began late on the night of December 16th, and transited the western coast of South Vietnam in a thirty-six hour trip. Meanwhile, the USS Mercer with another Mobile Strike Force Company and a thirty-man underwater demolition team, including a explosive ordnance disposal divers' element, embarked USS Satyr and USS Iredell County and proceeded to the rendezvous point in the Gulf of Thailand in three separate transits via the South China Sea, around the southern tip of Vietnam.

Rough seas delayed the commencement of the operation, designed to destroy a series of twelve fish-trap-style barricades erected across the western end of the Cua Lon River. After encountering difficulty on the mud flats at the Cua Lon entrance, the task unit succeeded in transiting the shallows with the aid of a Vietnamese Navy junk pilot. Strike forces were positioned on the bank while the diver units commenced destruction of the barricades. Meeting light enemy resistance, the "Silver Mace" forces completed the barricade destruction, with the task unit beginning to withdraw from the area.

On Christmas Eve, the boats of River Assault Divisions 151 and 152, with the 2nd and 3rd Battalions of the Vietnamese Marines, commenced a new phase of Operation SEA LORDS, pushing into a section of southwestern Kien Giang Province in the U Minh Forrest, where no government forces had entered in over five years.

The area proved difficult to subdue, as the Marines were unable to maintain contact with the evasive VC and the boats were subject to a number of highly accurate and costly ambushes. A total of thirty-six men of River Assault Squadrons 15 and 13 were wounded in the course of the fourteen-day operation. The squadron would claim the record for the longest sustained firefight as a result of a Viet Cong multi-company action, which extended down a line of almost two miles of weapons firing and lasted over one hour on New Year's Eve. The boats returned to the mobile riverine base after having been ambushed ten times. The operation resulted in fifteen Viet Cong killed and sixteen captured, along with a large enemy hospital complex destroyed and several hundred pounds of medical supplies captured. During this time, Commander D.R. Divelbiss relieved Commander Deal as Commander River Assault Squadron 15, while still in the area of operations.

Then for a short while, the Christmas season was upon them. Christmas was the one time of the year when everyone wanted to be home with family and loved ones. But regrettably, while one served a tour of duty in sunny Vietnam, it was not possible. To try and counter this problem, the supply departments of the force would order large stocks of fresh fruit, nuts, fruit cake, and other special items, which would be available for all hands during the holiday season. There would also be a grand Christmas dinner with roast tom turkey, accompanied by brown giblet gravy, and Virginia ham with raisin pineapple sauce.

Some of the cooks on those big boats were great and although we complained a little now and then, most of us had never had it so good. There were steaming deep trays of snowflake mashed potatoes, buttered corn and green peas, cornbread dressing, hot rolls, and tossed green salad, as the men all stood in a long line, waiting their turn to parade past the cooks with mouths watering. Albert "Cookie" Moore on the USS Benewah said he usually had a delicious dessert like pumpkin pie with whipped cream afterward. Then there was tea, Kool-Aid and coffee, which would sometimes be spiked with a little "Christmas cheer."

Of course, someone had gone out and gotten a hold of some Christmas trees, or something that looked like them. The men decorated them with everything imaginable, including hand grenade pins holding all kinds of strange objects. Of course, it was a little more traditional in "officers country," or at least that is what was rumored. Everyone looked forward to the care packages and letters sent from home. Those God-sent packages could be huge boost for a young man in a place so far from snow and Mom's home-cooking.

There were times in everyone's tour of duty when service to country had to come above personal preferences. So everybody made the best of it and hoped they would get the opportunity to spend the holidays with family and friends next year. Jingle bells, jingle bells, but until then, everyday was the same as the next, with the war raging on and the enemy trying to take advantage of every opportunity and holiday, so defenses had to stay strong.

At 2100 hours on December 27th, a patrol consisting of one Alpha, one Tango and three PBRs was proceeding south on the Rach Gia – Long Xuyen Canal when the patrol was attacked at a position three miles northeast of Rach Gia. One sailor was lost and three others wounded, with the Tango receiving three B40 rocket hits. Fire was returned as the patrol withdrew to the south with two Seawolf gunships scrambling and placing air strikes on the suspected enemy positions. The men lost during Christmas and holidays seemed to hurt the worst, not that losing them at other times felt any better.

At 0845 hours on December 31st, during a reconnaissance in force operation twenty miles southwest of Rach Gia, enemy ambushes against assault craft produced significant friendly casualties on two occasions. While on the way to land units of the 2nd and 3rd Battalions Vietnamese Marines, fifteen assault craft encountered B40 rocket and automatic weapons fire from both banks of a canal. Although enemy fire was returned and suppressed, one Tango and one Monitor were damaged by rocket hits, with seven U.S. sailors wounded. Later that same night in the same area, the river assault craft, again with Viet Marines aboard, came under attack three times, receiving fifty B40 rockets and heavy automatic fire. Tango-

151-12 received four B40 hits, Tango-152-13 received one hit and Tango-151-6 sustained three hits, producing heavy casualties of ten U.S. sailors, three Viet sailors and twenty-eight Viet Marines wounded. Enemy fire was returned by assault craft in all cases and at 2145 hours, two Seawolves and a U.S. Air Force Spooky aircraft attacked the suspected enemy positions.

Should old acquaintance be forgot, and never brought to mind. But seas between us broad have roared, for auld lang syne. And there's a hand, my trusty friend, and give us a hand o' thine. And we will take a goodwill draught, for auld lang syne.

During January 1969, Mobile Riverine Force units sought out and continued engaging the enemy throughout the delta. Offensive operations consisted of frequent employment of small unit forces over wide areas. This strategy was intended to have major effect toward the breakup of communist infrastructure, with the disruption of enemy plans and the demoralization of enemy forces. The activities of Mobile Riverine Group Alpha remained essentially stable as troop lift operations were continued mainly in Kien Hoa Province in support of the 2nd Brigade of the 9th Infantry. Constant pressure was applied to enemy forces in advancement of the accelerated pacification effort. The gradual wearing down of enemy forces was significant, yielding a daily average of fourteen Viet Cong killed, as the force continued to aggressively seek out the communists.

Mobile Riverine Group Bravo, operating mainly with the 3rd and 4th Battalions of the Vietnamese Marines, advanced into the southern delta provinces. Simultaneously, detached units of Group Bravo also conducted coordinated operations in the northern Mekong Delta, as components of SEA LORDS campaigns. Troops aboard these units discovered large quantities of enemy weapons and supply caches along the river banks.

On January 3rd, the U.S. Navy's Light Attack Squadron 4 (VAL-4), the "Black Ponies," was commissioned at Naval Air Station North Island, San Diego, California, and deployed to Vietnam. Its OV-10 two-seat, propeller-driven "Broncos" provided organic fixed-wing attack aircraft support. Armed with Zuni rockets and Mini-guns, the Black Ponies were a welcome addition to U.S. Naval forces and became a formidable enemy of the Viet Cong delivering devastating attacks on their troops.

A week later, the boats of the Mobile Riverine Force returned to Chuong Thien Province for an eight-day operation with the 4th Battalion, Vietnamese Marines, killing twenty VC and capturing five. The operation was marred by the mining of Tango-151-5 on the Rach Cai Nhut. Two sailors were killed, and the boat was a complete loss.

The following poem was written by Tango-151-5 Boat Captain Chief Lindsey, in honor of his two shipmates, Jose Campos and David Land, both lost on the "River Queen" on January 14th, 1969.

ODE TO THOSE I LEFT BEHIND

Greetings, stalwart sailor, who walked my decks with pride.
Who gave your all to protect me and those who bravely died.
A vote of thanks I give you, to all a job well done.
Your bravery was commendable, I never had to run.
To you who saved me faithfully, and helped me save face.
Who manned the guns with vigor to keep the enemy in his place.
What can I say, "Oh brave ones," to let you know my heart.
What can I say, "Ye sailors," you know we had to part.
Though no longer will you walk my decks and guide me to nest.
I keep you close to my heart, as I humbly go to rest.

The boats again set out on a large-scale blocking and interdiction operation on the Can Tho River. At the conclusion of the operation, over 7,000 sampans had been checked by patrolling boats. A first was marked for the squadron when the crew of Tango-152-12, assisted a woman in the birth of her baby while her sampan was alongside. The river assault squadrons continued to fight on through 1969.

By June 15th, 1969, River Assault Division 152 was again locked in deadly combat on the Ong Muong Canal in Kien Hoa Province. Lieutenant Thomas G. Kelley, while serving as commander of River Assault Division 152, was incharge of a column of eight river assault craft which were extracting one company of U.S. Army infantry on the east bank of the canal, when one of the Tangos reported a mechanical failure of its loading ramp. At approximately the same time, Viet Cong forces opened fire from the opposite bank of the canal. After issuing orders for the crippled Tango to raise its ramp manually, and for the remaining boats to form a protective cordon around the disabled craft, Lieutenant Kelley, realizing the extreme danger to his column and its inability to clear the ambush site until the crippled unit was repaired, boldly maneuvered his Monitor into the exposed side of the protective cordon in direct line with the enemy's fire and ordered the crew to commence firing. Suddenly, an enemy rocket scored a direct hit on the coxswain's flat, the shell penetrating the thick armor plate and the explosion spraying shrapnel in all directions. Sustaining serious head wounds from the blast, which hurled him to the deck of the Monitor, Lieutenant Kelley disregarded his injuries and continued directing the boats. Although unable to move from the deck or to speak clearly into the radio, Kelley succeeded in relaying his commands through one of his men until the enemy attack was silenced and the boats were able to move to safety.

Lieutenant Kelley's brilliant leadership, bold initiative, and resolute determination inspire his men to finish the mission after he had been medically evacuated by helicopter. His courage under fire and selfless devotion to duty resulted in Lieutenant Thomas G. Kelley being awarded the Medal of Honor for his actions that day.

The following is a letter written home to the families of the men of the Mobile Riverine Force from Commander, River Assault Flotilla One.

As I have said numerous times before, I have never worked with a more dedicated, resourceful and professional group of men than we have in our force. They are doing the job they came here to do.

I am sorry that I don't have the time to send a personal letter of appreciation to the many of you who have written to express their support of the task we are trying to achieve. In a country such as ours, no war should ever be described as a "popular" one. I cannot understand or excuse those Americans who are lending moral

support and encouragement to the Viet Cong to continue their
terrorist acts against their own countrymen, and their ambushes of
our forces. It is good to be reminded that this noisy group is definitely
in the minority.

Captain R. S. Salzer

The Mobile Riverine Force of Task Force 117 stood down
on August 25th, 1969, becoming the first major Navy command
deactivated in Vietnam. The sailors and soldiers of the Great Green
Fleet had completed their mission and delivered a devastating blow
to communist forces in the Mekong Delta. But it had come at a
high cost.

During 1968, the Mobile Riverine Force and the 9th Infantry
Division had engaged in bitter fighting in the Saigon area during
the Tet Offensive. Afterwards, General Westmoreland stated that
the 9th Infantry Division and the Mobile Riverine Force had saved
the delta. The 9th Infantry continued operating throughout the
Mekong Delta until two brigades were deployed to Hawaii as part
of the U.S. withdrawal. The 3rd Brigade stayed in Vietnam and also
fought in the Cambodian Invasion.

In October 1970, the last of the 9th Infantry came home.

SEAWOLVES

In the waning hours of the Tet Offensive, the enemy continued to harass and attack Naval Support Activity detachments, logistics craft, and Game Warden river patrol units. The communist insurgents employed rockets and automatic weapons in their attacks against support craft and PBR patrols with increased effectiveness, but did not deter the PBR's role of interdicting the enemy on the rivers and canals. Often the U.S. Navy Seawolf gunships of Task Force One-one-six were employed and scrambled to assist U.S. and allied forces lending their firepower to the battle and performing medical evaluations of the wounded, many times saving the day. This was never more evident than during the month of March 1968. While the Tet Offensive slowly wound down in Saigon, it continued to rage on for many more months in the Mekong Delta, crippling men and taking many more lives, both ours and theirs.

On March 1st, '68, the combined efforts of U.S. Navy, Coast Guard, Army, Air Force, and Vietnamese Navy units destroyed three of four enemy trawlers attempting to infiltrate supplies into South Vietnam. The fourth trawler turned back prior to entering the twelve-mile contiguous zone. This brought the total number of trawlers turned back or destroyed since February '65, to thirteen. There were no confirmed reports of successful trawler infiltration since the formation of Operation Market Time.

Three days later, the Nha Be detachment received an estimated thirty-five rounds of mortar and recoilless rifle fire. Fifteen rounds landed within the perimeter of the base and another twenty rounds landed in the water near by. As a result of the attack, four sailors were injured and the Public Works compound was damaged extensively. On the next day, the Qui Nhon detachment received approximately fifty rounds of harassment fire, but luckily there were no casualties.

Four days later, following Viet Cong attacks on three outposts just east of Tra On, Seawolves conducted air strikes along a tree line from which enemy fire had originated earlier that day. The Navy gunships opened their attack with low-level runs dropping twenty-pound bombs directly on the target, followed by rocket and machinegun passes, while enemy ground fire hit the lead bird twice, wounding one crewman. The Seawolves continued their attack until all rockets were expended, leaving six Viet Cong dead, five wounded, and several structures destroyed along with three tons of rice.

On the following morning, the maximum use of Navy teamwork was employed, resulting in a substantial enemy casualty toll. The action began when the SEAL 7th Platoon and an element of a Vietnamese Provincial Reconnaissance unit engaged the Viet Cong 531st Company and elements of the Viet Cong 509th at 0700 hours three miles north of Phu Vinh. Throughout the day, PBRs provided neutralizing fire as needed while Seawolves maintained constant air support. The ground units reported that many lives were saved by the coordinated fire by the patrol boats and gunships during the seven-hour operation. There were six known Viet Cong killed and twenty wounded. At least fifteen others were believed dead, but their bodies were not found. One of the dead was identified as the commander of the 531st Viet Cong Company. There were no friendly casualties from the day-long battle, which netted many captured VC weapons.

Also on March 6th, a Seawolf helicopter fire team on patrol in the Sa Dec area was called by the Kien Van sub-sector advisor to aid his men against enemy troops six miles northwest of Sa Dec. The Seawolf gunships received ground fire as they approached the target area and, in coordination with the Vietnamese ground elements, put in an air strike, routing a number of Viet Cong in trenches. Additional enemy troops remained in a tree line north of the initial strike area and continued to fire on the friendly forces. The Seawolves attacked the tree line, followed by a frontal attack by ARVN soldiers who bravely charged and overran the enemy positions. The Navy choppers killed seven of the enemy and were instrumental in aiding the ground forces in the capture of eighty more. There were no U.S. casualties, but one ARVN soldier was killed in the one-and-a-half hour battle. It was determined that the enemy had established an ambush area in which to attack river patrol boats, but thanks to the Seawolves and ARVN soldiers, this scheme was ended.

Later that evening, a PBR patrol intercepted a sampan with nine occupants crossing the river from the north bank about six miles northwest of Ben Tre. When the sampan ignored warning shots to stop for inspection, the patrol boats opened fire. The occupants were seen leaping over the side as the firing zeroed in. Five Viet Cong bodies were found. In view of the intensity of the PBR fire, it was highly suspected that the remaining four were either killed or seriously wounded. Thirty rounds of 7.62 Russian ammunition, six Viet Cong uniforms, a footlocker containing documents and the engine were taken from the sampan before it was destroyed.

The next morning about a half mile west of Ben Tre, a PBR patrol encountered heavy small-arms, automatic-weapon, and rocket fire. As the PBR gunners commenced return fire, a B40 rocket slammed into the aft .50 cal machingun of PBR 715, mortally wounding the aft gunner, Engineman Third Daniel D. Webb, and wounding three other crewmen. The boat cleared the area as additional rockets exploded in the water.

On March 8th, acting on intelligence that five to ten Viet Cong tax collectors were operating seven miles southwest of Tra On, on the southern bank of the river, PBRs landed Vietnamese Popular Force troops to conduct a ground sweep while Seawolves patrolled overhead. The Vietnamese troops soon made contact and drove the Viet Cong into a field where Seawolves delivered immediate air strikes on the enemy, who were seen running. The Popular Force troops later found seven dead Viet Cong. There were no friendly casualties.

On March 9th, 1968, Navy Lieutenant Commander Allen Ellis Weseleskey was leading a two-Huey Seawolf fire team when they answered a call sent out from river patrol boats on blocking positions in Kien Phong Province. It was a scramble one attempt to rescue two United States Army advisors who had been critically wounded when their Vietnamese battalions engaged a Viet Cong communist force. Commander Weseleskey and his fire team, with co-pilot Lieutenant Junior Grade Bill Macky, Crew Chief and door gunner Third Glenn Wilson, and door gunner Third John Bolton, upon arrival were caught in an intense crossfire during an attempt to land. Signaled to abort and clear the area by friendly ground troops, the choppers departed the kill zone with machineguns blazing but taking hits at the same time.

The Seawolves, as they called their UH-1B Bell-manufactured helicopters (as well as themselves), were armed with forward-firing machineguns and 2.75-inch rockets with two pilots up front and two enlisted men serving as door gunners in the back cabin, also manning machineguns. But the attack choppers had very little protection.

When Commander Weselesky wingman's Seawolf gunship commander, Lieutenant Junior Grade Hal Guinn, and door gunner were wounded, Wes ordered them to return to base while he and his crew remained on station to complete the mission alone. Witnessing a Vietnamese aircraft receive several hits which forced it to depart station, Navy Pilot Weseleskey renewed his determination to complete a successful rescue of the wounded Americans. Joined by an Army AH-1G Cobra gunship to cover his attempt, Wes again led his brave crew into the fire zone through heavy mortar bombardments and intense enemy automatic weapons fire from a communist large-caliber machinegun. Despite this, Weselesky made the ultimate penetration, by flying low under the tree tops, so the Viet Cong gunners could not track his chopper well. He was somehow able to land his bullet-riddled gunship on target, in an extremely confined zone. They then brought aboard the two critically wounded U.S. Army advisors and a seriously wounded Vietnamese soldier. Lifting his heavily laden copter out of the kill zone, with some difficulty, it must be said, Commander Weseleskey maintained absolute control of his helicopter despite adverse flying conditions and taking heavy hits galore. The Army Cobra's Mini-guns continued to suppress enemy fire. After clearing the hazardous fire zone, they flew the seriously wounded soldiers to the Dong Tam Army field hospital.

By his professional leadership and courageous fighting spirit, Wes served to inspire his men to perform to their utmost capability, thus ensuring the success of the mission. Lieutenant Commander Allen Ellis Weseleskey was awarded the Navy Cross for extraordinary heroism and bravery on March 9th, 1968. His crew was also decorated.

One of the Army advisors saved that day was First Lieutenant Jack Jacobs, who was torn up badly, with major head and body wounds. Lieutenant Jacobs had distinguished himself while serving as assistant battalion advisor, 2nd Battalion, 16th Infantry, 9th Infantry Division of the Republic of Vietnam Army. The 2nd Battalion was advancing to contact when it came under intense heavy machinegun and mortar fire from a Viet Cong battalion positioned in well-fortified bunkers. As the ARVN 2nd Battalion deployed into attack formation, its advance was halted by devastating fire. Lieutenant Jacobs with the command element of the lead company called for and directed air strikes on the enemy positions in order to renew their attack. Due to the intensity of the enemy fire and heavy casualties to the command group, including the company commander, the attack was stopped and the friendly troops became disorganized. Although wounded by mortar fragments, Lieutenant Jacobs assumed command of the allied company, ordered a withdrawal from the exposed position, and established a defensive perimeter. Despite profuse bleeding from head wounds, which impaired his vision, Jacobs, with complete disregard for his own safety, returned under intense fire to evacuate a seriously wounded advisor to the safety of a wooded area, where he administered lifesaving first aid. Jacobs then returned through heavy automatic weapons fire to evacuate the wounded company commander. Jacobs made repeated trips across the fire-swept open rice paddies, evacuating wounded soldiers and their weapons. On three separate occasions, Jacobs made contact and drove off Viet Cong squads who were searching for allied wounded and weapons, single-handedly killing three VC and wounding several others. His gallant actions and extraordinary heroism saved the lives of one of his fellow U.S. Army advisors and thirteen allied soldiers. By First Lieutenant Jack Jacobs's gallantry and bravery in action, he reflected great credit upon himself, his unit, and the U.S. Army. Jack Jacobs survived and was awarded the Medal of Honor. He would eventually become a military analyst for the MSNBC cable network.

On the evening of March 10ᵗʰ, 1968, a platoon of SEALs landed on the southern bank of the My Tho River one-and-a-half miles southwest of My Tho and, shortly after, made contact with a local Vietnamese civilian whose father had been killed by the Viet Cong. Because of his hatred for the Viet Cong, the civilian agreed to provide information concerning the local communist insurgents. The SEALs were then led to a house containing three Viet Cong, but as the team approached the enemy was alerted by a barking dog. As the communists attempted to escape, the SEALs killed all three of them. They were identified as the hamlet security chief and two of his assistants. The SEALs were then led to another house where they captured a female identified as a Viet Cong communication liaison. The female VC provided information as to the location of a Viet Cong tax collector; however, a search of the area failed to produce any positive results. The SEALs withdrew from the area the following morning, concealing the identity of the friendly civilian to protect him and his valuable source of information, which future operations would use to conduct successful operations.

The next morning, a 133-foot, twin screw, U.S. Navy refrigerated craft, YFR 890, in support of Game Warden forces, was headed down river from Vinh Long enroute back to Saigon with empty holds after having completed a resupply run. Suddenly, she received heavy enemy automatic-weapons and B40 rocket fire while transiting the Mekong River at a section affectionately referred to as the "Bottleneck," twenty miles west of My Tho. The delta resupply craft, commanded by Craftmaster Chief Boatswain's Mate Gideon W. Almy III, sustained eight rocket hits on the starboard side, which at the time sounded to the crew like the sky falling. The rockets caused extensive hull damage above the waterline, and one penetrated the hull and ended up in the block of the port main engine, causing considerable machinery damage. All weapons were manned quickly, with flak jackets and helmets donned while her crew returned fire with her starboard .50 cal and

M60 machineguns. Three sailors were wounded during the battle with the crew holding its own, as the support craft moved down river following specific orders to not stand and fight. The wounded were medevaced by PBRs shortly after the engagement. An hour later, YFR 890 met up with APL 55 at the head of the Ham Luong River, repaired her battle damage and then continued on her way.

Normally, when passing through narrow channels of the various delta waterways, YFR 890's crew members would throw apples and oranges to the children who lined the shore. This act of sharing had made many friends for the Navy craft, whose cargo holds were filled with fresh meat, fruit, and vegetables. Thankfully, these friends would mirror the situation at times. If the riverbanks were lined with people, there was little fear of enemy attack. If there were no people on hand to greet the craft, the crewmen stayed close to their weapons, knowing there was a chance they might get shot at. Craftmasters were briefed on "Red" areas before each delta run and were authorized to request PBR escort through these hot areas. They rarely ever did. They knew help was always only minutes away and didn't want to interrupt the regular duties of the patrolmen who put in long hours. Sailing up and down the rivers alone, seldom with escort, they knew their job was to deliver the cargo. But the small crews were always ready in either case.

On March 12th, a PBR blockade was established twenty miles up the Bassac River from Binh Thuy base that successfully engaged the enemy. The boats from River Section 511 were on station all night, encountering sporadic automatic weapons fire during the long wait. At first light, ARVN troops resumed a ground sweep in the area and began flushing out the enemy. A forty-foot junk with about thirty VC aboard tried to run the blockade, with PBRs opening fire on the junk destroying it. Then the PBRs directed their weapons' fire along the bank, reconing by fire. At the end of firefight, the river patrolmen had killed two Viet Cong and wounded seven others. In view of the overwhelming barrage of fire directed against the junk, it is highly likely that the other eighteen VC were killed as well. It is not unusual to lose sight of bodies once they enter the swift currents in the water. The PBRs concluded their action by destroying four enemy sampans.

The next day, a PBR patrol from River Section 511 was transiting the Bassac River seven miles southeast of Can Tho, when a sampan was detected crossing from the mainland to May Island. When the patrol closed in, a VC fighter in the sampan opened fire on the lead boat with an AK47 automatic rifle. The patrol immediately returned the fire, destroying the sampan and killing three insurgents. As the PBRs attempted to recover the remains of the sampan, they received intense automatic-weapons and small-arms fire from enemy positions on both the mainland and May Island. The patrol once again retaliated with all their weaponry in a thunderous return of fire, setting off a secondary explosion on May Island. A red fireball followed by smoke and flames rose ninety feet in the air, and the fire continued to burn for over an hour. The patrol made another firing pass at the island but was unsuccessful in suppressing enemy guns. The forward gunner on the lead boat sustained a serious wound during the action, so the PBRs cleared the area and called for a helicopter medical evacuation.

A second PBR patrol arrived on the scene shortly after and continued the engagement, along with a large Vietnamese Navy infantry landing ship which had also joined the river battle. Meanwhile, the air rescue of the wounded PBR sailor was aborted when the rescue copter and Navy armed choppers received intense ground fire. The wounded sailor was sped up river by boat to Can Tho, where an ambulance rushed him to the hospital. Action back at the scene of the ambush continued, and after three firing runs by the two PBRs and landing ship, the enemy fire was silenced. Three sailors were wounded in the fierce engagement, with three VC known dead. VC casualties ashore were undetermined but believed to be high.

On March 13th, undercover of darkness, the 7th Platoon of SEAL Detachment Alfa landed about thirteen miles east of My Tho off the Cua Tien River. After the SEALs were put ashore, they patrolled inland about a mile where the platoon split. Squad "Seven Bravo" moved to the north, as Squad "Seven Alpha" patrolled in a northwest direction. At 0200 hours, Alpha engaged and killed two Viet Cong. Upon hearing many voices to the east of its position, the squad evaded to the north followed by approximately fifty VC. The squad members then set up a perimeter defense and called for a Seawolf fire team to provide overhead cover and extract them from the area. Before the Seawolves arrived, the squad encountered and engaged about twenty VC moving in from the east. Seawolves put in air strikes while the SEALs were able to withdraw by a troop lift helicopter. Meanwhile, squad Bravo evaded to the south, where they established a perimeter defense to await a Seawolf strike and extraction. By 0330 hours, all SEALs were airlifted from the area, leaving sixteen dead Viet Cong behind. Four of the Navy raiders and an interpreter were wounded by grenade fragments during the incounter.

Later the same day, a new QT-2PC surveillance aircraft, designed to operate almost silently and utilizing very sensitive detection devices, proved its effectiveness during an evaluation flight when its crew provided intelligence to Game Warden units by detecting eight large junks transiting at night on a canal in the Dung Island complex near the mouth of the Bassac. Two PBRs and Seawolves responded by attacking and heavily damaging or destroying all eight junks.

Waiting in ambush on the next night nine miles west of Can Tho, SEALs of the 8th Platoon observed a man in a sampan approaching close to the bank where the ambush was posted. Two of the Navy raiders sprung into the sampan and captured the man, who was armed with a U.S. M-1 rifle. Upon questioning, the captive identified himself as a member of the Viet Cong Tay Do Battalion. The VC was then bound and gagged before the SEALs returned once again to silently wait in their ambush site. One hour later, another sampan with six VC approached. The SEALs spewed forth a hail of bullets, killing all six Viet Cong. Found in the sinking sampan were documents, grenades, ammunition, communication equipment and medical supplies. There were no friendly casualties.

On the morning of March 20th, a PBR patrol from River Section 534 detected and pursued a twenty-eight-foot sampan crossing the Ham Luong River about seven miles west of Ben Tre, in a known VC crossing corridor. Upon sighting the PBRs, the sampan, in violation of the established curfew, evaded to the south bank, ignoring all warning shots, electing to exchange fire with the patrol boats rather than heed their order to stop. The PBRs opened up with machineguns, setting the enemy craft on fire. Then patrol boats closed on the burning sampan and counted five dead Viet Cong. In addition, six males and four female insurgents were taken aboard and detained. Captured was one U.S. carbine, ammunition, and documents, including VC movement and personnel orders. The sampan was destroyed and the detainees turned over to Vietnamese authorities at Ben Tre.

Also on that day, four PBRs from River Section 535, a Seawolf fire team from Det-7, and SEAL platoon Delta-2 combined for Operation Quick-Kill seven miles southeast of Can Tho. The action began when two PBRs on a routine patrol were fired upon from three enemy positions on May Island. Within an hour, a quick reaction force of SEALs was landed by PBR, while Seawolves patrolled overhead. The SEALs commenced sweeping inland, following an initial air strike by the Seawolves, and made contact with one man believed to be a Viet Cong lookout. Seeing the SEALs, the man fled, although numerous trenches, bunkers, and an old base camp with two expended rocket boosters were found in a subsequent search. The SEALs began receiving automatic and small-arms fire from their right front. The Navy raiders returned fire while two SEAL scouts moved out to look for a flanking position from the right. Seawolves continued attacking the source of enemy fire, with little results. About five minutes later, the two scouts came upon the source of the enemy fire when they discovered four VC firing from a hooch. The scouts opened fire, and the Viet Cong dropped from sight. The scouts then returned to report their sighting when whistles were heard in front and rear of the squad. The SEALs withdrew to the river as the Viet Cong maneuvered around them, using whistle signals.

After the PBRs picked up the SEALs, the Seawolves swung in and raked over the area where the Viet Cong were maneuvering. The sector advisor later reported that twenty-seven VC were killed in the three-hour engagement. There were no friendly casualties. Later that evening, an enemy mortar attack on My Tho City had resulted in moderate damage to Naval support detachment's generator installation and a jeep, but there were no casualties.

In one two-day period, there were five separate incidents, scattered throughout the delta and the Rung Sat, in which three PBR patrolmen were killed and twenty wounded when their patrols were ambushed by Viet Cong employing RPG-2 and RPG-7 rockets. As a result, Game Warden units pursued the Viet Cong and exerted pressure. After three encounters with the enemy, SEALs seized a significant ordnance cache about ten miles south of Ben Tre.

On March 24th, five miles east of Vinh Long, PBRs 85 and 134 of River Section 522 came under rocket and automatic-weapons fire while on a routine patrol. The enemy attacked from several positions and fired at least seven RPG-7 rockets at the boats. PBR 134 took two hits, one in the starboard bow which exited through the port amidships. The second hit starboard amidships, destroying the radio and radar equipment, wounding two crewmen. PBR 134 cleared the area while PBR 85 continued to return fire on the enemy positions until the Seawolves arrived and suppressed the enemy with their 2.75 Zuni rockets and machineguns.

That afternoon, units of River Section 513 engaged in savage action with the enemy that claimed the lives of three PBR crewmen and wounded five more. The boats, PBRs 33 and 99, had just completed a medical evacuation of nine wounded and two dead Vietnamese soldiers from an outpost on the Nha Mau Canal, about seven miles southwest of Sa Dec. As the boats entered a curve in the canal leading to the Mekong River, the VC opened up with a deadly, continuous discharge of rocket and recoilless rifle fire. The first rounds hit PBR 99, the cover boat, which immediately capsized, dumping the crew and wounded Vietnamese into the canal. The boat sank, but the installed floatation material kept the bow above water. The crew swam to the opposite bank with several of the wounded Vietnamese and proceeded to a nearby outpost from which they were later recovered.

Meanwhile, PBR 33, the lead boat, still under heavy attack, was the target of numerous RPG-7 rockets. Direct hits killed the patrol officer, Boatswain's Mate First George F. Proffer, and the aft gunner, Gunner's Mate Third Ronald R. Lake, instantly. Boatswain's Mate

First Arthur O. Prendergast, the boat captain, though mortally wounded and intermittently losing conscious, stayed at the wheel of the boat long enough to clear the attack area, then he fell. He later died while en route to Dong Tam for medical treatment. Four additional PBRs and a Seawolf fire team were soon on the scene and commenced suppressing fire against the enemy positions while providing aid to the wounded crewmen on the stricken craft. The crippled PBR 33 was escorted to Sa Dec, and later that night, the sunken PBR 99 was towed from the area and refloated. Four additional PBR crewmen were also wounded in the battle.

On March 26th, Commander Task Force 116 conducted a combined Game Warden/River Assault Group operation against Tan Dinh Island, a Viet Cong stronghold in the lower Bassac River. Operation Bold Dragon III employed the USS Jennings County, LST 846, fourteen PBRs, four Seawolf gunships, a Mike-6 landing craft armed with a 106-recoilless rifle mounted on a wooden deck above the well deck, a thirty-six-foot-long armored personnel landing craft with.50 cal machineguns, and a SEAL platoon, all from Task Force 116, joined by RAG boats from River Assault Groups 25 and 29 with Regional and Popular Force troops embarked.

The attack began at 0900 hours with harassing and interdiction fire from the Jennings County, PBRs, Monitors and landing craft, with air strikes performed by the Seawolf gunships. By 1000 hours, the SEALs and Popular Forces landed to destroy a group of enemy bunkers and buildings. But after making contact with a sizable enemy force, they withdrew. The entire force then sailed down the narrow channel between the island and the mainland, putting in destructive fire on enemy fortifications along the banks. By 1300 hours, choppers had concluded the operation by dropping six gas canisters on the island, which released gas over a thirty-day period. Three buildings, four bunkers, four sampans and one ammunition dump were destroyed in the operation that netted a small VC body count with no friendly casualties. The following day, Dong Tam received nine rounds of 120mm mortar fire which resulted in only slight damage to a five-ton Navy truck.

In the early morning hours of March 29th, a Hoi Chanh led a SEAL platoon to a large enemy weapons cache and arms factory in Kien Hoa Province, about ten miles south of Ben Tre. PBRs proceeded two miles up a small canal off the Ham Luong River and, at 0600 hours, landed the SEALs within a hundred yards of the cache. As the SEALs moved into the village, they encountered and killed four Viet Cong. Sporadic small-arms fire was received throughout the operation as Seawolf gunships, six PBRs and USS Hunterdon County, LST 838, covered the operation. The Seawolves launched attacks, killing many of the VC fighters, while Hunterdon County provided harassment and interdiction fire between assaults. The cache was found in two concrete rooms, hidden beneath two houses being used as a weapons factory and storage area. Many of the captured items as possible were then loaded into patrol boats and the rest blown up before the SEALs withdrew at 0930 hours.

The former enemy soldier who led Game Warden units to the enemy locations and had rallied to the PBRs several days before, had related that he had been forced to go without food for two or three days at a time because PBRs had prevented the Viet Cong from moving food supplies on the river. He also stated that the river patrols had made it impossible for the Viet Cong to cross the river for the previous two weeks.

During the month of March 1968, Game Warden units, assisted by Seawolf gunships and quick-reaction forces under the operational control of Task Force 116, were involved in 151 firefights, killing 168 of the enemy while sustaining losses of four U.S. sailors and the wounding of sixty-four. Since the commencement of Game Warden operations, a kill ratio of forty-to-one had been attained by March '68. This did not count the river operations of Task Force Clearwater, which patrolled the dangerous waters of I Corps near the North Vietnamese border and performed equally as well. Navy Lieutenant Barry W. Hooper was killed while serving as a convoy commander assigned to Task Force Clearwater in March of 1968.

DUNG ISLAND

Enemy contact continued at a steady pace throughout the year, with Brown Water Naval Forces heavily involved. Time and time again, Seawolf gunships scrambled to support and rescue friendly forces, putting themselves into harm's way. VC insurgents aggressively transported resupply munitions and weapons from the Ho Chi Minh Trail into Vinh Long Province via the Mekong River trails. Routine procedures found the Viet Cong reinforcing crossing points with extra fighters to ensure safe passage along their routes deeper into the delta. One of these Viet Cong trails was Dung Island, which was a major Underground Railroad way point for VC logistics and operations. Located near the mouth of the Bassac River, midway in the stream, Dung Island provided refuge, shelter, and desirable cover for enemy elements transiting the land masses of the coastal plain of the Long Toan Secret Zone, on the north side of the Bassac. It was said to be a stop-off spot for the Viet Cong traveling between Saigon and the U Minh Forest with arms. It was a hot area which claimed the lives of many good sailors.

Less than a year earlier, on July 11th, 1967, Boatswain's Mate First W.V. Potter, Gunner's Mate Third O.P. Damrow, Seaman R.L. Center, and Fireman D.R. Nelson were lost when the enemy detonated a Claymore mine directed at their PBR near the northern tip of Dung Island. This happened when six river patrol boats of River Section 511 were in column returning to USS Garrett County, LST 786, on the Bassac. Moments after the mine showered PBR 58 with shrapnel, patrolmen on the other PBRs saw six Viet Cong fleeing the area and took them under fire, killing at least three. Seawolves launched and struck the enemy sites in the tree line.

The following recollection was provided by Seawolf Pilot Matt Gache, who flew Seawolf One-one off the USS Garrett County:

Our fire team had the duty that day. Lieutenant Tom Greenlee was the fire team leader in the lead gunship, with Lieutenant Webb Wright as his co-pilot. I was his wingman in the second bird, with Lieutenant Junior Grade Mike Jaccard as my co-pilot. Tommy Oleseski was my regular door gunner sitting behind me, and Chris Maher had the left door gunner position. We were out on the flight deck, enjoying the warm sun, observing a PBB patrol returning to the Garrett County. We were anchored up river from Dung Island on the Bassac. The PBR patrol was coming up river on the south side of the island when we observed one of the boats moving over to the shore. All of a sudden, we saw a burst coming from the tree line, most likely a Claymore set up in the trees. It hit straight on, and the boat went dead in the water. We scrambled to the island and put a strike into the tree line. I don't know for sure if we did any damage. In the meantime, the cover boat had gotten over to the PBR that had been hit and towed it back to the ship. At the time, we thought there were several wounded on the boat, so we were called back to the ship to medevac the wounded to Soc Trang, the nearest medical facility. Tom's crew took two wounded aboard their chopper and my crew took two, but when I looked in back of the bird, both of the PBR sailors looked pretty bad. Unfortunately, none survived. It was determined later that they had taken their helmets off, since their patrol was over and the home ship was in sight. I remember that the PBR river section officer in charge was furious with the survivors because they had thrown caution to the winds. The men that we medevaced had severe head wounds and might have survived had they been wearing their helmets.

Two days later, Seawolf One-seven was shot down at Dung Island and landed hard into a muddy rice paddy, killing Crew Chief, Aviation Machinist's Mate Third Donald F. Fee, and injuring the other three crew members of the downed chopper as well. Navy Pilot Lieutenant Commander Jimmy Glover did the best he could, but it was a beat-up old bird which, after she was hit, froze up and came down fast.

Petty Officer Fee, a West Virginia native who had just extended his tour and was one of the original Seawolves of Helicopter Support

Combat Squadron One, had his gunner's safety belt fully extended so he could lean well outside the aircraft and engage enemy troops from all possible angles, including underneath the bird. When the gunship smashed into the rice paddy, the copter's rolling momentum propelled Crew Chief Fee out to the full length of his restraint outside the cabin of the copter. As the fuselage rolled over, Fee became trapped outside the cabin door and was ultimately buried under the bird as it rolled onto its final resting position in the mud. As the crew was extracted from the wreck, Pilot Jimmy Glover saw an arm waving from beneath the fuselage. It was Fee, trapped in the thick mud. The crew tried to lift the copter up while Glover attempted to pull Fee free, but it was impossible. Glover held Fee's hand tight as Fee squeezed as if to say, "I'm trapped; Please help me." Glover squeezed back to say, "Hang on, we are with you and trying to dig you out," but there was just no way. Crew Chief Fee drowned in the sucking mud of Dung Island.

Losing Fee hit all of us hard, especially Jimmy. Our Seawolf Detachment Three leader, Lieutenant Commander Allen Weseleskey, had been replaced by a train wreck who had been trained by another detachment and would not take our advice on anything. He took his wingman back to the target area three times approaching from the same direction. Jimmy Glover advised the flight leader to not go back in from the same direction. You just didn't do that. The lead ship wakes everyone up, and the wingman takes the hits. Well, it only took one round that hit the fuel line and the engine flamed out. Jimmy was flying low over the rice paddy at an altitude where recovering from a flame-out is virtually impossible. In the rotor head world, it's called the dead man's zone.

Matt Gache

The second helicopter in the fire team rescued the surviving crew members and took them to Soc Trang for treatment. Fixed-wing aircraft struck the enemy positions, and a landing party from Vietnamese Costal Group 36, escorted by six PBRs, was dispatched to the scene. The landing party met light opposition in reaching the wreckage, which had already been partially stripped of weapons, ammunition, and documents by the Viet Cong. A search of the area by the Vietnamese sailors uncovered the missing items hidden in a hut. After the body of Petty Officer Fee had been recovered from beneath the stricken helicopter, it was extracted by a heavy-lift helicopter. The landing party withdrew under covering fire provided by the PBRs and Seawolves.

Shortly after Seawolf One-seven had gone down, PBRs had requested permission to go in and recover the crew of the downed bird, but were denied permission. The PBR crews had decided after this tragic event to never request permission again and agreed in the future to go in and assist any and all Seawolf gunships, on whom they relied heavily during combat actions. The PBR crews were saddened by the fact they were not allowed to go in and help their Seawolf brothers, and this would affect future decisions.

Battles raged on around the island for the next year, with light casualties. Then on July 13th, 1968, while on a routine surveillance patrol, Seawolves One-three and One-seven, which had been overhauled and drafted back in service, received permission to place a strike in the northeastern section of Dung Island. The two gunships dove in, receiving fire from all quadrants. Seawolf One-seven announced "going down" and was observed in a right descending turn with rotor RPMs decaying extremely fast. The chopper came to rest in heavy underbrush after crashing. Seawolf One-three broadcast "Mayday," and rescue aircraft were scrambled. SEALs who had been operating on the western bank of the Bassac across from May Island were told to abort their mission and return to USS Harnett County for transportation to the crash site. In the meantime, the wreckage was located by Coastal Group 36 personnel, who guarded it along with Popular Forces from Long Duc Outpost until the next morning, when PBRs inserted the SEALs for the completion of the salvage work. All four crew members, Lieutenant John L. Abrams, Lieutenant Junior Grade James H. Romanski, Aviation Metalsmith Third Raymond D. Robinson, and Aviation Metalsmith Third Dennis M. Wobbe, were lost in the crash. After removing as much of Seawolf One-seven as could be salvaged, the remainder of the copter was destroyed by C-4 explosives by the SEAL Team.

The SEALs continued to conduct special operations on Dung Island, and in the Viet Cong Secret Zones along the coast. Binh Dai, Thanh Phu, and the Long Toan Secret Zones were all well-known Viet Cong hideouts. The U.S. Navy and Coast Guard units fought the Viet Cong for control of these inlets to the Bassac and Mekong Rivers from the South China Sea, but the VC stubbornly refused to give them up.

Elsewhere in the delta, on September 4th, 1968, fourteen miles northwest of Sa Dec on the Mekong River, the merchant ship SS Heaven Dragon sustained three near-misses of B40 rockets. A PBR quickly reacted against the enemy firing position and killed two VC, breaking up the intended ambush of the five-ship convoy. On the Long Tau channel, two attacks occurred in the month of September when the SS Sea Train Texas, and the SS Kalydon, came under enemy attack. A PBR and Seawolf quick-reaction team once again thwarted the enemy by rushing in and surpressing fire both times.

At 1815 hours on September 12th, the communist aggressors proved more successful in an attack on the Game Warden support ship USS Hunterdon County. While sailing up the Ham Luong, Hunderdon was ambushed from both sides of the river five miles south of Ben Tre. The enemy directed heavy recoilless rifle fire and B40 rockets against the ship. The LST countered with her 20 and 40mm gun mounts and cleared the area. River patrol boats and Seawolves also hit the enemy firing positions. Two sailors on the LST were killed, with twenty-five wounded in the hail of gunfire. One ten-ton boom, one PBR, and one personnel landing craft were damaged.

Two days later, USS Kodiak, YF 866, with Quartermaster Chief Clarence G. Cooper as Craftmaster, was attacked north of Vinh Long on the Mekong River enroute to deliver much-needed supplies. The Task Force 116 supply craft had only light machineguns, other than the hand-held weapons of the crew members. The crew had specific orders: "You do not stand and fight. Your job is to deliver the cargo."

YF 866 had only a nine-foot draft and hauled dry cargo with a single ten-ton cargo boom to help load and offload. Her sisters,

YFR 889 and YFR 890, had refrigerated "holes" and all three craft were assigned to take care of the inland resupply of river firebases supporting river operations in the Mekong Delta. The term "resupply" meant that as they offloaded cargo, they loaded engines needing overhaul and cargo for return to Saigon or the Navy supply depot at Nha Be. The small World War II-class ships also did quite a bit of towing. But moving up and down the many rivers, with small islands located midstream, was dangerous work. YF 866 was ambushed from both sides of a narrow sharp turn in the river by well-hidden enemy enplacements, the same place where her sister, YFR 889, was attacked. Utilizing mortar, recoilless rifle, B40 rockets and crew-served automatic weapons, the enemy scored six direct rocket hits on the craft and raked the decks with machinegun fire.

While directing his crew's limited fire-power capabilities, Chief Cooper called for emergency Seawolf gunships and PBR support. During this almost one-sided heavy enemy blitz, six of the Kodiak's crewmen were taken down by wounds received from the Viet Cong's simultaneous discharge of guns. Chief Cooper went to full throttle, executing evasive manuvers in the restricted waterway. Observing his casualties, he ordered his men to take better cover and to conserve their ammunition. With composure, Cooper rallied his men to fire at well-identified targets and to make every shot count, trying to deter the enemy's fusillades of fire. The enemy strength was reconfirmed strong by the amount of continuous heavy fire being received by the U.S. Navy supply craft.

Noticing a severely wounded sailor hemorrhaging, Chief Cooper reached out to assist, bringing the man close by his station so he could direct first aid to control the loss of blood. Cooper helped preserve the wounded crewman's life and calmed the other sailors who were frantic trying to fend off the determined enemy attack. Chief Cooper's positive directions and calls for directing fire at the enemy's withering fire positions kept the superior Viet Cong force off balance. There was little doubt that the Viet Cong were trying to capture or sink the craft, which was full of cargo.

The arrival of a Seawolf gunship fire team from Det-3 surprised the enemy troops, but did not deter them from continuing their attack. Chief Cooper was able to direct the two gunships toward the major targets that were laying down devastating fire, hitting the severely damaged USS Kodiak and wounding its crew. Serving as the fire team leader of the Seawolf gunship fire team that had been called in to assist YF 866, U.S. Navy Pilot Lieutenant James Robert Walker, upon arrival, immediately commenced his attacks against the entrenched hostile emplacements on both sides of the river. After diverting the intense enemy fire from the badly damaged support ship to his gunship fire team, Lieutenant Walker continued to press his attacks. Using rockets and deadly accurate machinegun fire, the two Seawolves managed to silence the heaviest enemy firing positions, suppressing much of the Viet Cong fire. At this time, Chief Cooper alerted the lead Seawolf of his critically wounded sailor and the need to medevac him to a hospital as soon as possible. With his ammunition expended, Walker was prepared to leave the scene to rearm when he learned of the need to evacuate the critically wounded crewman aboard the support craft. Realizing that no medical-evacuation copters could approach the crippled ship due to the heavy fire, and that the badly wounded sailor might not survive, Lieutenant Walker volunteered to attempt the evacuation. With full knowledge that the ship had no landing capabilities for his chopper, and facing a tremendous hail of bullets, Walker and his crew hovered over YF 866 to extract the severely wounded man. Craftmaster Cooper then maneuvered his stricken ship to shield the "sitting-duck helicopter" rescue attempt. As if dancing with the copter, Chief Cooper kept the difficult positioning acceptable to the pilot's needs.

Seawolf crew chief and door gunner, Aviation Machinist's Mate Third Barry Waluda, continually exposed himself to enemy fire in order to deliver accurate return fire with his M60 machinegun. As he hung out the chopper, his suppressing fire silenced several enemy firing positions and provided cover for the supply vessel, his own gunship, and the wing gunship. Concerned about the critically wounded sailor on the vessel, and with complete disregard for his own safety, Petty Officer Waluda released his safety belt and climbed out onto the landing skid of the helicopter, exposing himself to enemy fire to help with the loading of the critically wounded man. Although almost thrown from his precarious perch several times, Waluda maintained his exposed position, without a safety harness, until the man was safely aboard the helicopter hovering over the bow of the ship. While returning to his position in the copter, Waluda noticed the landing skid of the hovering bird dangerously entangled in the ship's bow guard railing. Remaining in his exposed position outside of the cabin, crew chief Waluda calmly directed the pilot clear of the disastrous entanglement. During this extreme situation, the enemy continually engaged both the copter and support vessel with mortar fire and automatic weapons, raining down shrapnel over both. The second attack chopper continued to punish enemy positions with heavy return fire to break the surge. The hazardous medevac was finally completed just as the enemy's apparent will to fight started to dissipate. Chief Cooper then departed the scene, while he directed the care of his other five wounded crewmen. Lieutenant Walker flew the wounded man to awaiting medical attention at Vinh Long Airfield and quickly rearmed, returning to the scene of contact to press his attacks on the enemy positions. Forced to rearm once again at Vinh Long, Walker again returned to the ambush scene and succeeded in breaking up the fierce insurgents' attack and silencing all enemy fire.

As a direct result of Craftmaster Clarence Cooper's tenacity and daring, well-directed defense of his support craft while fighting off a determined enemy, there was no loss of life of his crew, with the six wounded sailors saved. They went on to complete their assigned mission successfully due to Chief Cooper's combat composure and determination to succeed. But because of Coop's characteristic modesty, very few knew of the attack. He would never receive proper recognition from the Navy for his part in the action.

Crew Chief Barry Waluda's sence of responsibility and devotion to duty were later recognized by the Navy with the Silver Star for his bravery during the attack on YF 866.

But a great deal of the credit for saving the day goes to Seawolf fire team commander Lieutenant James Robert Walker, whose tenacious and courageous gunship attacks, aided by an exceptional crew, turned a well-planned enemy ambush on a U.S. Navy vessel into a disastrous enemy rout. Walker's composure under fire and valorous dedication were later recognized with the Navy Cross, for his extraordinary heroism on September 14th, 1968.

After Tet '68, Commander of Naval Forces, Vietnam, reevaluated its intelligence organization and discovered shortcomings in its intelligence network. The biggest fault was that although the intelligence organization had good information, it often did not translate into timely operations based on that information. Instead, it was often analyzed and filed away. Naval Intelligence Liaison Officers throughout the Mekong Delta were often dependent on others for their communications, which presented problems.

On March, 22nd, 1968, Rear Admiral Veth Sends had this to say to Navy intelligence officers in Vietnam:

In general, the quality of intelligence information coming from our representatives in the field has been excellent and continues to improve. It is also interesting and useful. However, the primary value of intelligence is to enhance the effectiveness of combat operations in order to defeat the enemy. Whenever practicable, this headquarters attempts to convert intelligence into operational action. It is desired that you do the same. Whenever you have good hard information of enemy intentions or locations, get it to the nearest operational commanders in your area as soon as possible. Use your initiative and ingenuity, proselyting as necessary, to stimulate timely action. You will then be applying intelligence in the most effective role instead of as interesting reports for subsequent evaluation and filing. Keep the information flowing to us but convert it to action locally whenever possible. Keep in mind that, while it remains the prerogative of the commander to exploit intelligence, the Intelligence Officer is in the best position to stimulate enthusiasm and prod the operational planners into action. The extent to which field Intelligence Officers can provide basis for combat operations will reflect the effectiveness of liaison and rapport with commanders in your area. Report instances where it has been possible to translate intelligence to operations.

This message was the result of a post-Tet evaluation the staff of Naval Forces of Vietnam made of their pre-Tet intelligence, collection, analyzing, and promulgation. They gave themselves a very low mark. Intelligence officers in the field had a prominent role in operational planning, whether it was with the Mobile Riverine Force, PBRs or with the SEALs.

It is widely known that 1968 was the bloodiest year of the Vietnam War, with estimates from Headquarters U.S. Military Assistance Command, Vietnam, indicating that 181,150 Viet Cong and North Vietnamese were killed during the year. Allied losses were 27,915 South Vietnamese, 14,584 Americans, and 979 South Koreans, Australians, New Zealanders, and Thais. Contributing to the high casualty number was the Tet Offensive launched by the communists. Conducted in the early weeks and continued with several waves launched throughout the year, it was a crushing military defeat for the communists. But as with much of the Vietnam War, the news media misinterpreted the offensive, and it was reported as an overwhelming success for communist forces. Nothing could have been further from the truth. But early reporting of a communist victory went largely uncorrected in the media, and many say this led to a psychological victory for the communists. Had the truth been reported that the Viet Cong were nearly wiped out, in place of Walter Cronkite's assessments that the war was being lost, we may have been seen as succeeding in our mission. Instead, back in America, viewers heard of the heavy U.S. casualties incurred during the offensive each night on television, coupled with protesters' demonstrations fueling the growing disenchantment with President Johnson's conduct of the war. Johnson, frustrated with his inability to find a solution in Vietnam and his lack of support at home, announced on March 31st, 1968, that he would neither seek nor accept the Democratic nomination for president for another term. Johnson felt that, when he lost Cronkite, he had lost Middle America. This announcement surprised and shocked many, but did not dampen the wave of antiwar protests that climaxed with the bloody confrontation between protesters and police outside the Democratic National Convention in Chicago.

More than 31,000 U.S. servicemen had been lost in the Vietnam War by the end of 1968, with over 200,000 wounded, yet the Viet Cong had been severely beaten and control of the Mekong Delta had swung to the side of American and the Republic of Vietnam. Still, Hanoi continued to claim victory, and many in the media and America supported that claim.

General Vo Nguyen Giap, the designer of the Tet Offensive, would say many years later that Tet had been a military defeat for the communists, though they had gained the political advantages when Johnson agreed to negotiate and did not run for re-election. Giap admitted that the second and third waves of the Tet Offensive were costly mistakes. Communist forces in the south were nearly wiped out by the end of the year. It took until 1971, after America had withdrawn most of her forces, for them to re-establish their presence in South Vietnam again. But they had to use North Vietnamese troops as local guerrilla fighters. General Gaip also went on to say that, if the American forces had not withdrawn under Nixon, his forces would have been punished much more severely, and that they had already suffered badly enough in '69 and '70 as it was. But because North Vietnamese forces had solid backing in the north, a portion of the south and even in the States, they continued to fight on. Yet, when the GIs returned home after defeating the enemy, they were greeted by antiwar sentiments, with protesters calling them names and trying to shame them with guilt. This was yet another example of how the Vietnam War was reported incorrectly and used by many for political gains.

PBR 112 RIVSEC 533
top and bottom

Robert L. Blias *left*
Gary L. "Moose"
Merrit *on right*
RIVSEC/DIV 532

Duc *left*, Albert "Pancho" O'Canas, Jon Inskeep *right*

Boatswain's Mate William Taylor with Frank "Little One" Springer on top right.
Terry Sater manning 20mm gun mount with pictures of his wife Judy.
Mobile Riverine Force deploying in background

Top Charlie Grisert on MSR-7.
Mid Program IV-original Monitor.
Bot Swift boat.

General Westmoreland and General O'Conner. Matt Gache and Seawolf One-one. PBRs being turned over to South Vietnam. *Bot* MSBs, Alphas, and PBRs at pier.

THE 458th

The significance of those who served in what became known as the 458th Transportation Company, which was the one and only U.S. Army patrol boat company employing PBRs in South Vietnam, can hardly be overlooked. Even in today's light, veterans are able to document only small, detailed accounts of the unit's history. This is not the full story of the young men who volunteered to become soldiers and yet became sailors, but it is a start.

The roots of the 458th can be traced back to June 2nd, 1943, when the 458th was an amphibious truck company bound for England, France and ultimately Omaha Beach. During that mission, the 458th provided direct support, using a new two-and-a-half ton, six-wheel-drive amphibious truck called the DUKW, pronounced "duck" and originally designed and built by General Motors for transporting goods and troops over land and water. The 458th used it in approaching and crossing beaches in amphibious assaults. The 458th performed admirably during the Normandy Invasion and also participated in northern France, Rhineland and other operations, earning many awards.

By June 1964, the 458th had traded in its DUKWs for the new Lighter Amphibious Re-supply Cargo craft or "LARC-Vs," which carried five tons of material in ship-to-shore operations. The 458th was then assigned to the 10th Battalion, 4th Transportation Command. In preparation for deployment overseas to Vietnam, the unit received an influx of helicopter trainees who were converted to seamen. After the company adopted the nickname the "Sea Tigers," First Sergeant Flynn asked John Hoeker to draw a Sea Tiger for a logo. The only picture of a tiger that John could find was the ESSO tiger in a magazine ad, so he used that as his inspiration.

In September 1966, the company, under the command of First Lieutenant Walter D. Gruff, shipped out for Vietnam aboard the

USNS General Maurice Rose, T-AP-126, by way of the Panama Canal and then Long Beach, California. The company's destination was initially Vung Tau, but was later changed to Cam Ranh Bay, with the unit arriving on October 13th, 1966. At first, the 458th was the only logistical, amphibious unit in the operating theater. But unfortunately, its LARC-Vs and equipment went to Vung Tau while the 458th ended up in Cam Ranh Bay to support the LST landing beach. By the time its men were scheduled to reunite with their equipment, another LARC unit had arrived at Vung Tau. The 458th became an orphan unit and went whereever needed. Cam Rahn Bay had been built up by the Army to relieve the deep water ports at Da Nang and Saigon. After the 458th was reunited with all thirty-five LARC units, its mission and areas of operations were expanded to include Nha Trang, Phan Rang, Phan Thiet and Vung Ro Bay.

The first 458th waterborne security patrols were carried out by LARCs, equipped with single .50 cal machineguns mounted on their sides, and a couple whaler skimmer boats. At Phan Thiet, the 458th directly supported the 2nd Battalion 7th Cavalry Division during Operation Byrd, a hard-fought campaign where continuous fighting on steep, hilly terrain caused many difficulties to resupply.

Concerns and solutions were being developed involving ship and port security in the port areas of the Republic of Vietnam. In August 1967, Company Commander, First Lieutenant R.A. "Pete" Sellers was given six Boston Whalers, which were twelve-foot fiberglass, flat-bottom boats with outboard motors. They could search out VC sappers under piers and hard-to-reach shallow waters while conducting harbor patrols. As the buildup continued in Vietnam, the mission of the 458th also changed. Lieutenant Sellers was tasked to attend strategy meetings with the 18th Military Police Brigade to devise a plan to augment needed harbor security up and down the coast of South Vietnam. A plan was approved and put into motion for six detachments, with thirty-nine newly manufactured Mark II PBRs and the use of Boston Whalers, to backfill U.S. river patrol units being reassigned deeper into enemy waters. The 458th built its own pier for its boats on the south beach of Cam Ranh Bay so the men could remain in and near company operations area, rather than use the LST beach landing site. The unit grew to 162 enlisted men and officers, with logistics and maintenance performed at Nha Be Naval detachment.

At the time I joined the 458th in Vietnam, Chief Godwin was the maintenance officer. Unofficially, he was also the humorist and one of the "morale adjustment" leaders. His sense of humor and "don't let the day get you down" attitude most certainly contributed to being able to keep the unit's spirit up beat. As the 458th began transition from the amphibious cargo transport mode to the security mode, Chief Godwin was both flexible and valuable. As the Boston Whalers arrived, virtually no one else in the local Army community knew about them or had the time to provide support. Chief Godwin found the time and capacity to take on this mission and he did well. As I departed the unit, Chief Godwin was the Maintenance Officer for the PBRs.

Pete Sellers

The transportation corps provided one boat captain to serve as coxswain and an engineman to take care of the jet-pump propulsion system and the twin 6V53 Detroit diesel engines that propelled the boat to speeds of thirty knots plus. The 18th Military Police Brigade assigned MPs for gunners, and a South Vietnamese National Policeman acted as interpreter. Newly recruited Army PBR crew volunteers were sent through the U.S. Naval facility at Mare Island, Vallejo, California, for training with Navy instructors.

The PBRs, the first fast-attack fiberglass patrol boats of their kind, were introduced into the war theater by the U.S. Navy in 1966. It was also the first and only time the U.S. Army provided this style of watercraft within the transportation community. Due to the nature and firepower of the boat, there was much concern from higher-ups. Army PBRs were identical to the Navy's river patrol boats, and they were designed and constructed at Uniflite's shipyard in Bellingham, Washington, by Art Nordtvedt and his crew.

All 458th detachments came under direct authority of the 18th Military Police Brigade. Interdiction work was defensive in nature, and due to fears by the brigade officers, there was to never to be any freelancing, such as setting up unauthorized ambushes or patrolling outside given assignments. Those who did were removed in short order. It is believed by many that command harbored unfounded fears about enlisted E4 and E5 having control of the sort of firepower that the PBRs were equipped with. But evidence has shown that the daring initiative taken by these gallant young warriors when meeting the enemy was invaluable and that the 458th PBR crews shined brightly and served honorably in combat actions.

"Ever Vigilant," the Army crewmembers of the 458th PBRs searched sampans, set up night ambushes, conducted harbor and river patrols and, convoy duty, and provided security for ammunition ships and barges throughout their assigned areas of operations. The 458th is credited with removing mines from both military Sea Lift vessels and U.S. Navy war ships, often killing or capturing sappers from Viet Cong Swimmer Sapper Team Ten, which operated from Cat Lo to the upper Saigon River and as far north as Qui Nhon. These were capital ship killers, the elite communist mining operators made up of both Viet Cong and North Vietnamese trained underwater demolition teams, which were often equipped with Russian gear. The Army PBRs also worked with the U.S. Navy Inland Underwater Warfare Group One and the Royal Australian Navy Clearance Diving Team Three. Enemy mines posed a serious threat to port facilities, with the danger level very high throughout South Vietnam. It was a dirty, dangerous job which no one took for granted and which had to be done correctly or there could be grave consequences.

On January 29th, 1969, while flying his L19 "Bird Dog" spotter plane on a routine aerial observation flight, Captain Lermon N. Jenk spotted what appeared to be camouflaged sampans and bunkers along the edge of the harbor. Jenk radioed the enemy position to the Army PBR detachment out of Qui Nhon. Ten minutes later, three PBRs were nosing around investigating the dike, through dangerously shallow waters. The Vietnamese policeman, called Canh Sat, had confirmed that the activity was enemy. The MPs onboard the PBRs called for the VC to come out and surrender.

Several fighters emerged from the bunker and tried to escape on foot. The PBR's .50 cal machineguns opened fire, with Specialist Four James E. Brady's PBR coming under intense enemy return fire immediately. In the firefight that followed, Bradley was wounded by shrapnel in his left shoulder but continued to maneuver his boat, trying to give his crew the best firing positions possible. Captain Jenk wrote in his report that "the PBR crewmen maneuvered their craft and continually exposed themselves so they could place more effective fire on the enemy." All three boats continued to fire on the enemy positions while Captain Jenk flew overhead, staying in contact by radio.

Throughout the firefight, Brady refused medical attention and continued to command his patrol boat. At one point, one of the machineguns jammed and Brady left the helm to help the gunner fix the weapon. During the battle, the boats had to pull back several times for air strikes. Because Brady effectively blocked the escape routes of the sampans, he had sealed the enemy escape routes by water. After the last strike, they went back in. MPs searched the area and found fifteen dead, with ten enemy bunkers and twenty sampans damaged or destroyed. Captain Jenk concluded in his recommendation that "the courage and intelligent decisions of these PBR crewmen were in keeping with the highest traditions of the military and reflected on themselves, their unit, and the United States Army."

There was no such thing as a normal day aboard a PBR. Just ask the Navy River Rats who served on them. At anytime, the bravery of any man, no matter what age or rank, could be called upon to do what appeared to be impossible tasks. Such was the day of June 11th, 1969, when while serving on a patrol boat near Qui Nhon supporting combat operation, Sergeant Charles Lowe was requested to take his boat and evacuate five seriously wounded Vietnamese soldiers from a nearby ground action. The seriousness of their wounds demanded helicopter extraction immediately. This would take some time, so they took the wounded aboard and proceeded to rendezvous in hopes that the copters would arrive quickly.

The medivac helicopter arrived but could not land to pick up the wounded. It was then that Sergeant Lowe decided to remove the PBRs radio antennas and climbed on top of the canopy. Then as the copter hovered above, Sergeant Lowe handed up the wounded. This was extremely hazardous while the boat erratically pitched beneath him. As the last of the wounded was being past to the airmen aboard the copter, the copter swerved, knocking Lowe off the canopy, damaging the radar dome. Luckily, the sergeant was okay.

By December 1969, the 458th PBR unit had moved its floating dock and maintenance shed, nicknamed the "House Boat," and anchored it just southeast of the Dong Nai River Bridge. There it began operations with the 720th Military Police Battalion, which commanded six light cargo transport boats obtained from the Coast Guard. The House Boat provided sleeping quarters, a maintenance area, and a tactical operations room. On May 18th, 1970, Army PBRs moved out to assist a Navy tug boat ambushed on the Dong Nai River just south of the battalion's responsibility. Crew members of the tug had been wounded when the Viet Cong struck the boat with two rocket-propelled grenades. The Army PBRs provided security and evacuated the wounded crewmen safely. The Navy and 458th PBRs also provided close-in riverine support and transport assistance to the men of the 720th Military Police Battalion for river patrol, ambush, and recon teams throughout the span of Operation Stabilize.

At 0220 hours on June 28th, '70, USS Meeker County, LST 980, was tied up to the Delong pier in Vung Tau harbor when shots rang out. They were fired by one of the ship's sentries, who had duty and was standing watch. A Military Police roving patrol radioed that sappers were seen in the water by Meeker County's crew. The alert came about an hour after concussion grenades had been thrown in the water around the pier, to serve as makeshift depth charges. PBR-J7816 responded along with a Military Police skimmer also on patrol at the time. As both arrived at the area, Boat Captain Specialist Four Bob Brower immediately coordinated an assessment of the reported mine and transferred to the skimmer for closer inspection, leaving Private First Class Noland in charge of the PBR. The mine was eventually located one yard underwater, forty-five feet forward of the stern and tied to an eyelet with one line and to a second eyelet sixty feet forward on the portside with another line. It was decided not to wait for the EOD dive team. It was clear to all that if the mine exploded, the Meeker County would go down, thereby blocking use of the pier, possibly taking the lives of some of the sailors aboard ship as well.

A plan was quickly developed. The forward line would be cut on the way back to the PBR and the skimmer would go around the starboard side and cut the stern line to the mine. Specialist Four Brower transferred back to the PBR and instructed a Navy lieutenant aboard ship to get the men off of the port rail. The idea was to slowly drift the mine away from the hull, then tow it clear of the ship. But before the skimmer began its return, two Australian Clearance Team Three divers, John Kershler and G. Kingston, appeared at the stern of the ship. Kershler entered the water from a small floating dock and agreed to cut the stern line to the mine and steer it away. Boat Captain Brower instructed Noland to pull him out and away from the ship as Brower held the other line. Once they knew they would be able to clear the ship, diver Kershler let the line go, and the PBR pulled the mine out. Then Kershler and Kingston performed a dive below the ship to check for any additional mines while Brower and Noland secured the mine to a fish stake about a quarter mile away.

The fifty-pound C4 mine detonated near high tide around 0730 hours, with a twelve foot hole opening up in the water and spouting water forty feet in the air. It was quite a shock for the sailors to realize how close they had come. They knew that if they had waited USS Meeker County could have sunk, and the loss of life could have been significant. Although Army PBR sailors were never trained in ordinance removal, nonetheless, they did it, and often without recognition. And even to this day, they have received very little credit.

At 0830 hours, Boat Captain Brower, Engineman Noland, and one newly arrived Army crew member were greeted by a Navy chief on the LST and thanked by the commanding officer. The PBR crew was invited to stay for breakfast, but orders from Cat Lo were to return ASAP to replenish and prepare for the next patrol.

Although the mining attack had failed, it had taught the VC sappers that their plan was sound and needed another try. Later, the 458th PBRs intercepted another sapper team trying to take out the shipping at the same spot at Delong pier. Thanks to the alertness of Specialist Four Don Owens and Specialist Five Bob Elliott, and their PBR crews, two sappers were captured in the act. Divers later located two mines attached under the pier. The communists were relentless, however, and SS Green Bay and American Hawk fell victims to drift tactics of VC Sapper Team Ten in June and August of 1971, at Qui Nhon.

On April 3rd, 1971, Army seaman James Arthur Loux was riding on a 458th PBR, helping to escort a shipment of aviation fuel to combat units operating near the village of Cho Thu Bay. While on the way, the PBR Loux was aboard struck a mine, sending the boat up in flames. The crew found itself in the middle of enemy crossfire from both banks of a canal, while the boat, out of control, beached itself. Gravely wounded and unable to escape the kill zone, Loux manned the .50 cal machinegun, covering the convoy fighting its way out. He continued to battle at least two enemy positions until the communists broke contact and their guns fell silent. Jim Loux had put up a truly great fight but sadly died of his wounds two days later in the hospital. He was only twenty-one years old and was close to rotating back home. For his heroic acts of gallantry on the field of battle that day, James Loux was awarded the Silver Star and his second Purple Heart. As a tribute to him, the U.S. Army named a ship in his honor, LSV-6, James A. Loux.

Throughout its short history, the Army 458th military police river patrol units saw their share of hostile action, capturing enemy soldiers and supplies, thwarthing civilian criminals, and successfully completing hazardous combat and rescue missions. Many of the missions were performed while operating in total darkness on the muddy brown waters. The men who crewed the Army PBRs are respected by their Navy River Rat brothers and truly earned the reputation of being proud, brave, and reliable - PBR.

There is no history unless you can read about it one hundred years from today.

Bob Brower

SEA LORDS

By the summer of 1968, the Navy's three in-country task forces - the Coastal Surveillance Force of TF-115, the River Patrol Force of TF-116, and the Mobile Riverine Force of TF-117 - had collectively accumulated nearly seven years experience in performing their missions. For the most part, the three forces had operated independently of each other; however, there were times when units from two forces would join for a specific operation. Each force knew its capabilities and pushed the envelope attempting to improve effectiveness.

On September 30th, 1968, Vice Admiral Elmo R. Zumwalt Jr. relieved Rear Admiral Kenneth L. Veth as Commander of Naval Forces, Vietnam. Prior to his arrival in Vietnam, Admiral Zumwalt had been the director of the Systems Analysis Group in Washington, D.C. He had gathered information during briefings from reliable sources before arriving in-country, so he had an appreciation of the status of the Naval Forces in Vietnam. Admiral Zumwalt sensed that the Navy could be doing more and, in initial discussions with in-country commanders and some of his staff, confirmed that fact. It was suggested that consideration be given to having the three forces operate jointly rather than separately.

Within days, the suggestions resulted in what would become known as "Zumwalt's Wild Ideas." In this one, the admiral tasked his mini-staff to examine the feasibility of an operational merger. Representatives of the three operational staffs received a briefing on the new concept directly from the admiral and were tasked to put together lists of objectives they wanted to achieve.

On Saturday, October 19th, 1968, the three task force commanders, along with selected members of their staffs, assembled at the Naval Forces of Vietnam headquarters in Saigon. They were Captain Robert F. Hoffman, commander of TF-115:

Commander Wayne Beech, deputy commander of TF-116; and Captain Robert S. Salzer, commander of TF-117. Also present was Captain Earl F. "Rex" Rectanus, the assistant chief of staff for intelligence for the Naval Forces of Vietnam. The commander of TF-116, Captain Arthur W. Price Jr., was on temporary duty in San Diego, California.

At 0800 hours, Admiral Zumwalt and his deputy, Rear Admiral William F. House, walked into the conference room, and Zumwalt made a brief announcement explaining why he had called the representatives of the three forces together. It was to develop a new operational concept he identified as Operation SEA LORDS, and he went on to explain that SEA LORDS meant Southeast Asia Lake, Ocean, River and Delta Strategy. The basic concept of the plan was that the three Naval task forces would operate together and in conjunction with allied forces to interdict infiltration routes from Cambodia into South Vietnam while pacifying the Mekong Delta waterways and harassing the enemy in its base areas.

When he finished his presentation, Zumwalt along with House, left the room. The flag lieutenant remained long enough to announce, "Gentlemen, this will be a working conference. Lunch will be hamburgers, cheeseburgers, french fries and coffee or Coke. Who wants what and how many?"

Captain Salzer, who had the reputation as an operational organizer, began to conduct the meeting. In his opening remarks, Salzer stated the group was to utilize all of its assets to the maximum to achieve objectives. The old competitiveness and animosities between the forces was history. The group was to be innovative, creative, and focused on interdicting infiltration routes, wherever the riverine forces found them.

The discussion started with representatives of each task force identifying their priorities and what assets were deemed necessary to accomplish their mission. This process continued through the burgers, and by 1330 hours, a basic outline had been developed. Admiral Zumwalt rejoined the group at 1400 hours for a briefing led by Captain Salzer. A representative from each task force presented recommendations, prepared to explain and/or defend them. At the end of the briefing, Admiral Zumwalt stated that that was what he wanted. "Now write the operation plan." With that, he left the room.

The tables in the conference room were in a U-shaped arrangement. Captain Salzer took his position inside the U and tossed a pad and pencil to the nearest staff officer and told him to write what he dictated. A military operation plan has six basic paragraphs: situation, mission, execution, administration and logistics, and command and signal. Those paragraphs can lead to many pages of printed matter.

While Captain Salzer slowly paced in the U, he dictated the operation plan without reference to notes. His delivery was slow, clear, and deliberate. Should the recording officer miss something, Salzer patiently repeated what he had said without changing a word. When the first recorder tired, the pad and pencil was passed to another. That routine continued with new pads of paper and pencils added when necessary as the three Captains and staffs worked together.

Late in the afternoon when they finished drafting the operation plan, Admiral Zumwalt returned and received a short briefing. The draft was taken to the communications center to be put in message format, and Admiral Zumwalt personally carried the operation plan to General Creighton Abrams, Commander of U.S. Military Assistance Command, Vietnam. All of this had been accomplished in nine hours. General Abrams gave his approval to Operation SEA LORDS with the stipulation that Major General George S. Eckhardt, the Senior Advisor of IV Corps Tactical Zone, be briefed and also give his approval to the operations contemplated within his area of responsibility.

After General Eckhardt had endorsed the Navy's proposals, the Navy organized and initiated Operation SEA LORDS under the control of newly formed Task Force 194. Captain Salzer was designated First Sea Lord and assigned a staff of nine officers and six enlisted men at General Eckhardt's headquarters in Can Tho. Captain Salzer became first commander of Task Force 194.0 and exercised operation control, commencing October 15th, 1968, of the three major task groups: 194.5, Coastal Raiding and Blocking;

194.6, Riverine Raiding and Blocking; and 194.7, the Riverine Strike Group.

Captain Salzer was directed to designate one of the three task group commanders to command each specific SEA LORDS operation, with the commander of Task Force 115 expected to direct SEA LORDS invasions from the sea, and the commander of Task Force 116 involving large commitments of Naval ground forces. This was provided by NSA sailors who would man the many support craft and forward bases alongside of the river patrolmen. A series of small Navy firebases, interconnected with Vietnam Army and province force outposts, were organized to tie the different operations together into one long interdiction barrier. The Navy forward firebases were built and positioned, along with large river craft, to support the many river boats and gunships that had been joined together.

Spaced roughly a half mile apart, PBRs, Swifts, Monitors, Alpha and Tango assault craft were positioned side by side to block the Ho Chi Minh Trail. From dusk 'til dawn, U.S. and Vietnamese Naval Forces stood watch on ambushes called waterborne guard posts, linked by short range line-of-sight FM communication radios to small outposts and support ships on the larger rivers and sea.

The Swift boats of Market Time sailed up river assuming patrols along the Cambodian border on the Mekong and Bassac, taking over many of the inland patrol tasks formerly performed by PBRs. This freed up the river patrol boats and shallow draft assault craft, which pushed even further inland inserting into the canals deep into long-held VC areas. By 1969, the Mobile Riverine Force had started turning over its missions and assault craft to the Vietnamese Navy. The remaining assault craft and crews were reassigned to SEA LORDS, and all but the barracks ship USS Benewah were returned to the continental United States and decommissioned. The repair ships were reassigned to assist SEA LORDS operations and dispersed throughout the Mekong Delta.

The SEA LORDS barrier system had been created and designed to extend from the Gulf of Thailand on the Vinh Te Canal northeast to the Bassac River. Then over to the Mekong River, traveling east on the French Canal, continuing northeast across the Plain of Reeds on the Grand Canal, also known as the Kinh Lagrange, to the Vam Co Tay River, and around the Parrot's Beak connecting with the Vam Co Dong River, traveling north into Tay Ninh Province.

South of the Bassac was determined as one of the principal water routes to exploit for the purpose of stopping the communist flow of men and supplies entering IV Corps Tactical Zone from Cambodia. A series of small streams and creeks ran parallel to the Bassac flowing from Cambodia into the central part of the Mekong Delta. It was like a four-lane water highway flowing from the ports of Sihanoukville, Cambodia, where communist forces and supplies were being allowed to off load, then travel south into Vietnam. It was this system of waterways that for years went relatively unscathed for the simple reason that Task Force 116 could not operate in those areas due to the lack of logistic support, basing, supplies, and security. It was one of those situations where command leaders knew where the stuff was coming from and how it was crossing into the delta, but could do little about it. They had drawn a sketch of what they knew and had begun to act on it.

Since the Vinh Te Canal closely paralleled the border and the risk of border incidents dictated against placing a SEA LORDS barrier there until the plan had been tested in a less sensitive area, it was decided that two parallel canals, some thirty-five and forty miles southeast of the border, would be used to form a double barrier and to inaugurate the SEA LORDS campaign. This would also open the two canals for friendly water traffic and help block enemy strongholds to the south. In addition, river patrols would be strengthened from Long Xuyen on the Bassac, east through the Vam Nao Crossover to the Mekong River some miles away.

The second objective of SEA LORDS was to control the vital trans-delta inland waterways. This would be accomplished by the removal of obstructions to navigation in the Coa Goa Canal, linking the Vam Co and My Tho Rivers, and by strike operations along the Mang Thit-Nicolai Canal, which joins the Co Chien and Bassac Rivers, and by also reopening the Bassac-Bac Lieu rice route in the lower delta. Penetrations of rivers in the Cau Mau Peninsula, the third objective, actually began before formal proposals were made to General Eckhardt. A river patrol boat incursion of the Cau

Lon River on October 18th, 1968, is generally considered the first SEA LORDS operation, although a few earlier such operations were conducted by Market Time forces.

The communist soldiers would hike hundreds of miles south through the jungles and mountains of Laos and Cambodia, picking up Viet Cong guides along the way. Then they would split into smaller groups and try to sneak into South Vietnam at different locations in the wilderness. Brown water sailors were often the first to greet these forces. There is no doubt that some made it, but many did not.

The plan for Operation SEA LORDS began to take shape on November 2nd, 1968, when a Naval blockade was set by PBRs and assault craft patrolling two canals between Long Xuyen on the Bassac, and Rach Gia, on the gulf. Later given the name Search Turn, the operation involved South Vietnamese paramilitary ground troops helping Navy units secure the waterways in operations that resulted in twenty-one Viet Cong killed and sizable quantities of weapons captured. Then a permanent Navy patrol was established with the goal of securing the western ends of the barrier and the network of perpendicular canals and creeks running north from Rach Gia to Ha Tien.

According to intelligence reports, the principal messengers passed through this territory delivering Hanoi's orders to the VC strongholds in the U Minh Forest and Nam Can in the lower Cau Mau Peninsula. According to high ranking sources, River Division 531 really hurt the VC. Not only did the enemy sustain casualties, but it also lost its supply route, which was cut to ribbons. Prior to River Division 531's arrival, large quantities of supplies flowed across this area, which 531 cut to a trickle. But it did not come cheap; seven of its ten PBRs were hit with rockets and all were involved in firefights at one time or another.

Back on October 1st, 1968, River Division 531, commanded by Lieutenant Thomas K. Anderson, left My Tho and sailed to USS Jennings County, LST 846, in the Ham Luong River. At the end of the month, they were all moved up river near Long Xuyen on the Bassac River in preparation for Search Turn. Lieutenant Anderson remembers taking fire from the enemy when the LST moved up the Bassac, fire which both the PBRs and the LST returned and suppressed. Several days after arriving in position, the heavies of Task Force 117, with six PBRs from Task Force 116 sandwiched in positions in the column and some at the rear, proceeded all the way from Long Xuyen down to the Rach Gia/Rach Soi area, blasting its way along, with Vietnamese troops sweeping along the banks to take care of anything that might be left standing. This created a wonderful "vacuum" for almost two weeks. After the heavies left, that vacuum was quickly filled when the enemy found out that all that was left behind were a few fiberglass PBRs that could be disabled with AK47s and B40 rockets. A series of river battles followed in which both sides fought hard for control of the canal.

From about November 15th to December 17th, we suffered serious hits on seven boats, some small holes in all ten PBRs, and about fifty percent casualties, ranging from one killed, to many others wounded in various degrees of severity. At that point, we ended up not having enough boats or people to carry out our mission of patrolling that canal anymore. I think we had five fully operational boats, so we were relieved by River Division 514 so we could get replacement boats and repair the others as well as getting new men to replace the sailors that we had lost or were wounded and unable to come back.

Tom Anderson

One of these battles took place on the night of November 21st, 1968, when PBRs 110 and 109 were locked in heavy combat with the enemy in what was referred to later as a change of luck. The crew of PBR 110 consisted of Boat Captain Mineman First Cecil H. Martin, Engineman Harry Jones, Seaman William O'Donnell, Gunner's Mate Seaman Vernon Lucas, and Engineman Hartwell A. White. The crewmen of PBR 109 were Boat Captain Signalman Donald McClemons, Engineman Keith Erntson, Gunner's Mate Jackie Touchstone, Seaman James Drennan and Michael Eckhardt. The patrol was transiting from Rach Soi to Rach Gia with PBR 110 ahead and going around a cutoff in the canal when the boats came under attack with rockets and machineguns. PBR 109 went out of control and beached. The crew of PBR 110 opened up on the VC while Martin turned the boat and came back to help. Heavy fire continued while they evacuated the crew of PBR 109 with Martin manning the aft .50 cal returning fire when they received three more rockets off the stern of PBR 110. Martin decided that the better part of valor was to get out. So he crossed back over to PBR 110 and they left the scene with both crews onboard. They had gone only a short distance when they met PBRs coming from Rach Gia to assist them. In the meantime, they found that PBR 110 was taking on water and had to use the eductor hose to keep it afloat. The last three rounds had damaged the seals around their pump intakes and nozzles and the PBR was taking on water faster than the bilge pump could empty it. PBR 109 was still beached but was boarded by Lieutenant Anderson after arriving, who found the engines would still start up and run. So Tom Anderson and another sailor drove PBR 109 back to Rach Soi under its own power. The canopy was in shreds and still smoking. Bravery and heroism during this action was displayed by members of both crews. Some men, even though wounded, still returned and suppressed the enemy fire. Others returned fire and rendered first aid assistance while still under fire.

As Senior Boat Captain of the two-boat patrol, Mineman Cecil Martin displayed exceptional courage when his patrol came under heavy attack on all sides. During the initial hail of fire, his cover boat, PBR 109, received two direct rocket hits, wounding all the sailors aboard and causing the craft to veer out of control and run aground directly in front of the enemy firing positions. Boat Captain Martin ordered his coxswain to reverse course and reenter the ambush area to rescue the cover boat's crew members. As his unit approached the stricken craft, Cecil Martin directed effective counterfire and, placing his boat between the beleaguered craft and the blazing enemy batteries, took command of the precarious rescue effort. While affording exemplary leadership and inspiration to the members of his surprised and battered patrol element, he directed the major fire-suppression efforts of his gunners, personally manning and firing a machinegun at crucial intervals. Additionally, Martin rendered first aid to casualties, extinguished a fire in the beached craft, advised his commanding officer in the Naval Operations Center of the seriousness of the situation, and coordinated the transfer of wounded sailors to his unit. Through his courageous and determined fighting spirit, Martin succeeded in safely extracting his men, undoubtedly saving numerous lives. His great personal valor in the face of heavy and sustained enemy fire was in keeping with the highest traditions of the United States Naval Service. Mineman First Class Cecil H. Martin was awarded the Navy Cross for the action on November 21st, 1968.

It was my understanding that the Viet Cong had been told the boats were made of glass and would break apart when hit and then it was a simple matter to shoot the sailors in the water. I believe we were told this story by a Chieu Hoi VC that had been in both the November 21st and November 27th fights. He quit because he thought we were crazy as we would drive our boats right up on to the bank to carry the fight to them. He believed this as both PBR 109 and PBR 29 lost control and were beached when they were hit by a couple of rockets each.

Cecil Martin

We moved up river to the Mekong while refitting and had limited patrols on the Mekong up to the Cambodian border for the rest of December. During this time, Boat Captain Cecil Martin in PBR 110, and his cover boat were patrolling the Mekong River where it entered Cambodia on Christmas Eve night 1968. Later I was told that Martin cracked a bottle of snake medicine his brother-in-law had sent him for Christmas and everyone on both crews got one tiny taste, to ward off the snakes that might have been on the prowl, and then he dropped the nearly full bottle into the mighty Mekong. Or at least that was what Cecil told me. Then, when we got our full ten boats going in mid-January '69, we were sent into the Grand Canal on Operation Barrier Reef West. We came across a SEAL who was working for the CIA with a base load of PRUs, way up in the canal. These were Vietnamese who had been let out of jail if they swore to fight for South Vietnam and this poor guy was in charge, all by himself. He said we were the first round eyes he had seen, and he was real happy to see us!

Tom Anderson

While Operation Search Turn was in progress, additional SEA LORDS forces were employed in clearing the Cho Goa Canal. Later in November, Tan Dinh and Dung Island in the Bassac were sealed off by a Navy blockade, while ground forces conducted sweep operations. At roughly the same time, Market Time craft bravely moved into areas in the Ca Mau Peninsula that had long been considered exclusively the domain of the Viet Cong.

The second of the interdiction barriers was established on November 16th when PBRs, Swifts, assault craft, and Vietnamese gunboats started patrolling along the waterway from Ha Tien, on the Gulf of Thailand, through the Vinh Te Canal, which divides Cambodia and Vietnam, over to Chau Doc City on the Bassac River. Although the southern side of the Vinh Te Canal was Vietnam, Cambodia was plainly visible on the north bank, with established Viet Cong ambush sights and trails along the way. Off the coast in the Gulf of Thailand was stationed a LST with a two-Huey Seawolf gunship fire team aboard in support of Ha Tien and friendly outposts along the canals.

This operation was originally named Foul Deck, but as a symbol of the Vietnamese contribution to the combined effort, the allied command changed the name to Tran Hung Dao in honor of the early Vietnamese warrior sailor who was a hero to his people. It should also be mentioned that, although we had a support base at An Thoi, Phu Quoc Island was never cleared of VC and was a haven and sanctuary throughout much of the war, with perfect terrain for step transfers from sea-transport to the Cambodian border.

As these first two barrier systems grew in strength, two non-propelled repair barges, YRBM 16 and YRBM 20, were positioned on the upper Bassac River and manned by over 150 sailors each with both home bases to Seawolf fire teams, and river patrol units. Normally one YRBM was anchored at Chau Doc City in support of Tran Hung Dao, and the other down river at Long Xuyen in support of Search Turn.

On December 6th, 1968, against heavy enemy opposition, U.S. river forces fought their way up the Vam Co Dong and Vam Co Tay Rivers west of Saigon averaging two firefights a day. Given the code name Giant Slingshot, this campaign represented the longest and most productive segment of all the interdiction barriers. But it was costly.

When first initiated, Slingshot extended from Hiep Hoa down the Vam Co Dong to the junction of the two rivers, then up the Vam Co Tay to Moc Hoa fifty miles west. The Giant Slingshot campaign ran along and across enemy supply lines from the Parrot's Beak of Cambodia into the western approaches to Saigon. Operations by river patrol and riverine units with U.S. and Vietnamese ground forces were carried out on almost a daily basis on Slingshot. During January, significant quantities of enemy supplies were discovered in forty-four arms and rice caches near the two rivers.

These results were not achieved without cost, however, as patrol units encountered hostile fire sixty-eight times, including four booby traps. Losses were eight U.S. Navy, one U.S. Army, and fifteen Vietnamese. In addition, two U.S. soldiers were missing with fifty-one sailors, twenty-four soldiers, and thirteen Vietnamese were wounded. Twenty-three craft were damaged and two PBRs sunk. During river bank sweeps by ground forces, and while taking twenty-six evading junks and sampans under fire and suppressing hostile fire, Slingshot forces killed seventy communists and wounded nine others while capturing twenty and detaining an additional twenty-five suspects. But this was only the beginning of Slingshot, which went on to claim many more lives as it grew in size in the next few years.

West of Saigon, Cambodia's Parrot's Beak thrusts deep into Vietnam's III Corps and had long been known as a communist base camp from which supplies moved across the border with well-documented infiltration routes traced. One trail turned south into the delta, while another traveled east to supply the Viet Cong in the countryside surrounding Saigon. The Vam Co Tay and the Vam Co Dong flowed on both sides of the Parrot's Beak on converging courses, making them perfect for interdiction. The sisters joined in Long An Province, where the two rivers formed a giant slingshot shape from the air, hence, the name Giant Slingshot. Because of the distances involved and the impossibility of bringing large ships up river beyond the low bridges at Tan An and Ben Luc, a new basing and support system was devised for Slingshot. An Advanced Tactical Support Base, ATSB, was designated.

For ground support in Operation Slingshot, Rear Admiral William H. House, who had assumed the post of First Sea Lord upon Captain Salzer's departure, called on the commanding general of II Field Force Vietnam, Lieutenant General Frederick C. Weyland, to get his help.

Bases were first established at Tuyen Nhon and Moc Hoa on the Vam Co Tay, and at Tra Cu and Hiep Hoa on the Vam Co Dong. The site at Hiep Hoa was later abandoned in favor of Go Dau Ha. USS Askari, ARL 30, and a berthing and messing barge for underwater repair crews, were stationed at Tan An on the Vam Co Tay, and the USS Harnett County, LST 821, provided support at Ben Luc on the Vam Co Dong until the completion of the base.

The Vam Co Tay flowed west of the Parrot's Beak deep into Kien Thoung Province with ATSB Moc Hoa furthest out. ATSB Tuyen Nhon was south at the eastern entrance of the Grand Canal. The Vam Co Dong ran northeast of Parrot's Beak with ATSB Ben Luc being established above the confluence of the two rivers, followed by the ATSB Tra Cu, and then ATSB Go Dau Ha. All Navy firebases were built over time and manned before completion by river divisions and support sailors, who continued building alongside the Seabees while combat patrols were being conducted by river divisions.

From its very beginning, Giant Slingshot was characterized by frequent heavy clashes between patrol boats and enemy forces intent on maintaining the lines of communication to their Cambodian storehouse. The enemy fought hard, not wanting to surrender these important trails. Extremely large quantities of arms, munitions, and supplies were uncovered in catches buried along the twisting and turning river banks, proving beyond doubt that vital enemy infiltration lines had been cut.

But Operation SEA LORDS was not complete until the fourth and last of the interdiction barriers was established on January 2nd,

1969, when PBRs and assault craft patrolled westward from the Vam Co Tay River onto the Grand Canal through the marshlands known as the Plain of Reeds, to An Long Village on the upper Mekong River. Dubbed Barrier Reef, this operation joined Slingshot in the east with Search Turn and Tran Hung Doa in the west.

It should be noted that, from the Bassac River at Chau Doc City, there was an important barrier on the French Canal, also called the Chau Doc/Tan Chau canal, extending northeast to the city of Tan Chau on the Mekong River. The control center and mother ship of the green fleet, USS Benewah, was positioned on the upper Mekong in support of the Green Beret base at Thuong Thoi and Barrier Reef. In the summer of 1969, YRBM 21 was assigned to accompany Benewah on the Mekong and was home to Seawolf Det-9 and River Patrol Division 592, with others periodically stationed aboard.

All YRBMs had been configured specifically to support the operation of river patrol boats. The heavy assault craft were maintained by the repair ships USS Satyr, USS Sphinx and others.

Naval support bases were built by the Seabees from the U.S. Navy Construction Battalion and the NSA sailors, who also manned the lookout towers and mortar pits, providing a safe haven for the river patrolmen to recoup and get a short break from the insufferable heat. In many cases, strong bonds and friendships were made by these men who stood together on these lonely outposts for months at a time, living in hooches and eating out of cans. Periodically, Seawolf gunships staged from these bases and Navy OV-10 Black Ponies and Air Force Spooky gunships flew overhead in a continuous pattern.

All these barriers, support craft, gunships, and men combined to make up SEA LORDS, with sailors patrolling and standing watch blocking communist trails day and night. With relatively little disruption to existing organization and logistics, boats were shifted rapidly from one area to another. One such example was in mid-June of 1969, when U.S. Navy and Vietnamese boats quickly deployed north of Go Dau Ha on the Vam Co Dong in response to serious threats to Tay Ninh. This extended the last section of Slingshot, with patrols making heavy contact while ATSB Ben Keo was being built near a small fishing village. Then it all peaked in August.

River Division 531 Commander, Lieutenant Commander Thomas K. Anderson, directed an impressive display when he and his sailors, along with Vietnamese Airborne soldiers stationed across the river, successfully repelled enemy probes leading a 2000-man communist attack on Ben Keo August 13th. They fought for two-and-a-half days, with the Vietnamese Airborne fighting hand-to-hand, as they repelled the attack. At the end of the battle, the Airborne stacked three hundred enemy bodies near their fort, as the communist fighters limped back into Cambodia, dragging their wounded after losing all hope of crossing the river where over fifty river patrol boats remained in control. This ended communist plans to take Tay Ninh City.

A SEA LORDS campaign that did not meet with as much success occurred on April 12th, 1969. While performing routine sweep operations in the Ca Mau Peninsula with South Vietnamese troops onboard, eight Swift boats came under heavy enemy gunfire at Dung Keo Canal near Guong Keo River. Detonation of two Claymore mines from the northwest bank was immediately followed by recoilless rifle rounds and B40 rockets, which slammed into the craft and disabled PCF 43's steering gear while fatally wounding the boat skipper, Lieutenant Donald G. Droz. The Swift boat beached at high speed in the center of the ambush site, as B40 rockets continued to slam into her. Uninjured crewmen and members of an underwater demolition team who were onboard that day hastily set up positions around the boat, while PCF's 5 and 31 returned alongside to assist the stricken PCF 43, at the same time maintaining a heavy volume of return fire into enemy positions. Seawolf gunships scrambled and reached the location in minutes placing heavy fire into the area, suppressing enemy fire. All men were removed from PCF 43 and PCF 5 to safety. A fire in PCF 43 later reached UDT ammunitions stores aboard, triggering an explosion that destroyed the craft. Final results of the fight were three U.S. sailors lost and thirty-three wounded, with two Vietnamese Marines killed and thirteen wounded. PCF 43 was destroyed and two other Swifts badly damaged along with another two boats moderately damaged. Eighteen Viet Cong were killed.

Shortly after this, President Richard M. Nixon's Vietnamization policy started to take effect, as American Naval units struck their colors and began the process of turning over their boats and duties to the South Vietnamese Navy, which totaled 42,000 officers and enlisted men. It was the beginning of the end of U.S. participation, with America voting to bring the troops home.

SEA FLOAT

The scope of Operation SEA LORDS had been expanded by early 1969, after the new interdiction campaign, Barrier Reef, had been initiated to complete the interdiction line. Barrier Reef sailors contributed to an important enemy defeat when the presence of river patrol units supporting a Provincial Force ambush team eighteen miles east of An Long Village, twice turned back an enemy heavy weapons company attempting to cross the canal on its way from Cambodia to Sa Dec. The enemy company was spotted by a visual reconnaissance aircraft on the morning of January 14th, and most of its members were killed by gunship strikes or captured by the Provincial Force unit. Other enemy losses to patrol craft or ground forces operating with patrols included twelve killed, ten captured, and two detained, with one small-arms cache discovered. As with Slingshot, the enemy reaction to patrols was quickly answered with six hostile fire incidents, including the mining of two PBRs, which indicated to some extent how the interdiction campaign was hampering enemy logistics. Friendly losses in these actions included four U.S. sailors, with sixteen wounded, along with one Vietnamese. In addition, two patrol craft were damaged, two craft sunk or beached, and one helicopter shot down. The helo was recovered later.

The interdiction/pacification campaign continued in Kien Giang Province northeast of Rach Gia in the area, bounded by the Rach Gia to Long Xuyen and Rach Soi canals. Mobile Riverine Group Bravo, operating with Vietnamese Marines, continued to stage operations in Kien Giang, Chuong Thien, and Phong Dinh provinces. These campaigns, plus the numerous river and canal raids carried out by coastal surveillance craft, hit at enemy base areas and crossed previously unimpaired enemy supply routes.

This resulted in high enemy losses and provoked a strong response of attacks on river craft.

Defoliation operations were carried out along the Ha Tien to Rach Gia canal and Rach Giang Thanh River early in the month. But lack of cooperation by local officials delayed defoliation along the Vinh Te, increasing the threat of enemy-initiated action along the banks. The mining of a PBR near the entrance of the Vinh Te Canal wounded four crewmen and sank their patrol boat. The seriousness of the mine threat led to the halt of patrols until chain drag sweep operations by Vietnamese landing craft began, with operations by U.S. minesweepers commencing by the end of the month.

Operations in the Rach Gia campaign continued to meet intermittent enemy opposition, including the mining of an Alpha minesweeper boat. Patrols by PBRs and Alphas were taken under hostile fire six times during January, resulting in four Vietnamese sailors killed. One U.S. sailor and three Provincial Force soldiers were also wounded, with two craft damaged and one patrol boat sunk. Patrol operations discovered one arms cache in addition to killing two VC and detaining nine suspects. A week of mobile riverine operations southeast of Rach Gia, along the Cau Lon River, also encountered heavy enemy opposition, resulting in eight firefights with one Tango sunk by a mine. By the end of the month, operations were commenced along the Can Tho River in Phong Dinh Province.

For the Coastal Surveillance Force of Task Force 115, there was a slight increase in detections of junks and sampans. The percentage of craft detected, which were checked by visual boarding and search, remained at the high level. Operation Market Time units inspected 24,120 junks and sampans and boarded over half of them. As a result of the boardings, 1,679 people were detained for various violations. No suspicious activity was noted during the inspections of steel-hulled vessels. But, as in the past, a number of Swifts continued to operate under the operational control of Task Force 116 on the Soi Rap River, making several thousand detections and carrying out thousands of boardings. In addition, Swifts under Task Force 115 control patrolled approximately seventy miles of the lower Ham Luong and Co Chien Rivers in order to release PBRs for other employments.

River incursions into Ca Mau Peninsula continued to dominate offensive operations carried out by coastal force units as sixty river and canal operations and several naval gunfire support missions by Swift patrols were carried out during the month. In addition, two Swift boats supported by a Tango continued daily patrol operations on the Rach Giang Thanh River along the Cambodian border. Of fifty-four hostile incidents recorded in January '69 by coastal units, thirty involved craft operating on inland waterways, resulting in one U.S. sailor lost, nineteen wounded and twelve Swift boats damaged. An additional four U.S. sailors were wounded as a landing team from two Swifts was taken under fire while sweeping an area east of Phan Rang. Enemy losses to gunfire by Market Time units during river and canal operations, totaled over 1,500 junks, sampans, structures and bunkers destroyed, plus 154 communists killed and sixty wounded.

At the beginning of the month, PCF 13 carried out an effective psychological operation off the coast near two enemy-controlled villages twenty-five miles northwest of Chu Lai. After an hour of loudspeaker operations, approximately 150 Vietnamese civilians gathered on the beach for escort to a refugee village. As the escort operation by PCFs 13 and 69 commenced, an enemy ambush killed ten and wounded five of the refugees as they moved from their village. The Swifts called in American gunships to suppress the enemy fire as a Viet interpreter on PCF 13 announced to the refugees that help was on the way and sang them songs to prevent panic. Despite VC threats of death, by the end of the day more than 200 people had been relocated in order to escape enemy exploitation of their food and labor.

Although nearly all of the river operations represented significant incidents in the month's activity, two stood out, one for the size of forces employed and the other for extending operations into new areas. By the middle of January '69, the enemy bunkers that had frequently been the source of intense hostile fire two miles up the Bo De River, fifty miles south of Ca Mau, were dealt a final blow. A force consisting of ten Swift boats, EOD and UDT personnel, and mobile strike force troops, supported by two Coast Guard WPB cutters and an LST, moved up river under both helicopter gunship and fixed-wing aircraft cover. Following air strikes on the bunker complex, demolition teams and security troops landed unopposed to destroy the enemy positions. During the day's operation, seventy-four bunkers were destroyed and another six damaged.

The second unique river incursion took place at the end of the month, when four Swifts carried out a six-hour operation that took them more than forty miles across the Ca Mau Peninsula. Entering the Ganh Hao River, twenty-three miles east-southeast of Ca Mau City, the Swifts proceeded up river all the way to Ca Mau City, taking targets of opportunity under fire along the way. From Ca Mau, the four Swifts made their way to the Gulf of Thailand via the Ong Doc River, receiving hostile fire at one point, which disabled the engine of one Swift. The boat was towed the remainder of the journey out of the river, with no casualties suffered during the engagement. Enemy losses were seventy sampans, twenty-five structures, two bunkers and a fish trap destroyed, with many others damaged. Because of these brave new incursions into long-controlled enemy areas, it was decided that forward Navy bases were needed to support these operations.

The Navy Seabees in Vietnam were put to good use building roads, bridges, and just about everything else needed, but one of the most important jobs they accomplished was building the advance tactical support bases that the U.S. Navy had positioned on inland waterways in support of river craft. Many of the Navy bases were built on thirty-by-ninety-foot barges or ammies as they were called. The ammies had been used for transporting coal before being transformed into floating bunkhouses, chow halls with kitchens, maintenance shops with command post, and communications huts.

Seven ammies with wooden hooches were needed, with additional barges for a helicopter landing deck to support the Seawolves, and areas for supply and maintenance sailors to work. The shop would have a drill press and all the tools needed to repair the boats. At a time when America was withdrawing from Vietnam, a maximum effort was called on to be fufilled by Navy units, who made sure all boats were serviced daily so there were no holes in allied defenses at night. As more and more of the Army was being withdrawn, the Navy was being given more responsibility for patrolling and defending these areas.

In May '69, a request came in from the Chief of Naval Operations to Cam Rahn Bay Naval Headquarters to build a base immediately. Seabee Commanding Officer, Commander "Dutch" Filbrick, selected one of his best men, Chief Builder Ron Larrivee, and put him in charge, telling him to pick a team and get the job done. After Chief Larrivee picked the cream of the crop, thirteen builders and steel workers, the Seabees got together and looked the project over and then asked, "Chief, how much time do we have to build it?"

Larrivee replied, "Three weeks."

"How would you like to have it done in two weeks?" they inquired.

"That would be great," the Chief said.

So the team did it in one.

The Seabees set up a construction assembly line with one crew that did nothing but cut two-by-fours while another crew assembled the wooden pieces. There was a plywood crew and a crew that put on screening and tin roofs. Working twelve to fourteen hours a day, they built one sixteen-foot-by-forty-foot hooch a day. The work was going so fast that Commander Filbrick, who came down to check it out personally, was astonished.

"I can't believe you did it in a week," Filbrick told Larrivee after inspecting the new mobile base.

All the brown water sailors wore the same green fatigue uniforms, and the proud Seabee team wanted something that would distinguish them from all the others at the repair base. So Chief Larrivee had fourteen shoulder patches made at a sewing shop in Saigon. The patches displayed a dragon with "Seabee Team 30207" emblazoned across it. After the inspection, Commander Filbrick noticed the new patches on the shoulders of the Seabee team. Chief Larrivee explained that he had wanted a special patch for the Seabee team.

Dutch Filbrick looked at the patch for a moment, then turned to Larrivee and said, "Good job, Chief. Keep it going."

After completion of the nine-ammie floating base it was transported south by landing ships and positioned on the river. The hooches were at one end, with additional ammies added to provide two helo pads at the other end. The pads constituted a very small area and were not lit, so the Seawolves had some tricky maneuvering at night in order to get the choppers down safely. The barges were about two feet above the water, and there was not much visual reference for landing. There were around 150 people living on the ammies at first, with the Seawolf crews sharing a hooch with the SEALs, a ragtag-looking bunch that rarely shaved, blackened their faces and wore headbands for operations, making them more invisible. The SEALs usually had two to four bandoliers of bullets over their shoulders, hand grenades strapped to anything that would hold one, and enough fire power to end the war, or so it seemed.

At the same end of the barge where the copters were parked were thousands of rockets, hundreds of thousands rounds of ammunition, and crates of M-79 grenades to support operations. When the choppers needed fuel, they had to go ashore to refueling stations scattered throughout the delta. At the other end of the ammies were the hooches for the river patrol and river support units. All of the land surrounding the ammies was enemy-controlled, with Nam Cam being one of their centers of operations. The U.S. Navy had planted a base right in the midst of their forces, which up set them terribly and hampered their movement. This would lead to many river battles.

The ATSB was called Sea Float by the U.S. Navy and Tran Hung Doa III by the Vietnamese, when speaking of the twelve ammie complex positioned on the Cau Lon River. The advance tactical support base that was later built ashore, was named Solid Anchor by the Americans and Tran Hung Dao IV by the South Vietnamese. It was a joint U.S. and Vietnamese attempt to inject an allied presence into An Xuyen Province, 175 miles southwest of Saigon. Its purpose was to extend allied control over the strategic Nam Can region. Heavily forested, the area sprawled across miles of mangrove swamp. The site selected was on the Cau Lon, which connected to the Bo De and Dam Doi, and were all three rivers contaminated with saltwater. Any fresh or drinking water used afloat or ashore had to be brought in by ship. The entire area was a communist stronghold and had been solidly held by the Vietminh against the French, and by the Viet Cong against the Republic of Vietnam and its American allies.

The entrance to Sea Float from the eastern approach was up the Bo De to the junction of the Dam Doi and Cau Lon Rivers, with the western approach from "Square Bay" up the Cau Lon River. The western approach was very shallow and was only attempted at high tide. Oceangoing ships, tugs, and barges came in by way of the Bo De River. Commander of Naval Forces, Vietnam, begged, borrowed, and shanghaied materials for the operation from various in-country commands.

On June 25th 1969, three 7th Fleet dock-landing ships began off-loading the twelve ammi barges which would become home for many river sailors and SEALs for the next few years. One was Gunner's Mate Second Robert "Bob" Stoner, who was attached to Sea Float and Solid Anchor from May through November of 1970. Stoner worked for Mobile Support Team Detachment Charlie that operated and manned the guns of two light, one medium, and one heavy SEAL support craft. Another was Commander Art Schmitt, call sign Seawolf One-six, who was commanding officer of Seawolf Detachment One assigned to Sea Float and Solid Anchor in 1970.

There were approximately 700 officers and enlisted men at Sea Float and Solid Anchor by the peak of the operation, which did not include the crews of Vietnamese river assault landing craft and a large landing ship support (LSSL), or the U.S. Navy gas turbine patrol gunboats (PG) that all provided protection. Sea Float had a support staff, galley, intelligence section, communications section, supply department; a motley collection of Vietnamese Navy owned and operated RAG boats with American advisors, two Mobile Support Team detachments, three SEAL platoons, a UDT detachment, six to eight coastal junks, and some miscellaneous Vietnamese Navy and U.S. Navy Swift boats in addition to the Seawolves.

Security for Sea Float was provided by U.S. Navy Patrol Gunboats of the Ashville-class, and old American World War II landing ships converted to gunboats and given to the South Vietnamese Navy. One U.S. gunboat was normally anchored 1,000 yards east of Sea Float with the Vietnamese LSSL anchored 1,000 yards west on the opposite end of the barges. The USS Asheville (PG-84), USS Gallup (PG-85), USS Antelope (PG-86), USS Crockett (PG-88), USS Marathon (PG-89), and USS Canon (PG-90) were all rotated in and out, providing security beginning with USS Asheville on July 11th, 1969. The U.S. gunboats had diesel engines for cruising and gas turbines for high-speed running. Armament was a three-inch, rapid-fire gun forward, a 40mm gun aft, and twin .50 cal machineguns on either side of the stack on the zero-one level behind the bridge. The patrol gunboats rotated in and out on-station at Sea Float and provided a floating security trip wire.

In mid-July 1970, USS Canon was conducting harassment and interdiction fire off the entrance to the Bo De River, when while attempting to return to Sea Float the next morning, she was ambushed and received recoilless rifle and rocket damage that knocked out the pitch change controls on her propellers. USS Canon was temporarily disabled until the damage could be repaired. There was one casualty who was medevaced from Sea Float after Canon was escorted back by Swifts with Seawolves flying overhead. In August, while returning to Sea Float, USS Canon was again ambushed by VC forces, which this time fired rockets from both river banks. During the attack, Canon took eight rocket hits on both port and starboard sides. Out of the crew of twenty-four, fourteen were wounded, with five medevaced out. One was the captain. Swift boats and a Vietnamese vessel came to Canon's assistance and escorted her to Sea Float. USS Gallup escorted the badly damaged Canon to Cam Ranh Bay for repairs the following day. Then Gallup returned to Sea Float to assume Canon's patrol duties until relieved by USS Crockett, which was, in turn, relieved by Gallup later on. For its crew's heroic actions on August 11th, 1970, the USS Canon became the most decorated ship of the Vietnam War.

The Vietnamese had seven landing ship support large and five similar landing ship infantry large (LSIL), also in support of Sea Float and Solid Anchor. The Vietnamese gunboats had diesel engines and were conversions of old WWII American ships with the five infantry landing craft about 158 feet long and weighing around 250 tons. The bow ramps had been welded closed on most, which were then converted to gunboats by the addition of three-inch slow fire guns forward, two twin 40mm guns fore and aft, and four 20mm guns. They also had .50 and .30 caliber machineguns.

The original seven Vietnamese LSSLs were Nguyen Van Tru (HQ-225), Le Trong Diem (HQ-226), Le Van Binh (HQ-227), Doan Ngoc Tang (HQ-228), Lu Phu Tho (HQ-229), Nguyen Ngoc Long (HQ-230), and Nguyen Duc Bong (HQ-231). The Vietnamese rotated their ships supporting Sea Float and Solid Anchor similar to the Americans.

In September 1970, Nguyen Van Tru was mined and lost to a swimmer attack. The mines were floated down on a cable with the current. The cable caught the anchor chain of the ship, and the current carried the mines against the hull amidships. The explosion blew the ship in half and sank it within minutes. The American advisor stationed onboard of Nguyen Van Tru was transferred to Le Trong Diem, only to find she had been sunk on the Bassac River around the same time as her sister. The Le Van Binh was sunk in 1966. The Doan Ngoc Tang, Lu Phu Tho, Nguyen Ngoc Long, and Nguyen Duc Bong all made it out and steamed to the Philippines in the 1975 evacuation of South Vietnam.

Swift boats were involved in operations around Ca Mau on its rivers and large canals, as well as the sea, on almost a daily basis. When a Swift was at combat stations, the door to the pilot house was closed, and many crews actually did the conning of the boat from the emergency steering, just below the American flag on the port side of the deck house. The forward twin .50 gunner put flak jackets over his legs to protect himself from shrapnel wounds because the VC would shoot rockets and recoilless rifle rounds at the pilot house in an attempt to disable the boat. If the pilot house door was not closed, the boat's unit badge, normally placed on the inside of the door, was an excellent bull's-eye for the VC gunners, who were very accurate.

While operations were conducted from Sea Float barges, American Seabees began construction on a permanent shore base on the north bank of the Cau Lon River. The swampy nature of the terrain was clearly recognizable by the large areas of standing water. The Viet Kit Carson Scout camp was on the east side of a canal across from the base. The results of defoliation around the base to prevent ground attacks through the mangrove swamp were very apparent from a bird's-eye view. The area was formerly the old site of Nam Can, which had been flattened by air strikes during and after the 1968 Tet Offensive. Water-filled bomb craters from B-52 strikes were still evident. In order to build the base on such soggy ground, the Navy brought in six-million-dollars' worth of sand in barges to provide a foundation for everything. Even then, interlocking steel pilings were placed along the river and canal banks to keep the tidal currents from eroding the sand almost as fast as it was put in place.

When Sea Float had first been moored in the Cau Lon River by Nam Cam, special multiple-point moorings were required because the river currents typically were between six and eight knots, and because the Cau Lon, Bo De and Dam Doi rivers connected with the South China Sea on the east, and the Cau Lon with the Gulf of Thailand on the west. These currents would typically reverse due to tidal effects, so current reversal and water levels were significant factors in planning operations. At low tide ashore, the armored troop carriers were beached so the piers for the Swifts had to be positioned farther out, with Sea Float anchored in the middle of the river.

Gunner's Mate Bob Stoner was no stranger to the river craft that cruised the dangerous waters around the barges of Sea Float, as he had been transferred from the Mobile Riverine Force in the Mekong Delta after the force had been disbanded. After he and his shipmates sailed USS Nueces, APB-40, back to Long Beach Naval Shipyard for decommissioning, Stoner was transferred to Boat Support Unit One in January 1970, and shortly after found himself back in-country serving with the units deployed assets, the Mobile Support Teams.

At the time Stoner arrived, the most reliable boat available was the heavy SEAL support craft, which was actually a modified landing craft mechanized that ran very well. The same could not be said for the two light and one medium SEAL support craft. The two light craft (LSSC) were twenty-four-foot-long and aluminum hulled, powered by two Ford 427 cubic-inch gasoline engines. They were equipped with PRC-25, PRC-77 or VRC-46 FM radios, a small Raytheon search radar, and a .50 cal Browning and two M60 machineguns with ceramic armor tiles and flak curtains along the sides of the crew compartment for protection. The low-profile LSSCs, were normally crewed by two to three sailors and could haul six or seven SEALs in and out of missions, drawing only eighteen inches of water when fully loaded. But when Stoner first arrived, both of the light craft had already been sunk with one having been completely submerged and the other partially. The crafts' Styrofoam interiors, which had provided sound suppression and flotation, were partially waterlogged. This meant they couldn't get up to speed when they needed it most. One craft was sitting on its trailer on the beach with two bad engines. Its bow patch had been removed to allow access to the waterlogged Styrofoam. The foam was being scraped-out by hand before re-foaming. The second craft only had one good engine, but wasn't as badly waterlogged. It was used only as a water taxi until it got another engine.

Stoner never really liked the light crafts. They were cramped and crude for his taste. Two of his shipmates, Radioman Second Jimmy Wells and Radarman Second "Wally" Wallace, did, however, and they usually took them out when needed.

The medium SEAL support craft (MSSC) was a thirty-six-foot-long, aluminum boat, cathedral hulled and powered by twin Mercury Cruiser stern-drive engines. It had a VRC-46 FM radio, the Raytheon radar, and three .50 cal or two .50 cal and a 7.62mm General Electric Mini-gun, with four M60 machineguns. It carried a crew of five and up to eighteen SEALs. But this craft was also not operational when he first arrived. It had sucked a huge gulp of salt water in one engine at shutdown. The two Chevy 427 cubic-inch gasoline engines had a high-rise manifold for the underwater exhaust to prevent water from being sucked back into the engine at shutdown, but it did not always work.

The medium craft was fast and roomy and carried 300 gallons of gasoline in four seventy-five-gallon bladders, which were paired on either side of the hull at the waterline. The interior of the well deck was covered with ceramic armor tiles and flak curtains. Its weakest fault was in the steering cables, electrical cables, and engine throttle controls, which all ran down the starboard side instead of being split up. This almost caused the loss of the boat when a B40 rocket hit severed the steering and electrical cables, just missing the fuel bladder. Fortunately, the engines stayed in operation, and SEAL operator Dave Bodkin crawled across the engine hatches under fire to install the emergency tiller he used to steer the craft out of the kill zone.

The heavy SEAL support craft (HSSC) was a much-modified LCM-6 landing craft. With two GM 671 diesel engines to push its flat-bottomed bulk, the battlewagon carried armor and enough firepower to make up for its lack of speed. There was a piggy-back 81mm mortar, .50 cal machinegun behind the cut-down bow ramp. A helicopter landing pad had been welded across the top of the well deck, and a gun tub was attached to the front of the helo pad. The gun tub contained a GE Mini-gun, and a 106mm recoilless rifle graced the center of the helo pad. From below the helo pad, the snouts of four .50s and four M60 machineguns poked out, two on each side. Raytheon radar topped the afterdeck house and a .50 cal covered the stern. Bar armor protected the afterdeck house, gun tub, and hull above the waterline from B40 rockets and recoilless rifle rounds. Heavy flak blankets lined the inside of the well deck, engine room, and deckhouse to protect the crew from flying splinters if the sides were penetrated by a rocket. The only thing the crew couldn't defend against was a command-detonated underwater mine, and the bad guys were very good with those, if they could successfully lay them.

The heavy SEAL support craft couldn't hold its own against the currents caused by the tides. Operations had to be planned for when currents were weak or for when the tide was going out or coming in. All of the boats had to make sure they weren't stranded by the tide when working a canal. The rule of thumb was, if the tide is running out, and you're in doubt, get out. Operations were scheduled to take advantage of incoming tidal waters in the canals. If they were in one of the smaller canals, and the tide was going out, it was better get out, or they would be high and dry until it came back in. Operations in Square Bay, at the western mouth of the Cau Lon River, were especially hazardous. The main channel, which changed daily, was only twelve-to fifteen-feet-deep at high tide and three-to five-feet-deep everywhere else outside the channel. At low tide, the water level dropped so that everything except the main channel became acres and acres of mud flats. All things considered, this operational area was one of the most God-forsaken places anyone could imagine, and it was hard to understand why anyone would want it. The only good thing about the area was that it was a full-circle, thirty-mile-diameter free-fire zone.

When the first medium craft arrived, one of the main engines had to be replaced. So about six weeks after Stoner's arrival, his officer-in-charge and three of the boat crew took it down river to Square Bay, up the coast to Song Ong Doc, up river to Ca Mau, and by canal to the mobile repair team at Binh Thuy. The repair team detachment at Naval Support Activity Binh Thuy worked very hard to keep all the boats operational. They had two heavies, eight medium, over a dozen light craft, and a bunch of small boats to work on.

After being at Sea Float for awhile, visiting Binh Thuy was like living in luxury, with laundry facilities, a decent rack with clean linen and cold beer after work. It was almost paradise, the only concern being the security of the medium craft, for the Vietnamese would steal anything that wasn't locked up. The Ca Mau detachment's MSSC even had its twenty-four-volt instrument panel light bulbs stolen while it was tied-up near the MACV compound. All portable gear, weapons, and ammo were removed and locked in a container with the crew taking turns sleeping on the boat to make sure it left with everything it had come with. After the new engine had been installed, it really made the craft move out. She was a joy to drive and handled like a high-powered ski boat when at full throttle.

When they returned to Sea Float, their sister mobile support team, Detachment Bravo, had returned from operations. Now the SEALs had two medium craft from which to operate.

Gunner's Mate Bob Stoner was always on the lookout for more ways to beef up the firepower of the medium craft. He considered the Mark-19, 40mm automatic grenade launcher. But all the ammo on hand had been linked incorrectly, and it jammed. The detachment didn't have a linker, so the Mk-19 went into storage in the Conex box. Stoner did manage to get a .50 caliber Browning aircraft machinegun that the SEALs had captured. At first, the intelligence officer was convinced it was a Russian machinegun until Stoner showed him it had been made at Springfield Armory in Massachusetts. The SEALs then fought off attempts by the An Xuyen province chief to take it. In the end, the SEALs gave it to Stoner to spite the province chief. After swapping and adding parts gotten from the base armory, Stoner was ready to test fire the gun. He kept bothering his officer-in-charge to take the boat out so he could test fire the gun and finally got permission and went several times. Each time they went out, Stoner made adjustments to the gun, but it still needed additional work. Their officer and three of the crew took the medium craft up river past the village to test the gun one day, and as they were moving along, Stoner was resting on the gun and looked over at the beach. Suddenly he saw a puff of mud and debris, along with a big, black blob cartwheeling at them. It was an enemy rocket, and Stoner happened to see where it came from. He hit the triggers of the .50 cal, with the aircraft gun letting out a throaty roar and eating up over half of his 426-round ready service ammo can before he knew it. Just as quickly, they had pulled out of range, and the officer turned around and asked him what all the commotion was about. Stoner told him that someone had just fired a rocket at them and missed, and he had splattered them with .50 cal fire. The officer nodded and resumed conning the boat. Bob Stoner's test fire had worked better than planned, but the lack of spare barrels forced him to use the aircraft .50 cal for only special ops, where its fast rate of fire - 1,150 rounds a minute - could be decisive.

The SEALs had purchased sampans from the local Vietnamese, who lived in a ramshackle bamboo and thatch village called Ham Rong, which was nicknamed the "Annex" and was about three miles east of the base. They used the sampans to do stealthy insertions and extractions on canals that were too narrow and shallow for the support craft.

One time, for whatever reason, Bob got tagged to go with Jim and Wally for a solo night op, where they weren't using a cover boat for backup. They had received notice of an operation early in the afternoon. Briefing was at 1800 hours, and within a few hours, the two sampans had been secured to the light support craft with three crewmen and six SEALs getting underway. The mission was a simple recon up a side canal off one of the main canals that emptied into the river. One thing about the area was, when the sun went down, it got dark fast. On that night, they were favored with a clear sky with lots of stars and no moon. By 2200 hours, they had dropped off the SEALs and pulled back to act as a guard post to watch the mouth of the canal, while tied up to a fish stake that was near the middle of the canal. One of the crew manned the radio for an hour, another watched the banks through a starlight scope, and one rested or slept if possible. The jobs were rotated hourly, but as it turned out, no one slept that night. It was probably a combination of adrenaline or maybe some "stay awakes" (stimulants) someone had gotten from the SEAL corpsman. Stoner took them only once, and they started to put him asleep, so he avoided using them again. In other people, they acted to produce hallucinations. Because of their unpredictable effects, most of the boat crews didn't use the pills.

While on waterborne guard post, no one smoked, and the little talk done was in muffled whispers. Any kind of noise carried a long way at night, especially across water. The only break in the monotony was when there was a burst of radio static on the handset, every thirty minutes. This was done by the SEAL radioman keying the transmitter on the handset, to indicate all was okay. The boat crew's response was two bursts in return.

Dawn came early that time of year, and they received word to extract around 0430 hours. The extraction point was another canal about a mile away. They moved quietly down to the SEALs, with the team signaling by flashing a blue-lens strobe light at the boat to confirm their location. The coxswain set the engine throttles to idle, and the two sampans came out to meet them, with the sampans silently and quickly stowed. They then made their way back to the river with all safely aboard and hit the throttles, speeding home.

Halfway through Mobile Support Team Detachment Charlie's tour, headquarters, Naval Special Warfare Group, in Saigon decided to upgrade the medium support craft with the 7.62mm GE Mini-gun to replace the aft .50 Browning. The Mini-gun was an electric-powered Gatling gun scaled-down from the 20mm Vulcan cannons used on fighter and attack jets. The gun could fire 6,000 rounds a minute. But the motor controller allowed only two rates of fire: 2,000 and 4,000 rounds per minute. The gun ran off the boat batteries and carried 3,800 rounds of linked 7.62mm ammunition in its ready service magazine. It had two triggers, one on the left for 2,000 rounds, and the right for 4,000 rounds firing rate. The gunner always started with the left first and then the right to keep the gun from jamming. They said it sounded like a two-speed chainsaw when firing. Even with the flash suppressors, there was a large muzzle blast and a near solid streak of red tracers heading toward the target. It was impressive to shoot, but also took an impressive time to reload as well. They learned the hardway not to get lead-fingered on the triggers.

Mobile support team Charlie's sister detachment, Bravo, had gotten relieved. Some of the new personnel arrived aboard, and Charlie team's officer had arranged to show Bravo team's officer the operation area. They also felt like it might be a good time to test the new Mini-gun on the way back from Square Bay. They quickly made it down to the bay, pointed out the places of interest, and started back home. Suddenly, sniper fire erupted from the tree line. Things happened in a blur, with the officer hitting the throttles. The portside gunner and Stoner were taken by surprise by the acceleration and went tumbling to the deck. The aft gunner saw the muzzle flashes, hunkered down, and let the Mini-gun rip, not easing off the triggers until he ran dry. Meanwhile, the other gunner and Stoner kept slipping and falling on the Mini-gun's spent brass cartridges as they tried to get to their guns. Just as they were about to make it back up on their feet, the officer would fishtail the boat to give the aft gunner a better field of fire, and down they would go again. Soon they had cleared the ambush site and passed out of range. They set about reloading the Mini-gun and found out why it wasn't a good idea to run its magazine dry. It took ten minutes to link-up the 750 round sections of ammo into the 3,800 round belt and stow it in the magazine, then bring it through the feed booster and pull it through the feed chute. Not a good idea while under fire. They learned to fire short bursts to conserve the ammo.

For longer-range missions, the medium craft was invaluable as a radio relay point, and its larger size allowed them to carry larger sampans. A joint operation using both the light and medium craft was organized, with the bigger sampans loaded on the medium craft and smaller sampans on the light craft. The SEALs split up between the boats, with each boat providing cover for the other during the insertion and extraction.

Petty Officer Stoner was on the medium craft that night, with the light craft their cover-boat for the operation. They proceeded to the insertion point, and the light craft went in, while the medium craft covered to establish flank security. After securing the flank, the crew nosed the medium craft in also. Once beached, both boats off-loaded the sampans. The SEALs continued in the sampans up the canal, too shallow for either boat to follow. After the SEALs disappeared into the jungle, both boats retracted from the beach and moved to prearranged positions, where they could keep other canals and each other under observation.

While the SEALs were mucking about in the jungle, the time on the boats was usually spent keeping watch, sweating, monitoring the radio, sweating, and swatting giant mosquitoes flying around in bloodthirsty swarms. It was 0530 hours and the sun had just made it over the horizon.

"Black Bear, Black Bear, this is Tradewinds, over."

"Black Bear, go," the boat crew answered the SEAL team.

"This is Tradewinds, request emergency extraction, request emergency extraction over."

Two sets of engines grumbled to life as adrenaline pumped. Both boats were quickly underway headed for the extraction point. Both boats entered the dangerous canal, with the light craft in the lead and the medium craft providing cover. The canal narrowed as time seemed to slow and drag. Eyes and ears on the medium craft strained to pick out signs of the light craft or sampans.

Finally, the light craft emerged with the sampans in tow. The boats nestled together against the beach as the sampans were stowed. There were no casualties, but some of the SEALs weren't happy. As they came aboard the medium craft, the SEAL officer slammed his weapon against the bulkhead in frustration.

"Those dinks were three rice paddy dikes over against the trees, and we were out of range."

Because the boats were unable to penetrate farther up the canal, the SEALs were out of visual and hearing range. The boats were able to keep track of them only by radio. They could not hear the gunfight, which lasted almost an hour, from their location back on the boats, much less offer support. It was a Mexican standoff, with both sides at the edge of their effective small-arms range. It became a mutual disengagement, with both sides withdrawing. After everyone was back aboard, the boats got underway and out to the main river. From there, they proceeded at maximum speed back to base. The SEALs were still pissed.

The heavy SEAL support craft was a fortress. It had firepower, and it had armor. In short, just the kind of boat the bad guys loved to hate, which they did. There was a big canal just past the village that had been begging for exploration for some time. It was deep enough for the heavy craft even at low tide, and there were places where the fifty-six-foot craft could turn around.

The evening's adventure was to insert and extract a Beach Jumper Unit "Duffle Bag Team," which planted and monitored vibration and body-heat-activated sensors that helped track movements of the enemy around the base. On the way out, they were to play some "Wandering Soul" tapes that the Psychological Warfare guys had dreamed up to terrorize the guerillas. The idea was the Viet Cong would become so frightened, they would come over to the government side. But they never got to hear the tape, nor was the Duffle Bag Team ever able to plant their guerilla tracking sensors. Instead, they got ambushed.

Stoner's general quarters station was the forward 81mm mortar /.50 cal mount. Engineman Third Mike Meils was the starboard forward .50 gunner. Engineman Third "D.J." Desjardins was on the Mini-gun. Engineman Second Don King was on the aft .50 cal machinegun by his engine room. Lieutenant Fulkerson and Boatswain's Mate First Quincy Butler were driving from the coxswain's flat in the deckhouse. The crew had loaded the 81mm mortar and 106mm recoilless rifle with anti-personnel flechette beehive rounds. When fired, they acted like a gigantic shotgun and were ideal for ambush situations.

The team had entered the canal at low tide when the water was out. The banks of the canal were actually even with the top of the helicopter pad, which meant the water was approximately eight to ten feet below the top of the bank. Stoner's gun was covering the left bank, with the recoilless rifle covering the right. Stoner, who had gone over to ask Mike Meils a question, had noticed one of the psyops boys sitting behind Mike. The calm was torn by two fast, bright explosions, changing the black of night to day. Stoner looked up, and both men had gone to return fire. Then Stoner looked back at his gun, which seemed to be a half mile away, with the night sky lit up from muzzle flashes. A crazy rationalization was going through his head: "This is insane! That gun mount is lit up like a Christmas tree. You could get killed up there. Nope, the enemy has gotten their heads down by now. Better get up there and get the guns working, or I'm going to feel real stupid in front of the guys."

Stoner was at his guns in what seemed to be two giant steps. The 81mm beehive went first and was followed by 150 rounds of .50 cal armor-piercing rounds. Then the craft made it out of the kill zone and around a bend in the canal, where it beached.

"Seawolf, Seawolf, this is Black Bear, scramble, scramble, over."

"Black Bear, Seawolf, roger scramble one; have two chicks on the way."

It was then Stoner discovered the mortar and .50 could not fire forward at close range because the bow ramp had not been cut low enough. Great, he thought. The Mini-gun is jammed, the recoilless rifle may have shrapnel damage, and the two forward .50s can't cover the front of the boat with Stoner's gun mount unable to fire because the bow ramp was in the way. In Stoner's mind, he and his .45 cal grease gun, with three clips, was going to have to hold off the entire North Vietnamese Army. He was relieved to hear choppers and see their flashing anti-collision beacons.

"Black Bear, Seawolf One-six. We think we are close to your position, can you authenticate, over?"

"Roger Seawolf One-six, watch for my strobe, over."

It didn't register with Stoner immediately what the radio had requested until he caught the white flash of the strobe light in his peripheral vision and thought, damn, if the Viet Cong didn't know where we were before, they sure do now.

"Black Bear, Seawolf One-six, we will cover, over."

"Roger Seawolf One-six, extracting, out."

The heavy support boat backed off the bank and headed cautiously through the area where it had been hit. Good, the crew thought, almost through. Then BLAM! BLAM! And the boat was hit again. Same drill: Return fire and get past the kill zone beyond the bend in river and beach the boat. Then, for the next fifteen minutes, the two Seawolf gunships raked the ambush site with rockets and Mini-guns. Meanwhile, Lieutenant Fulkerson had asked Stoner if they had something special for their VC friends to remember them by. Stoner replied yes, and broke out eight, white phosphorous rounds for the mortar. After the gunships finished, the forward gunner and Stoner dumped four "Willie Pete" mortar rounds on both sides of the ambush site. The gunships orbited overhead and covered them until they arrived at the main river.

Back at Sea Float, everyone had heard about the ambush. Lots of anxious faces greeted the crew as it arrived. Everyone was still running on adrenaline, but luckily no one had been hurt. After securing the boat, crew members went to the mobile support team hut to debrief. At debrief, Lieutenant Fulkerson asked who was screaming just after they had been hit on the way in. D.J. Desjardins confessed he was the one, but he had good reason. When they got hit, D.J. had opened up with the Mini-gun and got off two or three bursts before it jammed. Then he grabbed a LAW rocket but it misfired. Then he grabbed his M16 and had gone through two magazines when it jammed also, and he couldn't clear it. After all this, D.J. was so frustrated that he had pointed his finger and yelled, "Bang! Bang! Take that, you son-of-a-bitch!" And with that he threw the empty magazines at the beach.

When the sun came up, they finally figured out what it was the bad guys had used on them. From all the leaves, twigs, and garbage found, it was evident the enemy had used Claymore-type, remotely-detonated, directional mines set in the trees, which were set to fire on Swift boat patrols at high tide. The team had crossed them up, going through at low tide. When they fired at the sound of the boat engines, the mines on both banks shot over the top of them, twice. Final confirmation came when Petty Officer Stoner found a piece of scorched olive-green sheet metal labeled with Chinese letters, about six feet from where he'd been talking to his gunner the night before.

After the Americans moved ashore from Sea Float to Solid Anchor in September 1970, the empty barges became the object of scavengers from Ham Rong village. Building materials used to construct the hooches on the ammies were recycled by the local Vietnamese, who stripped them of their plywood for building materials. These barges were later used to rebuild ATSB Song Ong Doc in Operation Breezy Cove after the ammie firebase was destroyed on the night of October 20th, 1970. Breezy Cove had been positioned at the mouth of the Song Ong Doc River and was even more exposed than Sea Float to enemy activity. The floating advanced tactical support base at Song Ong Doc was destroyed by mortars, recoilless rifle rounds, and a company-sized ground attack. The old Sea Float barges were used to rebuild a new Song Ong Doc several miles up river from the old base. In June 1971, the remaining barges were moved to Ca Mau. The Solid Anchor base was heavily rocketed and mortared in late January 1971 and was formally turned over to Vietnamese Navy on April 1st, 1971. The last Americans left Solid Anchor on February 1st, 1973.

THE FATE OF MSR-7

While operating on the upper Mekong River near Tan Chau City the night of November 4th, 1969, Patrol Officer, Quartermaster Chief Heinz Hickethier heard Minesweeper River Seven, MSR-7, trying to raise Mine Division 113 command center. Because MSR-7 was unable to get a response and the chief had just checked in with command, the chief offered to relay any messages to YRBM 16 for MSR-7. A young seaman responded over the radio that they wanted to relay their position to command. Chief Hickethier told him he would need to encode the information. The seaman then informed the chief that they had been hit in an attack and had several seriously wounded crewmen. Well, that changed everything, of course. The enemy already knew where the sweeper boat was, and the chief now knew that his quiet ambush had just ended as he quickly prepared his patrol to get underway. He guessed the vessel's problems with communicating may have been due to battle damage, and he was right. The chief listened attentively over the radio as he learned that the vessel was MSR-7 and it had been hit with multiple B40 rockets and small-arms and machinegun fire from both banks of a canal. The disabled sweeper boat had an engine out and had lost steering, going around in circles until it went aground up against the bank.

The caller that night had been Boatswain's Mate Seamen Clint Evens, and he and most of the crew of MSR-7 were wounded. Their boat captain, Boatswain's Mate Chief Charles Price Geisert, was down. At this point, Chief Hickethier requested their position, but Seaman Evens was not exactly sure of where they were. But he described the canal as best he could. Hickethier guessed that MSR-7 was in the French Canal and, after confirming, broke ambush and headed at full speed up river to the French Canal, to support the crippled minesweeper.

The French Canal was a narrow, shallow waterway that connected the upper Mekong at Tan Chau City to the upper Bassac at the city of Chau Doc. It was patrolled by the brown water units of Operation SEA LORDS who interdicted enemy infiltrators. It was a very dangerous area and within rifle fire of the Cambodian border. The two fiberglass patrol boats had been about seven miles away in a small canal off the Mekong River. The chief then radioed the command of MSR-7 and informed them of the sweeper boat's situation. Soon after, Chief Hickethier got another call from the wounded MSR-7 and could hear the heart-rending sound of loud gunfire in the background as Gunner's Mate Third Lee was laying massive fire from his twin .50 cal machineguns into the enemy positions. Unlike on the PBR, the sweeper boat's forward guns were fully enclosed and armored. Hickethier then asked the disabled boat for more information on its situation. The crew members responded that their boat was dead in the water and against the southern bank. The chief had no way of knowing what the condition of the wounded men was, but he did know that they were returning as much fire as possible and what seemed like a bad situation could turn into a disaster soon.

The PBRs were approaching the mouth of the French Canal from Tan Chau when "Pappy" Meeks' PBR picked up a fish net in its pumps. His engineman quickly took the pump cover off and started to pull the bits of net from the pump as the first PBR stood by. Because of the danger of using lights at night, all the engineman could use was his red flashlight and hope and pray they were not hit while he was on his hands and knees over the pump. He soon reported the pump was clear, and the engine started up again. Both boats had slowed while the clogged pumps were being cleared. It took a long, agonizing minute or two, and then they were finally able to return to full speed as the two PBRs rushed to the aid of the crew of MSR-7.

Upon arriving in the French Canal, the PBRs sped to the grounded MSR-7 with all guns blazing in a thunderous return of fire. The enemy immediately started firing at the PBRs instead of MSR-7. The smoke-covered sweeper boat was alongside the south bank in an area of little population in one of the few clear areas on the canal. MSR-7 had taken a direct hit forward by a recoilless rifle on the portside, a foot above the waterline, and the recoilless round had sprayed shrapnel throughout the craft, wounding five of the crewmen. Five B40 rockets had missed the boat exploding nearby, with an additional five B40s that struck the lifeline stanchions and several other locations covering her with debris. The sweeper was splattered with shrapnel with small-arms fire, leaving holes in the hull. Chief Hickethier was at least happy they did not have to take on the enemy in a bunch of hooches full of innocent women and children as the boats' gunners continued to lay down suppressing fire into the retreating enemy. The chief then embarked onto the burning, crippled craft. Pappy Meeks's boat took up a position aft and in the center of the canal. This would allow the PBR to cover both banks from which the attack had originated. It also gave the crew of the lead patrol boat a clear fire area of the north bank and forward. The chief took one of his crew members with him when they boarded MSR-7, to get the wounded personal off the disabled craft. While doing this, they found the body of Boat Captain Charlie Ceisert in the cabin behind the pilot house on a bunk.

They moved all of the crew off MSR-7 and onto the PBR, immediately starting first aid. Most of the crew had been badly wounded and were bleeding from numerous wounds. Boatswain's Mate Jerry Griffin was having trouble breathing. He had been wounded on one side of his body, in his arm, his ribs and one lung. The crew made a special effort to put him in a position that would make him more comfortable and help him breathe. Seamen Clint Evens was badly wounded in the knee. Chief Hickethier knew, that whatever first aid they were able to provide for the wounded, it would not be as important as getting them professional medical help quickly. One of the wounded said there was a Vietnamese interpreter on board, so the crew went back and searched the deck, down into the boat, and in the water nearby. But the interpreter was not found and believed to be lost over the side. The men went aboard MSR-7 one more time to retrieve the body of Boat Captain Giesert. As they prepared to make their departure, Chief Hickethier took up position on the M60 amidships on the engine covers, so that two members of the PBR crew could continue to patch up the wounded men.

They were all very happy to see the arrival of the Seawolf gunships, which had scrambled to provide cover for the disabled boat. The patrolmen continued to evacuate the wounded as the Seawolves laid down suppressing fire. Command center radioed that there were Swifts en route to tow the crippled vessel to YRBM 20, positioned on the Bassac River. Seawolves circled overhead low to the deck and provided fire support to make sure MSR-7 was not boarded by the enemy and to also provide cover for the Swift boats that tied up and towed the damaged, but still floating, MSR-7 back down the canal. The Swift boats cruised slowly with the crippled craft in tow, becoming targets themselves. The air cover that the Seawolves provided from overhead deterred the enemy from wanting to close in and attack, but enemy fire continued from a distance.

The two patrol boats ran at full speed, carrying the wounded to the YRBM 16, also on the Bassac, which had a fully equipped medical center with an American doctor. En route, Chief Hickethier was communicating with the commander of Operation Barrier Reef, Commander J.G. Storms, to arrange for the medical staff to meet them on arrival. Commander Storms had a number of questions about the severity of the wounded. Chief Hickethier could tell him only that two were very serious and the others were also fairly bad, but he felt that if they we were not attacked on their way over, he believed they would make it. Commander Storms also wanted to know the ammo expenditure, which Hickethier expressed as minor, maybe 500 rounds. The PBRs ran at full speed through the eighty-foot-wide French Canal and shot out the west end into the upper Bassac and headed down stream to YRBM 16. The chief was amazed and proud at the skill the PBR crews displayed as the boats raced down the dark narrow canal attempting to save the lives of the crew of MSR-7, with little consideration for their own lives if they happened to run into another ambush on the way. After arriving, the crews carefully transferred the wounded men to the doctors and corpsmen and stayed alongside to clean up their boats.

It may be hard for others who have not experienced combat to imagine how much blood and gore is involved when four or five badly wounded men are brought aboard your boat. Most would have probably frozen or turned away in fear or grief had they looked at the wounded sailors they had carried to safety. They may not have believed these critically wounded men could have made it back alive. One PBR seaman stepped on the pump cover which floated out from under his feet as he fell on his ass. The patrol boat began sinking, so the crew stopped cleaning to concentrate on bigger problems. The pump inspection plate had come loose and would not seat properly because there were still remnants of the net that had been sucked up into the pump in the French Canal. Quickly clearing the debris and resetting the inspection plate, they pumped out the water and cleaned up the rest of the patrol boat.

A couple of hours later, a corpsman came down and escorted the crews of the patrol boats to the hospital ward to see the wounded. They were bandaged all over their bodies, but they looked 1,000 percent better than they did when they were rushed to YRBM 16.

This is a description of the attack on MSR-7 by Tov Guarisco of Mine Sweeper Three, in a letter written to Charlie Geisert's sister, Mary Woodburn. Guarisco was one of the crew members of MSR-7 wounded in the attack:

You are right, MSR-7 was the designation for our boat, and although the boat was badly damaged during the firefight, it did not sink, at least not while we were on it. The attack began with B40 rocket fire. B40 rockets are launched from a 40mm tube which rests on the user's shoulder, similar to the old bazookas of WWII. The rockets themselves are not very stable in flight and therefore not very accurate, but when they found their mark, they could be very effective.

It was during the first few seconds of the attack that we were hit by rockets. The first of these penetrated the hull near the engine compartment. The explosion either cut or critically damaged hydraulic lines that served the helm, and the steering on the boat was lost. Normally that would not have been a problem. The boat was equipped with two engines, and steering could be accomplished using the throttle controls for each engine. But something else had happened: The blast from the rockets had also caused the port engine to fail. It could have been damage to the fuel lines or possibly the electrical system or some other critical component. In any case, the boat was left totally unable to steer. If we had been on one of the other rivers or tributaries of Vietnam, just the action of the current could have drifted us out of harm's way in only a minute or two. But because we were in the shallow canal, there was virtually no directional flow of water, and without steering, the best we could hope to do was go around in circles and try to create the most difficult target possible.

The attack was not just a quick hit-and-run effort on the part of the Viet Cong. The attack was well-planned, with enemy forces positioned on both banks of the French Canal. Most attacks on river boats were quick, short-lived fire fights which lasted only a minute or two. More like terrorist attacks, where one or two enemy troops would spray a few clips of automatic weapons fire and then quickly disappear into the dense foliage. The attack on MSR-7 that night was a well-planned and sustained effort. The attack lasted for at least ten minutes. When a minute can seem like hours, ten minutes can seem like an eternity. MSR-7 was hit by hundreds of rounds of automatic AK47 fire as well as 51 caliber machinegun and recoilless artillery. On my return to Mine Division 113, after recovering from my wounds, I was told that we had sustained hits from at least twenty B40 rockets. But, to the best of my knowledge, the boat did not sink. It was towed in for repairs and was already in service when I returned about two months later.

I feel that at least part of the reason for the ferocity and intensity of the attack was that we had established a very strong presence on the canal and a very good rapport with the local villagers. Looking back on it now, I feel that the VC felt that they needed to regain some measure of control of the area because we MSR-7 crewmen had made many friends along the canal amongst the local people. You can see it in the pictures of Charlie playing with the kids. This was not a one time event. We frequently stopped to interact with the local people. I feel that our boat was specifically targeted for this reason.

The following is an account of Boatswain's Mate First Charlie Geisert's last moments, given by his shipmate Boatswain's Mate Third Jerry Griffin:

Charlie had left the bridge to make the 2300 hours report. He would use the remote radio position in the bunk room because he could use a small red cabin light while talking on the radio. He would sit on the edge of the bunk while working on his report. It was the only place where he could have the code books out and see without light being seen and exposing our position to the enemy. He was making his report when the boat was hit by overwhelming rocket and machine gunfire.

The following is a description of MSR-7's bunk area given by Engineman Rulon Young:

Boat Captain Charlie Geisert had his bunk, or fold-up cot, attached to the bulkhead right in the passageway outside the pilot house door. There was Charlie and a five-man crew, so some "hot bunked it." The pilot house was surrounded by a four-foot-high by three-foot-wide passageway with aluminum bulkheads. The pilot house had a narrow door of about three-quarter-inch plate steel, which was also what the rest of the pilot house was made of. Compared to everyone else's pilot platforms, it was Fort Knox. The rest of the boat was made of aluminum, and that was the problem. Although Charlie was only a foot or two from the safety of the pilot house, a bullet came through the aluminum bulkhead and hit him in the back as he rose from the bunk. And that's what got Charlie. Later, when I was assigned to the crew of MSR-7, we hung some of those woven glass wool blankets from the hand rails outside to protect the bunk areas a little better.

The Vietnamese interpreter's body was recovered in the canal a couple days after the attack. Gunner's Mate Third Lee was the only man to return to Mine Division 113. Boatswain Mate Third Jerry Griffin was transferred to a hospital in Saigon for a couple of weeks then to Balboa Naval hospital in California. He was medically discharged from the Navy and went back to Texas. In January

1970, MSR-7 was attacked, burned and sunk in the Vinh Te Canal. Engineman Rulon Young was aboard and survived the attack.

Thirty-seven years later, Retired Chief Hienz Hickethier was honored to meet Charlie Geisert's wife and daughter at the dedication of the Vietnam Unit Memorial Monument in Coronado, California, on May 21st, 2005. Charlie Geisert's name is engraved across the wall along with 2,558 men that served within various units in the United States Navy, and seven Coast Guard men, that made the ultimate sacrifice while serving in the Vietnam War.

THE SIEGE OF LONG KHOT

During the month of December 1969, combined SEA LORDS Naval forces operating in border interdiction accounted for a total of 378 communists killed and forty-seven captured. This was a significant increase over November. On the other hand, friendly casualties for these campaigns were down, with twelve losses and eighty-four wounded. Although there were incidents of enemy contact in the northern regions of the Republic of Vietnam, communist attacks were primarily aimed against the government's pacification efforts in the Mekong Delta. Continued reports of enemy troop and logistic movements in I, II and III Corps Tactical Zones of South Vietnam were at a moderately low level in December. However, in the IV Corps region, a greater number of enemy contacts reflected activity two to three times what had been reported in previous months and was characterized by small unit crossings, mining incidents, and attacks against Naval units. Reports of increased infiltration across Barrier Reef, and Moc Hoa in Slingshot, indicated that this was an area of maximum enemy threat.

Tuyen Binh Outpost at Long Khot lies on the northern edge of Kien Tuong Province. It faces Cambodia across seven-hundred yards of flat marsh and rice paddies, in a sparsely settled area of the Plain of Reeds. Fourteen isolated hamlets, mostly along waterways of the Vam Co Tay, form the Tuyen Binh District. To the east, the boundary line with Cambodia forms the Parrot's Beak, providing safety for known communist sanctuaries. To the west, the Vam Co Tay intersects with the Rach Cai River, then forks north along the Cambodian border, while the Rach Cai flows northeast into Cambodia, and southwest into the plains.

The province seat was twenty miles to the southeast at the village of Moc Hoa, where ATSB Moc Hoa is the furthest western end of Operation Giant Slingshot, which was an important part of SEA LORDS. The Binh Thanh Thon Civilian Irregular Defense Group camp was five miles to the southeast of Tuyen Binh. Two small compounds, approximately two-hundred yards apart, formed the Tuyen Binh outpost along the narrow winding Vam Co Tay River. The larger square compound measured 100 by 125 yards and housed the district office of the 859th Regional Forces, with strength of eighty-nine soldiers, four Popular Force platoons of thirty men each, and a small Provincial Reconnaissance Unit. The senior advisor for the district was a U.S. Army Special Forces Captain with four Green Beret assistants, who were also quartered at the larger compound. In early November, '69, the 866th Regional Force Company, with strength of eighty-five Ruff Puffs, moved to the outpost and occupied the small triangular compound, with the District Chief in command. Both compounds were protected by earthen berms and surrounded on all sides by lines of barbed wire apron.

The South Vietnamese government-supported Popular Forces were platoon-size, about thirty men, and guarded their home village, manning watchtowers and road-side bunkers scattered throughout the Mekong Delta. Regional Forces were company-size, over a hundred men, and protected the district. The CIA-sponsored Provincial Reconnaissance Units were "hired guns," who wore black pajamas and who often would infiltrate Viet Cong enter-structures, gather intelligence and conduct Operation Phoenix, the snatching and assassination of communist leaders. The Civilian Irregular troops were employed generally along the Cambodian border as part of an effort to seal the frontier against Viet Cong and North Vietnamese movements of men, weapons, and supplies.

Tuyen Binh outpost had lived for many years with the threat from Cambodia, knowing the enemy was always near. In 1963, the base was overrun, the Green Beret advisors captured and dragged off. The communists were frequently detected moving in small groups along the border; there base camps were only a few miles away. There were ten light contacts in November '69, with the river craft of Slingshot heavily involved in blocking the enemy from crossing the river.

Operation Giant Slingshot was about to complete its first year. During the year, brown water units, in close coordination with ground and air support, interdicted enemy infiltration and cut supply lines along the strategically flowing Vam Co Tay and Vam Co Dong rivers. Thanks to brown water forces operating on Slingshot, there were slowdowns in the movement of enemy fighters and supplies. This lowered the threat of enemy attacks on major population centers such as Tay Ninh City and Saigon. But things were about to change. With monsoons over and waters receding, movement along the Ho Chi Minh Trail was again reported heavy, with thousands approaching.

In early December, the threat became a reality when the 504th Viet Cong Battalion, along with four companies of the 8th and 9th Battalions, 88th North Vietnamese Army Regiment, crossed the border behind a barrage of communist mortar and rocket fire and attacked the two small compounds, anticipating a quick, easy victory over the small Republic of Vietnam territorial forces.

As darkness had fallen on December 11th, the outpost deployed five ambush patrols as observation posts, to scan the area and the trails during the night. Shortly after 2130 hours, two patrols made contact with the enemy near the border. Several Alpha boats of River Assault Division 153 were nosed in to the beach at the Special Forces camp, where they received 82mm mortar, B40 rockets and automatic weapons hits. Four PBRs, which were a guard post nearby, were scrambled to the scene, along with Army Cobra gunships and Navy Black Pony aircraft, which were diverted to the area for support.

While approaching, PBRs took hits from automatic weapons and B40 rockets, which were fired from the west fork of the river. After an intense thirty-five-minute firefight, where both sides had been hurt, the enemy withdrew, leaving behind seven dead, three AK47s, three gas masks, a pair of binoculars and a field phone. The South Vietnamese outpost patrols suffered one killed and one wounded, while damaged Alpha boats departed for the Navy base at Moc Hoa with two American sailors lost in combat and two wounded.

Vietnamese reconnaissance patrol members brought the captured equipment back to the outpost before returning to the border. The Vietnamese commander and the senior American advisor examined the items and concluded that a forward observer element had been intercepted while performing a reconnaissance in force to find a position from which to direct fire on their two small compounds. The base commander was not unduly perturbed. Stand-off attacks were not common. He advised the tactical operations center at Moc Hoa by radio of the patrol contact and the nature of the captured equipment. Then the outpost continued its usual night-time activity, but its personnel were now alerted.

At 0200 hours, the first incoming 107mm rocket round arced over the border and impacted in the outpost, sending men flying. Then a barrage of mortar, rocket, and recoilless rifle fire quickly followed, coming from enemy positions to the north and northeast inside Cambodia. Then the enemy began to opened fire from a third position on the northwest. The intensity and duration of the fire indicated to the Long Khot commander that this might be more than just another attack. He opened his radio net to the Civilian Defense camp, five miles to the southwest, where the Binh Than Irregulars had their single 105mm howitzer registered on Long Khot, for support. The outpost now requested that the howitzer be placed on call if a ground attack commenced. The barrage continued and soon reports came in from the patrols that the enemy was crossing the border in strength and heading their way.

The outpost opened up with its mortars on enemy avenues of approach while requesting by radio that Binh Thanh 105mm howitzer fire commence. The Vietnamese executive officer of the 859th Reconnaissance Force positioned himself on the berm as a forward observer and adjusted fire through field glasses, as rounds thundered overhead and exploded in the swampy marshland. Binh Thanh was also requested to divert any air assets to Long Khot that it might contact, with the tactical operations center at Moc Hoa also asked to supply any air assets available. At that point, Black Ponies reengaged, and two additional PBRs were scrambled from Moc Hoa and raced to join the fight.

At 0230 hours the Black Ponies were forced to leave the area due to low fuel. Meanwhile, the PBRs continued to lay direct fire into the enemy. A Binh Thanh radio operator contacted a Night Hunter Team, whose Cobra gunship and UH-1B Huey helicopter, fitted with Xenon infrared light searchlight and Mini-guns, were completing a mission to the northwest. Hearing the call for help, the team headed immediately for Long Khot. The gunships circled the outpost and took the enemy under fire wherever they were sighted south of the border. After fifteen minutes of expending their remaining ammunition, the team was forced to pull off and departed, as the enemy continued to advance through the darkness from three directions. As mixed small-arms fire was received, along with mortar and rocket rounds, the friendly patrols from the outpost were ordered to slowly draw back in close to the outpost perimeter.

The tactical operations center at Moc Hoa had contacted the direct air support center at command for Tactical Zone IV and called for gunship support. The 44th Special Tactical Zone at Coa Lanh was also alerted for assistance. The U.S. Air Force's Shadow-77, a prop-powered fixed-wing AC-119 gunship nicknamed the "Flying Boxcar," armed with Mini-guns and flares and a crew of six to eight men, was airborne and ready for just such a contingency when the call came through to proceed to Long Khot. By 0300 hours, the gunship had lit up the battlefield like a night ball game. Its radio contact was the Special Forces Captain, who was located with the Vietnamese commander in the outpost. Working through a fluent English-speaking reconnaissance force officer, the Vietnamese commander passed details of the situation to the American captain, who in turn, passed it on to Shadow-77. After plotting the location of friendly patrols still in contact, Shadow-77 established an orbit and pummeled the battlefield with her four Mini-guns that fired a total of 24,000 rounds per minute, illuminating a visual trail of red tracers from the "Dragons Breath" to the ground, as she took the enemy under devastating fire. The enemy responded by returning fire to Shadow-77 from several firing positions inside Cambodia.

Gradually, the enemy tightened its noose and surrounded the outpost, while the regional defenders laid down a heavy counter-fire in all directions. When the last of the friendly patrols were brought back into the compound, the Vietnamese commander authorized Shadow-77 to fire within fifty yards on all sides of the two small compound perimeters. By this time, the outpost had received nearly 300 rounds of mortar and rocket fire as the enemy crawled forward. Backed by intense enemy machinegun fire, sappers with Bangalore torpedoes and satchel charges worked their way into the perimeter and blew the final defensive wire. A machinegun post in the north corner of the 866th compound was destroyed, and the enemy penetrated the barrier of the small outpost. Shortly thereafter, with the threat of being overrun, the Army captain requested emergency extraction and medevac. The extraction was begun by PBRs, as the enemy forces entered the camp and forced the defenders to retreat to the southern perimeter. Quickly, the 866th company commander led a group of defenders in a counterattack on the enemy-held gun post and, after a bitter ten-minute hand-to-hand fight, closed the breach and recaptured the position. While all this was going on, PBRs continued to lay heavy fire into the insurgents, cutting them down in waves.

Shadow-78, which had been alerted to replace Shadow-77, received a radio briefing from Shadow-77 while en route to Long Khot, arriving on station at 0455 hours. Shadow-78 then contacted the Army captain by radio and was informed that the outpost commander had declared a tactical emergency, requesting Shadow-78 to take immediate action to suppress the enemy hostile fire.

Spat-05, a night forward air controller, arrived on station shortly after 0530 hours to recon the border and search out enemy positions for air strike. The outpost defenders continued their heavy counter-fire from all sides of the compounds and, by 0600 hours, had successfully repulsed three assault waves as VC bodies cluttered the perimeters. Spat-13 then arrived to replace Spat-05 as night forward air controller and, at 0630 hours, directed its first air strike on the enemy. Shadow-78 remained on the scene, working closely with Spat-13.

The Army captain radioed Spat-13 and Shadow-78 that the enemy appeared to be pulling back; however, the outpost was still receiving mortar and small-arms fire. Shortly after, Bomber-32, a day forward air controller, came on site and directed four more air strikes in the vicinity of the border against mortar and machinegun positions that were still firing on the outpost. By this time, the enemy was widely scattered and disorganized.

At first light, the tactical operations center at Moc Hoa airlifted a reaction force of two Reconnaissance Force platoons and inserted them two miles southeast of the outpost. This force conducted a sweep up the Vam Co Tay and into the battle area, pursuing the retreating enemy to cut off his escape routes. Another Reconnaissance Force was readied for movement from Moc Hoa by patrol boats. By 0900 hours, a Civilian Irregular Defense Company had moved into a blocking position three miles to the south.

By early afternoon, villagers in a small hamlet three miles northwest of the outpost had reported that enemy troops were present in strength in their area, apparently unable to regain access to their sanctuary across the border. A Mobile Strike Force and two Civilian Irregular Defense Group platoons were airlifted and inserted south of the hamlet, where they made contact with an estimated fifteen enemy fighters. Contact was broken after ten minutes, and by late afternoon, enemy activity had ceased. The inserted reaction forces swept the battlefield, clearing the area of the remaining enemy forces and blocking their escape routes, preventing them from concealing their losses or retrieving weapons.

The action was not quick, it was not easy, and it certainly was not a communist victory. Hours later, the confused and defeated attackers were fleeing back over the border in disorder, leaving 160 of their dead on the battlefield, along with large quantities of rocket-propelled grenades, satchel charges and individual and crew-served weapons. There were only two captured Viet Cong fighters.

Friendly losses were sixteen territorial forces killed, and twenty-seven wounded, with two Vietnamese sailors also wounded. Boatswain's Mate Third Larry Ray Damerson and Fireman

Joseph Frank Benak were lost, with two other Americans severely wounded. There were also two wounded U.S. Airmen whose light observation helicopter was shot down. The people of the village reported that the VC killed four civilians and wounded six while destroying fourteen hooches.

The territorial forces at Long Khot, along with river patrol and assault boats, preplanned artillery, gunships and tactical air support, fought courageously and with great determination. They successfully repulsed and thoroughly defeated an overwhelming but decimated enemy force. The intelligence provided by the villagers was a contributing factor in the elimination of enemy forces. This was a strong indication that the inhabitants of the area identified themselves with the government and were actively participating in defending their homes.

It was a great victory, but nobody mistook it as the end of communist attacks. The VC continued monitoring brown water units to limit their support of regional fire bases in forthcoming attacks. Two days after the siege, Black Pony aircraft killed thirty VC in air strikes a mile and a half to the northwest of Tuyen Binh Outpost.

Major Ronald Menner, who had served as company commander of Charlie Company 3/47th Infantry, 2nd Brigade, was the last American advisor at Tuyen Binh Outpost and remembers a similar attack on the area in May 1972, during his second tour of Vietnam.

BORDER INTERDICTION

During the month of February 1970, U.S. Navy units continued to hamper communist efforts to move troops and logistics across the Cambodian border. The number of enemy contacts and sightings in the SEA LORDS areas indicated that the enemy was still trying to move through the Tran Hung Doa and Barrier Reef interdiction barriers. During the month, the enemy suffered thirty-four killed in his many attempts to infiltrate the area. The U.S. Navy suffered two lost and sixteen wounded.

At 0100 hours on the morning of February 4th, 1970, four river patrol boats were in their assigned guard post on the Vinh Te Canal, ten miles southeast of Chau Doc City, when the PBR to the southwest sighted over a hundred black pajama Viet Cong on the north bank and approximately fifteen swimmers in the water, about 150 yards distance from their guard post. The PBR immediately took the large body of enemy under fire. Simultaneously, the patrol boat furthest east sighted almost 200 Viet Cong on the south bank, also approaching the canal. The other three PBRs took this group under fire as the startled infiltrators started running to the south. Seawolves were immediately requested and scrambled from Detachment Five. The Seawolves placed rocket and machinegun strikes on the retreating Viet Cong. Black Ponies relieved the Seawolves at 0130 hours and continued the air strikes until relieved by Shadow-77, which arrived at 0200 hours.

A daylight sweep of the action area was conducted, and the amount of captured material indicated that the patrol boats had interrupted a large Viet Cong canal crossing. A partial listing of the materials captured included twenty-five hand grenades, five boxes of mortar booster charges, two rounds of 82mm high explosive, three 60mm mortar rounds, 51 caliber rounds, uniforms, backpacks, thirty-eight bamboo rafts, gas masks, ponchos, one kilo of documents, 150 pounds of rice and miscellaneous cooking utensils.

At 0020 hours on February 7th, four PBRs with Patrol Officer Signalman Chief Dunnuvant and Quartermaster Chief Liggett incharge were in their ambush guard post with soldiers of a Mobile Strike Force embarked on the Vinh Te Canal about five miles from Vinh Gia City. Twenty-five VC and NVA were spotted a hundred yards south proceeding north with the enemy taken under fire and the Mobile Strike Force inserted.

At 0035 hours, four River Division 512 PBRs under Patrol Officer Quartermaster Chief Sneed and Boatswain's Mate Chief Hudson proceeded to the area, carrying additional Mobile Strike Force soldiers and ammunition, with Seawolves arriving on the scene and providing air support. The strike force swept south and came into heavy contact with an entrenched force of about forty North Vietnamese soldiers, suffering one U.S. sailor and three Vietnamese Strike force soldiers wounded in a heated exchange.

At 0250 hours, a Seawolf landed in the contact area to medevac the wounded while additional Seawolves provided overhead cover. Within an hour, a U.S. flare ship had arrived on the scene, providing continuous illumination. Black Ponies arrived shortly after, and after extraction of the Mobile Strike Force, commenced air strikes. At 0700 hours, the strike force was reinserted and conducted a sweep of the area, capturing three NVA and discovering eleven more dead.

A week later, patrolmen of Vietnamese River Patrol Group 54 were returning on a PBR from guard post when they sighted a Claymore mine on the north bank of the Vinh Te Canal. At that time, Explosive Ordinance Disposal assistance was requested. The EOD team, led by Lieutenant Junior Grade Valentine, arrived shortly after and destroyed the mine in place. The team reported that the mine was facing the canal and had been rigged with monofilament line which led to a spider hole on the north bank. From there, the mine could have been command detonated.

On that same afternoon, Mine Division 113 units, MSR-3 and MSR-6, were on routine day patrol in the Giang Thank River. Both units were at modified general quarters but were allowed to smoke and move around as long as they could get to their loaded and cocked weapons quickly. It was hot as usual, with the crew members wearing their fatigue pants, boots, flak jackets, and helmets, about half of them shirtless under their flak jackets.

They were proceeding south at three knots with MSR-3 in the lead and MSR-6 trailing about seventy-five yards behind. At 1548 hours, the units rounded a blind corner of the river and were ambushed from both banks by automatic weapons, B40 rockets and recoilless rifle fire. Aboard MSR-3, one B40 round hit the starboard side of the hull above the waterline, directly aft of the twin .50 cal mount, piercing the hull and hurling shrapnel throughout the compartment. Some of the shrapnel continued on through the port hull and out into the water. The heat of the explosion caused a fire in a clothing locker, a fire that eventually spread to the coxswain's flat before it could be controlled. One recoilless rifle round hit two feet aft of where the B40 round had hit and went out the other side of the boat without contributing to the fire and shrapnel damage. Another B40 round exploded on the forward compartment hatch, which was dogged down. The entire surface of the hatch was destroyed, although the porting remained in place. A second recoilless round hit the deckhouse just aft of the coxswain's stand on the starboard side. The round penetrated the deckhouse bulkhead and both bulkheads of the coxswain's flat, and fragmented pieces of shrapnel were imbedded in a fold-down cot mounted on the port bulkhead. A third B40 rocket, fired at the stern of the boat, hit port .50 cal gunner Gunner's Mate Third Thomas Copp in the chest. The impact of the round threw Boat Captain, Boatswain's Mate First Charlie J. Robertson forward, causing him to hit his head on the gauge console, receiving a gash and passing out for twenty seconds or so. But luckily when he fell forward, his hands were on the throttles and the forward motion of his body pushed the throttles to maximum turns, propelling the boat out of the kill zone. He regained consciousness just in time and steered the boat clear.

MSR-6 was hit at the twin .50 cal mount, with the B40 round piercing the hull while some of the shrapnel went through the hull and out the portside. Another B40 round hit the starboard side of the deck house just aft of the coxswain's stand, piercing the bulkhead and expending itself against a fold-up cot and the bulkhead of the coxswain's flat. The heat of the explosion caused the cot to ignite. Eight inches aft of that B40 round, a recoilless rifle round went through the starboard deckhouse bulkhead, through both bulkheads of the coxswain's flat, and expended itself against the port deckhouse bulkhead. A third B40 rocket hit the stern on the portside where the hull joined the main deck and transom. The impact of these explosions knocked Boat Captain Boatswain's Mate First Jerry F. Obsworth, who was coming out of the coxswain's flat, through the deckhouse door and into the berthing area immediately adjacent. He was knocked unconscious, suffering minor internal bruises and smoke-inhalation damage to his wind pipe and right lung. A crew member firing an M60 machinegun from the drone operator's platform was unaware that the boat captain had been knocked off the helm. The boat continued down the middle of the river until it had cleared the kill zone then veered toward the northwest bank and ran aground. The impact threw the M60 gunner clear of the boat and onto the beach. Luckily, he was unhurt. The forward twin .50 cal gunner received minor shrapnel wounds from a B40 rocket, which hit forward. Shrapnel from the B40 hit aft on the portside, seriously injuring a man standing two feet from the point of impact. One other man on the fantail also received minor shrapnel wounds while the third man was unharmed. The unharmed man later sustained third degree burns on both hands while fighting a fire on the boat.

The calculated attack was well-planned and executed. It appeared that the enemy on the northwest bank was tasked with hitting the forward .50 cal mount and the coxswain's flat, since all of their rounds landed in those areas. The enemy on the southwest bank was tasked with hitting the crewmen on the fantail, since all of the rounds from that bank hit the fantails of the boats.

Without doubt, flak jackets and helmets saved three men from death or more serious injury as several jackets and helmets showed signs of shrapnel damage. In addition, boat crewmen from both minesweeper boats had secured three-by-six foot flak curtains to the outboard side of the stanchions around the entire fantail of their boats. The B40 rocket which hit MSR-6 on the portside aft at the junction of the main deck and the hull detonated right below a flak curtain. Judging from the damage to the curtain, it absorbed at least sixty percent of the shrapnel, which undoubtedly saved the life of the man who was injured standing only two feet from the point of impact and also the lives of two other sailors.

During the attack, the units returned fire and then cleared the area to the south. The boats reported their situation and requested assistance. Four PBRs of River Division 532, under Patrol Officers Lieutenant Junior Grade Bomato and Boatswain Mate Chief Garrett, and two Swift Boats of Costal Division 11, with Lieutenant Junior Grade Ellington and Lieutenant Junior Grade Hill, embarked near the area of the attack and were directed to proceed to the assistance of the minesweeper boats under attack. The PBRs entered the area and suppressed the fire by 1558 hours.

The MSRs proceeded south to rendezvous with the Swift boats. On rendezvous, all units received automatic weapons fire from the west bank. The units returned the fire and requested air assistance. Seawolf gunships placed strikes in the second contact area and then medevaced the most seriously wounded at 1620 hours.

Gunner's Mate Third Thomas Copp was lost, with Boatswain's Mate Third Henry P. Wilcox and Gunner's Mate Third Edward B. Yost seriously wounded in the ambush. In addition, Fireman Gerry W. Abbott, Engineman Second Charles A. Brown, Gunner's Mate Third Elwood W. Arnell, Engineman Second Edward K. Fry, Boatswain's Mate First Jerry F. Obsworth, Boatswain's Mate Third Timothy R. Flynn, and Boatswain's Mate First Charlie J. Robertson were also wounded on that awful day.

In February 1970, Command Naval Forces Vietnam notified Chief Naval Officer that U.S. military representatives were prepared to receive the remains of three U.S. Navy helicopter crew members killed when their helicopter crashed in Cambodia on April 28th, 1969. On the afternoon of February 20th, 1970, the Cambodian government returned the remains of three crewmen. The mortuary service was able to confirm the identity of Lieutenant Junior Grade Hal Cushman Castle and Aviation Ordnance Third Michael Edward Schafernocker. The mortuary service certified that no remains were received of the third Navy helicopter crewman, Lieutenant Junior Grade Richard John Reardon, United States Navy Reserve. Commander Naval Forces Vietnam requested to have the American Embassy in Phnom Penh to search at both the crash and burial sites for a possible unopened grave or other evidence of the third crewman.

By the end of the month, the water level in the Vinh Te Canal had dropped so low that boats were no longer capable of operating in certain parts of the canal. Ground forces, sensors, and air support were the only means of interdiction in these areas where low water conditions prevailed.

The following poem was written by Electronic's Technician First E. Summerhill, in honor of the men who served with Mine Division 113. In the reference to "Red," he was speaking of MSR-3 Boat Captain, Boatswain Mate First Richard L. Schreifels. The gunners he refers to are Gunner's Mate Third Thomas Copp and Boatswain's Mate Third Timothy R. Flynn. "Little Robbie" was Boat Captain Boatswain Mate First Charlie J. Robertson:

They ride on the rivers, those sons of bitches. They ride the canals that they called shit ditches. They ride on the waterways, the big and the small, the Bassac, the Mekong, the Vinh Te and all. Though the boat's a minesweeper, and the captain a lush, tonight they'll go out on another ambush. They go looking for Charlie in hopes that they might catch him crossing the river in the dark of the night. One day it was Red's boat, MSR-3, searching the Bassac for the enemy. Then without warning, they came under attack. B40s I think. They were given no slack. A junk alongside was sunk straight away. Red called for his men to return fire and pray. The rockets kept coming, but somehow they missed. But they shouldn't have done it, because now Red was pissed. Red grabbed for the radio and yelled into the mike. "Bring on the Seawolves. We need an air strike!"

But his gunner replied in dubious tones. "You can't call them, Red, on these powered phones."

They got their air strike, and the fire suppressed. They got away clean, no wounds to be dressed. This time they were lucky, this time they weren't hit. But next time they'd land in a big world of shit.

One night little Robbie, first class boatswain's mate, took out MSR-7, for her date with fate. The seven was hit, nearly sunk and on fire. Red, in the three boat, was filled but with one desire. Get the men off, before the ammo explodes! So he returned to the kill zone, his number three boat exposed. But to the men trapped on MSR-7, Red must have looked like something from heaven. The men all returned from the battle that night. They were all very weary, but still full of life. Red got a medal, the great Silver Star that gleams in the sunlight, even from afar.

There was a young chief, an engineman by rate. A new generator arrived, I don't remember the date. But the chief was right there to assist and advice. The testing of the engine he'd supervise. The Commodore too came down for a look, and there was the chief with the instruction book. The chief ran around like a young frisky spaniel, shouting out orders as he read his manual. They got it running and it tested all right. It was time to secure it for the rest of the night. The chief said, "Don't touch it without the right tool. This engine won't quit till it runs out of fuel." Dopp looked at the chief and started to scoff. Reached into the engine and turned it right off. The chief was amazed for a short little while. The Commodore shrugged and broke into a smile.

Then there was Flynn, a stout Irish lad. Flynn came from Boston, an accent he had. One day while Flynn was sitting around, he picked up a revolver and chambered a round. Ever so carefully he aimed at his toe. He squeezed on the trigger, ever so slow. But there right before him was a hole in his boot. He called his boat captain. "I think I've been shot! I think I've been wounded, but I really hope not." The bullet passed between two of his toes, how he was so lucky, nobody knows. But when the seven boat sank, on that fateful night. Flynn was right there, in the midst of the fight. When Red brought the three boat back into the fray. There was a man in the water, but Flynn saved the day. He dove into the river, dirty with mire. He swam to the man through enemy fire. He pulled him aboard MSR-3, to the arms of his friends and safe company. There are other men too, with medals and glory. I'm afraid I've not time to tell the whole story. But they are all heroes, hell they have seen, these glorious men, of Mine Division 113.

Boat Captain Dick Schreifels had this to say about his shipmate and forward gunner Tom Copp:

I was assigned to Mine Division 113 as the boat captain of Minesweeper River Three, MSR-3, from June 1969 through December 1970. Gunner's Mate Third Tom Copp was the gunner's mate assigned to my boat. During the time Tom and I served on MSR-3, we went out on numerous patrols and engaged the enemy in many firefights. Tom was responsible for our boats weapons and always performed his duties in an outstanding manner. Tom was easy to get along with and promoted good morale among the rest of the crew, as well as with anyone he came in contact with. Tom had a good sense of humor along with a quick smile. Tom always maintained a neat appearance and wore his uniform with pride. The crew of MSR-3 was a proud group made up of six men who worked and lived together on a fifty-foot boat under arduous conditions in the Mekong Delta of Vietnam. Among all the minesweeper boats, Tom was considered to be one of the most experienced and knowledgeable gunner's mates in Mine Division 113. Other gunners' mates from other boats would often ask Tom for advice about servicing their weapons. Tom took care of our weapons, and from time to time, Tom would have weapons-cleaning day where the entire crew of MSR-3 would disassemble and clean all the weapons. We relied on Tom to supervise us and make sure we cleaned and reassembled them correctly.

I was not aboard MSR-3 on February 13, 1970 when Tom Copp was lost. I was in Hong Kong on a five day R and R.

PARROT'S BEAK

It was March 17th, 1970, another beautiful moonlit night in the Mekong Delta, as two patrol boats of River Division 551 set in their night guard post positions just south of the Parrot's Beak area of Cambodia. The boats had been ordered to leave support base Tuyen Nhon and patrol the Vam Co Tay River on Slingshot and bear off into the Industrial Canal, taking up positions spaced roughly 100 yards apart, near a mound of dirt called the Old Fort. They had secured their PBRs parallel to the beach, to bring all weapons to bear to either shore of the narrow, shallow canal. The four-foot elephant grass swayed lightly in the swirls of an intermittent breeze in the vast, open plains, allowing the two units a good view off into the distance of the swampy, no man's land. Quartermaster Chief Heinz Hickethier was assigned Patrol Officer of the two-boat patrol, with Torpedoman First Don Fallons Boat Captain of PBR 742 and Machinist's Mate First Robert D. Hinds Captain of PBR 772. The crews kept close to their .50 caliber machineguns, knowing they were near a major communist base camp just across the border. They were part of SEA LORDS, patrolling the brown water. It was the end of the Ho Chi Minh Trail and known to be a major infiltration zone for the North Vietnamese fighters trying to make their way into Saigon to disrupt the struggling democratic Republic of South Vietnam.

It was several hours past sunset when a South Vietnamese crewmember reported seeing movement through the starlight scope which, with the help of the moon, illuminated the field with a green glow, exposing groups of moving black dots. A large number of enemy soldiers were moving out of the cover of the jungle into the open plains, exposing themselves as they advanced toward the two thirty-two foot man-of-wars. The nearly full moon was beginning to rise into the sky when Chief Hickethier requested the starlight scope to assess the situation, while the two boat captains set up fields of fire to protect the boats and their crews. The Chief took a long look but could not see the enemy at first. After he was directed by the Vietnamese sailor where to look more closely, he noticed groups of black dots moving everywhere. Each group consisted of six or more members, and there were twenty or more groups. They had spotted the infiltrators so far out that it was almost impossible for the advancing enemy to see the American boats in their hiding spots along the bank. This allowed an enormous amount of time for the two small, brave PBR crews to prepare for the ambush of an enemy vastly superior in numbers.

The Chief put together ten sets of coordinates for artillery fire and radioed back to Fire Support Base Gettysburg, giving instructions for his plan to catch the enemy in the open. This plan would allow him to quickly direct artillery by calling in and simply specifying fire position one, two, or whatever number coordinates the enemy had congregated in. This allowed the Army firebase time to load and aim their 105mm and 155mm howitzers in the direction of the communists, who were rapidly advancing toward the patrol boats.

The Chief also radioed back to the command center and arranged for Seawolves to be flying over Ap Bac, which was only minutes away from the boats, but still far enough as not to attract attention and alert the enemy. The two crews had now all become gunners, maintaining noise discipline, standing fast to their weapons, waiting for the approaching infiltrators.

Chief Hickethier took up his position, on the engine covers, in the open, with the hand radio set strung up around the post holding the flag. As usual, he got the remaining weapons that were left by the crew. So on top of the canopy next to the radio hand set he placed an M16 with an M-79 grenade launcher and a couple LAW rockets. Both crews of gunners had settled into their battle stations, in full battle dress, wearing sixteen-pound flak jackets, helmets, and heavy arms with all safeties off. Adrenaline flow started to rise as the sound of the enemy drew closer, and closer. The crews waited until the closest groups were within thirty yards and almost on them. Still, the North Vietnamese were unaware of the boats as they prepared to start crossing the canal.

It was 2200 hours when Chief Hickethier finally gave the order to open fire. Both PBRs began blasting away at the startled enemy. The twin .50 cal machineguns on the bows, in combination with the aft .50s and M60s and grenade launchers amidships, immediately started chopping into the enemy lines as soldiers fell and scattered, trying to take up positions to return fire on the two floating forts that were cutting down their ranks. The sight and smell of smoke filled the air as red and green tracers, punctuated with RPG and LAW rockets, exploded and ricocheted into the night sky. The patrol boats received return fire from multiple directions as both boat captains coordinated their crews' fire into the exposed enemy positions. But it was hard to cover every group in the field at the same time, so they had to concentrate on the closest groups. In the first ten minutes of firing, the patrolmen observed a huge explosion as their fire took its toll on the devastated enemy fighters. By now several groups had stopped firing, motionless bodies lying on the blood-soaked mud and in the water, which was littered with debris as well. The gunners of the PBR crews adapted rapidly to the changing directions of fire from the dispersed groups, who were trying desperately to blow up and overrun the two thirty-two-foot fiberglass islands, rocking in the boiling and exploding water.

Moments after the fire fight started, the Chief had called in artillery fire to the rear of the enemy. He now started walking the air bursts and contact rounds toward the enemy positions, trapping the soldiers, not allowing them to withdraw. The Chief set his initial coordinates 1,000 yards out from the bank, to make sure there were no mistakes in initial aiming by the Army firebase. Ears perked up and shells flew overhead, crashing into the earth, sending mud, water, and men flying into the air. Army artillery fire was a mixed bag, with some rounds hitting the coordinates the first time and others needing to be walked into the positions, so as not to fire on their own troops.

The Army did not know how close the Chief was calling in the fire support, especially the air bursts. The Army higher-ups had many rules and quirks and if they had known the relationship of the boats to the position where the shells were dropping, they would have stopped firing immediately, knowing the rounds were too close and dangerous to our own units. There were times when firing stopped just when the shells were the most effective and desperately needed. Chief Hickethier also had the Army artillery put up 105mm flares. The placement of these flares gave the sailors additional problems. In order to get the flares up over the enemy, it meant that the canisters from the flares would be splashing in the water near them. The Chief then coordinated the end of the artillery fire with the arrival of the Navy Seawolves. He didn't want any birds shot down by friendly fire, so he called the choppers and had them set up above the boats, just behind their positions. This would allow both air and water forces to expend the maximum amount of fire and maneuver without coming into harm's way from each other's fire, while they both continued to lay waste to a dwindling enemy force.

At that point, the sailors on the boats became very excited, cheering the 7.62 Mini-guns and rockets firing from the Seawolves pods, as their door gunners hung out the sides with their machineguns, raining down fire on the enemy from a couple of hundred feet above. At the same time, the machineguns and grenade launchers of the two patrol boats were hitting the enemy at ground level. With the deafening combination of noises coming from the rotors of the two Seawolves, all the weapons thundering fire together, and the launching and exploding rockets all over the battlefield, it was impossible to hear anything. The crews of the PBRs could hear the shrapnel from the enemy rocket explosions hitting all around them, but luckily, not one rocket had hit the boats. The Chief stood in the open, firing his M-79 grenade launcher and LAW rockets, and then jumped to the M16 rifle, when he wasn't calling in strikes on the severely hurt communist fighters, as all gun barrels burned and crackled from prolonged firing and all hearts raced from fear and the excitement of the moment.

As the fight progressed, numerous spent brass shell casings and litter scattered all over the decks, the heavy smell of gun powder in the air. The sky filled with smoke, with flares drifting slowly down to the earth in the distance. The crews had done a remarkable job in repelling the enemy, as they set in their fixed position along the smoky ditch. The only PBR casualty was Machinist's Mate First Robert D. Hinds, who suffered minor shrapnel wounds to his right arm. The element of surprise and the overwhelming firepower brought to bear on the enemy troops made all their weapons and B40 rocket fire totally ineffective. The firefight had lasted for only around thirty minutes, it had seemed much longer to the brave men who had stayed at their posts and received intense small-arms, machinegun and rocket fire. That they had all survived the battle was a great blessing and a relief.

At midnight, the Army sent twenty soldiers from Artillery Fire Base Gettysburg to sweep the area, but they did not want to move into the kill area without additional support. They did, however, provide additional support in case of a counterattack. But no one really expected an attack after the enemy troops had been so severely mauled and were seen limping back into Cambodia. Chief Hickethier took steps to insure that they maintained control of the area, not wanting to lose anything that they might have gained. The crafts maintained their positions and used harassment and interdiction fire to control the area for the rest of the night. A Black Pony from VAL-4 was called in to make firing runs in the area of the badly wounded, retreating enemy, in hopes of catching the remaining communists still out in the open.

The Chief expressed his disappointment in the Army sweep effort by the fire support base soldiers. Lieutenant Smelly, River Division 551 Commanding Officer, arranged for ten NSA sailors and ten duffle bag river division sailors to join the two PBR crews at first light. The Army sent an additional thirty troop as units started the sweep and immediately started finding bodies, equipment, and supplies everywhere. The Chief and an Army lieutenant argued to get everything brought to one point for inventory and evaluation. The Chief expended a lot of energy trying to keep both Army and Navy personnel from pilfering souvenirs, but still many items disappeared, with the approval of the officers, into the Mike boat that had brought the Army troops up. When Chief Hickethier asked the Army officers if they would let him inspect the boat, they said no and refused him permission to board.

The area of contact was very large, 250 yards along the bank and 1,500 yards or more toward the Cambodian border. The entire area was covered with elephant grass, mud and water that varied between a few inches to a foot or more deep. This meant everyone had to slog through the mud. One of the problems soldiers and sailors always encountered in these types of conditions was the heavy presence of leeches. It was always a joy to go looking for those little fellows attached to one's body. If the water was to the waist, then one always had the fun of finding one attached to a favorite body part. Sweeps like this meant, when they finished, the men would be wet and covered in mud and leeches. Most of the sailors thought only Marines and Army field personnel did this sort of thing. "I thought I joined the Navy."

The Army also had a K9 unit, with two German Sheperd dogs and their handlers. The dogs quickly became excited and tried to follow every blood trail. And there were many. One of the handlers worked very well with his dog, checking for bodies. They followed blood trails, looking for wounded enemy soldiers that might be still hiding in the tall elephant grass. The other handler wanted to look for souvenirs and was getting madder by the minute at his dog, which couldn't understand the difference between looking for souvenirs and rooting out the enemy. It didn't take long before the handler was beating the hell out of the dog. The Chief told the Army first lieutenant that, if the handler didn't stop beating the dog, he was going to shoot the handler. The handler was separated from the dog and sent back onto the Mike boat. The Chief later made a report to the Army on the incident, in hopes it would make the dog's life a little better.

Everyone had to move slowly and be on the alert for booby traps and live ammunition. Everything found had to be carefully examined before it could be moved. Eight of the NVA/VC were dead, and there were seven blood trails within thirty yards of the two boats. Further out, there were many more blood trails everywhere and paths made by the enemy force in hastily retreat. The NVA apparently were not able to help evacuate their comrades at the bank, but had helped those that were farther out. The dogs had found pieces of flesh, ten feet of intestines, and a number of other body parts. Everyone knew that the two battle-hardened boats and their crews had defeated a large enemy force.

The enemy cache consisted of thirty packs, assorted weapons and supplies of all types scattered all over the place. The crews had found two RPG launchers, eight B40 rockets with boosters, three AK47 rifles, four 9mm pistols, three AK clips, 315 rounds of AK ammo, fifty-five rounds of 9mm ammo, one anti-tank grenade, two boxes of fuses, thirty non-electrical blasting caps, two zero-time booby trap grenades, seven packages of C4 totaling twenty pounds, seven gas masks, a huge assortment of medicines, fifty battle dressings, three pounds of documents (including code books), forty green plastic bags for floating supplies across the waterways, over 100 pounds of rice and other food, fifteen pounds of clothing consisting of NVA uniform items, a infrared optical sight, and an untold amount of items pilfered by Army and Navy personal that were not part of the inventory. It was very interesting to see just how many items popped up at the support base a few days later. There were rockets, 9mm pistols, belt buckles, patches and so much more found among the duffle bag personal that had helped with the sweep. One can only guess how many items went aboard the Mike boat to Firebase Gettysburg.

Most of the medicine recovered had U.S. markings. There were blood expanders, antibiotics, dressings, and many other types of medical items from the good old U.S. of A. Many of these medical supplies were probably donated to the children of North Vietnam by people back in the United States, but had instead been intercepted by two units of River Division 551 while on its way to support communists forces fighting in the south, the very same forces that American and South Vietnamese forces faced in battle everyday.

THE INCURSION

Through the years, Operation SEA LORDS proved to be an overwhelming success, thanks to the planners and the men who patrolled and paid the toll in the backwaters of South Vietnam. On two separate occasions, the mobility of the boats was increased when giant Army skycrane helicopters were used to lift them into areas of operations. Six river patrol boats were skyhooked to the upper Saigon River, and six more were lifted to the otherwise inaccessible Cai Cai Canal. Both operations achieved tactical surprise.

As each operation progressed, jointly planned efforts were made to integrate units of the growing South Vietnamese Navy. It seemed obvious that the Vietnamese Navy's hopes of relieving the U.S. Navy of its operational responsibilities in the war as soon as possible would be greatly enhanced by the success of SEA LORDS. The operation, remarkably organized, came to symbolize both unity of command and rapid response to changing tactical situations. Junior officers and enlisted men were often placed in positions of extraordinary responsibility. Tactics and techniques were employed and tested in the heat of combat, and at times, even borrowed from the enemy, improved upon, and used against him. For example, the waterborne guard post was a refinement of the enemy tactic of ambush. By using silent running boat techniques and night observation devices, the U.S. and Vietnamese boats stalked the would-be Viet Cong ambushers and trapped them, bringing an end to their journeys. Imagination and leadership provided the plan, and dedicated sailors, soldiers, and airmen made it work.

By 1970, the Mekong Delta was somewhat pacified and under the control of South Vietnamese forces, with Americans' turning over their boats and combat duties, while leaving behind advisors to guide the newly formed Vietnamese river and coastal forces in patrolling and standing waterborne guard post, using the beloved boats the U.S. had left behind. This didn't mean there wasn't any fighting going on, only that the Republic of Vietnam was in control of the Mekong Delta, and the Viet Cong were fighting to get it back. The U.S. Navy craft and vessels turned over to the Vietnamese Navy were used to support Vietnamese Marine and Army units. Operations were conducted in the style of the Mobile Riverine Force, but greater emphasis was placed on leaving security forces behind in areas that had been cleared, so the Vietnam government could protect and control them.

By May '70, SEA LORDS forces pushed into Cambodia by order of President Richard M. Nixon, with American River Division 532 slipping its ten PBRs up the Bassac River into Cambodia, but making little contact with the enemy. Newly formed Vietnamese river patrol groups, with American advisors aboard, steamed into the Parrot's Beak with Vietnamese River Patrol Groups 54, 56, and 53 brawling with the 9th NVA Division and a Viet Cong force for three days. And a flotilla of over one-hundred American and Vietnamese boats and ships sailed up the Mekong, relieving Neake Luong, Cambodia, from the communists who had dropped everything and run, with Vietnamese Marines disembarking and chasing them halfway across Cambodia.

Ordered to enter Cambodia on May 4th 1970, after reequipping at ATSB Ben Keo and refueling, members of River Patrol Group 54, accompanied by elements of RPG-56, fought their way into a major communist sanctuary along the Rach Cai Cay River, suppressing enemy fire as they went. After they sat an assigned guard post all night, they were attacked the next morning in the end, forcing the South Vietnamese PBRs to back out while under heavy enemy fire. The Vietnamese Navy suffered one man killed on the front 50s, and fifteen wounded. Nine U.S. Navy advisors were wounded, with fifteen boats heavily damaged.

Navy engineman worked through the day and into the night to repair the damaged boats, switching engine components from the severely damaged PBRs to the ones that could be quickly serviced. Radiomen repaired shot-up radios, with over half the radios out of service and communications on the blink. Communist rockets and

.51 caliber machinegun rounds had entered the fiberglass boats at one end and traveled through and out the other end, leaving mechanical components, radar and radios, and guns damaged as men rushed to get them back up to battle conditions. Then the Vietnamese river patrol groups were ordered back up the Rai Ca Cay into Cambodia and fought for two more days and nights, ultimately succeeding in their mission of cleaning out the enemy santuary. The Vietnamese river patrol groups that had entered Parrot's Beak from the Vam Co Tay River met with very little resistance.

On the morning of May 9th, 1970, a combined Vietnamese-American Naval task force steamed up the Mekong River to wrench control of key waterways away from North Vietnamese, Khmer Rouge, and Viet Cong forces and rescue Neak Luong from the communists. The flotilla was led by a Vietnamese Naval officer and was composed of American Swifts, PBRs, STABs (Strike Assaul Boats), and assault craft from River Assault Squadron 15, who disembarked Vietnamese Marines who attacked the enemy and kept them on the run. The command and control ship USS Benewah, repair ship USS Askari, LST USS Hunterdon County, YRBM 16 and YRBM 21 were all deployed, with several moving into Cambodian waters to support the many river boats in the operation.

At the town of Neak Luong Cambodia, the communists had seized and sunk three vehicle/personnel ferries, cutting off Highway One between Phnom Penh and Saigon. U.S. forces were stopped at the twenty-one mile limitation placed on them at Neak Luong while Vietnamese Marines and sailors fought on alone, chasing the communists. It was one last gallant charge before Congress ordered all U.S. forces to withdraw by the end of June. South Vietnamese and American forces had done more damage to the communists in the first two weeks of the invasion than they did in the remainder of the year of 1970. They attacked the communists in their sanctuary strongholds in Cambodia, chasing them off, but there was no doubt that they would rebuild.

The Cambodian Incursion on the Mekong served many missions. One was a humanitarian effort to stop the slaughter of innocent refugees, with South Vietnamese LSTs bringing out over 70,000 Vietnanese from Phnom Penh to be repatriated and placed in Red Cross camps along the Mekong River south of the Grand Canal. Another was to re-raise the three ferries and give them back to Cambodia, re-opening Highway One. Vietnamese Marines and joint Navy forces made up of American, South Vietnamese, and Cambodian river boats took the opportunity to attack the communists on the feeder canals also. It was to be a South Vietnamese victory, with American and Cambodian units in support. Prince Sihanouk of Cambodia had been overthrown by pro-American General Lon Nol, who took over the government while the prince was visiting Russia. From that point on, Cambodian forces were in support of South Vietnamese and American forces.

After U.S. forces were ordered to withdraw from Cambodia, all units were reassigned back into SEA LORDS barriers, working alongside South Vietnamese forces in the Vietnamization and Accelerated Turnover Programs. By December 1970, the Commander of Naval Forces of Vietnam had transferred the remaining river combat craft in his command, which included 293 PBRs and 224 Riverine assault craft, over to the Vietnamese Navy. That month, the River Patrol Force was disestablished and the Task Force designator reassigned to Commander Delta Naval Forces, a new headquarters controlling SEAL and Naval aircraft units. The Navy continued to spearhead a drive in the Mekong Delta to isolate and destroy weakened communist forces. The gradual U.S. withdrawal from Southeast Asia was reflected in reduced casualty figures. The number of Americans killed in action in 1970, 4,204, dropped to 1,386 in 1971, with South Vietnamese losses totaling 21,500 men, while the combined Viet Cong and North Vietnamese losses was estimated at 97,000 killed for the year of 1971. After ten years of U.S. involvement in the Vietnam War, a total of 45,627 American GIs had been lost. U.S. troop levels at the beginning of 1971 were 280,000, but dropped to 159,000 by year's end. YRBM 21 and other river support craft stayed on, with American engineers and logistic personnel in support of the South Vietnamese brown water naval forces until 1972. Then YRBM

21 was turned over, giving the last U.S. war-machines and gear to the South Vietnamese. By 1972, the American troop level in South Vietnam had reduced from 159,000 to only 24,000. The troop reduction was a direct result of the shifting American goal, which was no longer to attempt a military victory, but to gracefully disengage itself from the situation by transferring responsibility for the war to the South Vietnamese. It was the end of U.S. Naval involvement in South Vietnam, with many sailors being reassigned or given early outs after returning home.

With the end of Linebacker II, the most intense U.S. bombing operation of the Vietnam War, U.S. and communist negotiators prepared to return to the Paris peace talks, which were scheduled to reconvene. In a statement issued in Paris, the Hanoi delegation to the peace talks claimed that the U.S. bombings did not succeed in weakening the Vietnamese people and called attention to the losses of U.S. planes and the unfavorable world reaction to the raids. Despite the public denial that the bombings forced them back, the communists returned to the negotiating table. When the negotiators met in January, the talks moved along quickly, and on January 23, 1973, the United States, the Democratic Republic of North Vietnam, the Republic of South Vietnam, and the Viet Cong signed a cease-fire agreement that took effect five days later. By March 1973, all U.S. combat forces had finally left South Vietnam.

Operation SEA LORDS was a brilliant strategy that never got the recognition that it deserved, with many feeling that, had it been employed earlier, it might have possibly changed the course of the war. Although the operation was never mentioned at the Paris peace talks, one still can't help feeling that it had some small effect on communist decisions being made, since it heavily impeded enemy troop movements down the Ho Chi Minh Trail, taking serious tolls on enemy forces. In the first year of SEA LORDS alone, U.S. forces killed 3,000 enemy troops and destroyed 500 tons of weapons and supplies. But, as I have said before, it all came at a high price.

After most of us sailors returned home, it was apparent to us that the Navy's contribution was not well known. Even our fellow

Vietnam veterans knew little about us or the river and coastal war in which we fought. But we who were there knew how important it was and what it accomplished. The men who were sacrificed to achieve its success will never be forgotten. Today, only a few remain to tell these stories. I am proud to be one.

The state which separates its scholars from its warriors will have its thinking done by cowards and its fighting done by fools.

Thucydides

AT THE END

M ost Americans do not really know how the war in Vietnam came to an end. The image that was shown over and over again was of North Vietnamese tanks busting down the gates of the U.S. Embassy, in Saigon with the helicopters lifting off the roof, flying the last Americans away. Many thought the South Vietnamese were cowards who did not put up much of a fight. Nothing could be further from the truth. The last major battles for control of South Vietnam took place in the month of April 1975, climaxing on a short section of Route One, forty miles north of Saigon. For it was there that South Vietnamese forces bravely united in one last stand to save their country. But although it was a gallant defense for democracy against the communist way of life, everyone knew that, without American intervention, it was doomed from the start.

During the closing days of the war, the Vietnamese were left to fend for themselves, with American politicians voting to cut off funding to our allies. When President Richard Milhouse Nixon, who the communists feared, was forced out of the White House, the North Vietnamese began planning for their offensive. Although there were mistakes made, with the rout at the DMZ being the first, the South Vietnamese did fight, as unit after unit of troops, ARVN Infantry and Airborne, along with Regional and Popular Force, went down fighting while communist tanks pushed down the coastal road like Sherman on his march to the sea. If not for the Republic of Vietnam Air Force, which consistingly attacked North Vietnamese troops, inflicting heavy casualities, the advance would have been much quicker. But, for the first time, the American press was not there to see it, so very few reports came out. All of this took place with both sides fighting savagely, while we watched the helicopters evacuating American Embassy personnel to carriers in the South China Sea.

On April 1st, Nha Trang fell to North Vietnamese troops, who moved in to occupy the harbor while the evacuation of Cam Ranh Bay continued at a fast pace. Farther south, Phan Rang Air Base came under increasing enemy pressure, with its evacuation underway, although the South Vietnamese 6th Air Division continued limited operations from the field, bombing the NVA, slowing its advance. A forward command post for III Corps was established at Phan Rang under Lieutenant General Nghi, and on April 7th, the 2nd ARVN Airborne Brigade was flown in to reinforce the airbase. Two days later, the brigade moved to Du Long, north of Phan Rang on Highway One, to block the 10th North Vietnamese Army Division, which was taking heavy losses while moving south from Cam Ranh Bay, in the face of intensive air strikes.

One of the critical battles for the capture of Saigon took place on April 9th in Long An Province, when the 5th NVA Division, moving down from Parrot's Beak, Cambodia, launched a strong attack near Tan An with its 275th Regiment. The Long An Regional and Popular Forces fought well and were reinforced by the 12th Infantry, 7th ARVN Division from IV Corps. Taking only light losses, the 2nd Battalion, 12th Infantry killed over a hundred soldiers of the NVA regiment, forcing its commander to request reinforcements. The next day, the NVA attacked the Can Dot airfield in Tan An and, after closing Highway 4 for a short time, were driven off with heavy losses by Long An Regional and Popular Forces. In two following days of heavy fighting, the three Long An battalions of the 301st, 322nd, and 330th, accounted for over 120 NVA killed and two captured. Around the same time frame, the 12th ARVN Regiment, fighting two regiments of the 5th NVA, killed over 350 fighters and captured sixteen.

The ARVN 22nd Division, whose tough resistance at Nha Trang in Binh Dinh Province was considered one of the most remarkable feats of determination, courage, and leadership of the war, was in better shape than other divisions. Reassembled at the Van Kiep National Training Center in Vung Tau, the 22nd had about 4,600 men, one-third of whom were Regional and Popular Forces from

II Corps, but the division was short of all types of equipment. Although it had enough artillerymen to man three battalions, it had no howitzers. Sparsely equipped and barely organized, they were ordered to deploy to Long An with the rebuilt division heavily committed in the battles around Tan An.

Meanwhile, Phan Thiet, the town and air base southwest of Phan Rang in Binh Thuan Province, came under enemy attack. Binh Thuan Regional and Popular Forces fought extremely well, but they could not hold for long against the large NVA formations approaching through the hills from the north.

As of the second week of April, about 40,000 South Vietnamese troops who had withdrawn from I and II Corps Tactical Zones had reported to training camps, being reassigned to units in III Corps to repel the North Vietnamese. The 2nd ARVN Division, which had been reassembled at Ham Tan, had grown to 3,600 men, including two Regional Force battalions who had been sent in from Gia Dinh Province, surrounding Saigon. The ARVN reconstructed 4th Infantry Regiment was sent to Phan Rang, relieving the 2nd Airborne Brigade, but the division would have only four light battalions when the outfitting was complete. Sadly, the ARVN 4th Infantry was destroyed for the second and final time in the defense of Phan Rang.

The ARVN 3rd Division had about 1,100 men at Ba Ria and Phuoc Tuy and were assigned another 1,000, but they too were short all types of weapons and equipment. The Vietnamese Army 1st Division was also at Ba Ria, but with only two officers and forty men. Near Ba Ria at Long Hai was the ARVN 23rd Division, with about 1,000 men and twenty rifles.

The NVA kept pressure on Bien Hoa and Tay Ninh Provinces, with frequent heavy attacks during the first two weeks of April. Rockets hit Bien Hoa Air Base and the military training center and schools at Bear Cat, while Tay Ninh was struck repeatedly by 105mm and 155mm artillery as well as rockets. The ARVN maintained control of Trang Bang and Cu Chi, but skirmishes with enemy forces were relentless. The communists seemed to be sacrificing their forces to whittle down South Vietnamese troops, which they knew could not be replaced. This set the stage for the last bloody battle of the war, in which four North Vietnam divisions advanced against a small ARVN force dug in along the hills near the city of Xuan Loc, in Long Khanh Province.

Advancing in strength down the coastal highway were the Vietnam Peoples' Army 5th, 6th, 7th and 341st Divisions, massed with artillery and T-54 tanks. Defiantly blocking their way were the ARVN 18th Divisions, the Vietnamese 82nd Ranger Battalion, and Long Khanh provincial forces, with additional South Vietnamese military eliments and volunteers massing to face the communists. The prolonged fighting at Xuan Loc in the beginning was interpreted as a test of the ARVN's remaining will to fight. "I vow to hold Xuan Loc," declared the 18th Division Commander, Brigadier General Le Minh Dao. "I don't care how many divisions the other side sends against me. I will knock them down."

After the first communist attempt to seize Xuan Loc had been soundly repulsed, the 341st NVA Division began a second assault on the town. Infantry and tanks were preceded by one of the heaviest artillery bombardments of the war, about 4,000 rounds. With tanks firing down the streets, hand-to-hand fighting developed in a fierce battle that lasted all day. By nightfall, the 43rd ARVN Infantry had driven most of the shattered enemy force from the town, and the 52nd ARVN Infantry base on Route 20 was still in South Vietnamese hands. But the communists were relentless and resumed the attack the next day, this time committing the 165th Regiment of the 7th NVA Division, along with regiments of the 6th and 341st NVA Divisions. Again the attack failed, with the North suffering heavy losses, leaving bodies sprawled across the road.

West of Xuan Loc, between Trang Bom and the intersection of Highways 1 and 20, two battalions consisting of the ARVN 322nd Task Force and the 1st Airborne Brigade were fighting their way east against stiff resistance. The 1st Airborne Brigade, made up of four airborne battalions and one airborne artillery battalion, had executed an air assault into the area of operations earlier by helicopter. The NVA attacked the rear base of the 52nd ARVN Infantry on Route 20, the 43rd Infantry in the Xuan Loc, and the 82nd Ranger Battalion on the third day of the battle. The ARVN battalion of the 48th Infantry secured Ham Tan and then went back to Xuan Loc, where the 1st Airborne Brigade had moved in closer to the town. Task Force 322 was making very slow progress opening the road from Trang Bom to Xuan Loc, so General Toan ordered Task Force 315 from Cu Chi to reinforce them.

On the next day, battalions of the 52nd ARVN Infantry were still in heavy fighting north of Xuan Loc, but the city, although demolished, was still held by the 43rd ARVN Infantry. Three NVA battalions advanced and were repelled by day's end, with NVA losses in excess of 800 fighters, with eleven T-54 tanks destroyed, not to mention all the wounded and captured men and weapons. South Vietnamese losses were considered moderate. Most of the 43rd ARVN Regiment was holed up east of town, with the 48th Infantry positioned southwest. The 1st Airborne Brigade was south but moving north toward the 82nd Ranger Battalion, with the 322nd and 315th Task Forces on Route 1 west of the Route 20 junction, attacking toward Xuan Loc.

It has been said that the South Vietnamese fought bravely at Xuan Loc, but the NVA high command used the battle as a meat grinder, sacrificing its own units to destroy ARVN forces who were irreplaceable. Meanwhile, the North Vietnamese were moving troops from I Corps south, setting the stage to attack Saigon from the west. But the South Vietnamese stood their ground, with many of the battles that followed involving units of divisional size, with devastatingly effective Vietnam Air Force airpower using sophisticated U.S.-made bombs. Fierce fighting took place for the next week, as battalion after battalion of North Vietnamese soldiers attacked, but gained only one mile a day, with South Vietnamese forces counterattacking against impossible odds. In contrast to the general impression of total collapse on the part of the ARVN and South Vietnamese forces, the battles were described as heroic and gallant by the South Vietnamese defenders. It was one of the few places where the ARVN, though thoroughly outnumbered, stood and fought bravely, an act which stunned their opponents. The stand of the ARVN so impressed the rest of South Vietnamese forces, that previously routed units grew confident again and gathered to join the determined defense. The fighting was said to have been horrific, as the tanks slowly advanced over the dead and wounded.

After twelve days and nights of ferocious combat with North Vietnamese forces, the south was low on ammunition and called in air strikes on their own lines, with the defensive line at Long Khanh holding. The forces of the North Vietnamese 4th Corps that were engaged in the battle had suffered heavy losses. For this and other reasons, the North Vietnamese changed their plan for the attack on Saigon. The North Vietnamese 2nd and 3rd Corps forces in Tay Ninh were used to advance and capture Saigon, but they still had to fight their way in. The North Vietnamese 4th Corps would abandon its efforts against Xuan Loc and would become a reserve force. Xuan Loc was never taken.

A tall statue now stands in the middle of the chaotic traffic intersection on Route One, surrounding a small park dedicated to the North Vietnamese soldiers who died in the battle for Long Khanh. But I could not help for thinking about the South Vietnamese defenders who died fighting for freedom, but were not even mentioned. Maybe it was because I worked along side the South Vietnamese and had trained a few. Or maybe it is because I was raised in old Richmond, Virginia, Southern capital of Jefferson Davis, and it sort of reminded me of General Grant finally overrunning Bobby Lee after two years of sacrificing northern troops. There are a lot of statues in Virginia also, but it still looks like home to me. Saigon, on the other hand, has grown like crazy, but the people are the same.

EPILOGUE

Vietnam today lives in peace, for the most part, with younger generations knowing very little about the war in which the Americans fought alongside South Vietnamese Forces and the Republic of Vietnam. On my trips back in 2000, and 2005, it was evident that the Vietnamese still despise the Chinese, French, and Russians, who all stole from them. The Chinese and French ruled Vietnam for hundreds of years, and they called the Russians, "Americans with no money." They have all left Vietnam now, and the Vietnamese are once again reaching out to the United States. Although American GIs fought a tough, brutal war against communist forces, the Vietnamese still see us as good guys. Many of the children with whom we shared our food and provided medical services to, have grown to become leaders of their country and still remember Americans as kind, loving people who had a heart and care. Many stories have been related to me of how we GIs touched the people.

One such story was from a Vietnamese gentleman who has gone on to become a successful engineer who as a young boy received a penny from a GI, which he has never forgotten. That one simple act touched him and his story touched me. Even one of the Viet Cong fighters, who has gone on to become a senior provincial police officer, said "Please bring more of your friends next time to visit. We are your friends, and we share worst enemies together." I was once invited to a dinner where a man later introduced himself as a North Vietnamese officer who had fought at the battle of Khe Sanh. By the end of the conversation, he confessed to me that if he had it all to do over again, he would fight on our side, for his country was still struggling and he now realized that we Americans only came to help the Vietnamese and stop communist expansion.

This is true: Americans took nothing from Vietnam. We only gave, which I feel is true of all U.S. forces before and after us. We are not the policemen of the world, but rather the caregivers of the many people who have begged us to come and help them, time and time again. This was not done by choice, but rather out of necessity. We send food and medical staffs to help the starving and sick, and with them, we sent troops to protect our care providers and the different people that needed our help.

Many veterans have returned to Vietnam to visit and support the people, building medical clinics and moving freely among the Vietnamese who love to be around us. My shipmates, Sam and Bac Eaton, who live north of Saigon, have done much to help the people by donating money to different Vietnamese groups and by helping to build a church in An Long Village, where we served and where many of their family still live. Scores of Vietnamese who came to live with us in the United States have done well and proven highly successful. They, too, have traveled back to help their people, sharing their wealth and good fortune. I am very proud of them, and they have proven to me that any nationality that comes to live with us in the land of the free and works hard, adopting our way of life, will be successful and do well.

If any moved here to try and change us to the ways of their country, they shouldn't have bothered. We have been doing just fine. The American dream lives for all men whatever origin they are from. We welcome this in our society with open arms. But those who come to make money and yet criticize us should just stay home and save us the misery. If they choose to embrace our way of life and contribute, they are welcome and wished much success and good health. This is our way.

We veterans of the United States Armed Forces live in this country which we love, going about our lives and asking for very little, although many gave much. We are a proud bunch and, for the most part, have been doing just fine. Many of the images of us seen in the media and in books are distorted and wrong. There are many falsely claiming to be Vietnam veterans, telling stories that are untrue, dishonoring themselves and the men who served, fogging history and tarnishing our legacy. Most of my shipmates and the veterans I met are great guys and have led good lives, being rewarded children and grandchildren. And that is who I really wrote the book for: the kids.

ACKNOWLEDGEMENTS

I would like to thank the many veterans and friends who came forward to help me in this effort to record a small part of Navy history. There are so many that it is hard to know where to start, but I feel I must begin with Albert Moore, president of the Mobile Riverine Force Association, who kept whispering "Mobile Riverine Force" and "9th Infantry" in my ear, so I had to go research for myself. And he was right. What a tremendous group of warriors.

I also must thank Major General William B. Fulton, who led the 2nd Brigade of the 9th Infantry and has been described as a soldier's soldier who fought with honor, pride and, distinction in three wars. Still loved by the men who fought under his command long after he passed away, his book is considered the Mobile Riverine bible and was of great help to me in studying and trying to tell these important stories. Although I never had the honor to meet the man, I have become a big fan of his and of the Riverine battalions he commanded.

Thanks also to General Lucien E. "Blackie" Bolduc Jr., who led the 3/47th Infantry and advised and counseled me. Blackie is still the man. Thanks also to General George A. Crocker, Ron Menner, Terry Stull and my buddy Michael Richey of the 3/47th Infantry, who shared their stories with me. And what stories they are. As well, thanks to Jack Benedick, Phil Bateman, Chaplain WindMiller, and my friends Bill Reynolds and Jim Henke all of whom served with the 4/47th Infantry and contributed greatly. It was a huge honor for me to work with these 9th Infantry legends, and one I will not soon forget. Thanks to all for taking the time to look back with me one more time, and it is my hope that it did not cause you too much pain or discomfort.

I would also like to thank Tom Glickman, who spent forty years in the United States Navy, working his way up from a seventeen-year-old seaman to a Naval officer working in areas of great responsibility. Thanks for sharing your memories with this third-class petty officer, teaching me what you witnessed firsthand. I am forever in your debt.

Thanks to Phil Ferrier, who took the time to sit down on a park bench at the Vietnam Memorial in Washington D.C., on a rainy day, and to all the rest of the Mobile Riverine Force, like Al Breininger, Padre Johnson, Terry Sater, Jerry Berry, Joe Wall, Ralph Bigelow, and Bob Stoner, and the many others who came forward and contributed greatly, volunteering their words, pictures, and stories to me. Thanks to Melissa Binder for her words of support and pictures of her dad and his glorious shipmates. Thanks to Jerry Sampont and Bob Shirley of Operation Market Time. I would also like to thank to my buddies Larry Bissonnette, Fred McDavitt, Steve Watson, Ken Delfino, Albert O'Canas, Jerry Gandy, Heinz Hichetheir, Clarence Cooper, Gideon W. Almy, Woody Arnell, Tom Anderson, Cecil Martin, Bob Brower, and Tom Restemayer and their shipmates for opening up their hearts and souls, sharing their real-life experiences while serving with Game Wardens. To the many Seawolves like Frank Koch, Matt Gache, Wes Weseleskey, Art Schmitt, Mike Worthington, and many others, thanks for your continued service to keeping the memory of our Navy past alive. Thanks for covering our "Six" so long ago. If it had not been for these aviation daredevils, fewer of us would have survived. There was always a degree of comfort afforded to us by them, in the fact that enemy troops knew if they came out into the open to attack us, the Seawolves and Black Ponies would make their lives a living hell. My family and I will be eternally grateful for what you did and what you deterred from ever happening. You are truly the best of the best.

And to the brilliant Dave Chase, who designed and created the cover, back, and maps and who painfully cleaned and labored to bring our old pictures back to life. And also to Rodney Richey, who came through at the last minute and bailed me out after my editor became ill. Thanks, Dave and Rodney: you are both very talented men, and it was my good fortune that I was able to work with you.

I hope the book reflects well on you and brings you some feeling of accomplishment. You both certainly deserve it.

To my shipmates Sam and Bac Eaton, who continue to live in South Vietnam helping the Vietnamese people: Your views and descriptions of how the Vietnamese remember and see the war and us old Vietnam veterans is both enlightening and important to these writings, for without their point of view, it would just be another one-sided story told one too many times. And also thanks to the many who came forward and contributed that I have mentioned in the book. I hope these stories return the pride and honor you earned many years ago, pride and honor stolen by others claiming to be us, who tried to diminish our service, tell untrue stories, and make us out to be bad guys, which we were not. You are all heroes and legends to me, and I hope that someday you all are awarded your place in history with the other great men who served democracy and freedom. It is one thing to go into harm's way for your own freedom. It is another to fight for liberties of others. This fight is of the highest honor and the noblest of them all.

My deepest apologies to anyone I may have left out. Please forgive me and know that, without you and your words, I could have never completed this labor of love for our shipmates and the many who sacrificed and were lost. You, who were the heroes of my youth, have remained in my heart through the years and continue to be an inspiration to all the work that has gone into my books.

And last but not least, thanks to Commodore - Captain Michael L. Jordan and Command Master Chief Norm Giroux and River Squadrons I, II and III for your hospitality and continued support. Also thank you to the special boat units and the men and women serving on the USS James E. Williams and with the Navy around the world. The honor you have bestowed on us River Rats by embracing our river history is greater than you will ever know. Remember that wherever you might go in this time of need, you are in our hearts and prayers. God bless America and our men and women serving in our armed forces, for to them the torch of freedom has been passed, and rest assured, it is in good hands.

CPSIA information can be obtained at www.ICGtesting.com
Printed in the USA
266102BV00001BA/64/A